The Fight for Canada

Four Centuries of Resistance to American Expansionism

DAVID ORCHARD

Foreword by Kenneth McNaught

For Alexandra Florence

Here's for our country — enjoyed meeting you in Montreal!

David Orchard

November 26, 2004

Toronto

This book contains the complete text of the
first 24 chapters of the original edition
with five new chapters added – Chapters 8, 26, 27, 28, and 29

Printing History

First published April 1993 by Stoddart Publishing
Reprinted June 1993, June 1994, March 1998
Revised edition with new Chapters 8, 26, 27, 28, 29
published by Robert Davies Multimedia Publishing, February 1999
Reprinted November 2002
Revised edition issued in French under title:
Hors des griffes de l'aigle,
Éditions Multimédia Robert Davies, November 1998

Book store ordering information

Canada/USA:
General Distribution Services,
1-800-387-0141/387-0172 (Canada)
1-800-805-1083 (USA)
FREE FAX 1-800-481-6207
PUBNET 6307949
or from the publisher:

Robert Davies Multimedia Publishing Inc.
330-4999 St. Catherine St. West
Westmount, QC H3Z IT3, Canada
Tel. 514-481-2440 Fax 514-481-9973
e-mail: rdppub@netcom.ca

Private and group orders:

Citizens Concerned About Free Trade
Box 8052, Saskatoon
Saskatchewan, Canada S7K 4R7
Tel. 306-244-5757 Fax 306-244-3790
e-mail: ccafttor@sympatico.ca

David Orchard can be reached at
RR1, Borden, Saskatchewan, Canada SOK ONO
Tel. 306-652-7095
e-mail: davidorchard@sasktel.net

The publisher wishes to thank the
Canada Council for the Arts,
the Department of Canadian Heritage,
and the Sodec (Québec)
for their generous support of its publishing programs

To my father,
Ralph Orchard (1916-1992),
who could not wait to see this book in print,
and fought, to his last breath,
for a better Canada in a better world,
and to my mother,
Margaret Anna Orchard, née Ballard, (1917-2002),
who served her country in wartime,
her community in peacetime and
her family without fail.

Contents

Foreword

WITH THIS FORTHRIGHT, carefully researched book, David Orchard shows himself heir to an old and honourable Canadian tradition: that of the farmer activist. The deep concern expressed by this young Saskatchewan farmer for the survival of a just and tolerant society north of the 49th parallel matches that shown by the leaders of the Progressive movement in the early years of this century. Those earlier activists, people such as W.C. Good, E.A. Partridge and E.C. Drury, drew up Farmers' Platforms, organized rural education and cooperatives and entered provincial legislatures and the House of Commons as independent Progressives in an endeavour to curb the irresponsible power wielded by the great corporations of central Canada. Some of the specific issues have changed, but the fundamental patriotism that moved the Progressives is that which motivates Orchard.

As a society deeply suspicious of windy declarations and hand-on-breast loyalty, Canadians do not talk much about patriotism. But in an era of crumbling federal states, or reinvigorated ethnicity and tribalism, and of enormous pressure to seek shelter in harmonizing economic blocs, it is time to talk a little about love of country. Orchard does this intelligently, perceptively. Moreover, he has taken the trouble (a great deal of it) to provide a convincing historical analysis of the struggle waged by generations of Canadians to maintain their right to forge a society different from – and perceived by them as more humane than – that of their republican neighbour.

As a leader in the fight against the Canada-U.S. Free Trade Agreement (and now its even more ominous extension, NAFTA), Orchard knows well the strength of the corporate drive to overcome the often unarticulated wishes of the great majority of Canadians. It is the same power that successfully subverted the Progressives. It is the power which is now being deployed to prevent abrogation of the FTA and to achieve ratification of NAFTA.

Like the Progressives, Orchard is particularly aware of the danger that traditional party loyalties may, as they did in 1988, divide the majority who oppose the two misnamed trade agreements. His call for a concerted political effort by all concerned Canadians to prevent what might well be a fatally irreversible step provides a forceful conclusion to a distinctly moving book.

KENNETH McNAUGHT
Professor Emeritus
Department of History
University of Toronto
Spring 1993

Preface

IT HAS TAKEN eight years to complete this book. It had its beginnings long before that, when I was a boy growing up on a prairie farm. Like most farm children, I began operating machinery at an early age. I wondered why the identification plates on the machinery mostly bore the names of faraway places like Wisconsin, USA. Couldn't Canadians build tractors, engines and combines?

My brothers and I attended a one-room school. In winter we drove a horse and sleigh the five-mile round trip, and in the summer a horse and cart, made by my father. I watched my parents struggle to raise crops, pay the bills and meet mortgage payments.

My mother was a nurse turned farmwife. In the moments stolen from the never-ending work of raising four boys and keeping a large farmhouse, she would tell us how her family lost their farm in the dirty thirties in southern Saskatchewan, and how her first full-time job paid her five dollars a month. Or of her experiences overseas as a nurse during the Second World War.

My father spent endless hours in political and community work on top of running the farm. Election nights I recall him, in a rare pause from work, sitting next to the radio, an intense expression on his face, listening attentively to the results, pulling for Tommy Douglas.

One day when I was a teenager, U.S. Air Force jets came suddenly screaming out of the Saskatchewan sky, right over our barn. At barely treetop level they came so fast and so loud as to be from another planet, scattering the livestock in panic. For months they came, without warning. Later I learned they were conducting exercises and were on their way to bomb farmers in a place called Vietnam – farmers struggling to raise their crops and livestock just as we were. I first saw some of the people from that small country speaking in a Vancouver church in the early 1970s. They were so slight, frail almost, and spoke with such dignity and calm. How was it possible for them to stand up beneath the bombs?

In 1970, I went, with a few dollars in my pocket, to explore the world. I saw the sugar cane fields of Fiji, picked tobacco in New Zealand, worked on construction in northern Australia, picked grapes in France and was fascinated by the marketplaces of Morocco. I felt humbled by the dignity of the people of Spain, carrying the weight of Franco, and could see why Leonard Cohen loved Greece.

It amazed me to see the American control of other countries, their military bases, oil companies and supermarkets. I discovered that companies I'd grown up with, assuming they were Canadian, were not. When I returned to Canada I realized that American control of our country exceeded anything I'd seen in any other country of the world, and that the treatment of Native people here was as bad as the racism I'd seen in the Australian outback.

Perhaps these things could be changed. I thought that a law degree would help, and enrolled in law school. Valentine Nighttraveller, the only Cree person in our class, told me Joseph Kinsey Howard's book *Strange Empire* was the best written on Louis Riel. I read the late American writer, moved and amazed, not only that history could be told this way, but that I knew so little of it. At Batoche, the site where Riel and his general, Gabriel Dumont, made their stand, Stanley John, nephew of Almighty Voice, gave me a tour of the battlefield and introduced me to history from a Native point of view that had nothing to do with anything I'd learned in school. Our farm was barely fifty miles from Batoche, and our whole school had been taken to Regina for a tour of the RCMP museum, where we saw a piece of the rope that hanged Louis Riel, but we had been taught nothing about what he stood for and why. How could this be?

I left law school to find answers I couldn't find in the casebooks. I worked as a logger in B.C.'s interior, a longshoreman in Vancouver and New Westminster, a taxi driver and waiter in Saskatoon.

In 1973, I met Marjaleena Repo, an editor, organizer and writer, in Toronto. She'd come from Finland, yet knew, and cared, more about Canada than anyone I'd ever met. She was not intimidated by the Americans. She encouraged me to study my own country and to fight the colonial mentality she saw Canadians labouring under. She said it was not inevitable that Canada be controlled by the U.S. She believed that Canada could be free of foreign domination and that Canadians had the courage and ability to achieve their independence. It was important, she said, to organize seriously to accomplish this goal.

In 1984, when I first heard of the coming negotiations for free trade, I had been back on the family farm for nine years, had one hundred beef cows and was farming 1800 acres of land. I didn't know exactly what free trade meant, or the history behind it. But as farmers we'd had free trade with the United States in beef and farm machinery for years, and I knew about the problems it had caused those industries. And Brian Mulroney's apparent willingness to take Canada even more tightly into the American embrace spoke to me of a political danger ahead. I began to read all I could on free trade. It became clear that Canada's history had turned on whether we would have an economic border between ourselves and the Americans. I learned with surprise that Canada had had an election in 1891 and again in 1911 on the issue. That John A. Macdonald had called free trade "veiled treason" and that, for over 125 years, prominent figures had warned their fellow Canadians that without an economic border we soon would not have a political border either.

A newspaper article I wrote on the subject in the fall of 1985 resulted in a number of phone calls and soon a small meeting. All of us at the meeting were shocked by a recently leaked document from the Prime Minister's Office revealing that the government planned to use a deliberate strategy of withholding information on the topic and misleading Canadians – to ensure "benign neglect" from a majority of the population while a free-trade agreement was put into place. Marjaleena Repo was at the meeting, and under her organizational touch Citizens Concerned About Free Trade (CCAFT) grew into a national force. We began to sponsor public information meetings, and a whirl of events followed (all carried out without a cent of government money, paid for by donations received and what came from our own pockets): perhaps the largest debate in Canada on free trade, held in Saskatoon; 1200 turning out to a rousing meeting in Vancouver; 900 in Edmonton; 700 in Halifax. One hundred public information meetings and debates were held in two years, culminating in the November 1988 election. After the election, the pace hardly slackened. At these meetings people said the historical background between Canada and the United States was what moved them, and they wanted more. They bought our video and audio tapes, circulated them across Canada, and urged me to write a book. "We need it in our hands." I hesitated:

I'd never written a book; I had a farm to run. The public meetings were taking every spare moment and then some.

Finally, the lack of historical background in all the existing free-trade critiques that I could find, to say nothing of the mainstream media, forced the creation of this book. There was a crying need to respond to what Thomas D'Arcy McGee, the assassinated orator of Canadian Confederation, called "the warning from without – the American warning."

This book has been made possible only by those who helped, encouraged and inspired its production. I profoundly regret that women have been so completely cut out of our historical record that their contributions are so little acknowledged in this account. Women have carried the lion's share of the recent and ongoing fight against free trade; their role in previous battles for Canada would, without a shadow of doubt, have been equally great. Finding the documentation of those facts has proved to be beyond my skills.

For eight years my involvement in the fight against free trade, the work on the book and the running of the farm (the cattle are gone and the acreage cut back!) have been made possible only with immense and ongoing help from family and friends and the constant inspiration, encouragement and insistence of hundreds of Canadians determined that their country will not cease to be. For those who have felt deprived of the red thread of Canadian history and of their country's truly historic struggle to survive, I hope that this book helps weave together the pieces.

I WOULD LIKE to thank the following people who read all or parts of the manuscript and generously offered criticisms, comments or encouragement: Mel Clark, Kenneth McNaught, Foster Griezic, Palmiro Campagna, Stephen Clarkson, Claire Culhane, John L. Orr, William Loewen and others, including Mexican sources who, for their own safety, cannot be named.

None of these individuals is in any way responsible for the final use to which their suggestions have been put nor for any errors or shortcomings which remain.

Without the strength, help and encouragement of many individuals, this book could not have been written. I am deeply grateful to all those who offered assistance in the myriad ways it takes to put out a book. To name only a few: Rose-Marie Larsson for her generosity of reaction to the initial manuscript and hundreds of hours of crushing detail work on the final; Lisa Shaw for finding all the impossible sources and always answering her phone; Margaret Orchard, my mother, for a lifetime of care and support, for thinking about the practical details and for sending all the food so that farming and writing could go on; Grant Orchard, my brother, for finding time to read the chapters and for the long hours of help running the farm, which made it possible for me to write; Cady Williams for her helpful attention to substance and detail, both literary and practical; Raven Wilson for inspiration when most needed and encouragement to reach for the heights; Antoinette Martens for suggestions on deepening the content and for hours of background work; Satu Repo-Hendsbee for thorough and scholarly manuscript improvements and blinding speed at the computer; Leonard Shockey for the hours of typing and his advice to "just keep pecking away at it"; Bill Metke for finding valuable books in the most unusual places, and Monty Orr, Eileen Linklater, William Butler, Peggy McIntosh, Joe Durocher, Elaine Griffith, Aiyanas Ormond, Graham and Evelyn Linklater, Kelly Lamorie, Liam Grayer, and all the others who took time to comment on the manuscript.

Special thanks to my editor, Dan Liebman, for encouragement, patience and his keen eye for improvements throughout, to Donald G. Bastian at Stoddart for understanding the importance of history and imposing deadlines for which he may someday be forgiven, and, finally, to Marjaleena Repo, for solving the fantastic range of problems all along the way and without whose reworking of the manuscript, and ever-present helmswomanship, this work would long ago have been stillborn.

David Orchard
March 1993

Five years have passed since *The Fight for Canada* first appeared. In the revised edition five new chapters have been added covering some key events since *1993*. This book is now also available in French under the title *Hors des griffes de l'aigle*, Éditions Multimédia Robert Davies.

David Orchard
RR 1, Borden, Saskatchewan
December 1998

Economic union is political union. The nation which is eager to die sells to a single country.
José Marti

Fear of annexation has been a dominant factor in the psychology of politically alert and concerned Canadians and, consciously or subconsciously, has led them to weigh proposed policies, in any way connected with the United States, in light of their possible relationship to annexation.
Donald Warner

It might be that the lion and the lamb would lie down together but the lamb would be inside the lion.
John A. Macdonald

History is not dead, it is not even past.
William Faulkner

The man who would trade independence for security deserves to end up with neither.
Benjamin Franklin

The acquisition of Canada was the first ambition of the American Confederacy, and never ceased to be so.
Thomas D'Arcy McGee

Canada as a separate but dominated country has done about as well under the United States as women, worldwide, have done under men; about the only position they've ever adopted toward us, country to country, has been the missionary position, and we were not on top.
Margaret Atwood

Those who put shackles on the propagation of the French language from one end of Canada to the other are, some without knowing it, others perhaps knowing it... the most efficient instruments which the Americans could employ to absorb the Canadian confederation gradually.
Henri Bourassa

Part One

First Ambition

The Battle of Stoney Creek, June 5-6, 1813. Seven hundred British and Canadians made a surprise attack on 3500 invading American troops. This battle, along with the Battle of Beaver Dams, drove the Americans out of the Niagara Peninsula. (ILLUSTRATION BY C.W. JEFFERYS; USED BY PERMISSION OF THE JEFFERYS FAMILY; NATIONAL ARCHIVES, C70260)

This map appeared in the December 1, 1888, issue of the New York *World*, with this editorial comment: "What a majestic empire the accompanying map suggests; one unbroken line from the Arctic Ocean to the Torrid Zone. The United States is here shown as embracing nearly the whole of the North American continent. Having conquered the Western wilderness the star of Empire northward points the way."

1

A New Breed of People

ON SEPTEMBER 8, 1535, Chief Donnacona met Jacques Cartier on the St. Lawrence River, invited him into his canoe and welcomed him to the Iroquois town of Stadacona. The area to the west of Ile d'Orléans, Cartier was told, marked the beginning of the country known as Canada. Sailing further up the "great river of Canada," as the explorer wrote in his diary, he was welcomed by a thousand people and given a tour of Hochelaga by "one of the chiefest lords of the city." Taken to the top of Mount Royal, he was treated to a view "as fair ... as can possibly be seen." Cartier spent the winter, his men dying of scurvy until the Iroquois gave them the recipe for a cure.

On May 3, 1536, after celebrating the festival of the Holy Cross and erecting a 35-foot-high cross dedicated to the king of France, Cartier ordered his men to kidnap Donnacona, whom he called "the king of Canada," his two sons and seven other Iroquois. The captives, to be taken back to France as proof of Cartier's achievements, were boarded on the ships anchored in the St. Lawrence. Cartier wrote: 'At nightfall a large number of Donnacona's people came opposite to our ships ... howling and crying like wolves all night long, calling out incessantly, *Agouhanna, agouhanna,* in the hope of being able to speak to him." The following day, concerned about an attack by the gathering Iroquois, Cartier promised them that, after an interview with the king of France, Donnacona would be returned to Canada within a year. At this pledge, the Indians gathered gave "three great shouts in sign of joy," and Cartier's ships weighed anchor for France. Except for a young girl, all the captives died in France within five years.[1]

IN 1605, THE FIRST French settlement was founded in North America at Port Royal in Acadia (now Nova Scotia). Two years later,

3

the English established their first permanent settlement at James-
town, Virginia. In 1608, Samuel de Champlain, the "father of
Canada," founded the village of Quebec.

In 1613, the governor of Virginia, Sir Thomas Dale, upon hearing
of the settlement to the north, declared that the continent was not
large enough to contain both French and English. He hired a force
of mercenaries to drive the French out of Acadia. Samuel Argall and
his sixty soldiers attacked Port Royal, looted it and burned it to the
ground. Fifteen settlers were set adrift in an open boat, and a dozen
more were taken back to Virginia as prisoners. Acadia was inside
the northern boundary of Virginia, claimed the governor. Those
Acadians who managed to escape returned from the woods and, as
they would be forced to do more than once again, rebuilt their
homes and their settlement.

By 1690, Stadacona was Quebec City, and Hochelaga was Montreal.
Panic was sweeping through both towns. The delegates of an
intercolonial conference in Boston had decided to invade Canada.*
A leading New England theologian and writer of the time, Cotton
Mather, explained the need for a massive invasion: to get at the crows,
why not cut down the tree? Cotton Mather wrote: "The Indian Rooks
[crows] grievously infested the Country ... The French Colonies to
the Northward were the Tree in which those Rooks had their Nests
... the New-Englanders might very justly take this Occasion to
Reduce those French Colonies ... and so at once take away from all
the Rooks for ever, all that gave 'em any Advantage to Infest us."[2]

The American colonists numbered 200,000, the French Canadians
about 10,000. But the American colonies were beset with friction
among themselves, and the task of taking Canada fell largely to the
wealthiest and most powerful colony, Massachusetts, with a population
of 50,000, with some help from New York and Connecticut.

Borrowing an enormous 50,000 pounds, Massachusetts put forth
its best energy. In August 1690, a fleet of thirty-four ships carrying
2300 men under Admiral William Phips left Boston to attack
Quebec. Despite the lack of expected help from England, the fleet
set off, confident that Quebec would fall in the face of the colonists'

---

* Until 1700, the terms Canada and New France were used interchangeably.
  After 1700, New France became the term used for all of French North
  America, including Canada, Acadia, Louisiana and the trading posts in the
  West.

assault alone. At the same time, troops from New York under the command of John Schuyler moved overland towards Montreal.

Smallpox struck the troops from New York after they attacked La Prairie, a farming village just south of Montreal, and they were unable to reach Montreal. Admiral Phips, meanwhile, had problems moving his large fleet up the St. Lawrence. It was October by the time he reached Quebec, and already ice was forming at night on the edge of the river.

Hopeful that the mere sight of his armada would lead to capitulation, Phips sent a messenger with an ultimatum to the town to surrender. Count Frontenac, the "fighting governor" of Canada, made his famous reply: "I will answer your general only with the mouths of my cannon and the shots of my muskets."[3]

The Canadians "fought like Indians," and the invaders were driven back to their boats.[4] In the end, starving and miserable, with winter approaching and smallpox in their ranks, Phips and his officers sailed for home, "beaten and humiliated, with a heavy burden of debt to hang round the neck of a too ambitious Massachusetts."[5]

Canada had fought hard and won. A shot from the ramparts had knocked the flag of Phips's ship into the river. It was rescued and brought ashore as a precious trophy.

In defeat, in debt and with a thousand men lost, New England turned inward. The search for scapegoats began. "Brooding on this judgement, and the search for the sin that had prompted it, were to contribute to the hysteria of the Salem witchcraft trials of 1692."[6] At least twenty victims, mostly women, were hanged before the witch hunt subsided.

But the troops from Massachusetts vowed to return, and they did, twenty-one years later.

In 1711, the British joined forces with the American colonies, and under the command of Admiral Hovenden Walker, forty-five ships carrying 6500 men set out to attack Quebec, while an additional 2300 troops moved overland towards Montreal via Lake Champlain. "Canada was being invaded by three times as many men as had threatened her in 1690, an attack by a force of almost half of the total population of Canada."[7] (Some sources put the armada at seventy-one ships and 12,000 men.) A storm hit Walker's armada in the St. Lawrence, and nine ships carrying 900 men were smashed to pieces. Faced with this disaster, the invaders withdrew.

In Quebec, where a frantic mobilization was under way to meet the invaders, there was a great outburst of joy. In celebration, a

Quebec City church called Nôtre-Dame de la Victoire (Our Lady of Victory), in tribute to Frontenac's defence of the city in 1690, was renamed Nôtre-Dame des Victoires (Our Lady of Victories), the name it bears today.

IN 1750, ENGLAND held only a narrow strip of colonies along the Atlantic and a few scattered posts on Hudson Bay. France and its Indian allies controlled most of North America – from the North Atlantic coast to the Rocky Mountains, and from the sub-Arctic to the Gulf of Mexico. The French settlers had opposed the king's attempt to call their country New France. They were not French, they insisted. They were "a new breed of people, *Canadiens.* "[8]

The American colonies, except for New York, which enjoyed a profitable trade with Canada, agitated for war to drive the French out of North America. Britain agreed, and in 1755 a mighty force of more than 2200 soldiers under General Edward Braddock and Colonel George Washington and a train of artillery and baggage wagons four miles long set out to take the Ohio Valley from the Canadians. The rows of British troops marching in formation were ambushed and picked off by 900 French, Indians and Canadians at the battle for Fort Duquesne (present-day Pittsburgh), in one of the most remarkable battles in American history.

"We have been beaten," Washington wrote, "shamefully beaten, by a handful of French, who only expected to obstruct our advance. Shortly before the action, we thought our forces were equal to all the enemies in Canada; we have been most unexpectedly defeated, and now all is lost."[9]

At the other end of Canadian territory, after being handed back and forth between Britain and France for one hundred years, part of Acadia (Nova Scotia) had been permanently ceded to Britain in 1713, along with Newfoundland and Hudson Bay. By the mid-1750s, the French-speaking population of Nova Scotia approached 20,000, four times greater than the English. These long-time settlers pos–sessed the best land in the province. New England was expanding and short of land, and Yankee soldiers and fishermen had observed, and coveted, the fertile Annapolis Valley.

As early as 1710, New England had raised the subject of "whether the said French inhabitants may not be transported out of the province of Nova Scotia, to be replaced by good Protestant subjects."[10] Yielding to unrelenting pressure from New England, the governor of Nova Scotia, Colonel Charles Lawrence, on

September 5, 1755, called all the male inhabitants to the local churches of Acadia to "hear the King's orders." The unsuspecting people gathered, to be told that all their property – farms, homes and livestock – had been confiscated and that they were to be expelled from Nova Scotia. "They are not," said the order, drafted on the recommendations of Chief Justice Jonathan Belcher, recently arrived from Boston, "to be permitted to carry off even the smallest object." The church doors were locked, the soldiers emerged from their hiding places, and the incredulous men were herded at bayonet point onto waiting ships. Two thousand Massachusetts troops scoured the countryside, rounded up the women and children and torched the homesteads. "The women, most afflicted, bore their new-born children in their arms," recorded Colonel John Winslow, the New England officer in charge of the deportations, in his diary. "Some of them were pulling their infirm parents . . . in carts" to the ships.[11]

Those who survived the storms, starvation and disease in the crowded holds of the ships were dumped, destitute, in various Atlantic ports, where they were, according to Lawrence's instructions, "disposed of in such a manner as may best answer our design of preventing their reunion."[12] Four hundred Acadians sent to Connecticut were dispersed to fifty towns. Up and down the coast they were jailed, forced into servitude, and exiled to other lands, including the West Indies, France and Corsica.

One young Acadian, Joseph Girouard, with the help of his mates, overpowered the captain, seized control of the ship he was deported on, and sailed it back to Saint John, releasing its cargo of prisoners. Some 110 Acadian boys and girls managed to return all the way from Georgia to New York, only to be captured and dispersed once again. Others tried to begin new lives as far away as the French colony of Louisiana – where they would become known as Cajuns. Still others made their way back over the years. Some spent the rest of their lives searching for the members of their scattered families.

By late fall 1755, "over six thousand persons had been forcibly deported, while the rest of the population had been driven to the wilderness and their homes laid waste. Some wandered to the Isle St Jean [Prince Edward Island], and others to New Brunswick and Canada."[13] Not only the Acadians, but also the Abenaki Indians were driven from their land to make way for the New England settlers.

The deportations continued for six more years, during which time the Acadians fought back with guerrilla warfare and piracy. At first, the American settlers were afraid to move in, but by 1759 they started to arrive and take over the fertile, well-cared-for farms. The roundup moved on to Prince Edward Island, from where 3500 more Acadians were seized and sent to France, which provided no help. In total, about 11,000 were driven off their land.

The Boston contractors responsible for the removal of the Acadians made large profits by illegally selling cattle – up to 60,000 head – seized from the Acadians by the Crown. Each of them – Thomas and John Hancock, Charles Apthorp and Massachusetts governor William Shirley's son-in-law, John Erving – came out of the experience immensely wealthy men. John Hancock went on to be the first signer of the American Declaration of Independence.

In 1756, England declared war on France, and what Churchill would later call the first world war was under way. The Seven Years War, a great conflict involving almost all the major powers of Europe, saw Austria, France, Sweden, Russia and Saxony lined up against Prussia and Britain. The war was already under way in North America as well as in colonial India.

At stake in North America was, initially, the rich land of the Ohio-Mississippi valleys. The American colonies wanted to expand into the area. As Governor Arthur Dobbs of Virginia wrote: "How miserable must be the condition then of all our colonies when confined within the mountains, deprived of all the inland trade of the continent."[14]

Canada, however, was already in the Ohio. The American colonies wanted war because they desired Canada's land, trade routes, resources, furs and fish. The governor of New France, Pierre Vaudreuil, explained that the Ohio was Canada's natural and only direct link with Louisiana. Any concession there "would completely cut off communication between the two colonies [Canada and Louisiana] whose maintenance depends upon mutual aid."[15]

The American colonies outnumbered Canada in population almost twenty to one, approximately one million to 55,000. Britain easily outclassed France at sea. The war for the Ohio would, it seemed, be a short affair.

Canada, however, was like a wasps' nest under attack. The Canadians understood very clearly the meaning of the Acadian expulsion. Defeated, their fate could be the same. They fought ferociously. Learning from the Indians, Canadians had mastered the techniques of guerrilla warfare – using swift attack where least expected, ambush and, above all, surprise.

From Carolina north to New York and back down the eastern side of the Allegheny Mountains to within thirty miles of Philadelphia, the Anglo-American settlements were set aflame. The American colonies, although much larger in numbers, found the Canadians better organized and more skilled at war. For three years, from 1755 through 1757, the French, Canadian and Indian allies were winning. The British and Americans did not achieve a single goal, except for the expulsion of the Acadians. In 1756, the governor of Pennsylvania offered a bounty of 130 Spanish dollars for "the Scalp of every Male Indian Enemy above the age of Twelve Years produced as Evidence of their being killed." Fifty dollars was the bounty for "the Scalp of every Indian Woman."[16]

A factor hampering the Americans was their fear of a slave uprising in the south, which prevented effective troop mobilization. It was clear that without Britain's army and navy and its diplomatic clout, the American colonies could not take possession of all of Canada. But the British government needed to be convinced.

"The conquest of Canada ... was essentially an American idea," wrote Quebec historian Guy Frégault. "And although advanced British opinion adopted it as a political program, it nonetheless remained American in its conception. It was, moreover, in a certain sense an idea that would be imposed on the mother country by America."[17] Ten years earlier, Governor Shirley of Massachusetts had advocated the conquest of Canada. Now, not only was the pressure growing, but the right man in Britain was convinced.

William Pitt, a brilliant organizer and strategist, had come to power in 1756. Britain had regarded Canada as having little value, but under Pitt that view changed. The ongoing war had become a struggle between Britain and France for world supremacy, and Pitt decided the entire war could be won in North America. Subsidizing Prussia to carry the weight of the war in Europe, he poured an enormous four million pounds into the operation to take Canada — eighteen times the total budget of Canada for the six years of the war. In addition, the American colonies contributed large sums. Some 50,000 soldiers, almost half from the American colonies, were mobilized, along with 20,000 sailors — in total, more than the entire population of Canada. In building the most powerful empire the world had ever known, Pitt imposed taxes and doubled Britain's national debt. All other considerations were subordinated to one end — the conquest of Canada.

This decision caused jubilation in America, the source of the pressure on the British government. The New York *Gazette* said: "We have the fairest prospects ... of destroying at a blow that power that has so long harassed us ... Canada must be destroyed ... let it echo from our hills and vales."[18] Twenty-one thousand of the men attacking Canada would be American colonists in blue uniforms. The first men to land on Canadian soil at Quebec, and the first to die, were from Connecticut.

Pitt's plan was a three-pronged attack — against Quebec and Montreal, lle Royale (Cape Breton) and Fort Duquesne. At Cape Breton, the Canadians were outnumbered five to one by the British and American attackers, and in July 1758 the mighty French fortress of Louisbourg fell after a seven-week siege. France no longer held a single port on the Atlantic coast. In the Ohio Valley, Fort Duquesne, defended in 1755 against Braddock and Washington, now fell and was renamed Pittsburgh, after the British prime minister.

The church bells in Boston rang almost an entire day. "Blessed be God," wrote the Boston *News Letter,* "the long looked for day is arrived that has now fixed us on the banks of the Ohio." Governor Thomas Pownall of Massachusetts said, "We have put our hand again to the plow and if we do not look back it must go over the very foundations of the enemy's country."[19]

In addition to being vastly outnumbered, Canada faced a problem of a divided command and hostility between the French and the Canadians. General Louis-Joseph Montcalm, sent from France to direct the war, spent much of his time in conflict with the first Canadian-born governor, Pierre Vaudreuil. Montcalm, who wanted to fight a European-style war by European rules, had contempt for the Canadians, who wanted to fight a guerrilla war using Canada's great distances and natural ambushes against the overwhelming force of its enemies.

The British and Americans prepared to move on Quebec. After years of war, Canada was bled dry, men had been taken from their farms to fight, and famine stalked the land. Ships of supplies sent from France had been seized by the enemy. Arms, ammunition and soldiers were in desperately short supply. Men were so weak they could barely walk. The response from France was to tell Canada to redouble its efforts. "When the house is on fire, one doesn't bother about the stables," Louis XV is said to have remarked.[20] The government at Versailles complained bitterly about the cost and threatened to abandon its colony, under attack from three directions. Canada was bankrupt, and no more credit would be extended. In the words of Canada's first historian, François-Xavier Garneau, the "Canadians, who believed that the home government ... meant to make great efforts to save them ... were deceived." The court at Versailles, "enervated by orgies," abandoned Canada to its fate. A "wretched country," Voltaire said, "covered with ice eight months in the year, inhabited by barbarians, bears and beaver."[21] For its defence of Canada, France spent one-tenth of what Britain did to conquer it.

By contrast, the American colonies, their war costs subsidized by Britain, prospered, with war contractors, entrepreneurs and merchants enjoying a booming business. And, in England, Pitt was stronger than ever with his victories, the darling of the English public.

In June 1759, General James Wolfe was in front of Quebec City. His convoy of 200 ships carrying 37,000 soldiers and sailors – American and British – extended fifty miles down the St Lawrence.

Unable to force the defenders out from behind the walls of the city, Wolfe ordered the "systematic destruction" of the colony. "Bombs, cannon-balls, shells, fire bombs fell on the town" until there was "not a single house without a hole in it."[22] Wolfe, who had played an active part in crushing the Scottish highlanders at Culloden, issued a manifesto warning that those who resisted would be "punished with fire and sword, treated as Indians," who, he said, merited extermination. "It would," he wrote, "give me pleasure to see the Canadian vermin sacked and pillaged." Wolfe gave free rein to the American Rangers ("the worst soldiers in the universe," he had once called them) to burn the buildings and crops in all the settlements up and down the river. Resisters were shot and scalped by the American troops; 1400 farms were burned. Abandoned by France, the Canadians fought back fiercely. Wolfe, astonished, wrote: "Old people of seventy years and boys of fifteen fire at our detachments and kill or wound our men from the edge of the woods."[23] And Governor Horatio Sharpe of Maryland thought almost all of Canada had risen to defend the capital.

The night of September 12, 1759, Wolfe's troops scaled the great cliff of Quebec, and the next morning they were lined up on the Plains of Abraham. Montcalm, in "fatal precipitateness," without waiting for reinforcements and against the advice of his commanders, marched out from behind Quebec's walls onto the plains. His men were mowed down by the British. The Canadians, fighting for their country in their traditional manner, fired from the trees and bushes and for a time stopped the British and the Americans. Within the week, however, Quebec had fallen.

The following year, the French and Canadians nearly recaptured Quebec. Under the command of François-Gaston Lévis, who, in contrast to Montcalm, respected Canadians and inspired their confidence, they defeated the British just outside Quebec in April 1760. "One frigate, if it had arrived before the English fleet, would have achieved the surrender of [the English at] Quebec," Lévis later wrote. But no ship came from France. Instead, English frigates arrived once again. Lévis and his men were forced to withdraw, and 17,000 British troops moved on to Montreal, surrounded it and forced its capitulation. Canada had been conquered at last.

In London, the king proclaimed a day of thanksgiving and Wolfe was named "Conqueror of Canada." But the real winners were the British Americans. The joy in Boston was unbounded; New Yorkers were ecstatic. The Philadelphia *Gazette* proclaimed the fall of Montreal as "the most important event ... that has ever happened in favour of the British." The Boston *News Letter* "shouted for joy." A leading clergyman of that city, Samuel Cooper, thanked heaven from the pulpit: "God has heard our prayers ... the power of Canada is broken." In Albany, the celebration went on uninterrupted for three days. Reverend Thomas Foxcroft of Boston said: "Long has the conquest of Canada been the object of our attention and the matter of our prayers . . . and now at length we see the happy day of its accomplishment." Within ten years, Benjamin Franklin predicted, immigrants from the American colonies would swamp the French-speaking Canadians, who would then "be blended and incorporated with our people both in language and manners." In Franklin's view, with their constant competitor, Canada, eliminated, the growth of the American colonies would be unrestricted.[24]

Britain imposed martial law on Canada for four years. Farmers and businesses were destitute, and Quebec City lay in ruins after two months' bombardment. To describe the misery, said the new military governor, Brigadier James Murray, "is really beyond my powers and to think of it is shocking to Humanity."[25]

The Royal Proclamation of 1763 attempted to repudiate all things Canadian. The colony was dismembered and renamed the province of Quebec. Labrador was annexed to Newfoundland, and Prince Edward Island and Cape Breton were handed over to Nova Scotia. Largely as a result of the efforts of Chief Pontiac of the Ottawas, who in 1763 allied with the Hurons, Ojibways and Potawatomis and drove back the American and English settlers and military, the region south of the Great Lakes was not given to the American colonies. It was made into a neutral Indian Territory, from which white settlement was excluded. In Quebec, French law was abolished. Canadians were required to swear an oath to the King of England and give up their arms. Catholics were barred from holding any government or legal position.

If Governor Murray was stern, a "soldier-like sympathy" encouraged his respect for those who had bravely fought him in the battlefield. He refused to enforce the proclamation and issued a decree that French legal use and custom would continue. If the laws against the French Canadians were to be applied with vigour, he would resign, Murray told London. "I cannot be the Instrument of destroying, perhaps, the best and bravest Race on this Globe."[26] The American militiamen, filled with hatred for the Catholics, were sent home. British soldiers were put under strict orders to be civil to the people.

The merchants who had come from the American colonies were outraged. Although representing less than one percent of the population, they demanded control. They called for an assembly, knowing that the anti-Catholic laws would prohibit all Canadians from participating. "The most cruel, Ignorant, rapacious Fanaticks who ever existed," Murray said of them.[27] They clamoured to London for Murray's downfall. He was replaced in 1766 by Guy Carleton, who, married to a French-speaking woman, had little more sympathy for the anti-French merchants who demanded domination of the Canadians. Both Carleton and Murray urged London to reverse its policy of assimilation and, pointing to the rising tide of revolt in the American colonies, they succeeded. In 1774, the *Quebec Act* was passed, which provided for a return to the "Laws and Customs of Canada" on all civil matters. It abolished the ban on Catholics holding office and allowed freedom of religion. And, most significant for the American colonies, it re-established most of Canada's old boundaries, returning to it Labrador and the Ohio-Mississippi Indian Territory, which the Americans coveted.

The protests in the American colonies at the passage of the *Quebec Act* were violent. American land companies had moved into the Ohio Valley. The Sons of Liberty, formed to overthrow British rule and win independence, were riding the roads of the American colonies. Their slogan was "Liberty and Property" — and a good deal of the property they wanted was in Canada. (George Washington of Virginia, one of the richest men in the state, with large holdings of both land and slaves, who would soon become the first president, had investments in the upper Mississippi area. So also did Thomas Jefferson, another wealthy Virginia land and slave owner who would be the principal author of the American Declaration of Independence and the third U.S. president. Another prominent and prosperous framer of the Declaration of Independence, Benjamin Franklin, held a large grant of land on the Ohio River.)

In protest against taxation without representation, American colonists disguised as Indians had dumped several shiploads of tea into the Boston harbour. English retaliation was immediate and drastic. The British Parliament passed a series of "Intolerable Acts," which banned town meetings in the American colonies and dissolved the upper House of Assembly, henceforth to be appointed from Britain, and forced the compulsory quartering of British troops. To respond to these laws, the First Continental Congress met in Philadelphia in late 1774. At the top of its agenda was the *Quebec Act*, "the worst of laws." A letter was sent inviting Quebec to attend the Congress: "Your province is the only link that is wanting to complete the bright strong chain of union."[28] Noting that the land speculators, who wanted to take the Ohio Valley from Canada, were prominent in the Congress, Quebec did not respond to the invitation.

The *Quebec Act* was to take effect May 1, 1775. But just a few days before that came the shots "heard around the world." The American Revolution was under way to throw off the chains of British control over her trade and her destiny.

For 150 years, the Canadians, the French and the Indians had defended Canada against invasion from the south and from Britain. In a twist few could have foreseen fifteen years earlier, French-speaking Canadians, English-speaking British and the Six Nations Indians would shortly be fighting side by side. Once again the invaders would be from the south, but there would be an added dimension: France would be allied with the Americans.

At stake would be the very existence of Canada.

2

The Fourteenth Colony

THE AMERICAN DECLARATION of Independence was still nine months in the future when George Washington, commander-in-chief of the American Revolutionary Army, chose Colonel Benedict Arnold to lead one column of 1200 battle-hardened troops to invade Canada from Maine, and General Richard Montgomery to head another, larger force, to come up from New York. On November 13, 1775, Montgomery marched into Montreal and gave the residents four hours to surrender on his terms. He called for a provincial convention to "elect delegates to the Continental Congress, and declare Canada the fourteenth American colony."[1]

Congress mobilized almost 8000 troops for the task. The British force in all of Canada was only about 600 soldiers. With Montreal taken, the walled fortress of Quebec City was all that stood between the American troops and their goal of the fourteenth colony. "Till Quebec is taken, Canada is unconquered," Montgomery declared.[2]

As the American troops approached Quebec, rumours swept the city. Some of the merchants, fearful of losing their property, spoke openly of capitulation. American spies and messengers, disguised as traders, spread out across the province circulating Congress's Address to the Inhabitants of Quebec, which exhorted Canadians: "Seize the opportunity presented to you by Providence itself. You have been conquered into liberty, if you act as you ought. This work is not of man. You are a small people compared to those who with open arms invite you into fellowship. A moment's reflection should convince you which will be most for your interest and happiness, to have all the rest of North America your unalterable friends, or your inveterate enemies."[3]

In Philadelphia, Congress waited "in a state of the most anxious Suspense for Accounts of the total Reduction of Canada and their accession to our League."[4] On November 8, 1775, Arnold's troops had reached the south shore of the St. Lawrence opposite Quebec, where for three days a gale prevented them from crossing the river.

At the same time, Colonel Allan Maclean, second in command of the forces in Canada, was handed a letter by an Indian messenger carrying it from Arnold to Montgomery. Warned of the coming American attack, Maclean rushed to Quebec with a regiment of 200 armed men, mostly Scottish Highlanders, before Arnold could cross the river.

A town hall meeting was in session at one of the churches, with a speaker, a merchant named Williams, advocating negotiations with the Americans and surrender. Maclean, a grim old Scot, ejected the man from the pulpit and proceeded to mobilize the defence of the city "with red-hot energy and zeal."[5]

"Had I been ten days sooner," Arnold later wrote Washington, "Quebec must inevitably have fallen into our hands, as there was not a man then to oppose us."[6]

Guy Carleton, governor of Quebec, meanwhile had escaped from Montreal and was racing for Quebec, while Montgomery was racing for him. The Americans had set up a full blockade of the roads and of the river at Sorel to catch the fugitive governor. In the dead of night, Carleton, disguised as a habitant in the boat of a French-Canadian skipper named Bouchette, slipped past the American guns, the crew paddling silently with their hands lest the splash of an oar alert the American sentries. "It was a moment of breathless excitement; for the hope of Canada was in their keeping and no turning back was possible."[7] Carleton arrived in Quebec on November 19, to the "unspeakable joy" of the defenders and the "utter Dismay" of the Americans. He reinforced Maclean's organization of the city's defenders, regrouped the French-Canadian, British, Scottish and Newfoundland troops, and let it be known there would be no negotiation or capitulation. While he recognized the fate of the town as "extremely doubtful, to say nothing worse," he intended "to sink, if sink he must, with pennant at masthead."

Fresh from the fall of Montreal and his experience with collaborators there, Carleton issued a proclamation ordering every able-bodied man who would not sign up for the militia expelled from the city of Quebec in four days — or else face the loss of his property. A "long and wrathful" procession of prominent American and English merchants and lawyers, along with their sympathizers, filed out of the City.[8] "Cabals then ceased," said one of the militia commanders. "That order strengthened the garrison considerably. We could guard against open and avowed enemies, but not against those lurking about town."[9]

On December 2, Montgomery's force completed the march from Montreal, joined Arnold's troops on the Plains of Abraham, and laid siege to Quebec. As the weeks passed, Montgomery, who had hoped to secure Quebec's surrender by "alarming the timid, stimulating the disaffected, or fatiguing the garrison into discontent," had another foe to contend with — the cold, which "possessed the terrors of Arctic night for people to the south." He and Arnold decided on an assault.

"If shot and shell cannot remove the prejudices of the Quebecers, we are determined to storm," Montgomery's Lieutenant Copp stated. "The more Danger, the more Glory." To encourage his men, Montgomery promised them the right to loot the city. He would, he declared, "dine in Quebec on Christmas day or in Hell."[10]

At 4:30 a.m., December 31, under the cover of a raging blizzard, the Americans stormed the city. "A 'fatal' hour had come, for the town blazed, and the thunder of its cannon shook their stone walls ... The city was one ring of fire, one crater of tumult ... in the midst of it all, Governor Carleton, calm, alert, fearless."[11]

From the windows of houses, the defenders shot the invaders, who wore slogans pinned to their hats: "Liberty or Death." When the Americans placed their scaling ladders against the walls, a "Canadian Hercules" by the name of Charles Charland seized them from the hands below and wrenched the ladders up and over.[12]

In the morning, Montgomery was dead, on his back, with one arm sticking up through the new fall of snow. Arnold had been shot through the leg, and the invaders had been driven back outside the walls. Almost half the American force had been captured, killed or wounded.

This news was delivered to the American commander, General Philip Schuyler, owner of one of the largest estates in New York, at his stately mansion. (Schuyler was a member of a prominent family whose head, John, had commanded New York troops invading Canada in 1690.) "The gallant Montgomery is no more," Schuyler observed. "The brave Arnold is wounded; and we have met with a severe check."[13]

John Adams, who would become the second president of the United States, would not give up. "The Unanimous Voice of the

Continent is Canada must be ours!" he declared from Philadelphia. "Quebec must be taken!"[14]

Six thousand more troops were ordered to march north. Washington wrote to Arnold: "I need not mention to you the great importance of this place [Quebec], and the consequent possession of all Canada, in the scale of American affairs ... I already view the approaching day, when you and your brave followers will enter this important fortress, with every honor and triumph attendant on victory and conquest. Then will you have added the only link wanting in the great chain of Continental union."[15]

Benedict Arnold, now a brigadier general and still nursing his leg wound, maintained the siege of Quebec throughout the winter.

Congress, alarmed by the lack of support from the Canadians — "seven-eighths" of whom, both French and English, "would wish to see our throats cut" — sent Benjamin Franklin and two other prominent signatories to the American Declaration of Independence, Samuel Chase and Charles Carroll (the richest man in America), to Montreal. Instructed by Congress to tell Canadians the American invasion of Canada had no ulterior motive — it was in their interest to become "inseparably united" with the American colonies — they were to organize elections in the "Liberated Territory."[16]

Franklin and his entourage arrived from Philadelphia on April 29, 1776, with a printing press (the first in Montreal) and a French printer to publish an American newspaper and pamphlets. But it was too late for Benjamin Franklin and the rest of the Americans. On May 6, British ships with reinforcements arrived at Quebec, and Governor Carleton marched out of the city, dispersed Arnold's men, and took the Plains of Abraham in ten minutes. Arnold's soldiers fled, abandoning their freshly cooked meals. News of this defeat reached Franklin in Montreal and, on May 11, he and Father John Carroll (brother of Charles), a priest sent by Congress in a futile attempt to win over the Quebec clergy, added to the panic in the American ranks by "hastily quitting the city."

Shocked, Philadelphia received news of "a rout," "a disgraceful flight" and a "shameful retreat" as the American troops, decimated by smallpox and pursued by the British, Canadians and Indians, fled from Quebec.[17] Arnold evacuated Montreal in four hours, attempting to burn the city as he retreated.

Arnold's doctor later described the ten-month invasion as "a heterogeneal concatenation [confused series] of the most peculiar and unparalleled rebuffs and sufferings that are perhaps to be found in the annals of any nation." The estimated American dead were five thousand. "The subject is disgusting to me — I will dismiss it," said Samuel Adams, father of the American Revolution.[18]

Without Carleton's military ability and far-sighted leadership, the result could well have been very different. Above all, without the loyalty of the French Canadians there would not today be an acre of land north of the 49th parallel where the Stars and Stripes did not fly.

At that moment in 1775-76, French Canadians held the destiny of the continent in their hands. By refusing to support the American invasion of Canada, they ensured the survival of Canada. However, their unwillingness in the following months to support the British army in its counter-offensive against the American Revolution was a major factor allowing the Americans to win their independence.

Britain and the newly independent United States met at the negotiations for the Treaty of Paris, in 1783, to formalize American independence and, more importantly, to define the new republic's borders. Having failed to take Canada by force, the Americans attempted diplomacy. The chief U.S. negotiator, Benjamin Franklin, opened by smoothly suggesting that to allow the Americans and the British to be "perfectly reconciled," Canada should be entirely transferred to the United States.[19] This was necessary, Franklin said, to prevent future wars. Although Britain replied that there were other ways to prevent war, its prime minister, Lord Shelburne, "cherished the delusion that it was possible to make the Americans grateful and friendly by generous concessions."[20]

France, followed by Spain and Holland, had thrown its weight — including its navy — behind the Americans. To split this alliance against her, Britain was anxious to regain the goodwill of her former American colonies and would make tremendous concessions to do so. And so, what historian Donald Creighton called "the greatest blow in their entire, history" was about to fall on Canadians. By that treaty, Canada lost forever all its territory between the Ohio and Mississippi rivers (the present-day states of Michigan, Wisconsin, Illinois, Ohio and Indiana) which had been surveyed by the great explorers — René-Robert La Salle, "discoverer of the Mississippi Delta," Louis Jolliet, "co-discoverer of the Mississippi," Jesuit linguist Jacques Marquette and many others — and which had been administered by the Intendants of Canada, including the energetic and capable Jean Talon, for more than one hundred years.

All of this territory, including its settlements and posts built to serve the Canadian fur trade, and for which numberless battles bad been fought, was "surrendered to an enemy which had been incapable of effecting the capture of a single one of them."[21]

The Great Lakes, also explored and occupied by Canada, were either given entirely to the United States (Lake Michigan) or divided jointly. All this, together with the lands of the Six Nations, "was ceded without a shadow of military necessity, for the goodwill of the United States."[22] Joseph Brant, chief of the Six Nations, had been an unswerving ally of the British throughout the American War of Independence. The Mohawk Valley, promised to him by the king of England, was given to New York. Neither the Canadians nor the Indians were consulted. They would hear of these terms only after the treaty was signed.

This immense loss of rich territory south of the Great Lakes threatened to restrict Canada permanently to a limited area of eastern North America and prevent it from ever developing into a major continental nation. The great West presented the only hope of replacing this vast area and its rich furs. The North West Company of Montreal, an alliance of Scottish businessmen, English merchants and French-Canadian voyageurs, fought with desperate energy to secure the West for Canada. The French-Canadian coureurs de bois and voyageurs were individuals of immense strength and endurance. It was not unusual for a man to carry on his back, for sustained periods, a load of 400 pounds or more while travelling not at a walk, but at a dog-trot.

Alexander Mackenzie was the first white man to cross the continent. Relying on the advice of Natives — in all his contacts with Indians, Mackenzie wrote later, he had "never fired a shot in anger" — and transported by French-Canadian voyageurs, the explorer, in 1789, followed to the Arctic the great river that now bears his name.[23] He was 25 years old. In a second journey, he reached the west coast at the mouth of the Bella Coola River, where he scrawled on a rock overlooking the Pacific his famous words: "Alexander Mackenzie, from Canada by land, July 22, 1793." His work — backed by that of David Thompson, North America's greatest geographer, and the explorer Simon Fraser — helped give Canada a Pacific coast. The North West Company, with its explorers and voyageurs, was the first Canadian organization to span the continent. It would be ten years before their nearest American rivals, Lewis and Clark, reached the Pacific.

The war hawks in the U.S. Congress, however, had a solution to put an end to the competition for the northern part of the continent. Once again, it would be a military solution.

3

To Rival the Exploits of Rome

IN 1812, THE LONGEST and largest American invasion of Canada began. In June of that year the United States declared war on Britain, hoping to take Canada while Britain was tied down in war with Napoleon's France. Thomas Jefferson, who had recently served as president, declared: "The acquisition of Canada this year, as far as the neighbourhood of Quebec, will be a mere matter of marching and will give us experience for the attack of Halifax next."[1] William Eustis, the U.S. secretary of war, announced: "We can take Canada without soldiers. We have only to send officers into the Provinces and the people ... will rally round our standard."[2] Gouverneur Morris of Pennsylvania, another leader of the first U.S. Congress, stated: "All of North America must at length be annexed to us — happy, indeed, if the lust for dominion stops there."[3] And Henry Clay, speaker in the U.S. House of Representatives and a persistent advocate of conquering Canada, proclaimed: "The militia of Kentucky are alone competent to place Montreal and Upper Canada at your feet ... I am not for stopping at Quebec or anywhere else; but I would take the whole continent from them, and ask no favors. I wish never to see peace till we do. God has given us the power and the means. We are to blame if we do not use them."[4]

Southern U.S. politicians desired Florida; the northerners wanted Canada. Senator William Hunter of Rhode Island explained that the "declaration that Canada should be conquered and retained was the exacted pledge of the Northern men who voted for the war." There was, he expounded, to be an enlargement and a rounding out of the territory at the two extremities: "a fair division of the spoil." Representative John Harper from New Hampshire said: "To me, Sir, it appears that the Author of Nature has marked our limits in the

South, by the Gulf of Mexico; and on the North, by the regions of eternal frost."[5] And, announced Major-General Andrew Jackson, future president: "We are going to ... vindicate our right to a free trade, and open market for the productions of our soil . . . to rival the exploits of Rome" and to carry "the Republican standard to the Heights of Abraham."[6] Prominent congressman John Randolph of Virginia said that the House of Representatives echoed to "but one word — like the whippoorwill, but one monotonous tone — Canada, Canada, Canada!"[7]

The U.S. army under General William Hull crossed the Detroit River and attacked Canada with 2500 troops, and the war that would decide the destiny of half the continent was on. From the town of Sandwich, present-day Windsor, Hull set up his headquarters, raised the Stars and Stripes and issued his proclamation:

Inhabitants of Canada!

The army under my command has invaded your country, and the standard of the United States now waves over the territory of Canada. To the peaceable, unoffending inhabitant it brings neither danger nor difficulty. I come to *find* enemies, not to *make* them. I come to *protect* you not to *injure* you ... I tender you the invaluable blessings of civil, political and religious liberty ... that liberty which has raised us to an elevated rank among the nations of the world ...

Remain at your homes, pursue your peaceful and customary avocations, raise not your hands against your brethren ... I have a force which will look down all opposition, and that force is but the vanguard of a much greater. If, contrary to your own interests and the just expectation of my country, you should take part in the approaching contest, you will be considered and treated as enemies, and the horrors and calamities of war will stalk before you. If ... the savages be let loose to murder our citizens and butcher our women and children, this will be a war of extermination. The first stroke of the tomahawk, the first attempt with the scalping-knife, will be the signal of one indiscriminate scene of desolation. *No white man found fighting by the side of an Indian will be taken prisoner;* instant destruction will be his lot.[8]

Canada's population was outnumbered by the Americans twenty-five to one. In terms of military force, the United States recruited more men during the war than the total population of

Canada. As a first step, Congress mobilized 35,000 regular troops, with a call-up of 100,000, while in all the Canadian provinces there were only 6500 soldiers. There were, however, north of the border, two of the greatest military commanders in the history of North America. The first was the British general Isaac Brock. The second was the Shawnee chief, Tecumseh.

Tecumseh, born in 1769 in the heart of the Indian Territory south of Lake Erie, grew up witnessing the massacre of his people and the invasion of Shawnee land by the Americans. A warrior from his teens, the orphaned boy developed into a gifted orator and incorruptible leader. He urged an end to intertribal warfare and advocated an Indian confederation to stand against encroachment by the white population. He resisted and condemned the chiefs who were prepared to trade historic lands for enough money to enrich themselves but leave their people destitute. Water, air and land, he said, were the common possessions of all Indians, not something that could be signed away by "peace" chiefs who, he said, did not own them.

To the Canadian side of the Detroit River in 1812, he brought one of the most formidable forces ever commanded by a Native leader on this continent.

Born on the isle of Guernsey in the same year as Tecumseh was Isaac Brock, soon to be known as the Hero of Upper Canada. By 1812, Brock had accumulated twenty-seven years of military experience and was in charge not only of the military, but also of the civilian administration of the province of Upper Canada. A farsighted planner, Brock, like Tecumseh, was daring and energetic. When Brock and Tecumseh met for the first time, August 13, 1812, at Amherstburg, legend has it that Tecumseh reported to his men: "This is a *man!*" Brock for his part wrote: "A more sagacious and gallant Warrior does not I believe exist. He was the admiration of everyone who conversed with him."[9]

At the beginning of the war, Brock found widespread disbelief that Canada would ever be able to resist the U.S. giant. Writing from York, now the city of Toronto, he said: "My situation is most critical, not from anything the enemy can do, but from the disposition of the people . . . A full belief possesses them that this Province must inevitably succumb. This prepossession is fatal to every exertion — Legislators, Magistrates, Militia Officers, all have imbibed the idea."[10]

More than 30 percent of the population of Upper Canada

(Ontario) were recent American immigrants, and they offered little resistance to the enemy. Another group of former Americans, the United Empire Loyalists, driven out of the United States in 1783, had a very different point of view. In the words of historian Hugh Keenleyside, they "supplied the hatred and inspired the enthusiasm" that helped turn the scales.[11]

The British and Canadians looked to the Indian tribes, whose very existence was threatened by the American army and the never-ending U.S. takeover of their lands, as their main allies. Fur magnate James McGill wrote: "The Indians are the only Allies who can aught avail in the defense of the Canadas. They have the same interest as us, and alike are objects of American subjugation, if not extermination."[12]

At a war council meeting called by Brock, almost all his commanders felt it would be folly to cross the border and attack the Americans. But Tecumseh said it could be done. Brock listened. Tecumseh and his men had only a week earlier ambushed a heavily armed convoy of General Hull's, capturing the mail — including Hull's military dispatches to Washington — and bringing it to Brock, who was able to learn of the American commander's situation and especially his fear of the Indians. Further west, a few British soldiers, 400 Indians and 180 French-Canadian voyageurs had three weeks earlier seized the strategic fort of Michilimackinac on Lake Huron, giving Canada command of the main routes to the west.

Brock knew that everything depended on swift and bold action, and with Tecumseh he decided that the best defence was a good offence. "Gentlemen," he said, "we shall cross the river. We gain nothing by delay. We are committed to a war in which the enemy must *always* be our superior in numbers and ammunition."[13] Brock's 400 Canadians, 250 British and 50 Newfoundland troops joined Tecumseh's 600 warriors representing more than a dozen tribes: Shawnee, Miami, Ottawa, Wyandot, Chippewa, Potawatomis, Winnebago, Dakota, Kickapoo, Delaware, Fox, Sac and Iroquois. Together they set out to attack Detroit.

Before they reached the fort at Detroit, Brock sent out a man carrying a fictitious message to an area where he was sure to be captured. The letter, supposedly from British colonel Henry Procter, said that 5000 Indians were on their way to join the attack on Detroit. When the Americans captured the man and searched him, they found that message: Tecumseh then had his men cross a clearing in single file in full view of Detroit and then circle back through the woods and cross again. By afternoon, the American general, thinking thousands of Indians were preparing to attack, sent forth an officer with a white flag of surrender. Using a combination of limited attack and brilliant strategy, Brock and Tecumseh, and their forces, thus compelled the complete surrender of Hull and 2500 American troops.

The capture of Detroit, which commanded the whole of west-central North America, affected the entire war. The greatest loss of territory ever suffered by the United States, it was a major blow to American morale, and it inspired the Canadians. Tecumseh was pleased, "his face perfectly calm, but with the greatest satisfaction beaming in his eye." He and Brock rode side by side into the fort as the Stars and Stripes was lowered. On the previous day, August 15, 1812, Indian forces had attacked the fort at Chicago, overwhelmed the Americans and burned the fort to the ground, ending the last remnant of American control in the western Great Lakes region.

Defeated in the west at Detroit, the Americans now mobilized more than 6000 troops to enter Canada by the Niagara Peninsula. Although vastly outnumbered, Brock was determined to "neutralize numbers by activity and vim." The American force crossed the river at Queenston the morning of October 13, 1812. Brock, knowing the outcome of the war could depend on this battle, rallied his men for an assault on the American invaders' position at Queenston Heights. The defenders — Canadian, British and Indian — defeated the Americans in that historic battle. The Indians, under chiefs John Brant, son of Joseph Brant, and John Norton, who although Scottish born had become an adopted Mohawk chief, "particularly distinguished themselves" (in the words of Brock's successor, General Roger Sheaffe.)[14] The Americans were driven back across the river, with 900 taken prisoner. Brock, a perfect target in red with his distinctive cocked hat, was leading the charge in the teeth of enemy fire when he took a fatal bullet in his chest.

At his funeral, described by a contemporary as the "grandest and most solemn . . . that has been seen in Upper Canada," his casket was carried through a double line of 5000 armed Indians and militia.[15] From across the river, even the Americans, it is said, fired a salute to their fallen enemy.

Almost exactly a year later, in the battle of Moraviantown, on the Thames River near present-day Chatham, Ontario, the British forces broke under a U.S. cavalry charge. His troops outnumbered three to one, the British General Procter turned and fled for his life. Tecumseh, though wounded, was everywhere in the battle, a heroic figure urging his fighters on. The Indians stood and fought long and hard, until they were overwhelmed and Tecumseh was cut down.

Two-thirds of the U.S. soldiers in the battle were Kentuckians, and each of them wore a scalping knife. After the battle, the American troops turned to the bodies and scalped and mutilated them. The method they used was described by British historian William James:

> A circular incision, of about three inches or more, in diameter, according to the length of the hair, is made upon the crown of the head. The foot of the operator is then placed on the neck or body of the victim, and the *scalp*, or tuft of skin and hair, torn from the skull by strength of arm. In case the hair is so short as not to admit of being grasped by the hand, the operator, first with his knife turning up one edge of the circle, applies his teeth to the part; and, by that means, quite as effectually disengages the *scalp*. In order to preserve the precious relic, it is then stretched and dried upon a small osier [willow] hoop.[16]

Tecumseh's body was rescued by his people and spirited away. Another body, mistaken by the Americans for that of Tecumseh, was "flayed' and the skin cut into narrow strips for souvenir razor straps to be taken to Kentucky. The Indian settlement of Moraviantown was burned to the ground as part of the American scorched earth policy.

Tecumseh, to whom we owe, along with Isaac Brock, the very existence of the Canadian nation, lies somewhere in an unknown and unmarked grave.

In 1814, Illinois passed a law offering a bounty of fifty dollars for each Indian killed by a citizen. If the citizen first obtained permission of a commanding officer, the reward was doubled. The famous "Indian fighter," Davy Crockett, in his autobiography described one of his 1813 battles to remove the southern Creek Indians from their lands:

> We now shot them like dogs; and then set the house on fire, and burned it up with the forty-six warriors in it ... We went back to our Indian town on the next day, when many of the carcasses of the Indians were still to be seen. They looked very awful, for the burning had not entirely consumed them, but given them a very terrible appearance, at least what remained of them. It was, somehow or

other, found out that the house had a potato cellar under it, and an immediate examination was made, for we were all as hungry as wolves. We found a fine chance of potatoes in it, and hunger compelled us to cat them, though I had a little rather not, if I could have helped it, for the oil of the Indians we had burned up on the day before had run down on them, and they looked like they had been stewed with fat meat.[17]

In Canada, the combination of British troops and Native forces had turned the tide. But Canadians — French- and English-speaking, men and women — also played their part. Men, including the elderly, left their farms to fight. The women stepped forward to work the land and harvest the crops, and also performed various military functions, including scouting.

One of the champions of the War of 1812 was a Queenston housewife and a mother of five, Laura Secord. American-born, Secord had moved to Canada as a teenager. At the Battle of Queenston Heights, 37 years old, she had saved her husband's life by rescuing him from the battlefield where he lay seriously wounded after fighting alongside Isaac Brock. She then played a critical role in the strategic Battle of Beaver Dams. On June 23, 1813, she delivered a warning of an impending American attack, enabling the British commander James FitzGibbon to prepare for and ultimately defeat the Americans in that battle for the Niagara Peninsula. As FitzGibbon wrote later: "Not a shot was fired on our side by any but the Indians. They beat the American detachment into a state of terror." He also gave full credit to Secord's warning, acknowledging that it had enabled him to plan the ambush: "I have ever since held myself personally indebted to her for her conduct."[18] (It nevertheless took more than one hundred years of persistent effort, first by Laura Secord herself and then by women historians, to give her name its place in history. Laura Secord's wish to be assigned the care of Brock's monument was denied by government officials. She was 87 years old when she received the first official recognition of her role — one hundred pounds from Prince Edward of Wales. Secord's memorial now stands at Queenston Heights, not far from that of her hero Brock.)

In July 1813, the Americans looted and burned the Parliament buildings of York (now Toronto), the capital of Upper Canada. Their move on Montreal, however, was stopped at Châteauguay in October of that year, when fewer than 500 French Canadians under the bold and able command of Colonel Charles-Michel de Salaberry defeated an American invading force of 4000 and drove them back across the border. Allied with de Salaberry's French Canadians was a small force of Caughnawaga Indians, whose brilliant tactics of bluff and deception terrified the Americans into thinking that their numbers were hundreds rather than tens. This crucial French-Canadian and Native victory, along with the victories of Tecumseh and Brock, was instrumental in setting the course of the war.

The following year, British forces under Admiral George Cockburn and General Robert Ross seized Washington in retaliation for the destruction of York. President James Madison, his wife, and the U.S. secretary of war fled the city as the House of Representatives, the White House and the Capitol itself were put to the torch in a spectacular fire seen for miles. That evening at supper, Cockburn extinguished the candles so he and his men could eat by the light of the flames. For forty-eight hours Washington burned, until the British withdrew, unmolested. "In short, sir," Cockburn — said to be scrupulous about avoiding damage to private property — reported to his senior officer, Alexander Cochrane, "I do not believe a vestige of public property, or a store of any kind, which could be converted to the use of the government, escaped destruction."[19]

At the Treaty of Ghent to end the war, the American negotiators once again were more than a match for the British, who were pre-occupied with Napoleon and the fate of Europe. Although unable to conquer any of Canada, the American negotiators in 1814, as they had in 1783, opened by demanding all of it. Britain, although it controlled northern Maine and parts of New York and had a total naval blockade of the Atlantic coast, refused to use its power. The Americans walked from the table with a treaty providing a return to prewar boundaries, a position the United States had summarily rejected three years earlier when Russia had offered to mediate. The British, contrary to Brock's written recommendations to London, betrayed their Native allies — who were barred from any place at the table, as was Canada itself — by agreeing to U.S. claims over Native lands and dropping completely the Native demand for a neutral Indian territory in the region of the upper Mississippi. Victory was declared in the United States, with great celebrations of triumph. "The United States," observed author Bruce Hutchison, "had lost a war and won a conference."[20]

In Canada, a national war had been fought. Success in this life-and-death struggle against overwhelming odds gave French- and

English-speaking Canadians a new respect for each other. Without their joint effort, allied with the skill and energy of the Native forces and the discipline of the British troops, Canada would have been lost. Under the slogan "Independence and Liberty" the United States had tried to deprive Canadians of both, and had failed. The invader had been repulsed. The Montreal *Herald* summed it up. Canadians were, it said, "convinced of the future necessity of keeping their neighbours at a respectable distance, whether in peace or war."[21]

The U.S. failure to take Canada in the War of 1812 left a legacy in Canada of resistance to U.S. aggression and determined the shape into which the nation would develop over the next hundred years.

The War of 1812 deflected American expansionism from the north, and the United States turned to the south and southwest. In 1819, it seized Florida from Spain because, as Henry Clay told Congress, "it fills a space in our imagination."[22] Some Americans then began to make plans to take Texas from Mexico.

But U.S. designs on the Canadian colonies had by no means ended. U.S. business interests began taking over the rich timber areas of the Ottawa Valley and New Brunswick. The 1820s saw riots along the Miramichi River when Maine lumbermen came across the border and began to claim New Brunswick timberlands. In 1825, Maine declared as its own the New Brunswick settlements of Aroostook and others on the Madawaska. When U.S. officials arrived to plan an election and began to take a census, New Brunswick arrested them. Congress then called out the militia, authorized the recruitment of 50,000 men and voted $10 million for war. The governor of Maine ordered U.S. troops in to occupy the area. Nova Scotia then moved to support New Brunswick, calling a special legislative session in which $100,000 was voted for the immediate support of New Brunswick. "Amid scenes of great popular enthusiasm," as one historian wrote, Nova Scotia "promised to place at the disposal of the junior province every dollar and every man ... should war become an actuality."[23]

The United States reversed itself and withdrew its troops. Canada had won the Aroostook War! But the victory soon proved hollow. The United States began talks with Britain, through which it succeeded in gaining by negotiation most of what it had failed to gain by force. The British negotiator, Alexander Baring (Lord Ashburton), head of the Baring bank group, was married to the daughter of William Bingham, a U.S. senator who owned a million acres of Maine timber. (No doubt having his wife's estates in mind, Baring, at the negotiations ending the War of 1812, made an impassioned speech in the British House of Commons against asking America to give up Maine. And, to future president John Quincy Adams he wrote: "I wish the British government would give you Canada at once. It is fit for nothing but to breed quarrels.")[24] The chief U.S. negotiator, Daniel Webster, about to become U.S. secretary of state, was the agent for Barings in America. As a result, Maine received that large wedge of territory almost up to the St. Lawrence River, cutting Canada's coast off from the interior and cutting Saint John, New Brunswick, off from Montreal. By the Webster-Ashburton Treaty of 1842, Canada also lost Point Rouse on Lake Champlain, and Isle Royale in Lake Superior (near present-day Thunder Bay). Webster declared after the settlement that seven-twelfths of the territory and four-fifths of the value at stake went to the United States.

Not satisfied with this victory, some voices in Washington began to argue for the annexation of what is now southwestern Ontario. Matthew Maury, superintendent of the U.S. Department of Charts and Instruments, wrote in May 1845 that it was intolerable there should be this "long slip of foreign territory obtruding itself between two states of the Union, and reaching down ... into the very heart of the country." A straight line from Lake Ontario to Lake Huron, he wrote, "is the natural boundary of the United States," and every effort should be made to conquer and annex the "State of Toronto."[25] His efforts failed, however, and the focus of American expansionism moved to the West, where the dramatic struggle for the continent's Pacific coast was already under way.

4

54°40' or Fight

IN THE 1820S, MEXICO made a generous offer to Americans to settle in Texas, after the United States had by treaty given up all claims to this Mexican province in return for validation of its seizure of the Florida territory from Spain in 1819. Mexico hoped that, by populating Texas with white Americans, it would protect itself from U.S. aggression. It soon realized it had made a mistake. Some 20,000 Americans and their slaves moved into the province between 1820 and 1830. In 1826, some of the American immigrants staged a short-lived revolt and proclaimed a Republic of Fredonia. Then, in 1827, the United States attempted to purchase Texas; Mexico rejected the offer and, in 1830, stopped further immigration.

The American immigrants ignored Mexico's prohibition against slave labour, settled in areas reserved for Mexicans, and then in 1836 rose in revolt and demanded "independence" and admission to the United States. Mexican general Antonio López de Santa Anna came north to put down the revolt, trapped a garrison of Americans at the Alamo in San Antonio, and eliminated them. One of the "independence" fighters killed was Davy Crockett. In subsequent battles, American general Sam Houston, vowing never to bow his head to a "greaser yoke," defeated and captured Santa Anna and then forced him to sign a treaty, agreeing to Texan independence, that was promptly repudiated by the Mexican government. Houston, a Tennessee lawyer, one-time governor of that state, and U.S. congressman from 1823 to 1827, became the new president of Texas and promptly offered his country to the United States. For a few years, Texas had a separate existence while Houston urged the United States to annex it. In 1843, ex-president Andrew Jackson said his country must have Texas, "peaceably if we can, forcibly if we must."[1] In 1845, in spite of a strong opposition from the antislavery states, the United States completed its seizure of Texas, which was annexed as a slave-holding state.

Soon, "Manifest Destiny" and "Divine Right" would become the justification for the U.S. claim to all of North America.

IN 1579, FRANCIS DRAKE had sailed around South America and then north, becoming, it is said, the first European to lay eyes on the west coast of future Canada. Retreating southward, he anchored and "took possession" of the surrounding country in the name of the English queen. By the early 1800s, Russian, British and American traders were competing in a relentless rivalry for the west coast. In 1822, the Convention of Commerce fixed the international border between British North America and the United States across the prairies to the Rocky Mountains at the 49th parallel. West of the mountains, Britain and the United States agreed, would be a joint occupation of the Oregon Territory by British subjects and American citizens. The Oregon Territory was a large area bounded on the south by Spanish America (after 1821, the Republic of Mexico) at 42° — the present border between California and Oregon — and on the north by the southern tip of Russian America (present-day Alaska) at 54°40'.

By its charter of 1670, the Hudson's Bay Company had the exclusive right to trade in the British American northwest, and its domination of the fur trade in the Oregon Territory assured Britain control of that area. In 1842, U.S. president John Tyler offered to settle the border at the Columbia River if Britain would agree to pressure Mexico to sell California to the United States. Britain did not respond, and the U.S. government financed a group of missionaries and settlers from Missouri to travel to Oregon where, upon their arrival in 1843, they promptly declared a provisional government in spite of opposition from the Canadians and British already there. They demanded "all of Oregon" and the expulsion of Canada and Britain from the entire Pacific northwest – even though the Hudson's Bay Company, allied with the Canadians of the North West Company, controlled the region, and despite the fact that in the whole area north of the Columbia River there were fewer than a dozen Americans.

Because, as a leading American historical account put it, "England had both history and law on her side," American politicians discovered a "higher law" upon which the "true title" to Oregon should be based. James Polk rode to victory in the 1844

U.S. presidential election on the campaign slogan "Fifty-four forty or fight," claiming all of the west coast of North America clear up to Alaska.[2] In defending this slogan, which lacked any historical or diplomatic foundation – there was no treaty recognizing any American rights to the Pacific coast – John L. O'Sullivan, editor of the New York *Morning News,* coined a phrase that would run through American politics and sow fear in the hearts of that country's neighbours. Under the heading, "The True Title," O'Sullivan wrote: "We have a still better title than any that can ever be constructed out of all these antiquated materials of old black-letter international law. Away, away with all these cobweb tissues of rights of discovery, exploration, settlement, continuity, etc ... And that claim is by the right of our manifest destiny to overspread and to possess the whole of the continent which Providence has given us. Shortly before penning that piece, O'Sullivan had written: "Texas, we repeat, is secure; and so now ... who's the next customer? Shall it be California or Canada?"[3]

Congressman Edward Baker of Illinois informed the U.S. House of Representatives in January 1846 that he had little regard for "musty records and the voyages of old sea captains, or the Spanish treaties because we have a higher and better title under the law of nature." And William Sawyer from Ohio said: "We received our rights from high Heaven, from destiny, if you please."[4]

The aging ex-president John Quincy Adams, now a member of the House of Representatives, asked the clerk of that chamber to take a Bible and read from Genesis: "Be fruitful and multiply, and replenish the earth, and subdue it." "That, sir," Adams told the House, "is the foundation of the title by which we are now called to occupy the territory of Oregon." He asked the clerk to read again, this time from the second Psalm: "Ask of me, and I shall give thee the heathen for thine inheritance, and the uttermost parts of the earth for thy possession." This passage, Adams said, gave the United States a better right to Oregon than its present British and Canadian occupiers. Congressman Andrew Kennedy of Indiana thundered that if the British lion "refuses to move at a peaceful command, he will run his nose in the talons of the American eagle, and his blood will spout as from a harpooned whale."[5]

In his inauguration speech, President Polk declared once again that the American title to the west coast extended up to Alaska. He then gave legal notice to Britain that the United States was withdrawing from its joint-occupancy treaty and was preparing for war. To avoid war, Britain offered to surrender all the territory on the west coast below the lower Columbia River. But the Americans, who wanted the excellent ports of the Puget Sound and Juan de Fuca areas, refused. So Britain retreated all the way to the 49th parallel, and the United States succeeded in getting not only one of the world's finest harbours at present-day Seattle, but also the entire Columbia Valley, and what are now the states of Washington, Oregon and Idaho. Polk said that he doubted "whether the judgement of the civilized world would be in our favor in a war waged for a comparatively worthless territory north of 49°."[6] Thus, by the Oregon Treaty of 1846, the 49th parallel became the border, with Britain retaining all of Vancouver Island.

This settlement gave the U.S. government a free hand for a re-newed war on Mexico, whose territory, also by "divine right," the New York *Herald* said belonged not to indolent Mexico but to the United States, which would use it properly. Former Texas president Sam Houston, now a senator, declared the war was "the Divine Being ... carrying out the destiny of the American race" to civilize the continent. Senator Daniel Dickinson of New York called for *"a more perfect Union:* embracing the entire North American continent,*"* and pointed out that "new races are presented for us to civilize, educate and absorb."[7]

The "all-of-Mexico" movement, supported by most of the press in the United States, pushed Polk to seize the country, whose population of approximately seven million was 75 percent Indian. The problem, as one newspaper put it, was for Americans to unite with the "degraded' Spanish-Mexican race. Polk's secretary of state, James Buchanan, asked pointedly: "How should we govern the mongrel race which inhabits it?"[8]

The press offered a solution. Wrote the influential *Democratic Review:* "The process which has been gone through at the north, of driving back the Indians, or annihilating them as a race, has yet to be gone through at the south."[9] The New York *Evening* Post said that "Providence" had ordained that the Mexican people could not exist independently beside the United States: "The Mexicans are *Aboriginal Indians,* and they must share the destiny of their race." And the *American Review* explained that Mexico must give way to a "superior population ... oozing into her territories, changing her customs, and ... exterminating her weaker blood."[10]

Senator Lewis Cass of Michigan in February 1847 told the Senate: "We do not want the people of Mexico either as citizens or subjects ... All we want is a portion of territory which they nominally hold, generally uninhabited, or, where inhabited at all, sparsely so, and with a population which would soon recede or identify itself with ours."[11]

On February 2, 1848, by the treaty that ended the war, Mexico was forced to confirm the American title to Texas and cede outright New Mexico and California.

IN 12 YEARS, in total, the United States had seized one-half of Mexico's entire territory, including — besides Texas — nearly all the area that makes up the present-day states of California, New Mexico, Arizona, Nevada and Utah, and parts of Colorado and Wyoming.

The enslavement of Indians, started under the Mexicans, continued with a vengeance in New Mexico and California. Thousands of Indians perished under the relentless attack of American scalp-hunting teams. Public holidays featured Indian hunts as a form of celebration. As many as 50,000 Indian deaths occurred in California from 1849 to 1856.

Further north, the settlement of the boundary dispute defining British Columbia's southern border with the United States ushered in what was called the "friendly era" in U.S.-Canada relations. The Americans now chose to use trade rather than military force as a method of gaining control.

And this time around, they had help from some of the richest men in Canada, who would sign a call for the annexation of their own country.

5

The American Warning

IN THE MID-1800S, what is now eastern Canada was made up of five completely separate British colonies — Newfoundland, Nova Scotia, New Brunswick, Prince Edward Island and the United Province of Canada, the last-named formed in 1840 by the union of Upper and Lower Canada — each with its own government, trade arrangements (including tariffs) and even banking and money systems. And far away, on the west coast, were the little colony of Vancouver Island and the soon-to-be colony of British Columbia. Stretching between the east and west and over much of what is now northern Quebec and Ontario lay the immense land mass of the Northwest Territories, controlled by the Hudson's Bay Company.

In the late 1840s, Britain repealed the Corn Laws. These laws had provided for a preference, or lower tariffs, on grain from the colonies, in contrast with grain from the United States or other countries, going into Britain. With Britain moving to free trade, Canadian grain and flour exports fell dramatically, and Canada was hit by a severe economic depression. In 1849, Lord Elgin, Governor General of Canada, observed: "Property in most of the Canadian towns, and more especially in the capital [Montreal], has fallen fifty per cent in value within the last three years. Three-fourths of the commercial men are bankrupt, owing to free trade."[1]

Some of Montreal's most prominent businessmen formed a committee of "gentlemen of wealth, education and influence" to consider the problem and devise a solution. The city was alive with rumours that a public manifesto calling for annexation was about to be published. On October 11, 1849, there appeared in the Montreal *Gazette* the most important document in the history of the annexation movement.

Entitled "An Address To The People Of Canada," the lengthy manifesto began by calling upon all citizens to unite to solve the severe economic problems afflicting the country:

> The reversal of the ancient policy of Great Britain, whereby she withdraws from the colonies their wonted protection in her market, has produced the most disastrous effects upon Canada ... our country, stands before the world in humiliating contrast with its immediate neighbours, exhibiting every symptom of a nation fast sinking to decay ... amongst all classes, there is a strong pervading conviction that a political revolution in this country is at hand.

The manifesto looked at a number of possible remedies, including reviving protection in the United Kingdom, protecting Canada's own industries, forming a union of the provinces, and free trade with the United States. All were found lacking in merit. Those fighting for an independent nation were dismissed. An independent country was beyond the capability of Canadians, the wealthy authors of the manifesto maintained:

> The consolidation of ... new institutions from elements hitherto so discordant — the formation of treaties with foreign powers — the acquirement of a name and character among the nations, would, we fear, prove an over-match for the strength of the new republic.

With that, the document moved to its main recommendation:

> Of all the remedies that have been suggested for the acknowledged and insufferable ills with which our country is afflicted, there remains but one to be considered ... THIS REMEDY CONSISTS OF A FRIENDLY AND PEACEFUL SEPARATION FROM BRITISH CONNECTION, AND A UNION UPON EQUITABLE TERMS WITH THE GREAT NORTH AMERICAN CONFEDERACY OF SOVEREIGN STATES.

Then followed a long list of advantages to be had from joining the United States:

> The proposed union would render Canada a field for American capital, into which it would enter as freely ... as into any of the present states. It would equalize the value of real estate upon both sides of the boundary, thereby probably doubling at once the entire

present value of property in Canada ... Nor would the United States merely furnish capital for our manufactures. They would also supply for them the most extensive market in the world, without the intervention of a Customs House officer. Railways would forthwith be constructed by American capital . . . and railway enterprise in general would doubtless be as active and prosperous among us as among our neighbours ...

In place of war and alarms of war with a neighbour, there would be peace and amity between this country and the United States ... As citizens of the United States, the public service of the nation would be open to us — a field for high and honourable distinction, on which we and our posterity might enter on terms of perfect equality ...

The authors summarized the advantages of the union for the United States and concluded:

Fellow colonists, — we have thus laid before you views and convictions on a momentous question, involving a change which, though contemplated by many of us with varied feelings and emotions, we all believe to be inevitable; one which it is our duty to provide for, and lawfully to promote. We address you without prejudice or partiality — in the spirit of sincerity and truth — in the interest solely of our common country, and our single aim is its safety and welfare.[2]

Some 325 signatures were obtained in five hours. Within ten days, more than one thousand had signed. In all, over 1500 signatures representing the cream of the financial and political elite of Montreal appeared on the manifesto, including those of John Redpath and William and John Molson, surnames still familiar to Canadians.

A Kingston newspaper described the atmosphere thus: "The Montreal Annexationists doubtless desire to retain their loyalty but they flatly declare they can no longer afford the luxury." *Punch in Canada* published a "business flourometer":

Flour, 33 s. [shillings] per barrel — loyalty up

Flour, 26 s. per barrel — cloudy.

Flour, 22 s. per barrel — down to annexation.[3]

Leading Montreal newspapers, including the *Herald*, the *Courier* and the *Witness*, came out for union with the United States. The *Gazette* tried to straddle the fence, announcing it would support the annexationists when they were right and criticize them when they were wrong. The excitement in the city was at a fever pitch.

Although 96 percent of the signatories to the manifesto were English Canadians, Louis-Joseph Papineau, the French-Canadian leader in the long battle for responsible government that had culminated in the Rebellion of 1837, and the group around him (soon to become the Parti Rouge), joined the movement. Their newspaper, *L'Avenir*, published an article supporting the Annexation Manifesto. They introduced what would become a refrain among Quebec annexationists: the myth of Louisiana, which claimed, with more fantasy than fact, that the French-speaking Creole population of Louisiana was proof that the French culture could thrive within the United States.

The Montreal Annexation Association, an unlikely alliance of English Tory businessmen and French-Canadian radicals, ran candidates for the legislature, arguing that political union with the United States would improve Canada's economy. Its president was sugar tycoon John Redpath, and Denis-Emery Papineau, nephew of Louis-Joseph, was vice-president. Other officers included brewery owner William Molson and leading French-Canadian Rouge politicians Rodolphe Laflamme and A.A. Dorion. Alexander Galt, railway promoter and member of Parliament, joined the movement, as did John Abbott, a future prime minister.

The annexationists failed dismally to win support among the general population for their drive to make Canada part of the United States. The first protest, and it came swiftly on the heels of the manifesto, was from French Canadians. A counter-manifesto, signed by George-Etienne Cartier and other French-Canadian members of the government, was published: "We, the undersigned," it began, "have read with astonishment and regret a certain address to the people of Canada ... we consider ourselves urgently bound to protest publicly and solemnly against the opinions enunciated in that document." The counter-manifesto called upon the public to oppose "by every means in their power" the movement to subvert Canada.[4]

In rural Canada — French- and English-speaking — the annexationists were hated as "mercenary traitors, prepared to sell their heritage for Yankee gold."[5] The governing Reform Party of

Louis-Hippolyte LaFontaine and Robert Baldwin, which held every French-Canadian seat in the United Province of Canada, vigorously opposed the annexationists. Anyone holding a government position or appointment who had signed the manifesto was dismissed. The list included justices of the peace, officers in the militia and magistrates. Lawyers holding the status of Queen's Counsellor were asked to return their gowns. The annexationists protested loudly the "tyrannical conduct" against them.[6] But to no avail. Within less than a year, the annexation movement was in retreat.

A national spirit was developing, and its advocates argued that the alternative to looking to England for salvation was not to turn to the United States, but for Canadians to look to themselves.

In 1889, four decades after he had signed the manifesto, Sir John Abbott in a speech to the Senate said:

> The annexation manifesto was the outgrowth of an outburst of petulance in a small portion of the population of the Province of Quebec, which is amongst the most loyal of the Provinces of Canada ... There were a few people of American origin who seized a moment of passion into which the people fell, to get some hundreds of people in Montreal to sign this paper. I venture to say that, with the exception of those American gentlemen, there was not a man who signed that manifesto who had any more serious idea of seeking annexation with the United States than a petulant child who strikes his nurse has of deliberately murdering her.[7]

ALTHOUGH THEY FAILED to have Canada annexed to the United States, the backers of the annexation movement were able to push the British government to negotiate, on behalf of its five eastern North American colonies, a reciprocity agreement with the United States.* The Reciprocity Treaty, signed in June 1854, provided for free trade in natural products, opened Canadian waterways to U.S. shipping, and gave the United States free access to the Canadian maritime fishery.

The U.S. government was actively involved. One of its secret agents, Israel D. Andrews, sent up to influence the course of events,

---

* Reciprocity refers to the mutual reduction of duties or tariffs charged on each other's products by Canada and the United States.

made the mistake of leaving behind his expense account. It revealed that in an attempt to push the annexation and free-trade movements in Canada, he paid $5000 to an editor, $5000 to an attorney general, $5000 to an inspector general and $15,000 to a member of the New Brunswick Assembly. Andrews worked tirelessly and reported regularly to his state department. On May 13, 1854, he wrote: "I have therefore taken such measures as the circumstances of the case required in N.B. to moderate the opposition and keep the public mind in a quiet state ... I was able to reach Fredericton before the N.B. Legislature adjourned, and prevent any discussion of the proposition now under consideration, or any legislative action of an adverse character."[8]

In all, he spent more than $100,000 — equivalent to several million today — trying to persuade prominent individuals in Canada to support either annexation or, his second choice, free trade with the United States. But the amount was a mere trifle, he wrote, "in comparison with the immensely valuable privileges to be gained *permanently,* and the power and influence that would be given forever to our Confederacy."[9]

The term of the Reciprocity Treaty was ten years, after which time it was to continue indefinitely, subject to either party's right to terminate on one year's notice. It lasted from 1854 until 1866. After the treaty had been in effect for six years, the American consul in Montreal reported to his secretary of state, Lewis Cass, that the treaty was "quietly but effectually transforming these five provinces into States of the Union commercially speaking."[10]

Some in Canada viewed things differently. James Little, a lumberman, in 1862 described the situation: "As regards lumber — Canada lost millions by that treaty ... The raw material which would now be worth millions of dollars, were it standing in the forests, never returned a farthing to the operators or the country ... labor expended in manufacturing it went to add to the wealth of our neighbors across the line, while their own timber was so far preserved for future use. They and they only were the gainers by reciprocity in lumber, while nearly all on this side engaged in supplying their wants were ruined."[11]

U.S. lumber companies moved in on some of the finest timber in the Canadian colonies, leaving behind, in the words of Canadian historian A.R.M. Lower, "desolated, stump-filled regions" suggesting an invading army. A New York lumber company destroyed one of the largest stands of high-quality pine in Canada, in the region between Lake Simcoe and Georgian Bay. Some of the profits apparently were channelled into the endowment funds of Cornell University in New York. The forests above Lake Erie were destroyed, leaving behind "often nothing but a break-water, a few buildings and a waste of sand."[12]

As for the fishing industry, a Charlottetown newspaper wrote: "Our neighbors had so long trampled upon our privileges, that they imagined they had a perfect right to use our fishing grounds for their own benefit."[13] American vessels came in such numbers that, in the words of a British observer: "As regards fishing rights, the U.S. appeared largely to have the advantage."[14]

Because trade between the United States and the Canadian colonies increased during the period, and because the time was one of increased prosperity, free-trade advocates for the next 125 years pointed to free trade as being good for Canada. In fact, the period was one of phenomenal development in both countries for reasons that had nothing to do with the treaty. The increase in trade was part of a growth period that had begun before the treaty and would continue after it was terminated. These were boom years of railway construction in Canada. Large amounts of public and private money were spent building the Grand Trunk and Great Western lines. In 1850, there were sixty-six miles of rail in the colonies; by 1860, more than two thousand. The Crimean War, 1854-56, increased the demand and price for Canadian agricultural products. Sailing ships built in the shipyards of Quebec, New Brunswick, Nova Scotia and Prince Edward island were in strong demand. Above all, the American Civil War, 1861-65, disturbed the normal course of trade. The export of certain products from the United States was prohibited during the war, and Canada saw a huge demand created for its products.

During the years of the treaty, exports from Canada to the United States consisted almost entirely of raw materials, while about 60 percent of Canadian imports from the United States were manufactured goods. At the same time, the Canadian colonies changed their currency from the pound sterling to the dollar, tying their economy more closely to that of their neighbour.

The United States repealed the treaty unilaterally in 1866, not only as a result of pressure from some American businesses — in 1865 and 1866, the balance of trade favoured Canada for the first significant period of time in the treaty — but also, and more significantly, because many advocates of U.S. expansion felt that by cancelling it they could force the Canadian colonies to ask or beg for entry into the United States.

THE PERIOD ALSO saw tension rising between Britain (and Canada) and the United States over the American Civil War. President Lincoln and Congress had declared that the North was fighting not to put an end to slavery, but to preserve the Union. This declaration was followed by Queen Victoria's proclamation of neutrality, which implicitly recognized the right of states to secede and outraged Washington. In 1861, a U.S. (northern) warship had forcibly removed two Confederate (southern) commissioners from the English mail ship *Trent* on the high seas, creating an international incident known as the Trent Affair. Adding friction between Washington and London were the many among the English nobility and well-to-do commercial class who wanted to see the North defeated. As well, three Confederate ships, the *Alabama,* the *Shenandoah* and the *Florida,* were built in British ports, leading to the accusation by Washington that Britain favoured the South. Later, outside Britain, the *Alabama* was fitted with guns. By the war's end, it was said, the *Alabama* had sunk 62 northern vessels valued at $6.5 million. That ship's role in the war would have serious consequences for Canada.

Canadians were overwhelmingly opposed to slavery. Upper Canada had abolished slavery in 1793, the first British colony and the second jurisdiction in the world, after Denmark, to do so. But Canadians, as people repeatedly threatened with American attacks, also felt that the South, whether part of the United States or not, was a counterbalance to the relentless expansionism of the North. If the South broke away, the power of the United States to threaten Canada would be reduced.

For a time it appeared inevitable that the Trent Affair would lead to war between Britain and the United States. Britain dispatched 14,000 troops to Canada, and the colonies braced themselves to fight once more against the United States.

Meanwhile, the U.S. fever for annexation was rising. The New York *Herald* campaigned ceaselessly: "Let them remember," it pronounced, "that when the termination of our civil conflicts shall have arrived ... [f]our hundred thousand thoroughly disciplined troops will ask no better occupation than to destroy the last vestiges of British rule on the American continent, and annex Canada to the United States."[15] The men marching in the north sang a popular version of "Yankee Doodle":

Secession first he would put down
Wholly and forever,
And afterwards from Britain's crown
He Canada would sever. [16]

The Chicago *Tribune* declared in January 1866 that, following cancellation of the Reciprocity Treaty: "The Canadians ... will stay out in the cold for a few years and try all sorts of expedients, but in the end will be constrained to knock for admission into the Great Republic." Canada, the paper stated two weeks later, "will be snatched up by this Republic as quickly as a hawk would gobble up a quail."[17] The Massachusetts legislature passed a resolution for the annexation of Canada. Then, on July 2, 1866, General Nathaniel P. Banks, representative from that state and chairman of the Foreign Affairs Committee, introduced into the U.S. Congress "a Bill for the Admission of the States of Nova Scotia, New Brunswick, Canada East and Canada West, and for the organization of the Territories of Selkirk, Saskatchewan and Columbia ... as States and Territories of the United States of America."[18]

It was this threat from the United States that led the leaders of the Canadian colonies to begin negotiations for the purpose of joining forces to create the Confederation of Canada.

THE *ACT OF UNION* in 1840 had united the two largest colonies, Upper and Lower Canada (Ontario and Quebec), under one parliament with an equal number of seats for each. By the early 1860s, dissension was rife. George Brown's Ontario-based Reform Party, decrying "French domination," was demanding representation by population ("rep by pop") because Ontario had recently surpassed Quebec in population. This arrangement would have torn the fragile union apart — Quebec had accepted an equal number of representatives in 1840, although its population was then far greater. The Parti Rouge in Quebec, forerunner to the Liberal Party, was demanding repeal of the *Act of Union* for completely different reasons; it advocated universal suffrage and annexation to the United States. By early 1864, the future looked bleak: three Canadian governments had fallen in the space of thirteen months and Parliament appeared deadlocked. The Canadian colonies, divided and unorganized, wrote historian W.L. Morton, "having not so much as a flag, much less the uniforms of soldiers or police, to exhibit sovereignty ... drifted spellbound, incapable of moving ... to face the perils the end of the [Civil] war would bring."[19] (To prevent the northward movement of Union troops in railway cars, the gauge of Canadian railway tracks of the period was almost ten inches wider than in the U.S.)

Then the unexpected, almost unbelievable, happened. In a moment of dramatic and far-reaching significance, George Brown, leader of the Reform Party, decided he would support his enemies, the Tories, in order to make union of the colonies possible. Responding to tentative proposals from Conservative leader John A. Macdonald, Brown approached this long-time and bitter foe of his and offered to form a coalition. Brown's speech to the Canadian Parliament in June 1864 was one of the greatest of his life. He "almost broke down during it, but he carried the whole House."[20] Said Brown:

> For ten years I have stood opposed to the honourable gentlemen opposite in the most hostile manner it is possible to conceive of public men arrayed against each other ... I am free to confess that, had the circumstances in which we are now placed been one whit less important, less serious, less threatening than they are, I could not have approached honourable gentlemen opposite, even with a view to these negotiations. But ... if a crisis has ever arisen in the political affairs of any country which would justify such a coalition as has taken place, such a crisis has arrived in the history of Canada . . . Mr. Speaker, party alliances are one thing and the interests of my country are another.[21]

At the end of the speech, amid enthusiastic and sustained cheering, Brown was surrounded and congratulated from all sides, and some of the members from Quebec reached out and kissed him on both cheeks. The Great Coalition — of Conservatives led by John A. Macdonald, Reformers by Brown, and Quebec's Parti Bleu, forerunner of the Conservative Party in Quebec, by George-Etienne Cartier — was the most successful coalition in Canadian history. It made possible the Confederation of Canada.

ON SEPTEMBER 1, 1864, delegates from Nova Scotia, New Brunswick, Prince Edward island and Canada gathered at Charlottetown.

Would it be possible to join together in one united country, strong enough to overcome its internal divisions and powerful enough, in conjunction with Britain, to resist the power of the United States? George-Etienne Cartier opened the week-long conference with the case for a federal union. John A. Macdonald spoke for almost an entire day. Alexander Galt had long since reversed his earlier support for annexation to the United States, and now strongly advocated union of the provinces. Dr. Charles Tupper, premier of Nova Scotia, warned that the end of the Civil War could see the U.S. armies moving north against the provinces.

The conference moved on to Halifax. Delegates drew up plans for a follow-up convention in Quebec to hammer out the constitutional details of the new nation. For seventeen days, delegates to the Quebec City conference, including representatives from Newfoundland, worked in haste. The plan that emerged was for a grand transcontinental federation, with British Columbia, Vancouver Island and the great Northwest to be admitted on terms to be agreed by all.

The Parti Rouge attacked the proposal, and the debate raged throughout 1865. The prime minister of the United Province of Canada, Etienne Taché, argued: "If the opportunity which now presented itself were allowed to pass ... we would be forced into the American Union by violence, and if not by violence, would be placed upon an inclined plane which would carry us there insensibly." Solicitor-General Hector Langevin asked: "What would be the fate of the French Canadians in the case of annexation to the United States? Let us profit by the example of the French race in the U.S., and enquire what has been the fate of the French in Louisiana? What has become of them? What has become of their language, their customs, their manners and their institutions?"[22]

Thomas D'Arcy McGee, journalist, poet, historian and Canadian minister of agriculture, was the great orator of the Confederation movement. Warning Canadians "to sleep no more except on their arms," he urged a Canadian union and spoke of "the warning from without — the American warning."[23] Speaking in the Canadian Parliament on the Confederation resolution in 1865, he said:

> "Another motive to union . . . is this, that the policy of our neighbors to the south of us has always been aggressive. There has always been a desire amongst them for the acquisition of new territory ... They coveted Florida, and seized it; they coveted Louisiana, and purchased

it; they coveted Texas, and stole it; and then they picked a quarrel with Mexico, which ended by their getting California. They sometimes pretend to despise these colonies as prizes beneath their ambition; but had we not had the strong arm of England over us, we should not now have had a separate existence. The acquisition of Canada was the first ambition of the American Confederacy, and never ceased to be so, when her troops were a handful and her navy scarce a squadron. Is it likely to be stopped now, when she counts her guns afloat by thousands and her troops by hundreds of thousands?"[24]

George-Etienne Cartier, the leading father of Confederation from Quebec, summed up his position: "Confederation was at this moment almost forced upon us ... The matter resolved itself into this, either we must obtain British American Confederation, or be absorbed into an American Confederation."[25]

THE U.S. SECRETARY OF STATE, William H. Seward, strongly opposed Canadian Confederation. "I know," he told an appreciative audience in Boston, "that Nature designs that this whole continent, not merely these thirty-six states, shall be, sooner or later, within the magic circle of the American Union."[26] Backed by the New York *Times*, Seward worked relentlessly to make it so.

In 1858, the Irish Revolutionary Brotherhood, known as the Fenians, had been set up in Dublin to fight for Ireland's independence. An American branch of the Fenian Brotherhood established itself, and in 1863, at a large convention in Chicago, proclaimed the Irish Republic, elected a Senate and House of Delegates, and established an army. In early 1866, Major Thomas Sweeny, formerly of the Union Army, was made secretary of war in the Fenian Cabinet, and one faction of the Fenian Brotherhood announced plans for the invasion of Canada. Raids on Canada could strengthen its bargaining hand with Britain, this faction felt, or even trigger a war between Britain and the United States, which might enable Ireland to break away from the iron hand of British rule.

William Seward pledged not to interfere with the Fenian attacks on Canada. His president, Andrew Johnson, said he would recognize the establishment of a Fenian republic north of the border. Arms and ammunition were collected, and the Fenian military felt it would be able to take all of Canada, with the stiffest resistance coming from Quebec. Their marching song went:

> We are the Fenian Brotherhood, skilled in the art of war,
> And we're going to fight for Ireland, the land that we adore,
> Many battles we have won along with the boys in blue,
> And we'll go and capture Canada, for we've nothing else to do.[27]

On April 14,1866, the Fenians launched a raid on Indian Island, New Brunswick, near the New Brunswick-Maine border, where they burned several buildings before being driven back. Six weeks later, on June 1, 1866, a force of 2000 crossed the Niagara River and took Fort Erie, intending to move on Montreal. They were met by a massive Canadian mobilization and driven back across the border — nine Canadians were killed and thirty-seven wounded. Watching the results from Buffalo, some 8000 more men decided not to cross the river. On June 4, a second invasion of 1800 crossed into Quebec from Vermont, and were driven back by Canadian troops. The Fenian general, Michael Heffernan, bitterly complained afterwards: "We have been lured by the Cabinet and used for the purpose of Mr. Seward ... They encouraged us on to this."[28]

Seward urged an American banker to buy out the rights of the Hudson's Bay Company in Rupert's Land (today, northern Quebec, northern Ontario and much of western Canada) before the government of Canada could do so, and in March 1867 he negotiated the purchase of Alaska from Russia, taking control of the northwest corner of the continent in a move openly admitted to be an attempt to head off the confederation of Canada.

Historian P.B. Waite described the scene:

For Confederation the American purchase of Alaska was a significant flanking movement. The Queen signed the British North America Act on March 29, 1867. In Washington that same night the American Secretary of State, William Seward, and the Russian Minister were up until the small hours completing the agreement for the purchase of Alaska. It was signed then and there — about 3 o'clock in the morning on March 30, 1867. It went to the Senate a few hours later ... Charles Sumner [Massachusetts] urged the Senate to ratify the purchase of Alaska on the ground that it was a "visible step in the occupation of the whole North American continent." The Senate did ratify the Treaty, by a vote of 37–2. The American newspapers gave some indication of how Americans felt. Alaska may or may not have been the "sucked orange" that the New York *World* said it was, but the justification for its purchase was often the hope of gaining the territory between Alaska and the United States ... The *Morning* Post said the reason for the American purchase was not the intrinsic value of Alaska but the hope of acquiring the territory south of it.[29]

In the House of Representatives, while debating the bill annexing Alaska, Ignatius Donnelly of Minnesota declared:

I shall vote for this bill . . . because I consider it one of the necessary steps in the expansion of our institutions and nationality over the entire domain of the North American continent ... But the great significance this purchase possesses is found in the fact that it points the way to the acquisition by the United States of that great and valuable region, Western British America ... With our great nation on the south of this region, and our new acquisition of Alaska resting upon its northern boundary, British dominion will be inevitably pressed out of western British America. It will disappear between the upper and the nether mill-stones. These jaws of the nation will swallow it up ... Nothing less than a continent can suffice as the basis and foundation for that nation in whose destiny is involved the destiny of mankind.[30]

The name Kingdom of Canada, proposed for the new nation by the Maritime delegates, had been chosen by the fathers of Confederation. Maine's legislature passed a resolution opposing the name, and the issue was raised in Congress. London, concerned about its relations with Washington, asked the Canadians to find a name less objectionable to Americans. Accordingly, the struggling new country became the Dominion of Canada, a term practically impossible to translate into French.

The British Parliament in London passed the *British North America Act* on March 8, 1867. Watching anxiously from the gallery were John A. Macdonald and his new wife, Susan Agnes, Charles Tupper, Thomas D'Arcy McGee, Samuel Leonard Tilley of New Brunswick, and the other delegates, all of whom had been living in a London hotel for three months while shepherding the bill through the British houses of Parliament.

As Canada's birthday present, at the passing of the *British North America Act*, the U.S. House of Representatives unanimously passed a resolution of "extreme solicitude," condemning the formation of Canada as a separate nation on their northern boundary.[31]

NOBODY WAS EVER charged in the United States for the actions of the Fenians. Over the next half-decade, the American government repeatedly demanded payment from Britain for damage done during the Civil War by the ship *Alabama*, because it had been built in a British port. Charles Sumner, chairman of the Senate Foreign Affairs Committee, demanded outrageous compensation for "indirect claims." Britain could pay the bill of from two to as much as eight billion dollars, he indicated, by transferring its North American colonies to the United States. Senator Zachariah Chandler, chairman of the Military Affairs Committee, told Congress that Britain was responsible for half the costs of the Civil War. "I put on file a mortgage upon the British North American provinces for the whole amount," Senator Chandler thundered, "and that mortgage is recorded and the security is good."[32]

In 1872, Britain paid the United States in final settlement $15 million, more than twice what the Americans would shortly pay for Alaska. Yet all claims by Canada for damages, loss of life, injuries and cost involved in the Fenian raids were rejected out of hand by the U.S. government, which had openly assisted and encouraged them. And Thomas D'Arcy McGee, whose words had moved, inspired and mobilized Canadians to the vision of a united and independent country, was "shot down for his Canadian patriotism by a Fenian skulker in Ottawa," on April 7, 1868, at the age of 42.[33]

WITH THE TERMINATION of the Reciprocity Treaty and the birth of the Dominion of Canada, 1867 saw the end of the "friendly era." The expansionist forces in the United states turned again to direct annexation as their method of operation, and the theatre of action once more moved west.

6

Prophet of the New World

IN DECEMBER OF 1867, Minnesota senator Alexander Ramsey abruptly rejuvenated the annexation movement by introducing into the U.S. Senate a bill that would reinstate the 1854 Reciprocity Treaty. In return, the bill stipulated, "Canada ... shall cede to the United States the districts of North America west of longitude 90°" — all of that huge expanse of present-day Canada west of the Great Lakes. The United States would pay the Hudson's Bay Company six million dollars for its rights, take over British Columbia's debt, "not exceeding the sum of $2,000,000," and build a railway to Puget Sound.[1]

Senator Ramsey's bill did not pass. Instead, it speeded up negotiations between Ottawa and the Hudson's Bay Company for the transfer of Rupert's Land to Canada. These negotiations were denounced by a resolution rushed through the Minnesota legislature calling for Canada to be ceded to the United States — a transfer "which shall remove all grounds of controversy between the respective countries."[2]

In the House of Representatives, Rufus P. Spaulding of Ohio took strong offence when one of his colleagues spoke of acquiring "foreign possessions." "Sir," Spaulding retorted, "as an American citizen, and a republican at that, I deny that any territory upon this western continent is to be deemed foreign to the Government of the United States when it seeks to extend its limits ... This proud Republic will not culminate until she rules the whole American continent, and all the isles contiguous thereunto." To which Frederick Pike of Maine interjected: "Including South America." Whereupon Spaulding replied: "Including South America, by all means."[3]

The election in 1868 of Ulysses S. Grant as U.S. president and Grant's appointment of Hamilton Fish as secretary of state provided a big boost to the annexation forces. Secretary Fish repeatedly told Britain that, if it withdrew from North America, the problems of

"Indians, Fenians, disorderly soldiers &c." would be removed and the *Alabama* claims settled. Grant instructed his Cabinet to delay negotiations over the *Alabama* claims until Britain was ready to cede Canada.[4]

One of the special agents sent up by the Secret Service Branch of the U.S. Treasury to the Red River area of present-day Manitoba was James Wickes Taylor, known as "Saskatchewan Taylor" because of his knowledge of western Canada and his desire to gain it for the United States. A lawyer and one-time Ohio state librarian, Taylor was a tireless researcher. Recognized as the foremost American authority on western British America, he clipped from a wide selection of international papers — English, American, Canadian — every item that concerned the West. For twenty-five years Taylor, clever and discreet and operating under various covers, worked ceaselessly for his dream of a vast American empire in the northwest. As early as 1865, he announced from Fort Garry (outside present-day Winnipeg): "The Americanization of the fertile belt is inevitable ... Indeed it is for the interest of the settlers here that annexation should take place at once." The way to political union, he argued, was through economic union. With the end of the Reciprocity Treaty in 1866, Taylor turned to promoting outright annexation. In June that year he presented to the U.S. Congress a detailed plan for continental union. "The United States may interpose ... and if so, why shall we not combine to extend an American Union to the Arctic circle?"[5]

Meanwhile, Canada was negotiating with the Hudson's Bay Company to take over the Red River territory as if the area had no inhabitants. The 12,000 residents of Red River, 90 percent of them of mixed Native and European descent, called Métis, were opposed to being made a colony within a colony without being consulted by either Ottawa or London. They set up a provisional government in late 1869 to represent the Métis — both French- and English-speaking — to negotiate with Canada the terms under which the West would enter the Dominion.

LOUIS RIEL SR., a miller, trapper, trader and community leader, was born at Île-à-la Crosse in what is now northern Saskatchewan. His wife, Julie Lagimodière, was the daughter of the first European woman in the northwest. In 1844, in St. Boniface (part of today's Winnipeg), they had a son who would become one of Canada's most famous leaders, orators and spokespersons for the oppressed.

Educated in Fort Garry and in Montreal, young Louis Riel decided in the final year of his seminary training that he would not become a priest. He entered the study of law and then returned to Manitoba, to be chosen by the French and English Métis settlers to lead the new provisional government.

When the Riel government took power, the American annexation movement thought it saw its moment of opportunity and rushed to seize it. "The Red River revolution," wrote the *Press* of St. Paul, Minnesota, on February 8, 1870, "is a trump card in the hands of American diplomacy ... if rightly played." Minnesota congressman Ignatius Donnelly told a packed meeting organized by the St. Paul Chamber of Commerce: "If the revolutionists of Red River are encouraged and sustained by the avowed sympathy of the American people, we may within a few years, perhaps months, see the Stars and Stripes wave from Fort Garry, from the waters of Puget Sound, and along the shores of Vancouver." Minnesota's "geographical necessities," he said, dictated that "This country [Rupert's Land] belongs to us, and God speed the Fenian movement or any other movement that will bring it to us!"[6]

Colonel Enos Stutsman, a brilliant lawyer, although born without legs, rode fearlessly throughout the west in his specially made saddle. From 1862 to 1866, Stutsman served as a member of the territorial legislature of Dakota. Then, like James Wickes Taylor, he worked for the U.S. government as a special agent under several guises (real estate agent and reporter, among them), moving constantly between Minnesota and Fort Garry.

The American general Oscar Malmros, had arrived in Winnipeg in August 1869 as the new American consul. The headquarters of what then was called the American Party was set up in Emmerling's Hotel in Winnipeg. As jubilant Americans toasted annexation, the U.S. flag was raised over the hotel. General Malmros notified his department of state that the situation was volatile; he would be pleased to set up a force and seize the area when the moment was right.

In Minnesota, the press, the politicians and the merchants clamoured for Manitoba. The former governor, William Marshall, arrived in Winnipeg pledging financial and military backing if Louis Riel would declare for annexation. Jay Cooke, the railroad tycoon, pledged the money and organization to take the territory for the United States. Oscar Malmros urged his state department to act. "The sum of about $25,000 promptly sent," he wrote in a consular dispatch, "would materially aid and I think secure the success of the independence movement" — which he said meant "annexation to the U.S." To Senator Ramsey he was more direct: "$100,000 would make the annexation movement a success."[7]

Malmros, Stutsman, Taylor and W.E.B. O'Donoghue, an American of Irish origin who served as treasurer in Riel's government, besieged the Métis leader, urging annexation.

Another American agent, Major Henry M. Robinson, arrived in Winnipeg and began publishing a newspaper, *The New Nation*. A leading article of the first issue, entitled "Annexation Our Manifest Destiny," urged the colony to follow its economic interests and become part of the United States, rather than be tied by sentiment to the British Empire. Commercial links were impossible across the "dismal waste of rocks and water" between Winnipeg and Canada. "In fact," the article explained, "we have nothing in common with that country or its government." Nature had joined Rupert's Land to the republic to the south, the editorial argued, and "it is evident that the United States is the only Nation to whom we can look."[8]

The third issue carried bold front-page headlines: "Consolidation!" "The Future of the American Continent," "One Flag! One Empire!" "Natural Lines must Prevail." Its editorial called for the golden day when "but one flag shall wave" over the continent and painted "a vision of a grand consolidation of peoples and interests, such as can be paralleled nowhere else among all the Kingdoms of the Earth." Editorials from American newspapers were reprinted. The New York *Times* judged it a foregone conclusion that American influences would decide the future of the rebellion — to think otherwise would be a mistake. Under the headline "A Magnificent Future," the New York *Sun* wrote: "The tendency of events of this North American Continent is plainly toward the consolidation of all the people dwelling upon it into one great nation, around the present United States as a nucleus ... there will in time be but one government, and one national power. Canada, Rupert's Land, Victoria, Mexico will have but one flag and eventually Cuba and her sister islands will join us. Thus united, we can defy the world ... Who among us can say that ours is not a glorious destiny, or reflect without exultation that he is an American citizen!"[9]

At that moment, the future of all North America west of the Great Lakes clear to the Arctic Circle hung in the balance. From Ottawa, John A. Macdonald wrote: "It is quite evident to me ... that the United States government are resolved to do all they can, short of war, to get possession of the western territory and we must take immediate and vigorous steps to counteract them."[10]

But Macdonald was too late. The Canadian government had no presence in Manitoba. President Grant's Cabinet, hoping that without a road over Lake Superior the troops would be blocked, refused permission for the Canadian military expedition to Red River to pass through the locks at Sault Ste. Marie. Then, on April 22, 1870, Zachariah Chandler, the senior senator from Michigan, rose in the U.S. Senate. Although Canada was, he said, "a mere speck upon the map," it was "an intolerable nuisance." And if it ever reached the Pacific, it would become "a standing menace ... that we ought not to tolerate and will not tolerate." Britain should give the United States the deed to all North America, and in return the U.S. would forgive what Britain owed from the *Alabama* claims. He warned Canada not to send troops to the Red River. Both Fenians and frontiersmen were marching north, he said, and in support of them was "the strongest military Power on earth ... Mr. President, this continent is ours."[11]

Louis Riel was only 25 years old, but he stood his ground. He ordered the Union Jack raised over Fort Garry. When O'Donoghue tore it down, Riel replaced it and stationed his uncle André Nault under it, armed with a rifle and orders to shoot the treasurer of the provincial government or anyone else who tried to take it down.

Major Robinson, now the American vice-consul, was arrested and forced to give up his keys to the *New Nation's* office. In the next issue of the paper, annexation was "knocked on the head," according to Alexander Begg, a prominent local merchant.[12] The power and influence of the American Party vanished almost overnight. The American flag came down, not to fly again. General Oscar Malmros learned that some of his letters to Washington, asking for money and troops, had mistakenly been published by the State Department. He declared his position had become "untenable, impracticable and, in fact, intolerable"; and, although ill and despite a raging blizzard, he abruptly left the colony in the middle of the night.[13]

Faced with President Grant's refusal to let westward-bound Canadian troops pass through the locks at Sault Ste. Marie, Macdonald's Cabinet threatened to close the Welland Canal in retaliation. The Americans reversed their position.

According to official testimony provided by Bishop Taché of St. Boniface, the Americans offered Riel and members of his provisional government more than four million dollars, in addition to men and guns, in exchange for supporting the annexation of western Canada to the United States.

But Riel remained "thoroughly patriotic and no less thoroughly incorruptible" (this description by Montana historian Nathaniel P. Langford, the brother-in-law of James Wickes Taylor).[14] Using consummate diplomatic and political skill, he secured basic rights for the French- and English-speaking population and achieved most of what his government sought from Canada. In 1870, Manitoba was admitted as the fifth province of the Canadian union, with the rest of the West, east of British Columbia, to be administered as a territory. Provincehood for this territory was promised within five years.

James Wickes Taylor, now U.S. consul in Winnipeg, saw his dream go up in smoke. Riel, he reported to Washington, "could not be persuaded to abandon the Queen, and Riel was still 'chief of the Métis.'"[15]

The annexationists complained bitterly that Riel had used them as a bargaining lever to get the political arrangements he wanted from Ottawa, then "discarded them when his purposes were served."[16]

O'Donoghue, now working openly for annexation, returned to the United States to raise a force to invade and seize western Canada. With the active support of Senator Ramsey and the eager assistance of Stutsman, O'Donoghue met with President Grant and then toured the United States, giving speeches and passing the collection plate for funds for the invasion. He met twice with the Fenian Council and requested troops.

Rumours reached Winnipeg in October 1871 that O'Donoghue had an army of 3500 troops assembled in St Paul for the invasion. In his tent at the border, Manitoba's militia commander, Major Acheson Irvine, with only eighty men at his command, sent off a frantic message: "I shall require reinforcement at once."[17]

Riel's council voted to organize an armed force to meet the invasion. A letter signed by Riel, his general Ambroise Lépine, and Pierre Parenteau went to the lieutenant governor of the new province, Adams Archibald: "Several companies have already been organized, and others are in process of formation ... you may rely on us."[18] When Governor Archibald arrived to review the force, between two and three hundred well- armed "wardens of the plains" greeted him by firing their traditional salute.

The invading force at O'Donoghue's command turned out to be

fewer than fifty men, who were subsequently arrested by the U.S. military with the assistance of local Métis and then promptly released. O'Donoghue, who escaped arrest, tried again. Captured on the Canadian side of the border by a party of Riel's Métis horsemen, he was delivered back to the United States.

Governor Archibald wrote later: "If the half-breeds had taken a different course, I do not believe the Province would now be in our possession."[19] Historian W.L. Morton summed up Riel's accomplishments:

> By the Resistance Riel saved the French element in the North-West from neglect and oblivion. He saved them both from the heedless aggression of Ontario and the parochial indifference of Quebec. By the Resistance Riel challenged Quebec to play a positive part in Confederation, to maintain French institutions throughout Canada and not merely in Quebec. He challenged Ontario to recognize that the dual character of Canadian nationality was not a temporary concession to necessity, but the foundation and framework of the federation. Riel, in short, forced the new Dominion to consider the full implications of the work of Confederation; and he demonstrated that Canada was not to be governed, as the North-West was not to be annexed, without the co-operation of French and English Canadians. Above all, the Red River Resistance revealed, in its full course and in full perspective, to what extraordinary lengths French and English Canadians would go, in spite of much mutual irritation and many mutual wrongs, to preserve a common allegiance and to share a common country.[20]

For ten months, Riel, in the face of tremendous pressure from Washington, Ottawa and the might of the British Empire, had held together a provisional government of varied and volatile forces. He had done so with "courage, energy, and decision" (in the words of Captain W.F. Butler, a British officer who had visited Fort Garry — and no friend of the Métis).[21] All this had been achieved with a single execution: that of Irish-born Orangeman Thomas Scott from Ontario, court-martialled by the Métis council, found guilty, and shot after his second armed attempt to overthrow Riel's government.

For this death, Riel — French, Catholic and part Native — would be relentlessly pursued for the rest of his life by Protestant Ontario. Although elected three times to the House of Commons by the voters of Manitoba, he was never allowed to take his seat. After his third election, Riel was condemned in absentia by the Commons to five years' exile. The province of Ontario offered a reward of $5000 for his capture.

Volunteer soldiers from Ontario, who had come west in the Canadian military expedition of 1870 to shoot "down any Frenchman" connected with Scott's execution, were anxious to collect such a considerable sum.[22] Recently released from military discipline, they "began to roam the country drunk with rage and alcohol." Ten of them, heavily armed, broke into Riel's home, threatened his mother and sister, and ransacked the humble dwelling. Riel and his general, Ambroise Lépine, were forced to flee to the United States, where the bounty hunters soon followed. Lépine, unable to live a life on the run, returned to his farm, where he was arrested, charged and convicted by the Canadian government for the "murder" of Thomas Scott, an action undertaken by a duly constituted provisional government before the government of Canada had jurisdiction in Manitoba. Four days before Lépine's scheduled execution, the sentence was commuted to two years in prison and loss of all civil rights.

The Métis people were terrorized and brutalized. Governor Archibald wrote: "Many of them actually have been so beaten and outraged that they feel as if they were living in a state of slavery."[23] Elzéar Goulet was chased by a civilian and two Ontario soldiers to the river, where he was stoned until he sank in the water and drowned. François Guillemette was murdered, and André Nault was stabbed with a bayonet and left for dead on the plains. Thomas Spence, the new editor of *The New Nation,* was horsewhipped. James Tanner, described as "a Protestant Half-Breed, who enjoyed a reputation of perfect honesty among his own people," was killed leaving a political meeting.[24] Baptiste Lépine, brother of Ambroise, was killed in a bar. The names go on: Letendre, Jolibois, Hallett ...

Many of the Manitoba Métis left the province for Saskatchewan. By 1885, the rest of the prairies still had not received the provincehood promised Riel in 1870. Instead, the Northwest Territories was run as a virtual dictatorship by a lieutenant governor and council — appointed by Ottawa. The residents, Native and white, began to organize. Conditions throughout the West were desperate. The United States government deliberately exterminated the buffalo in order to eliminate the Indians, who depended on the animal for survival. It is estimated that between 50 and 125 million buffalo were slaughtered in the United States between 1870 and 1880. According to an 1887 report by the Smithsonian Institute, the American buffalo range was "one vast charnel-house. Putrefying carcasses, many of them with the hide still on, lay thickly scattered over thousands of square miles of the level prairie, poisoning the air and water and offending the sight."[25] In the same period, an estimated one billion of the now-extinct passenger pigeons, another primary source of Native food, were killed in the United States in one year alone, 1878.

Hunters in Canada helped finish off the buffalo. Twelve thousand Natives on the Canadian prairies, almost half the population, were starved to death between 1880 and 1885 to clear the land for settlers and the railway. Louis Cochin, a priest from the North Battleford area, wrote about the conditions of Natives rounded up onto reserves and colonies: "I saw the gaunt children, dying of hunger come to my place. Although it was 30 to 40 below zero, their bodies were scarcely covered with torn rags."[26] The government refused to release rations or supplies to the starving people.

Louis Riel, in exile, was teaching in Montana. In 1885, a delegation of Métis, including Gabriel Dumont, the famed hunter, marksman and leader whose word, it is said, was law throughout the Saskatchewan country, asked Riel to return. The white settlers, under the effective leadership of Will Jackson, secretary of the Settlers' and Farmers' Union, joined forces with Riel and the Métis to petition the federal government for elected and representative government and land rights. Ottawa replied by sending 5000 troops, one for every five Indians and Métis living on the prairies. The soldiers came west under the British general Frederick Middleton, who had fought the Maoris in New Zealand and put down resistance to British rule in India. With them was a veteran U.S. "Indian fighter," Lieutenant Arthur Howard of the Connecticut National Guard, who brought with him three mounted Gatling guns.

The Gatling, invented during the U.S. Civil War, was the first successful machine gun. Now improved, with a capable man on the handle, the machine could fire 1200 bullets a minute. Howard, who knew as much about the gun as anyone alive, had petitioned to join the Canadian government forces, and had trained himself to the peak of perfection for this test of his beloved gun. As American historian Joseph Kinsey Howard described the event: "He had travelled more than twenty-five hundred miles into a foreign country to kill men against whom he had no feeling whatever ... His interest in the mass murder of Métis was wholly scientific ... Batoche was to be his laboratory."[27]

A military verse of the day tells us something about the role of the Gatling as used against the Métis, many of whom were forced to make do with nails and stones for ammunition:

Music hath charms even midst war's alarms
To soothe the savage breast;
None can hold a candle to that music "by Handle"
That lulled Riel's "breeds" to rest.
And they sleep that sleep profound, so deep,
From which shall awaken none;
And the lullabies that closed their eyes
Were sung by the Gatling gun.
All honour's due — and they have it, too —
To the Grens. and the Q.O.R.*
They knew no fear, but with British cheer,
They charged and dispersed afar
The rebel crew; but, 'twixt me and you
When all is said and done,
A different scene there might have been
But for Howard and his Gatling gun![28]

The bullet holes from the Gatling gun can today be seen in the rectory at Batoche, Saskatchewan. The mass grave of the vastly outnumbered Métis who fell can be found at Batoche as well.

When the battle was over, Riel gave himself up. After, in his own words, "being hunted like an elk for fifteen years," charged with treason, he would now face his accusers in court. The government succeeded in moving Riel's trial from Winnipeg, where, under the constitution of Manitoba that he had helped draft, he would have had the right to a twelve-man jury, half French-speaking. The trial would be held in Regina, in the Northwest Territories, under federal jurisdiction, where Riel got a six-man jury, none of whom spoke French. The greatest state trial in Canadian history would be conducted by a petty magistrate with an axe to grind: Judge Hugh Richardson had lost his property in the resistance fighting. The six Protestant jurors all were chosen from a list drawn up by the judge

---

* Royal Grenadiers and the Queen's Own Rifles of the Toronto Expeditionary Force.

himself. Crucial testimony would have to be translated by opinionated, and inexperienced, translators.

Denied all access to his papers, struggling with his lawyers who argued that he was insane, Riel was not allowed to question Crown witnesses or to bring his own key witnesses, now fugitive in the United States.

When finally allowed to speak on July 31, 1885, after the trial was over and after his lawyers had stated they would not be responsible for "any declaration he may make," Riel stood to face the sweltering courtroom.[29]

Struggling with the English words — "I cannot speak English very well, but am trying to do so, because most of those here speak English" — Riel began:

> When I came into the North-West ... the first of July 1884, I found the Indians suffering. I found the half-breeds eating the rotten pork of the Hudson's Bay Company and getting sick and weak every day. Although a half-breed, and having no pretension to help the whites, I also paid attention to them. I saw they were deprived of responsible government, I saw that they were deprived of their public liberties ...
>
> I know that through the grace of God I am the founder of Manitoba ... I did all I could to get free institutions for Manitoba; they have those institutions today ...
>
> In 1871 the Fenians came ... I brought to the governor 250 men, Governor Archibald was then anxious to have my help ... But the Canadian Government, what reward would they give me? ... He comes to the help of the Government with 250 men and the reward is $5,000 for his head.

Riel had a dream that the Northwest would be a place to which all the oppressed of the world could come:

> I say my heart will never abandon the idea of having a new Ireland in the North-West by constitutional means, inviting the Irish of the other side of the sea to come and have a share here; a new Poland in the North-West by the same way ... a new Italy ... and I want the French-Canadians to come and help us ... and the Jews who are looking for a country for 1,800 years ... the waves of the Pacific will chant sweet music for them to console their hearts for the mourning of 1,800 years ...

My ancestors were amongst those that came from Scandinavia and the British Isles, 1,000 years ago. Some of them went to Limerick and were called Reilson, and then they crossed into Canada and they were called Riel; so in me there is Scandinavian, and well rooted; there is the Irish, and there is the French, and there is some Indian blood. The Scandinavians, if possible, they will have a share, it is my plan, it is one of the illusions of my insanity, if I am insane, that they should have on the other side of these mountains, a new Norway, a new Denmark, and a new Sweden ... the Bavarians, the Italians and ... the Poles ...

If it is any satisfaction to the doctors to know what kind of insanity I have, if they are going to call my pretensions insanity, I say humbly, through the grace of God, I believe I am the prophet of the new world.[30]

Under massive pressure for Riel's death, the jurors nevertheless recommended mercy. But there would be no mercy from Ottawa. "He shall hang," Macdonald said, "though every dog in Quebec bark in his favour."[31]

Will Jackson, an intelligent, passionate man and a forceful speaker, offered to die in Riel's place. Jackson, too, as one of the main leaders, had been tried for treason, but he was acquitted on the basis of "insanity" by a government that did not want to hang a white man.

On the morning of November 16, 1885, in a Regina jail surrounded by so many police that even Gabriel Dumont was unable to rescue him, Riel stood in dignity on the scaffold trap door.

Riel's new-born baby had died just before the hanging. His Cree wife, Marguerite Monet, crushed by the weight of anti-Riel hysteria, tuberculosis and grief, would die within six months; their only daughter, Angélique, would follow within a decade, from starvation and tuberculosis. Their son Jean, forced to change his name to Louis Monet, "so reviled was the name Riel," died young and without children.[32]

Louis Riel's body was shipped in a boxcar on a midnight freight out of Regina to Winnipeg, where he was buried and rests today. Within a week, Montreal saw the greatest public meeting ever held in the province of Quebec. Wilfrid Laurier told the 50,000 people who had gathered in grief and rage: "If I had been on the banks of the Saskatchewan, I, too, would have shouldered my musket."

Honoré Mercier, who would go on to found the Parti National based on this momentum and win the premiership of Quebec within two years, "won the leadership of French Canada at this moment of crisis with his opening words: 'Riel, our brother, is dead, victim of his devotion to the cause of the *Métis* ... In killing Riel, Sir John has not only struck a blow at the heart of our race, but above all he struck the cause of justice and humanity.'"[33]

A LEADING HISTORICAL account of the period sums up the fight for the West: "With distinctly superior diplomatic skills, Canada's first Prime Minister, Sir John A. Macdonald, bested his American adversaries, won the Northwest for his young country, and assured it of a transcontinental greatness." In doing so, "he damped down the expansionist fires in Minnesota and elsewhere in the United States."[34] Macdonald's insistence that the military expedition be manned with British soldiers as well as Canadians was a brilliant move. The United States, war-weary and carrying massive debts from its Civil War, now knew that military intervention in Manitoba would involve Britain, something President Grant was not prepared to face.

Macdonald's victory would, however, be forever stained by the blood of Louis Riel and by the treatment meted out to his people, Native and Métis. Had Riel and the Métis succumbed to the bribes, intrigues and pressure of the Americans, it is a virtual certainty that all of the West — two-thirds of present-day Canada — would have been lost to the United States.

Defeated in Manitoba, the annexationists were now also about to lose their high-stakes battle for British Columbia.

7

The Uncrowned King of
the Masses

TWENTY YEARS FOLLOWING the settlement of the boundary between British Columbia and the United States, the area north of the 49th parallel no longer looked as "comparatively worthless" as President Polk had thought in 1846.[1] Gold had been discovered on the Fraser River.

In 1857, Victoria had been a quiet British settlement. A year later it suddenly became an American tent city, with 30,000 miners, most of them American, pouring into the area. The currency was American, flags flown were American, and American holidays were celebrated. The American gold-seekers even took steps to set up American courts.

Annexationists pressed for union with the United States and promised a rail line to the south. President Grant's secretary of state, Hamilton Fish, demanded that Britain cede British Columbia as settlement for the *Alabama* claims. Rumours circulated that the Fenian Brotherhood of California had enrolled up to 40,000 armed men "willing and anxious to go north."[2] The bishop of California asked: "May we not, by getting British Columbia, extend our territory in an unbroken line from Mexico to the Arctic Sea? How natural when one has four volumes of a work, to desire the fifth!"[3]

It seemed inevitable that the United States would gain the entire west coast. Britain seemed almost resigned. The *Times* of London wrote that if the colony wished to join the United States, "the Mother Country will in no way seek to prevent annexation."[4] Then, in a virtual replay of the seizure of Texas two decades earlier, and then of Oregon, Senator Corbett told the Senate that British Columbia should be admitted to the republic because a large number of U.S. citizens residing in the territory demanded it!

Under the nose of the governor in Victoria, the annexation movement grew. A petition for admission to the Union was sent to President Grant. From Ottawa, John A. Macdonald wrote to the British government: "No time should be lost ... in putting the screws on Vancouver Island, and the first thing to do is to recall Governor Seymour, if his time is not yet out. We shall then have to fight only the Yankee adventurers and the annexation party proper, which there will be no difficulty in doing if we have a good man at the helm."[5]

The "good man," however, was already in the colony, and he had come not from London but from a humble family in Nova Scotia. William Alexander Smith had left his native province to spend eight years travelling and working throughout the United States. In 1854, by an Act of the California legislature, he had changed his name to Amor De Cosmos (lover of the universe) because, he said, it conveyed what he most loved: "order, beauty, the world, the universe."[6] He arrived in Victoria in 1858, founded a newspaper, the *Times-Colonist*, and began to do battle with the annexationists. He advocated union of the colonies of British Columbia and Vancouver Island, which finally took place in 1866. Using the *Colonist* as his weapon, he rejected annexation and demanded responsible government and a transcontinental railway. Without a railway, one contributor to the paper wrote, "British Columbia might as well be confederated with the Pyramids of Egypt. Canada could not defend a Pacific province in case of war with the United States."

The *Colonist* developed the largest circulation in the west coast colonies. Its short-lived American-published competitor was, in De Cosmos's words, "managed by a proprietor from San Francisco like European states once imported Swiss mercenaries to do their bloody behests and drill their native subjects into submission."

Sir James Douglas, the governor of the now united colony, enraged by the *Colonist's* independent spirit, its attacks on corruption, "toadyism ... and incompetence, compounded with whitewashed Englishmen and renegade Yankees," and its demands for responsible government, ordered De Cosmos to post $3000 for a licence or cease publication immediately. In response, the public staged a large meeting that raised the money. Within ten days the *Colonist* was back on the street.

De Cosmos wrote: "It is too late in the day to stop men thinking. If allowed to think, they will speak. If they speak they will write, and what they write will be printed and published."[7]

Along with other prominent community leaders, the government assembly members, "vain, puffed up, tyrannical, corrupt, short-witted, conceited mummies and numbskulls," as De Cosmos referred to them in his editorials, tried repeatedly and unsuccessfully to muzzle him, using court action, electoral fraud and direct attack.[8] R.P. Rithet, one of the first mayors of Vancouver, went after De Cosmos with his fists, and the head of the Hudson's Bay Company, Roderick Finlayson, is said to have beaten De Cosmos physically after the editor exposed his receipt of patronage from the Douglas government. De Cosmos began carrying a stout walking stick for self-defence, but despite threats of violence, he refused to soften his criticisms.

The U.S. purchase in 1867 of neighbouring Alaska quickened the annexationists' momentum. All the coast would soon be American. De Cosmos wrote repeatedly of the danger posed to the colony by the United States. The only solution, he said, was confederation with Canada. He spoke across the province at large meetings and rallies, supported by the miners and by the people who, he said, "took the matter into their own hands, which they had a perfect right to do," by demanding Victoria ask for union with Canada.[9] In 1868, De Cosmos organized a convention at Yale, B.C., which set up the Confederation League and called for immediate union with Canada.

During years of bitter fighting with the annexationists and the colonial authorities, De Cosmos advocated his dream: "From the time I first mastered ... geography, I could see Vancouver Island on the Pacific from my home on the Atlantic, and I could see a time when the British possession, from the United States boundary to the Arctic Ocean, and extending from the Atlantic to the Pacific, would be consolidated into one great nation. And if I had my way, instead of the United States owning Alaska it would have been British today."[10]

A new governor, Anthony Musgrave, was appointed, and he quickly became convinced Confederation was the will of the people. De Cosmos, although denied by the governor a seat on the delegation negotiating provincehood with Ottawa, was elected to the B.C. legislature by the voters of Victoria. "I would rebel if there were enough like me in the colony," he declared, "and arrest every member of the government that I thought was robbing me of my rights." Meanwhile, Colonial Secretary Philip Hankin complained bitterly to England about those here who "hold out for ... Responsible

Government; and that they certainly are not fit for." Their leader, De Cosmos, was "a thorough Democratic ruffian" who is "a great nuisance in the House, & abuses the officials & the Government generally."[11]

By the close of 1870 the fight for Confederation was won and De Cosmos was the people's hero. The Canadian government had agreed to the monumental task of constructing a transcontinental railway. The new province of British Columbia would have three seats in the Senate and six in the House of Commons. Responsible government would be granted. The terms agreed to by Ottawa were virtually the same as De Cosmos had advocated for years. De Cosmos was promptly re-elected to B.C's legislature in Victoria, and at the same time was sent as a new member of Parliament from Canada's sixth province to Ottawa. In 1872, he became the second premier of British Columbia, a position he resigned in 1874 when dual representation was forbidden.

In later years, De Cosmos was callously treated by both Ottawa and Victoria. No gesture was ever made to recognize the contribution to Canada of the man who had "stood behind the gun." Deeply hurt, he "retreated with a wounded intensity into private life."[12] He was said to suffer from mental breakdown, and the courts, unable to tame him before, now had their way. The *Times-Colonist* reported in late 1895: "A man who once swayed the destinies of this great province and who, not many years ago, was the un-crowned king of the masses — a political power in the land — is now at the point of death ... Yesterday he was judged insane."[13]

Not long afterwards, in July 1897, hardly a handful watched as the casket of the man largely responsible for British Columbia's entry into Confederation was lowered into the ground. Yet without De Cosmos's fearless mind and the courage to use it, the beautiful resource-rich west coast of Canada would, in all likelihood, be American soil.

Canada now extended from sea to sea, and Manifest Destiny had been checked. Failing in their latest attempt to take Canadian territory physically, the American expansionists turned once more to methods of trade.

8

The Lightning Striker

THE INDIVIDUAL WHO, perhaps more than any other, made possible both the Confederation of Canada and its survival in its early tenuous years, was a man known as the "Lightning Striker." George-Étienne Cartier was born in 1814 into a well-to-do farming and grain exporting family in the Richelieu Valley at Saint-Antoine, not far from Montreal. Both his uncle and his father had fought against the American invaders during the War of 1812. During his tumultuous life, Cartier's energy and his vision for Canada played a major role in shaping Confederation, building the railroad to hold it together and negotiating the entry of the West into the young Dominion. At each step of the way Cartier too would face down powerful U.S. adversaries.

While still a teenager, George-Étienne Cartier became an early supporter of Louis-Joseph Papineau in his great battle for democratic rights. At the age of 20, he was a founder and first secretary of a patriotic association called the Saint-Jean-Baptiste Society. The maple leaf was chosen as the society's emblem, and for its founding meeting, June 22, 1834, those present stood and sang Cartier's national song, "O Canada, mon pays, mes amours," which he had composed for the event, and which likely inspired Canada's national anthem. His marching song, "Avant tout je suis Canadien [Before all else I am a Canadian]," composed during the rebellions that erupted in both Upper and Lower Canada in 1837, became his life's motto.

During the 1837 battles, he fought at Saint-Denis along with Wolfred Nelson and the other Patriotes with a courage, perseverance and steadiness that were the hallmarks of his whole life. On the Patriotes' side more than 300 died, about 1000 were arrested, over 50 were exiled to Australia and Bermuda[1] and 12 hanged. In Upper Canada, where William Lyon Mackenzie led an armed rising against the abuses of colonial rule, two were hanged, over 90 exiled and another 1000 arrested.

With Papineau in exile in France and William L. Mackenzie banished to the United States, the leadership of the Reform movement in Lower Canada was taken up by Louis-Hippolyte Lafontaine, and in Upper Canada by Robert Baldwin. Charged with high treason himself, Cartier escaped to the United States with a price upon his head and a banishment order forbidding his return under pain of death. After the amnesty of 1838, he immediately returned to support Lafontaine in the ongoing struggle to wrest power from the hands of officials appointed by London and put it into those elected by the people. Within a decade Lafontaine would become in effect the first prime minister of the United Province of Canada.

Meanwhile, when several hundred thugs drove Lafontaine's supporters from the polls to defeat him in the 1841 election, Robert Baldwin, the Reform leader from Upper Canada, who had won election in two seats (a legal practice at the time), offered his North York riding to Lafontaine. Baldwin wrote to the farmers of his riding, asking them to support Lafontaine as "a substantial pledge of our sympathy with our Lower Canadian friends."[2] Baldwin's father, Dr. William Baldwin, took Lafontaine around the riding and introduced him before each speech. Lafontaine was elected overwhelmingly. A year later, when Baldwin was defeated, Lafontaine returned the favour – bringing him to Rimouski, where the unilingual French-speaking voters elected him as their representative!

In 1842, Lafontaine told the legislative assembly of the United Province of Canada, "The mass of the two populations of Upper and Lower Canada have common interests and they will work out how to get on together."[3]

The striking and effective alliance between Baldwin and Lafontaine achieved its goal in 1848 when responsible government — control of the executive by elected representatives — was finally achieved. No longer could colonial governors overrule at will the elected assembly. As F.D. Monk, a prominent Quebecer, later wrote, "the day when Lafontaine accepted the charge of Premier and took the oath, stipulating that Robert Baldwin, his lifelong friend, should be his colleague, the 11th of March 1848, was without doubt a triumph dearly bought."[4]

Cartier and Lafontaine had by now split with Papineau, their former leader, who, after his return from exile in France, had declared that annexation to the United States was inevitable.

Cartier quickly rose to be co-premier of the United Province of Canada with John A. Macdonald in 1857-58 and again 1858-62. From this position he set in motion the move to Confederation, travelling to London with his finance minister, Alexander Galt, who had insisted on Confederation before joining the Cabinet, to recommend in writing that the subject of a federal union of the Maritime Provinces and the United Province of Canada be considered:

> At present each colony is distinct in its government, in its customs, its industries, and in its general legislation ... and the only common tie is that which binds all to the British Crown. This state of things is considered neither promotive of the physical prosperity of all, nor of that moral union which ought to be possessed in the presence of the powerful confederation of the United States.[5]

For years Cartier had the largest following of anyone in Parliament and sustained his ally John A. Macdonald, who was often in a minority position in his own province of Upper Canada. (Upper and Lower Canada had an equal number of members under the 1840 Act of Union.) The alliance between the two men formed the basis of the Conservative Party. As early as 1852, Cartier spoke out in favour of protecting Canadian industry. He authored a plank in the Cartier-Macdonald government, which he headed from 1858-62, that would "encourage Native industries and domestic manufacturers."[6] For the first time, a policy of protection had been adopted by a Canadian government.

Cartier opposed direct taxation of the population and insisted that government revenue should come from duties on imported goods. "I have never been a free trader in the absolute sense of the term," he explained. "The tariff should be regulated in a manner to serve the needs of the public service." His government intended to tax imported articles "which can be made in the country, protecting the manufacturers without increasing the price to be paid by the consumer."[7]

The key to French-Canadian survival, Cartier believed, lay in working with those in English Canada who also wanted to resist absorption into the United States. In advocating a Canadian union, Cartier warned eloquently and often of the threat he saw of assimilation of French Canada into the United States – followed soon by English Canada. To a banquet audience at the close of the 1864 Charlottetown conference he urged union with the Maritime Provinces:

> Can we not find the means of reuniting the great national units which constitute ... the British North American provinces, and to make of them

a great nation, or shall we continue to be separate provinces ... divided politically? We have in Canada, it is true, the two principal elements of nationality – population and territory – but we also know what we lack. Great as is our population and our territory, there is wanting that other element absolutely necessary to make a powerful nation, the maritime element. What nation has ever been powerful without the maritime element?

... There are no obstacles which human wisdom cannot overcome. All that is needed to triumph is a strong will and a noble ambition. When I think of the great nation we could constitute if all the provinces were organised under a single government, I seem to see arise a great Anglo-American power. The provinces of New Brunswick and Nova Scotia represent the arms of the national body embracing the commerce of the Atlantic. No one will furnish a finer head to this body than Prince Edward Island, and Canada will be the trunk of this enormous creation. The two Canadas extending far westward will bring into Confederation a vast portion of the western territory. When we possess a federal government, one of the most important questions will be the defence of the country ... Everyone familiar with public opinion knows that the dominant question is one of defence."[8]

On February 7, 1865, Cartier rose in the Canadian parliament for the most important debate in the nation's history, proclaiming:

Confederation, so to speak, is a necessity for us at this time. It is impossible to close our eyes to what is going on on the other side of the line ... It is for us to act so that the five colonies inhabited by people whose interests and sympathies are the same shall form a great nation. The way is for us all to unite under a general government. The question reduces itself to this – we must either have a Confederation of British North America or be absorbed by the American union. Some are of the opinion that it is not necessary to form such a Confederation to prevent our absorption by the neighbouring republic, but they are mistaken. When we are united the enemy will know that if he attacks any province, either Prince Edward Island or Canada, he will have to deal with the combined forces of the Empire ...

The absorption of Canada by the American union has long been contemplated, as will be seen by Article 7 of the original draft of the American Constitution, which I ask permission to read:

"Article 7. Canada, according to this confederation and joining in the measures of the United States, shall be admitted into and entitled to all the advantages of this union, and shall be equally with any other of

*the United States solemnly bound to a strict observance of and obedience
to these articles ... except Canada, no other colony shall be admitted into
the confederacy without the assent of eleven or more votes."*

By that article, no other colony could go into the Union except by a
vote of the number of states required to admit a new partner. But as
regards Canada it was exempt from that condition; all that was needed
was the wish to form part of the union.

To the powerful opponents of Confederation, Cartier turned and spoke:

Those persons of British origin who are opposed to this project seem to
believe that the English element will be absorbed by the French-
Canadian element, while its opponents amongst the French-Canadians
declare that it may have as a result the extinction of the French-Canadian
element. The annexationist party of Montreal ... oppose Confederation
on the ground that they see in it a danger to the English of Lower
Canada. Their desire is to throw Canada into the American Union ... it
is not surprising that the French-Canadian annexationists betray their
purpose in opposing Confederation, and that their English-speaking
allies profess a fear for their rights if it takes place. They know that
once this union is adopted, no one will want to form part of the
American Union.[9]

Cartier won over even influential opponents like Joseph Cauchon,
the editor-politician of Quebec City. Cauchon now told his followers
Confederation was immensely preferable to becoming another
Louisiana, annexed to the United States. Better to be a minority of one
in three than of one in thirty, he said, and became a staunch defender
of Confederation.

With Confederation, an alternate power was born in North America,
its achievement one of the significant events in world history. If
successful, the northward expansion of the United States would be
stopped — permanently — and a new northern nation would step onto
the world stage.

At Cartier's return from London after passage of the British North
America Act, thousands welcomed him at Quebec. When he stepped
from his train at Montreal 10,000 were waiting. In response, Cartier
said:

Yes, gentlemen, as you have said, I return after accomplishing a
great political act, after the complete and entire elaboration of a
constitution. This act, this constitution, has as its result the union

under the one government of the two Canadas, New Brunswick and Nova Scotia and this union has as its object to make us a nation.

Do not lose sight of the fact that with this federal union we become the third maritime trading nation of the world ...

In France it is understood that Confederation is the only means for the British North American provinces to escape annexation by the United States, and in the country of our forefathers they realize it is to the interest of the rest of the world that the United States should not further extend its frontiers. That is why, apart from ties of blood, Frenchmen follow with interest the progress of political events in that Canada which they regret they no longer possess.

... We went to England, and we were treated justly and generously ... The Canadians, said the English ministers, come to us with a finished constitution, the result of an entente cordiale between themselves ... They are the best judges of what will be suitable to them ... We required her sanction; she gave it; without hesitation ...

"Now," he concluded, "everything depends on our patriotism."[10]

In the first government after Confederation, Cartier assumed the defence portfolio because, he explained, it was the most difficult of all and "I have always liked to overcome difficulties."[11] In a five-hour speech in which he presented his first militia bill, he outlined a careful and far-reaching measure containing over 100 clauses involving the mobilization across the Dominion of 700,000 men capable of bearing arms. "Fortune favours the brave," he said, quoting Virgil. "No people can lay claim to the title of nation if it does not possess a military element — the means of defence."[12]

Cartier knew that "to stand effectively on guard for Canada, to ensure its survival, it was absolutely essential to create a viable transcontinental nation, a whole state with a will to live and the frontier to sustain that will. And it was necessary to fight the United States every inch of the way. The Americans expected it, the British knew it and Cartier felt it in his bones because if the battle were won it would mean the sure survival of the French-Canadian people. If it were lost first the English, then eventually the French-Canadians, would be assimilated into the North American melting-pot."[13]

In reply to an opposition motion in 1870 demanding free trade with the United States, Cartier reacted fiercely, "What will be the consequences of industrial reciprocity? ... the factories of Canada will lose the advantages ... they now possess ... and eventually the largest manufacturing industries will be concentrated in the U.S."

The end result would be union with the United States — "that is to say, our annihilation as a country."[14]

It was Cartier who went to London and successfully concluded negotiations for the transfer to Canada of the Hudson's Bay Company territories (now western Canada), outmanoeuvering the U.S. envoy who was in the city at the same time, attempting to negotiate their transfer to the United States. On Cartier's return home he told the crowd in Montreal that "in a few months the Dominion of Canada will extend from the Atlantic to the Pacific ... I hope we shall then no longer hear of annexation."[15]

And it was Cartier who warmly welcomed the delegates from British Columbia when they arrived in Ottawa to negotiate B.C.'s possible entry into Canada. Reading the diary kept over a three-week period by J.S. Helmcken, one of the B.C. delegates and an early opponent of Confederation, one is struck by the sincere desire of Macdonald's government to make a generous agreement with B.C. and by the portrait of Cartier. After a boat trip from Victoria to San Francisco, a train journey across the United States, then back up into Canada, the B.C. delegates had arrived in Ottawa:

JUNE 6, 1870:

According to appointment we proceeded to the Government Buildings and met Sir G. Cartier, whom we found in his shirt sleeves, hard at work. He, as usual, was exceedingly pleasant, gave us a sherry, and introduced us into the Privy Council ... It appeared as though the Government of Canada would grant everything they possibly could ...

JUNE 7, 1870:

It is astounding how Sir G. works – morning, noon, night, brings no cessation.

JUNE 25, 1870:

A very long discussion took place about the Telegraph service but Sir George Cartier decided it by saying the Telegraph would be valuable and fall in with the plan of the Government to build a Telegraph to Red River, from there to B.C. would follow ... [16]

When the B.C. representatives asked for a railway to the foothills of the Rockies and a road the rest of the way, Cartier told them, "No, that will not do. Ask for a railway the whole way and you will get it."[17]

The B.C. delegates were stunned. They had been offered more than they had requested. Anthony Musgrave, lieutenant-governor of British

Columbia, was ecstatic. The terms were "outstandingly better ... than what we asked for. And the Railway, Credat Judaeus! is guaranteed without a reservation!! Sir George Cartier says they will do that or 'burst'."[18]

The Liberal Party unanimously opposed the railway agreement. "All the resources in the British Empire" could not build such a line. How could a country of three and one-half million, not yet four years old, promise to build the world's greatest railway — more than 1500 kilometres longer than the first transcontinental railroad across the United States, just completed by that country of 40 million? "It was," opposition leader, Alexander Mackenzie, told the House, "an act of insane recklessness."[19] Even a bloc of Cartier's own Conservatives from Ontario tried to amend the railway contract to include the clause, "if the financial ability of the Dominion will permit." But Cartier wouldn't hear of it and he brought the B.C. delegates in to speak directly to the Ontario members. And then, as reported by J.W. Trutch, one of B.C.'s negotiators:

> He told them that if they shrank from their engagement with B.C. he and his friends from Quebec would vote alone in fulfilment of the Treaty he had made and if defeated in this matter he would dissolve the House ... But for the pluck and determination of the 'lightning striker' they would have given in, the measure would have been defeated and the Gov't broken up. We must all remember in B.C. that to Sir George Cartier and his followers in Lower Canada we owe the position we are now in and especially the Canadian Pacific Railway.[20]

Helmcken's diary concludes by relating Cartier's optimism about British Columbia's and Canada's future. "I am to tell from Sir George Cartier," the B.C. delegate reported, "that it is necessary to be Anti-Yankee. That we have to oppose their damned system — that we can and will build up a northern power ... The Dominion is determined to do it."[21]

On April 26, 1872, his bill for construction of the Canadian Pacific Railway was printed, ready to be presented to Parliament. Cartier was exuberant. "Here," he roared to a happy group in his office, "is a bill that has attraction for a man! Here are ideas! We are going to tie the oceans together ... This bill is my pride and joy."[22] After it passed the House in June, Cartier leapt to his feet and said, "All aboard for the West!"[23] Then he went slowly to his office, gathered together the legislation that he had authored, including all the Dominion Railway acts, the Manitoba and British Columbia acts, Militia bills, Canal and Steamship acts, and asked that they be bound. In a year he would be no more, gone at the age of 58.

Powerful U.S. railway promoters, including Jay Cooke and J.J. Hill, strove mightily to stop the building of the CPR or divert it to a U.S. terminus, preferably Boston. In the West they wanted to run feeder lines up into western Canada to bring the traffic down to their lines. Cartier and Macdonald were adamantly opposed.

Moreover, Cartier said, he would resign before letting an American company get the contract to build the CPR. There were, he said, enough Canadian companies to do the work. "As long as I live," Cartier asserted, "and as long as I am a member of the Ministry, never will a damned American company have control of the Pacific. I will resign my place as a Minister rather than consent to it."[24]

American money poured into Cartier's Montreal riding to undermine him. No secret ballot existed in Canada until 1874, so bribery was effective — not only could agents bribe, they could also check how people voted. Strong-armed men could, and did, keep people physically away from the polls. These methods, and more, succeeded, and Cartier, ill, legs swollen in pain from rapidly advancing Bright's disease, went down to defeat in the 1872 election.

His government, however, survived. "I have reason to believe," said Macdonald, "that the U.S. Northern Pacific Railway also subscribed largely in order to place Mr. Mackenzie at the head of the Government, as he would have handed over our Pacific Railway to them. This nefarious design has, however, been defeated. We are, I think, fixed in the saddle ... and shall take good care that the Yankees have nothing to say to our Pacific Railway."[25]

Further reflecting on the election, Macdonald observed that "a party, like a snake, is moved by its tail. The tail of the Grit party is the Annexation section."[26]

From the West, Louis Riel, who had repeatedly won his Red River seat in Manitoba, agreed to step aside to allow Cartier to run in his riding, where within three weeks he was returned unopposed.

But now Cartier was fighting a battle his doctors told him he would not win. Before leaving for medical treatment in London, he and Macdonald had a long talk — their last. They would complete the Pacific Railway, whatever the cost. And it would be an all-Canadian road. It was a question of national survival.

If Canada did not build a railway and bring settlers to the West, Cartier and Macdonald both understood, then the United States quickly would.* "Old Tomorrow" and the "Lightning Striker" would become known as the Siamese twins of Canadian politics. Their relationship was perhaps the most important in the country's history: Macdonald, the brilliant tactician with his deft touch and winning ways (significantly, his singular failure — the disastrous treatment of Riel — happened when Cartier was no longer at his side), and Cartier, the driving, visionary man of action — the railroad-building poet.

An editor friend described Cartier: "In the same half hour of conversation he would unfold a vast political plan, expose an important measure, relate the latest trick he had played on his adversaries, interject a commentary — often new and always just — on European politics, seek information on the health of your children whom he would remember as well at the end of 15 years as if he had seen them yesterday, and never forget an amusing tale."[27]

Cartier's alert energy, his determination, and his mastery of Parliament — on which Macdonald relied heavily — were legendary. "Having made a speech of six hours' length in English, he is quite willing if need be to speak six more hours in French."[28] Cartier called Macdonald "a statesman who has never yet been surpassed in Canada and who probably never will be."[29] Macdonald, in turn, said, "Cartier was as bold as a lion ... he was afraid of nothing ... But for him Confederation could not have been carried.[30]

On May 20, 1873, Macdonald received from London a telegram that his friend was dead:

The news spread fast. By three o'clock the galleries of Parliament were packed, and nearly every member in his seat. They watched silently as a pathetic Macdonald took his seat, front row centre, next to a desk whose emptiness now seemed so frighteningly real; and there they listened, as he rose and said: "Mr. Speaker. I have a painful duty to fulfill to this House. I have received a telegram this morning from Sir John

---

* A report by the U.S. Senate Committee on Pacific Railways had declared its intention unmistakably: "the line of the North Pacific ... when built will drain the agricultural products of the rich Saskatchewan and Red River districts east of the mountains, and the gold country on the Fraser, Thompson and Kootenay rivers west of the mountains ... The opening by us first of a Northern Pacific railroad seals the destiny of the British possessions west of the ninety-first meridian [roughly west of Thunder Bay]. They will become so Americanized in interests and feelings that they will be in effect severed from the new Dominion, and the question of their annexation will be but a question of time."

Rose, which I will read to the House:

'Sir George Cartier had a relapse last Tuesday and he died peacefully at six o'clock this morning. His body will be sent by Quebec steamer on the 29th.

Rose'

I feel myself quite unable to say more at this moment."

Sir John A. Macdonald sank back into his seat and his eyes filled with tears. Now sobbing uncontrollably, he placed his right hand on Cartier's desk and buried his head in his left, while his whole body shook with grief. The House sat stunned until his sorrow fell and he was quiet.[31]

In 1914, Lomer Gouin, the premier of Quebec, wrote of Cartier:

He was a big man. He was imbued with large ideas ... and the Canada of today is largely the result of his instructive statesmanship ... He exposed the futility of the contention that it was impossible to make of Canada a great nation ... The range of his vision, like that of his great namesake — the first European to set foot in Canada — extended far beyond the boundaries of Lower Canada, and he was fond of asking his fellow countrymen whether they desired to limit the influence of their race to the narrow boundaries of their own province ... The name of Cartier will live as long as this Dominion — of which he was one of the master builders — endures ... until time shall be no more ...[32]

9

Veiled Treason

DURING THE LATE 1880s, Canada's economy fell into a depression. Again, as in 1849, free trade with its southern neighbour was the answer, said the advocates of the "commercial union" movement. As before, right behind them were those pushing for the annexation of Canada to the United States.

John A. Macdonald was prime minister and, except for the years 1874-78, had been in power since Confederation. Many Canadians, resentful of American attempts to crush and absorb their nation, were determined to develop Canada's own resources into an economy separate from and independent of the United States. Macdonald saw these people as his constituency, and he promised that Canada would have a national economy. To achieve this goal, he advocated that Canadian manufacturing be protected from U.S. competition, and to protect goods "we ourselves are capable of producing," a tariff policy could be introduced.[1] The income from these tariffs (also called duties or taxes) on imports would be the new Dominion's main source of revenue. Thus was born the famous National Policy, which would allow Canadian manufacturing using Canadian resources to develop, protected by tariffs against the flood of U.S. imports. And to achieve an independent Canadian economy and create a real union of the far- flung and until recently separate provinces, a national railway must, Macdonald believed, be constructed.

For more than ten years, Macdonald fought for his dream — the completion of the transcontinental Canadian Pacific Railway. Scraping funds and virtually begging in foreign financial markets, he faced a powerful and unrelenting opposition within Canada, and encountered indifference in London and outright hostility in the United States.

The railway, Macdonald insisted, must follow an all-Canadian

81

route over the top of Lake Superior. This was "monstrous folly," said the Liberal opposition with hearty support from the United States and England; the rail line should follow the cheaper, less rocky and shorter route south of the Great Lakes, through the United States, up to Winnipeg and then west. The difficult, expensive northern route was viewed by them, in the words of historian Donald Creighton, as an example of the "criminal absurdity of nationalism which ought to be abandoned at once."[2]

Such a route would not be a Canadian transcontinental railway, Macdonald replied, but only a prairie line joined up with the U.S. rail lines, which would end up siphoning off the flow of trade from the Canadian West. Common sense and patriotism, Macdonald said, called for an all-Canadian railway, which would "give us all we want … a great, an united, a rich, an improving, a developing Canada, instead of making us tributary to American laws, to American railways, to American bondage, to American tolls, to American freights, to all the little tricks and big tricks that American railways are addicted to for the purpose of destroying our road."[3]

Finally, on June 28, 1886, the first ocean-to-ocean train pulled out of Montreal bound for the west coast. The completed railway was Macdonald's "second crowning triumph … second only to that of Confederation."[4]

Macdonald had always hoped to travel the new railway, "before I am just quite an angel," as he expressed it. On his first trip west on the new CPR, he told a crowd in Winnipeg that while his friends had often felt he would have to see the finished railway from heaven above, his enemies had assumed he'd be forced to look up at it from the place below. "But," he said, "I have now disappointed both friends and foes and am taking a horizontal view."[5]

Beneath the banter was the reality that the grim struggle for the railway had very nearly finished the 71-year-old Macdonald, whose always precarious health was more fragile than ever. An American historian summed up the building of the railway thus: "The sledge hammer that drove the last spike cracked the knuckles on the feebly outstretched hand of American Manifest Destiny."[6]

Yet Macdonald's great and final campaign was yet to come — the battle for an independent Canadian economy.

Provincial interests, allied to powerful U.S. ones, stood ready to oppose him. The Manitoba government had again begun to build a railway from Winnipeg south, to link up with U.S. lines. Macdonald told the House of Commons that if Canada's transcontinental railway were to be "bled at one hundred different points," all that would be left of "the magnificent stream of commerce that we had a right to expect to pass through Canada" would be a "miserable fragment."[7] After all attempts failed to dissuade Manitoba, Macdonald, using the power of disallowance over provincial legislation given to the federal government by the *British North America Act*, wiped Manitoba's *Red River Valley Railway Act* off the statute books as contrary to the national interest.

Meanwhile, under the leadership of Quebec's premier, Honoré Mercier, who would soon openly advocate annexation to the United States, the provincial governments proposed Canada's first federal-provincial conference. On October 20, 1887, amid an avalanche of press coverage, the premiers met and declared they were going to amend the Constitution. Prince Edward Island and British Columbia did not attend but, in the words of historian Donald Creighton, the premiers of the five other provinces, led by Ontario's Oliver Mowat and Quebec's Mercier, "strutted about ... in a bright spotlight of publicity ... formulating resolutions, and talking, with interminable volubility, about their virtues and their woes."[8] They "abolished the federal power of disallowance, reformed the Senate in the interest of the provinces, and voted themselves a large increase in the subsidies" from the federal government. Most significantly, the provinces, with the exception of New Brunswick, called for an end to Macdonald's National Policy, and they called for free trade with the United States.

Macdonald, knowing full well the Constitution could not be amended without federal government approval — he'd written a good part of it himself — reacted with scorn. Not only did he refuse to attend the conference, but he also studiously refused to acknowledge it had ever taken place.

In the week preceding the conference, one of the leading figures of the federal Liberal Party, Richard Cartwright, had come out in favour of free trade, or "unrestricted reciprocity." Now, the movement for Canada-U.S. "commercial union" grew rapidly through rural Ontario, with forty farmers' institutes endorsing it within a few months.* One of the longest and strongest movements for annexation in Canadian history was under way.

---

* Commercial union meant the removal of all tariffs and even the elimination of customs houses at the border between Canada and the United States.

The annexationists knew that speaking openly about their goal would be politically fatal, but they saw in free trade a way to achieve their real objective. The commercial union movement of the late 1880s, like the one that would emerge one hundred years later, was well organized and amply financed.

Goldwin Smith, a wealthy British professor, left his post at Cornell University in New York and moved to Canada to become one of the leading intellectual proponents of both the free-trade and annexation movements. In his book *Canada and the Canadian Question,* Smith laid down arguments still widely used by those advocating free trade. Canada, he said, is an unnatural country; the "natural" flow of trade is north and south, and the sooner the geographical absurdity that is Canada joins in a continental union, the better. (More than one Canadian historian has replied to Smith by pointing out that the St. Lawrence River and the Great Lakes, the natural trade routes of North America, run east and west. Canada as a nation is no more natural or unnatural than any other country in the world, and it need not defend its existence on the basis of its "naturalness.")

For Goldwin Smith, the idea of a "United Continent of North America ... is no less practical than it is grand." Smith did not like the term "annexation": "An ugly word; it seems to convey the idea of force." He preferred "reunion" because, as he wrote with a remarkable reworking of history, the Anglo-Saxons of Canada and the United States have merely been separated by one century, and "only one war." He skipped entirely the 150-year defence of Canada by French Canadians prior to what Smith calls "the unhappy schism" of the American Revolution and the 1775 invasion of Canada. To those who fear American domination in the great union, Smith assured Canadians (based upon his twenty years of experience with Americans) that, with the "violence and unscrupulousness" of slavery now passed away, "Americans are a moral people" who have "no craving for more territory." In fact, he claimed, not even under the influence of a demagogue could the Americans ever be made to encroach on another country's rights. As part of the united continent, Smith assured his readers, Canadians would still be allowed to celebrate Canada's past victories, just as the Scottish celebrate theirs as part of Britain. "The Americans would only smile" at such celebrations. North America, he maintained, is "a continent which nature has forbidden to be divided," though a "perverse policy struggles to divorce" the two countries. In the West, all that separates it is an "imaginary boundary drawn across the prairie for 800 miles."

Union would "greatly raise the value of property in Canada," Smith continued. All that is needed is to allow "a free market, free inflow of American capital." The political future of the continent rested in America, and Canada would promote its ultimate interest by "recognising destiny without delay."

Having said this, Smith was reminded of another reason for not putting off the unification of the "English-speaking race" in North America: "it is perfectly clear that the forces of Canada alone are not sufficient to assimilate the French element."[9] Continental union would clear up the problem by swamping the French-speaking population and inspiring "the moral federation of the whole English- speaking race throughout the world." "Our presence in Canada," he had written earlier, "artificially preserves from absorption the French Canadian element, an antediluvian relic of old French society with its torpor and bigotry, utterly without value for the purposes of modern civilization."[10]

Erastus Wiman, a wealthy Canadian born businessman from New York, wrote pamphlets, spoke across Canada and, like Smith, provided the financial support to the commercial union movement. Commercial union would be like the German *Zollverein*, which was bringing prosperity to the twenty-seven German states. It would mean free trade between Canada and the United States, with common internal taxes and a common tariff wall to the outside world. Everyone would benefit from "a market such as the world has never equalled." Wiman, an articulate and persuasive speaker, directed one of his arguments to Canadian mothers. The cream of Canadian youth, he said, was being drained off to the United States. Commercial union would restore Canadian prosperity and stop this migration. "If commercial union could accomplish nothing else," he wrote, "than keep our young men at home, it would be a boon of the greatest magnitude. For there is not a mother ... but dreads the day when her boy, her precious boy, will look with longing eyes across the border."[11]

The Toronto *Globe,* the Toronto *Mail*, the Montreal *Herald* and the Manitoba *Free Press* jumped on board. Political unionists infiltrated the Liberal Party. The Young Liberals of Toronto endorsed political union, and then, in March 1888, the Liberal Party adopted a policy of "full and unrestricted reciprocity."

A commercial union bill passed in the U.S. Senate. Its sponsor, Senator John Sherman of Ohio, chairman of the Foreign Affairs Committee, pointed out that U.S. citizens had large sums of money invested in Canada. "I want Canada to be a part of the United States," he said. "Canada should have followed the fortunes of the colonies in the American Revolution ... The way to union with Canada is not by hostile legislation ... but by friendly overtures. This union is one of the events that must inevitably come in the future ... The true policy of this government then is to tender freedom in trade and intercourse, and make this tender in such a fraternal way that it shall be, an overture to the Canadian people to become a part of this Republic."[12]

The Chicago *Tribune,* on September 26, 1888, wrote that Canada's "safety lies in not provoking the United States by unfair or unfriendly dealing, for when the provocation comes, Uncle Sam will reach out and take her in, in order to ensure quiet, and neither she nor her venerable old mother can prevent it."[13]

In December, the New York *World* published a map of the United States as it would appear following the annexation of Canada. Entitled "The Future Great Republic; the Annexation of the Dominion of Canada would add Twenty-seven States and Territories," it appeared with the following editorial comment:

> What a majestic Empire the accompanying map suggests; one unbroken line from the Arctic Ocean to the Torrid Zone. The United States is here shown as embracing nearly the whole of the North American continent. Having conquered the Western wilderness the star of Empire northward points its way ... There would be no more trouble about fishing treaties or retaliation measures, and peace with all nations would be assured, by making the United States absolute master of the vast Western continent.

The paper suggested how this could be done:

> Nobody who has studied the peculiar methods by which elections are won in Canada will deny the fact, that five or six million dollars, judiciously expended in this country, would secure the return to Parliament of a majority pledged to the annexation of Canada to the United States. [14]

William C. Whitney, secretary of the navy, said that four armies, each made up of 25,000 men, could easily conquer Canada. Massachusetts congressman General Benjamin Butler, in words strikingly similar to those used by the U.S. officials just prior to the annexation of Texas, described annexation as Canada's fate: "Peacefully, we hope; forcefully, if we must."[15] To keep costs reasonable and inspire morale, he suggested the invading troops be paid in grants of Canadian land.

American money poured into the Liberal Party. The Toronto *Globe,* the voice of the Liberal Party at the time, received $50,000 from one U.S. company alone, the railroad and mining giant S.J. Ritchie Corporation of Ohio. Debate raged across the country, and for a time it seemed Canada would be stampeded into economic union with the United States. Ontario was the centre of annexationist fever, while in Quebec, Riel's execution had "opened a breach in the wall of French loyalty to the Dominion."[16]

But John A. Macdonald was not easily stampeded. He saw quite clearly "the inevitable toboggan slide towards annexation ... which would be created by any system of continental commercial union."[17] Macdonald had at first dismissed the commercial union movement as a "dead duck," even after the Governor General, Lord Lansdowne, had come out in favour of it. He had long known, he wrote, that Lansdowne was "a free trader to the bone, and all such men are deaf and blind to any other considerations but the blind teachings of abstract political economy."[18] However, when he realized the strength of the commercial union movement, Macdonald dissolved the House of Commons. The election of 1891, Canada's first full-blown free-trade election, was on.

MACDONALD'S DESIGN FOR the nation was an east-west trading system, protected by tariffs against competition from the south, but at each end open to trade with the world. The United States had always been Canada's main rival in this economic plan and its most dangerous enemy. Against this view, the opposition Liberals had fought the all-Canadian railway and had taken up the cry of "provincial rights," advocating more power to the provinces at the expense of the federal government; now they had come out for free trade with the United States and an end to the National Policy tariffs.

The Liberals, Macdonald said, had been bought up with Yankee gold, and if their views were to prevail, it was *"finis Canadia."*[19] "I believe that this election, which is a great crisis, and upon which so much depends, will show to the Americans that we prize our country as much as they do, that we would fight for our existence as much as they fought for the preservation of their independence."[20] Free trade, Macdonald said, was "sheer insanity," which would have "as its inevitable result, annexation to the United States."[21]

Edward Farrer, an editor of the *Globe,* had written a pamphlet for the U.S. Senate, outlining ways the United States could undermine Canada's policy and push its neighbour into annexation. "Political union with the United States is the manifest destiny of Canada," he maintained.[22]

Sir John A. Macdonald acquired a copy of the proofs of the pamphlet and made them public. Farrer was a traitor, he said, who would deliver Canada to the United States: "I say that there is a deliberate conspiracy, in which some of the members of the opposition are more or less compromised; I say there is a deliberate conspiracy, by force, by fraud, or by both, to force Canada into the American Union."[23]

Against the advice of his doctors, Macdonald threw himself into the campaign, issuing his famous manifesto. One historian called it "the most stirring appeal to ... Canadian loyalty" since Isaac Brock in 1812 spoke with the American armies moving towards Canada.[24]

Reciprocity with the United States, Macdonald said, would inevitably result in annexation to the United States. How could Canada keep its political independence after it had thrown away its economic independence? he asked. By threatening to terminate such an agreement, the United States could force the Canadian Dominion into union. Even if the Americans refrained from cracking this whip, ever-tightening economic ties would slowly draw the two countries together. Macdonald gave the example of the states that had formed a free-trade area called the *Zollverein,* which had become Germany and was dominated by Prussia, the strongest member. The Liberals, MacDonald said, "have as many aliases for their policy as a thief has excuses for his wrong-doing. It has been commercial union, unrestricted reciprocity, and latterly tariff reform; but there is another name by which it must be known, and that is annexation – which is treason."

In the United States, Secretary of State James Blaine, who according to American author Donald Warner, "consistently displayed a cold contempt for Canada," believed that a policy of refusing to deal with Canada would ultimately succeed in forcing

Canada into continental union. "Canada," James Blaine said, "is like an apple on a tree just beyond our reach. We may strive to grasp it but the bough recedes from our hold just in proportion to our effort to catch it. Let it alone, and in due time it will fall into our hands." Steady pressure on Canada would do the job, Blaine wrote to his president, Benjamin Harrison. "The fact is we do not want any intercourse with Canada except through the medium of a tariff, and she will find she has a hard row to hoe and will ultimately, I believe, seek admission to the Union."[25]

In Canada, Edward Blake, the former leader of the Liberal Party from 1880 to 1887, broke with his new leader, Quebec lawyer and journalist Wilfrid Laurier, when Laurier advocated reciprocity. Laurier begged Blake not to make his views public until after the election. "Restless and uncomfortable," Blake agreed to remain silent. A Truro, Nova Scotia, newspaper reported. "One old Liberal, at a political meeting in Colchester County, Nova Scotia, just before the election, asked, 'Where is Mr. Blake? We have heard nothing from him!' It was gently explained that 'Mr. Blake is not just with us in our policy this time.' 'Neither am I then,' said the old man, who reached for his hat and stick and made for the door."[26]

Macdonald, 76, was everywhere in the campaign, going at a punishing pace, always a joke on his lips, never forgetting a name or a face. He "saw not only his government but his life work in peril."[27] The question, he told the voters, "resolves itself into this: Shall we endanger ... the great heritage bequeathed to us by our fathers ... for the privilege of having our tariff fixed at Washington, with the prospect of ultimately becoming a portion of the American Union?"[28]

On February 25 at the town hall in Napanee, Ontario, the old man, his body wracked with illness and exhaustion, rose for what would be his last speech: "As for myself, my course is clear. A British subject I was born — a British subject I will die. With my utmost effort, with my latest breath, will I oppose the 'veiled treason' which attempts by sordid means and mercenary proffers to lure our people from their allegiance."[29]

Shortly afterwards he collapsed, and for the next two weeks, while the campaign swirled to a climax, he lay too ill to move. When the votes were counted, and the results brought to his bed, John A. Macdonald had won. Free trade had been defeated. But it had been a close fight, and without "the Old Man, the Old Flag and the Old Policy," it is hard to say what would have happened.

One day after the election, on March 6, 1891, Blake's famous letter was published, and it struck the Liberal Party like a thunderbolt. Free trade, Blake said, was the same as commercial union. And commercial union would lead inevitably to political union with the United States. Free trade, which must be a permanent arrangement to conserve credit and industrial interests, would be impossible without control of the Canadian tariff by the U.S. Congress. The intermingling of populations, the more intimate business and social connections, and Canada's constant fear of the United States terminating the agreement — all these would push Canada into political union with the United States. "I cling," he wrote later, "to the hope of a higher though more arduous destiny for the Great Dominion. I look for the regeneration of my own country. I cling to the hope that — sooner or later, and rather soon than late — there may be born into the world an independent Canadian Commonwealth, nerving itself to solve, after its own fashion, the many ... problems which confront us."[30]

Slowly Macdonald regained some of his strength, but on May 29 a devastating stroke left him paralysed and unable to speak. "He is dying," newspaper headlines declared. For a week, from his deathbed, he ruled the Canada that he had done so much to create, answering questions with pressure from his left hand, yes or no. On June 6, 1891, the pulse faded, and bells began to toll across Canada. By farm wagon, horse, train and carriage, thousands came to Ottawa to say goodbye to the man to whom they had shouted: "John A., you'll never die."[31] For his funeral, the CPR locomotive was draped in black and purple, and for 5000 miles along the track, every engine and every railway station wore the black of mourning.

THE 1891 ELECTION ended the annexationists' hope of winning their goal behind the cover of reciprocity. But the election had been close enough to embolden them, and now, with Macdonald gone, perhaps they could succeed. Too well known to operate in secret, they decided on a bold two-pronged approach — holding open meetings to promote their cause publicly and arranging private meetings to win over prominent leaders in the Liberal Party. Sir Richard Cartwright in Ontario and Honoré Mercier were among the supporters.

In the United States, a powerful group established the Continental Union League (CUL), with the goal of compelling annexation or political union by force if necessary. Its members included steel giant Andrew Carnegie, former secretary of the navy W.C. Whitney, Theodore Roosevelt, who would be president within a decade, John Hay, who would be his secretary of state, and Elihu Root, who would be his minister of war. An allied Canadian branch of the CUL had Goldwin Smith as its honourary president and Edward Farrer of the *Globe* and Harry Darling, the president of Toronto's Board of Trade, as members. The American organization raised money to publish pamphlets and support the Canadian organization as well as selected politicians in Canada.[32]

Oliver Mowat, long-time Ontario Liberal premier, decided to confront the movement publicly. He dismissed from their positions two Liberals who publicly supported annexation and, in a rousing speech delivered July 16, 1892, at the one-hundred-year celebration of the founding of Ontario, Mowat, in the words of an eyewitness, "sounded the death-knell of the annexation movement" in Ontario[33] as he asked the large crowd:

> Shall we give away our great country to the United States as some — I hope not many — are saying just now? [Cries of "Never."] Or … shall we go for the only other alternative, the creation of Canada into an independent nation? I believe that the great mass of our people would prefer independence to political union with any other people. And so would I. As a Canadian I am not willing that Canada should cease to be. Fellow Canadians, are you? [Cries of "No."] I am not willing that Canada should commit national suicide. Are you? [Cries of "No."] I am not willing that Canada should be absorbed into the United States. Are you? [Cries of "No."] I am not willing that … our hope of a Canadian nationality shall be for ever destroyed. [Cheers.] Annexation necessarily means all that … No, I do not want annexation. I prefer the ills I suffer to the ills that annexation would involve . . . I hope that when another century has been added to the age of Canada, it may still be Canada, and that its second century shall, like its first, be celebrated by Canadians unabsorbed, numerous, prosperous, powerful, and at peace. For myself I should prefer to die in that hope than to die President of the United States. [Cheers and applause.][34]

Mowat urged people to disrupt the annexationists' public meetings. Before long, speakers were challenged and interrupted from the floor and resolutions in favour of annexation were hotly debated and defeated. Goldwin Smith complained that Mowat was packing his meetings. The by-elections of 1892 were swept by the Conservatives. The year 1893 saw the United States plunged into a depression worse than Canada's, and abruptly the voices of the Canadian annexationists fell silent.

Quietly, unrestricted reciprocity was dropped from the Liberal platform. Two decades later, however, it would re-emerge to occupy centre stage once again.

10

The Yankee to the South of Us Must South of Us Remain

THE TWENTIETH CENTURY opened for Canada and the United States with a boundary dispute involving Alaska and the Yukon. The undefined boundary between Alaska and Canada, the roots of its dispute involving the Russians, British, Americans and Canadians, had become a burning issue with the discovery of gold in 1895. The resulting Klondike gold rush saw thousands of miners pour into the area claimed by both Canada and the United States. For twenty years, both Canada and Britain had made repeated approaches to the United States to have the boundary determined, but Washington had not responded. The U.S. secretary of state, John Hay, did not want the boundary dispute submitted to arbitration because he was afraid that the Canadians would gain a "foothold on the coast." Besides, he said, his government was so sure of its case that it was not "willing to put it in jeopardy before some chance arbitration."[1]

Following years of escalating pressure from Britain and Canada, the Americans suggested a tribunal of six, three on a side, a majority to decide. "In this case," wrote Secretary Hay to President Roosevelt, "it is impossible that we should lose."[2] Canada failed in its struggle for an odd-numbered panel and a neutral outsider as umpire. The United States and Britain agreed to have three American, two Canadian and one British panellist — a tribunal of "six impartial jurists of repute, who shall consider judicially the questions submitted to them." The Canadians appointed George Armour, a justice of the Superior Court, and Sir Louis Jetté, a former justice of the Quebec Supreme Court. Britain appointed its chief justice, Lord Alverstone.[3]

The American "impartial jurists of repute," appointed by President Roosevelt, were his secretary of war, Elihu Root, who had just mobilized 800 troops up to the Alaska boundary to face forty Canadian police constables; Senator George Turner of Washington State, who had led a relentless opposition to Canadian claims; and Massachusetts's Senator Henry Cabot Lodge, who had campaigned loudly for American troops to settle the Alaska problem.

In response to Canadian and British outrage and disbelief at hearing the names of the "impartial" American appointees, Roosevelt made it clear that if the U.S. case failed, he would ask Congress to vote the funds necessary for war so that he could "run the line as we claim it, by our own people, without any further regard to the attitude of England and Canada."[4] Roosevelt arranged to have this message passed directly to the British prime minister and his Cabinet during the tribunal sittings. In May 1902, Roosevelt told the British embassy in Washington that on the Alaska question he was "going to be ugly," and he made sure his words were reported to Ottawa.[5] In the end, Lord Alverstone voted with the Americans. The Canadian representatives, Sir Louis Jetté and Allen B. Aylesworth, who had stepped in after George Armour's death, refused to put their signatures to the document. In the settlement, Canada lost all the coastline above 54°40', including Skagway and Dyea and all of the Lynn Canal. The result left the northern half of British Columbia and all the Yukon landlocked, cut off from access to the Pacific.

Roosevelt, whose motto in foreign affairs was "speak softly and carry a big stick," was exuberant. The settlement was, he said, "the greatest diplomatic victory during the present generation."[6] His secretary of state, John Hay, was still jubilant over the recent U.S. invasion of Cuba and the Spanish-American War, which left the Americans in control of not only that island but also the Philippines, Puerto Rico and Guam — "a splendid little war," he called it.[7] (Cuba was forced to incorporate the humiliating Platt Amendment directly into its constitution, giving the United States the right to intervene in Cuba at its "discretion." Further, Cuba could not refuse to sell or lease lands wanted by the United States.) At about the same time, the United States had annexed Hawaii and taken control of Samoa. "I do not wonder," Hay now wrote about the Canadian reaction of outrage at the Alaska decision, "that they are furious. But ... serves 'em right, if they can't take a joke."[8]

The decision drove home in Canada a sense that no one but Canadians would defend the country. The beautiful "O Canada," created by Quebec composer Calixa Lavallée with words by Adolphe-Basile Routhier, was translated by Robert Stanley Weir and it began to be sung as the national anthem in English Canada as well.

In 1896, Laurier's Liberals won the first of their four election victories, and in none of them was free trade or reciprocity an issue. In 1898, a joint high commission was established for Canada, the United States and Britain to deal with all outstanding Canadian-American problems. The United States opened the first session by proposing complete free trade between Canada and the United States, with both countries to adopt the same external tariffs towards all other countries, including Britain. This arrangement, it was suggested, would bring an end to Canada-U.S. problems.

Dozens of influential American organizations flooded Washington with letters and resolutions of support. The Boston Merchants' Association wrote to the U.S. treasury secretary, Lyman Gage: "We are unalterably convinced that the magnificent resources of the entire North American Continent can, by a wise reciprocity between the United States and Canada, be made available for the unity, prosperity and the progress of the entire North American people."[9]

This proposal appeared to be too much even for Laurier, still sensitive over his 1891 defeat on the question of free trade. The matter, however, soon became academic; the Alaska boundary dispute took centre stage, and the ensuing explosion of anti-American feeling across Canada made any talk of free trade politically impossible. Equally important, by the early 1900s the long and costly effort to establish John A. Macdonald's National Policy of tariffs, to discourage imports from the United States and increase internal trade, was paying off. Canada's industries were growing, agriculture was booming and the country's trade was flowing east and west. About 70 percent of the federal government's revenue came from duties charged on imports, and there was no income tax. Canada, having turned its back on continentalism, was experiencing unprecedented prosperity. There were more miles of railway per capita in Canada than in any other country, and the trains were running full. In 1907, Canada had established a triple-tariff system — a high general tariff with the United States, a low tariff for Britain, and for other countries a tariff that could be negotiated. In the words of one observer, the reciprocity movement was "dead beyond all possibility of early resurrection."[10]

The U.S. secretary of state, Elihu Root, noted these developments ruefully: "Unfortunately, a policy which I must think mistaken, has carried the Canadian situation far beyond any possibility of general reciprocity. Canada has definitely entered upon a career of protection and of building up her own infant industries ... She is going to travel the same road that we have travelled."[11]

The United States was not pleased, and in 1909 it passed the *Payne-Aldrich Act* to "protect America's foreign trade without compromising domestic protectionism."[12] It would also, according to a memo written for the U.S. president — entitled "The Open Door to Canada," help to destroy the National Policy with its encouragement of east-west trade. A "natural movement of trade" would replace it, flowing from "north to south and south to north." Washington had realized that a continental economic system, arranged according to the needs of the United States, would be vital to the future prosperity of American industry. U.S. officials wanted to head off Canada's development into an advanced industrial country and a serious competitor. They wanted both to guarantee for the American economy a cheap and plentiful supply of Canadian natural resources and to secure the Canadian market for American industry. Control of Canada's agriculture and resources was necessary "to sharpen American industry's competitive edge in the world economy."[13]

In early 1910, a telegram arrived in Ottawa, conveying U.S. President Taft's "urgent desire to begin at the earliest possible moment negotiations with Canada."[14] The Laurier government hesitated briefly, but soon agreed to negotiations. Within months, Washington and Ottawa signed a reciprocity agreement that provided free trade in a broad list of natural products and reduced the tariffs on some manufactured items. Many Canadian agricultural products would be allowed into the United States tariff-free, while American farm machinery would enter Canada at low rates. For years, some western farm groups had pressured Laurier for this type of arrangement. Perhaps he could now win his fifth election.

The United States was pleased. "I regard this as the most important measure of my administration," said President Taft. In concluding the speech that presented the agreement to Congress, Taft stated that Canadians had come to the parting of the ways: "They must soon decide whether they are to regard themselves as isolated permanently from our markets by a perpetual wall or whether we are to be commercial friends." Free trade, he wrote to ex-president Theodore Roosevelt, "would produce a current of business between western Canada and the United States that would make Canada only an adjunct of the United States. It would transfer all their important business to Chicago and New York, with their bank credits and everything else, and it would increase greatly the demand of Canada for our manufactures. I see this as an argument against reciprocity made in Canada, and I think it is a good one."[15] The American press agreed. The Hearst newspaper chain threw the full power of its influence behind the treaty.

When the agreement was introduced into the House of Commons on January 26, 1911, the Liberals "cheered and cheered again."[16] Conservative leader Robert Borden wrote that "there was the deepest dejection in our party, and many of our members were confident that the Government's proposals would appeal to the country and would give it another term of office."[17] But opposition to free trade soon appeared. Once again, Canada entered into a free-trade debate. It would culminate in the famous 1911 free-trade election.

PRIME MINISTER Wilfrid Laurier declared in the House of Commons that the agreement would make Canada so rich that all forms of taxation could be abolished. His finance minister, W.S. Fielding, said his only fear was that Canada had made such a good bargain, the U.S. Congress might not approve it. (Fielding was the former premier of Nova Scotia who had won a provincial election in 1886 campaigning for Nova Scotia's secession from the Dominion.)

George Foster, the Conservative finance critic and former finance minister, stood in the House of Commons to reply to Laurier. In a long and powerful speech, still strikingly relevant today, Foster said:

> I may be wrong, but I have given a great deal of thought to trade matters in the course of my political life, and my conviction is that we have never had in Canada any question quite so important as this present one — any issue upon which hung more far-reaching consequences. The only one that, in my mind, approached it, was the struggle in 1891 ... around which centred one of the greatest political battles ever fought in Canada ...
>
> You talk about your foreign trade, and you bellow about it as though it were the greatest thing in Canada. I was going to say that it was almost the least thing in Canada. What is the greatest thing in Canada? The interprovincial trade . . . which is absolutely the life and essence of this country as a whole ...

Why are they solicitous for this trade treaty with Canada? It looks out upon every page of their argument; it slips off the tongue of every advocate of the proposal. It is that the United States of America covets the rich natural resources of the Dominion of Canada — covets these resources not with a view to coming where the resources are, bringing labour and capital, and working them up where they exist; not that, but covets them to draw them away to their own manufacturing industries, to the centres of their own country, to make them up with their own labour to their own profit, directly and with all the subsidiary gain which accrues to manufacturing in the United States ...

[D]ivide and destroy, that is the maxim. First, one industry will be attacked, and it will go by the board, then another industry will be attacked and it will go by the board. Do you mean to tell me that sensitive, long-sighted capital, looking for investment, will, under these considerations, invest itself in industrial establishments and enterprises on this side of the line? No Sir, it will make capitalists doubly sure to plant themselves and plant their enterprises on the side where the big population, the big market and greatest chances for themselves exist...

Two countries that show ideal conditions of reciprocity in trade would be the West India islands and Canada ... But in the case of the arrangement we are now discussing, you are trying to establish reciprocity between two countries, each of which has a surplus, and a surplus of exactly the same products...

Let a man with $8,000 go into business with a man with $100,000, and who manages that business? It makes no difference that the man with small capital is wiser than the man with large capital, the man with small capital sees his interests are not being well cared for and sees he is subjected to injustice, and he goes to the predominant partner and says: I want this thing changed, and the other says: You do, do you, well I don't want it changed; what are you going to do about it? So the United States can say to Canada ...

If a foreign army threatened us on the border every Canadian would rise and take up arms to defend his country, but have we no duty, no service to perform in defending our country in times of peace? Battalions of armed men are not the greatest menace to the country. Oft times the peaceful warfare of trade and pact is more fatal than open arms ...

It does not follow that, because you are friendly with your neighbour and doing each other good turns, that you should give him half or three-quarters of your house and install him in it. Neither does it follow that because we want to be on good terms with the United States we are to hand over the rich possessions we have hewn out and made for ourselves, and go into a dangerous partnership with them. Nor does it agree with our policy, our instincts and our ideals. It was the conquest of Canada aimed at in 1775; it was the conquest of Canada aimed at in the years around 1812, and since; it was the conquest of Canada and its incorporation with the United States aimed at by the methods I have spoken of in respect to our trade and the fisheries; and the dominant spirit in the United States that is pushing reciprocity through to a successful enactment today is not economic, it is political. It is still the conquest of Canada. But it is the conquest of Canada by peaceful means ... to bring about the time when from the frozen North to the Mexican gulf, there shall be but one power predominant, and that the United States of America.

"The best kick that Canada ever had," Foster said, was the abrogation of the 1854 Reciprocity Treaty. For then, "Canadian nationality" began to develop: "Canadian resources for Canadian developments," and "Canadian routes for Canadian trade." Then "new blood pulsed in our veins, new hopes ... new horizons and new visions." He ended his speech with a passionate declaration:

I utter the most solemn words I have ever uttered in my life, and I believe them to the very bottom of my heart, that there is danger, and deep danger ahead. This path entered upon leads us away from home to a strange country. I pray, Sir, that the full meaning of this first step may sink into the hearts of members of parliament and into the hearts of the people of this country until there shall burst forth a protest of such strength that the steps contemplated will be recalled to the old paths, leading east and west, in and out amongst our own people ... and which we may follow without uncertainty and without menace to our national existence.[18]

To counter the agreement, the Anti-Reciprocity League was set up in Montreal and the Canadian National League in Toronto. The leagues organized meetings, distributed petitions and published literature. The public protest became formidable. By March of 1911, the Governor General of Canada, Lord Grey, wrote that "the feeling in Montreal and Toronto against the Agreement could hardly be stronger if the United States troops had already invaded our territory."[19]

In a critical blow to the government, eighteen prominent Liberals, and Clifford Sifton, a sitting member of Parliament and Laurier's former minister of the interior, broke with the party over the issue. In the House of Commons, Sifton gave his reasons. First, he said, the government had no mandate from the people for such a radical change of policy. Next, some industries would be destroyed. What reason could there be for selecting certain industries which have not committed any crime and wiping them out of existence? The United States would control the grain and livestock trade of western Canada. "The best years of my life," Sifton said, "were given to the settlement of that country, and I cannot tell you how I feel about that great country being made a backyard to the city of Chicago."

Instead of binding the scattered provinces together, free trade would bind each province to the states south of it. Sifton could see "no possible answer" to George Foster's argument. To him it was perfectly clear that every day Canadians adapt to U.S. markets, and "adapt all our arrangements to catering to those markets strengthens the grip of the United States upon Canada." If the treaty went into effect, there would never again be a revision of Canadian tariffs "in which United States interests, United States lobbyists, and United States pressure will not be brought to bear on this parliament."

"If ever a government got it wrong on a subject from first to last," Sifton insisted, "my honourable friends have got it wrong on this subject ... Sir, I would not break away from the political party with which I have acted for 23 years, practically all my life, if I were not in earnest about it."

Sifton asserted that the one thing Canadians must do is be independent of the Americans; reciprocity was the opposite of that policy. It turns Canada "towards the path that leads to Washington. I say, so far as I am concerned: Not for me."[20]

William van Horne, the American-born ex-president of the Canadian Pacific Railway, came out of retirement and announced that he "was out to bust the damned thing." With reciprocity, he wrote, Canada "was making a bed to lie in and die in."[21]

There was some wishful talk, just as there would be seventy-seven years later in 1988, that the agreement would not go through the U.S. Congress. It sailed through, however, in a special summer session in July 1911. During the debate, Representative Charles Davis trusted that "a divine Providence ... may so use this so-called reciprocity treaty, this entering wedge, to further amalgamate these two countries and eventually make them one, with but one flag — the Stars and Stripes."[22] The speaker of the U.S. House of Representatives, James Beauchamp Clark, said: "I am for it [this reciprocity agreement], because I hope to see the day when the American flag will float over every square foot of the British North American possessions clear to the North Pole."[23] Congressman Prince of Illinois stated: "Be not deceived. When we go into a country and get control of it, we take it." And Senator McCumber concurred: "Canadian annexation is the logical conclusion of reciprocity with Canada."[24]

A near revolution in the Conservative Party took place over Robert Borden's "too gentlemanly conduct of the antireciprocity campaign."[25] A group of businessmen from the manufacturing, banking and railway sectors met the Conservative leader, urging him to stiffen up his spine and not be so polite in the conduct of the battle. Conservative MPs were receiving the same message from their constituents. Borden pledged to fight. For twenty-five days the Conservatives held up the House, forcing relentless debate on the agreement.

In Brandon, Manitoba, on a western tour, Borden was met by a delegation from the Grain Growers who lectured him on the benefits of reciprocity. He replied: "All I have to say about that agreement is that I am absolutely opposed to it and that if you gentlemen in the West were prepared to make me Prime Minister of Canada tomorrow if I were to support that agreement, I would not do it and I would not be fit to be Prime Minister of this country if I said anything else to you than that, having the convictions upon it that I have."[26]

In the end, Laurier was forced to go to the people in a general election. During the campaign, the Liberals repeatedly tried to talk only about economics and did their best to avoid the sovereignty issue. The Liberal strategy was to focus on the economic benefits they predicted from reciprocity: free trade would mean bigger markets for Canada's natural products and, hence, more prosperity, increased freight for the railways, a larger population and burgeoning land values. They downplayed the Conservatives' position that Canada would be absorbed by the United States, arguing that increased prosperity would strengthen Canadians' loyalty and independence.

But their strategy failed, and the Liberals were forced to spend most of their time dealing directly with the charge that reciprocity would push Canada into the United States. Time and again, the debate ended up on the central issue of free trade, which is, and has always been, Canadian sovereignty.

In Quebec, Henri Bourassa, prominent political leader and founder of the Montreal newspaper *Le Devoir,* fought against Laurier and reciprocity, allying himself with Quebec Conservative leader Frederick Monk. In 1899, Bourassa, then a sitting Liberal, had broken with Laurier's decision to send Canadian troops to help the British crush the South African Boers. He then founded the Nationalist League, which opposed Canada's involvement in England's imperialist wars, and advocated greater Canadian autonomy and economic independence from both England and the United States. "It is important," Monk wrote, "for us to remain independent of the American people, independent of their ways and their influence which will be fatal to our prosperity and national identity."[27]

Asked for his opinion by a Canadian newspaper, Rudyard Kipling, the renowned British author, wrote: "It is her own soul that Canada risks today. Once that soul is pawned for any consideration, Canada must inevitably conform to the commercial, legal, financial, social, and ethical standards which will be imposed upon her by the sheer admitted weight of the United States. Whatever the United States may gain, and I assume that the United States' proposals are not wholly altruistic, I see nothing for Canada in Reciprocity except a little ready money that she does not need, and a very long repentance."[28]

Distinguished humorist and economist Stephen Leacock turned out articles against the agreement, which were widely read. He described the campaign: "People lived on figures and the man who could remember most of them stood out as a born leader."[29]

In "Canadian Born," the famous poet Pauline Johnson, daughter of a Mohawk chief and an English mother, gave expression to the feelings of many:

The Yankee to the south of us
Must south of us remain
For not a man dare lift a hand
Against the men who brag
That they were born in Canada,
Beneath the British flag.[30]

The Montreal *Star* fought valiantly against the agreement. Its last issue before the election covered the entire front page with an editorial entitled "Under Which Flag?": "This is not a party election. It is a national crisis. We are, in truth, 'at the parting of the ways.' We will either continue to march on the highway toward national greatness with the flag of Canada floating in our clear northern air over our heads; or, we will turn aside toward absorption in the 'great and glorious Republic,' to the south of us, surrendering to a calculating smile what we have long defended from hostility in every form — armed invasion, tariff persecutions, bullying over boundaries, even insolent disregard of treaty obligations."[31]

Robert Borden, in his final message to the people of Canada before the election, on September 19, 1911, said from Halifax:

> As this campaign closes ... the solemn duty confronts us of deciding, very probably for all times, the most momentous question ever submitted to the Canadian electorate ... Throughout this Dominion the electorate now understand that they are called upon to determine not a mere question of markets, but the future destiny of Canada ... Even upon the economic side the reciprocity compact is but a step in a greater process. On each side of the boundary line its advocates realize perfectly that in its final outcome this treaty undoubtedly means the commercial and fiscal union of Canada with the United States ...
>
> Above all, do not forget that the momentous choice which you must make is for all time. If the tariffs of the two countries are interlocked by this treaty be assured that the stronger party will always carry the key. I believe that we are in truth standing today at the parting of the ways. This compact made in secret and without mandate, points indeed to a new path. We must decide whether the spirit of Canadianism or of Continentalism shall prevail on the northern half of this continent.[32]

Two days later, the Laurier government was swept from office. Eight Cabinet ministers, including W.S. Fielding, finance minister and the architect of the agreement, went down to defeat. "On September 25, Robert Laird Borden entered Ottawa in triumph, like a conqueror. A hundred men drew his carriage for miles through streets which were packed with crowds and brave with fluttering flags."[33]

The Toronto *Globe,* which had done its best to promote the

agreement, was bitter: "[The] lesson of yesterday's election" is that "the people of Ontario do not like their neighbours to the south ... Liberals ... joined the Conservatives ... to show their objection to having any 'truck or trade with the Yankees.' "[34]

Clifford Sifton analysed the election afterwards, explaining that at the beginning of 1911, the opposition Conservatives appeared completely out of the running. The Liberal government, strongly entrenched under a striking and statesmanlike leader, "went into a fight on the question of reciprocity and was hopelessly routed." It was not that the deal was not good enough, Sifton said, or that Canada's negotiators should have demanded more. Rather, "the people believed that the development of the two countries under the reciprocity policy was bound to interfere with the commercial independence of Canada and that idea was fatal."[35]

THE RECIPROCITY TREATY of 1911 was more limited than the unrestricted reciprocity of 1861 and far and away less sweeping than the free-trade agreement to come in 1988. Yet the voters saw it as a first step to annexation and it was rejected.

During the 1911 debate, a constituent asked his MP, Liberal William Lyon Mackenzie King, for three reasons for and three reasons against reciprocity. King replied: *For:* (1) increased prosperity through access to a market of 90 million; (2) prevention of monopolies or trusts through increased competition; (3) fostering of friendly feelings between Canadians and Americans "through the avoidance of the kind of friction which tariff matters bring." *Against:* (1) the threat to Canadian manufacturing; (2) that free trade may lead to annexation; (3) that there was no mandate from the people.[36]

Four decades later, the same young MP, now Canada's longest-serving prime minister, would have cause to remember his words and the fury of the 1911 election.

11

Working for Mr. Rockefeller

THE DEFEAT OF LAURIER in 1911 put an end to talk of free trade for more than twenty years. Then, in the Depression years of the 1930s, Conservative Prime Minister R.B. Bennett's government began negotiating with the Americans for a limited trade agreement. William Lyon Mackenzie King, now leader of the opposition Liberals, travelled to Washington. If elected, he promised the Americans, there would be an agreement with more concessions. King had taken his academic training in the United States and had worked for the Rockefeller empire for five years as a "labour expert." In fact, according to broadcaster Knowlton Nash, John D. Rockefeller Jr. later "underwrote King's entire future career, enabling King to be free of financial worry."[1] When Rockefeller died he bequeathed King, then prime minister of Canada, $100,000.

King went so far as to suggest to the U.S. government how to manipulate Bennett into a negotiating strategy favourable to the United States. The American government then stalled until Bennett was defeated in the election of 1935. Within three weeks of taking office, King signed in Washington an agreement that was, according to the U.S. under-secretary of state, William Phillips, "vastly more favourable to the United States than the one which was being considered with Mr. Bennet."[2]

Embarrassed to be in Washington so soon after his election, King joked to the U.S. ambassador that in Canada people called him "the American" and "with a good deal of reason," because he regarded closer ties with the Americans as a "blessing" rather than a danger. The U.S. ambassador in Ottawa, Norman Armour, reported to Washington that King made it clear to him "that there were two roads open to Canada, but that he wanted to choose 'the American road' if we made it possible for him to do so." The prime minister was not advocating annexation, because, as he told

Armour, "certainly you have enough troubles of your own without wanting to add us to them."[3]

In a long memo to his state department shortly before King left for Washington, Mr. Armour set out the importance for his government of signing the trade agreement with Canada, "not so much from an economic standpoint as from, well let us say, a political or international viewpoint if you will." In addition to being profitable for the American exporter, a trade agreement would have "the long range effect of bringing Canada not only within our economic but our political orbit." In recent years, Armour warned, Canadian industry, by protecting its economy, had developed the capacity to produce goods "destined to compete sharply with our exports on the markets of the world." If such a trend were to continue, Canada "may become before long our most intensive competitor." "There is still time," the ambassador continued, "while the Canadian economy is in a formative stage, to shift the impetus away from highly competitive production to complementary production." Through a trade agreement, the United States could, Armour argued, create "some Canadian industries that do not seriously compete with our domestic production." "Is it not," Armour asked, "vitally important for our political future that we have next to us a Canada ... supporting our policies in regard to Latin America ... the Far East and elsewhere, and feeling that in a thousand and one ways they are bound to us in practical things."[4] Ambassador Armour's memo is one of the clearest documents that has come to light expressing the modern U.S. view of eliminating Canada as a competitor.

On November 11, 1935, Prime Minister King and President Roosevelt signed the Canada-U.S. Reciprocal Trade Agreement. Although it was far from free trade, this agreement reduced many tariffs and set in place the economic structure that allowed American capital to take over large parts of the Canadian economy during the next fifty years.

The treaty worked as the Americans had intended: exports of Canadian raw materials increased rapidly, and imports of finished products from the United States grew. In four years, Canada's trade deficit with the United States tripled from $39 million to $107 million, meaning Canada imported almost three times more from Americans than it exported to them. John Hickerson of the U.S. State Department called the benefits of the treaty "staggering" for the United States and said the agreement was "so favorable to us that ... it will be recognized generally as a great economic and political asset."[5] By 1942, the United States had passed Britain as Canada's major customer for the first time. U.S. control of the Canadian economy grew so rapidly that by the time King understood the full meaning of developing "closer ties" with the United States, he was having second thoughts. He came to feel that "the long range policy of the Americans was to absorb Canada," and that "it might be inevitable for us to have to submit to it."[6]

King's misgivings materialized early in 1948, when the U.S. administration approached Canada and proposed negotiating a free-trade treaty. In response, King sent some of his bureaucrats, including a young Simon Reisman, down to Washington, and they negotiated an agreement entirely in secret. The Americans were proposing "ultimate free trade," a treaty for up to twenty-five years modified only by quotas at the beginning, and they wanted the whole agreement to go to Congress by May. The U.S. insistence on haste bothered King, and when he saw the far-reaching scope of the final draft, he changed his mind, stating: "What has been suggested to me today is almost the largest proposal short of war any leader of a government has been looked to to undertake."[7]

Woodbury Willoughby, the head of commercial policy at the U.S. State Department, wrote that the agreement would be a "momentous decision" for Canada that would "radically alter the pattern of her foreign trade from a predominantly East-West to a predominantly North-South movement."[8] The Canadian negotiators understood this as well. John Deutsch, chief negotiator from the Finance department, told a friend: "[The] price of a customs union* with the United States is the loss of political independence in the sense that we would no longer be in effective control of our national policies ... Policy would be shaped in Washington."[9]

King had worked hard to keep the negotiations secret, but the United States saw no necessity to hide its plans for Canada. *Time* magazine announced: "Canada has become an economic 49th state,"[10] and *Life* magazine made the plan public under the title "Customs Union with Canada: Canada needs us, and we need Canada in a violently contracting world." The Canadian press reacted immediately: "Customs Union Not the Answer," said the *Financial Post.* "Not on Your Life," announced the *Globe and Mail.* The Canadian conviction, as always, was that political union would

---

* Customs union: a free-trade agreement in which Canada and the United States also adopt a common tariff on imports from all other countries.

inevitably follow a customs union. King himself had become convinced of this inevitability: "I felt sure that the long objective of the Americans was to control this continent. They would want to get Canada under their aegis."[11]

King killed the draft agreement without ever making it public or even presenting it to his Cabinet. Having lost his seat in the free-trade election of 1911, he had no desire to repeat the experience.

12

Comic Union

THE 1940s WOULD SEE another epic battle, this time for the east coast and Canada's tenth province.

After eons of settlement by the Inuit and Beothuk, and almost 500 years after Leif Erikson and the Vikings established a settlement there, Henry VII of England awarded John Cabot ten pounds for "finding" the "new isle" in 1497. Four hundred and fifty years later, in 1947, the people of Newfoundland and Labrador elected delegates to a convention to decide their future. A referendum with only two choices was decided upon: continuing as a colony of Britain, or gaining independence as a Dominion. Joseph R. Smallwood was a former union organizer, radio broadcaster, pig farmer and an ex-journalist. The son of an alcoholic father, he was blessed with a mother who raised her thirteen children with "inexhaustible energy and a steel will" and Smallwood used both of these traits to change Canadian history.[1] He fought hard for a third option — Confederation with Canada — to be put on the ballot, and organized a massive campaign of 50,000 letters and telegrams to Britain, asking that Confederation be put before the people as a choice. London agreed, and the referendum was set for January 3, 1948.

Confederation was opposed by most of the professionals and businessmen of St. John's and by the Roman Catholic Church. Smallwood dubbed the businessmen "the 21 millionaires" and fought them with "the steam-roller drive of a man of action."[2]

Status as an independent Dominion would not long be viable, for behind it was a growing threat — the movement for union with the United States. The Economic Union with the United States Party was founded, led by Chesley Crosbie, one of the 21 millionaires. "For a brighter tomorrow vote for economic union with the United States today!" was Crosbie's slogan.[3] His party received immediate backing from a number of U.S. senators and from Colonel Robert McCormick, owner of the Chicago *Tribune,* who called for Newfoundland's entry into the U.S. as the forty-ninth state. McCormick also owned a paper mill in the company town of Baie-Comeau, Quebec, and on his visits to the town would give fifty-dollar bills to a young boy named Brian Mulroney to sing for him.

Harold Horwood, a young journalist and union organizer, and Greg Power, poet, satirist and sometime farmer, joined Smallwood, and the trio became known as "the Three Bolsheviks." Power dubbed Crosbie's party "the Comic Union," a title Smallwood used so often in his speeches and over the radio that many Newfoundlanders began to regard it as that movement's real name. Smallwood found support in Ottawa in J.S. Pickersgill, Prime Minister King's private secretary, one of the few, and the most influential person to back the idea of Newfoundland joining Canada. Pickersgill believed that if Newfoundland and Labrador joined Alaska as a second northern flank of the United States, Canada would be "strangled, not physically, but spiritually."[4]

Called, among other things, a traitor and a Judas, Smallwood took a level of personal abuse unprecedented in the political history of Newfoundland. Despite threats, attempted beatings, crowds shouting to lynch him, and being forced to carry a revolver and hire bodyguards, Smallwood, "the people's champion," never slowed down. In the last sixty hours of the tempestuous campaign, he mounted an incredible final effort, giving fifty-six speeches in thirty outposts, stopping only when he lost his voice.

When the votes were counted, there was no clear majority. A second ballot was set for July 22, and the bitter battle went on. Again, Smallwood repeated his visits to all the settlements and talked until he could no longer speak. "A gruelling, grinding, savage battle," Smallwood called it, "but it ended gloriously: Confederation, 78,323 (52.34 percent); responsible government, 71,334 (47.66 percent)."[5] The "crazy radical had become ... the hero of the hour and of Newfoundland history."[6] On March 31, 1949, Newfoundland and Labrador entered Canada as the country's tenth province. Smallwood became the province's first premier and remained so for the next 23 years. In retirement he penned the sweeping five-volume *Encyclopedia of Newfoundland and Labrador.*

As at so many other critical times in Canadian history, a remarkable individual had emerged. Had Smallwood not been there to guide the fight with his inexhaustible energy, his flair and his commitment to Canada, Newfoundland almost certainly would not have voted for Confederation — or even had the chance to vote for it. Forty years later, Chesley Crosbie's wealthy son, John, would carry on the family crusade; he would be Brian Mulroney's right arm in delivering all of Canada into economic union with the United States in the Free Trade Agreement of 1988.

The long process of Newfoundland's joining Canada as the nation's great eastern flank had been completed. Meanwhile, dramatic developments were taking place in the battle for control of key sectors of Canada's economy.

13

In a Class of Its Own

CANADA'S ONGOING STRUGGLE for its own economy was graphically demonstrated by an episode in the aerospace industry. It involved an airplane, a jet interceptor, that could fly to twice the speed of sound and was called the Arrow.

Until 1940, Canada had looked to Britain for its military supplies. With the declaration of war in 1939, Britain urgently needed a source of supply herself. C.D. Howe, an American-born engineer and businessman, was made minister of munitions and supply in the King government and given the job of organizing Canada's war industry. He recruited one thousand businessmen — "Howe's boys" — from across the country, set up twenty-eight Crown corporations and achieved dramatic results. Canada's gross national product — the total value of goods and services produced by the nation — jumped astoundingly, from $5 billion in 1939 to $12 billion in 1943, and Canada climbed to fourth among the Allies in industrial production. By the end of 1944, Canadian shipyards had turned out almost 600 ships; some 45 aircraft companies, running 24 hours a day and employing 80,000 workers, had produced 16,000 aircraft. Declared Howe: "Never again will there be any doubt that Canada can manufacture anything that can be manufactured elsewhere."[1]

Sir Roy Dobson of Hawker-Siddeley Aircraft, developer of 180 aircraft projects in England, came to Canada and was impressed by what he found. "It opened my eyes, I'll tell you," he said. "If these so-and-so's can do this during a war, what can't they do after. One thing this country would need is an aircraft industry of its own: design and development, not just assembling somebody else's stuff." Later he explained:

> I saw a great country full of natural resources, all kinds of metals, all kinds of minerals and oil, all kinds of capacity for growing

112

wheat and other kinds of food, and yet it seemed to me ... lacking
in the finer engineering developments ... in things like aircraft,
aircraft engines and so on. And I couldn't imagine ... a nation
with this sort of potential carrying on without demanding — not
just asking, or thinking about it, but demanding — its own aircraft,
its own aircraft industry, its own engine industry and indeed a lot
of other industries too ... So I said, "All right. That's my field. I'm
going to have a go at it."[2]

By 1945, the Royal Canadian Air Force was the third-largest in
the world in terms of men and equipment. Robert Leckie, chief of
air staff, had for years fought for an independent Canadian air force,
with aircraft designed in Canada and built to suit Canadian needs.
At the close of the war, Roy Dobson and C.D. Howe struck a deal,
and A.V. Roe (A.V.R.O.) Canada was set up in the Victory Aircraft
plant outside of Toronto "to give Canada," as Dobson told the press,
"a basic industry which, in our opinion, she badly needs. Canada
will become the aircraft production centre of the British Empire
within ten years."[3] Hamilton native Fred Smye, aircraft production
director at Victory, became the first employee and a driving force
behind Avro's future success.

March 17, 1949, saw the test run of the first Canadian jet engine,
the Avro Chinook. In August, the Avro Jetliner, the first North
American commercial jet aircraft and second in the world, made
its maiden flight, fourteen days after the British Comet had lifted
briefly a few feet off the ground in England. In April 1950, eight
years before the first American commercial jet airplane took flight,
the Avro Jetliner carried the world's first jet airmail, from Toronto
to New York, where its crew was welcomed with a ticker-tape parade
through the streets of Manhattan. The trip was made in half the
flight time of a conventional airplane.

Avro then designed and produced the Orenda jet engine, named
after the god of the Iroquois. Developed by a small group of about
forty young Canadian engineers, the Orenda was one of the most
successful turbojet engines ever built. By 1954, more than one
thousand had been delivered to the Canadian air force.

Avro went on to design and build the highest-rated all-weather,
long-range fighter in NATO, the CF (Canadian Fighter) 100. The first
of hundreds of Orenda-powered aircraft was delivered to the RCAF
in October 1951. By 1958, the Canadian content in the CF-100 was
90 percent, and in its Orenda engines 95 percent. Avro, following a

buy-Canadian policy, established a network of Canadian suppliers and sub-contractors, which created a beehive of development activity in nearly every other Canadian industry. By now, A.V. Roe was the third-largest company in Canada, employing 50,000 people in all divisions and carrying out 70 percent of all research in Canada.

October 4, 1957, saw the official roll-out of the first Avro Arrow — a supersonic jet fighter designed and built in four short years. With the Arrow, Avro had created a brilliant aviation industry that drew to Canada international specialists at the top of their fields. After the unveiling, *Aviation Week* reported: "Avro CF-105 Arrow has given Canada a serious contender for the top military aircraft of the next several years. The large, decidedly advanced delta-wing fighter was rolled out of the Malton plant a few days ago ... The Arrow's power, weight and general design leave little doubt of its performance potential." *Flight,* another international aviation magazine, called the Arrow "the biggest, most powerful, most expensive and potentially the fastest fighter that the world has yet seen."[4]

On March 25, 1958, the Avro Arrow Mark I — a "great, sleek, white bird," to one observer — lifted gracefully from the runway and was airborne for the first time.[5] The most advanced aircraft in the world, it exceeded all expectations. At three-quarter throttle, the Arrow flew at nearly twice the speed of sound — faster than the most advanced plane in the Canadian Air Force three decades later, the American F-18.

The world speed record in 1958 was 1404 mph. The first five Arrows, fitted with temporary, less powerful engines, flew at 1320 mph. Into the sixth Arrow was installed the most advanced and the most powerful engine in the world, the brand new Iroquois, Canadian designed and built from scratch. On February 19, 1959, the Avro Arrow Mark II, fitted with Iroquois engines, was on the tarmac, being prepared for the test flight expected easily to break the world speed record. Behind it, another thirty-one Mark IIs, Iroquois equipped, were ready to roll down the assembly line.

At the sprawling 400-acre Avro plant just outside Toronto, almost everybody felt good about their work. They saw themselves as contributing to Canada. Absenteeism was low and lateness was rare. The atmosphere was described by one aviation writer as touched by magic: "They were so proud of that airplane, and of the inescapable fact that they were producing something that was the best in the whole bloody world. You could sense it the minute you walked in the place." Joe Morley, the sales and service manager, explained:

"We were all possessed with one ideal — the Arrow. No one, even in junior management, ever punched a time clock; it would have been as much overtime as straight time."[6] The design and development people were top notch, as were the engineers. The Arrow "was in a class of its own and at least twenty, if not thirty, years ahead of its time in terms of design philosophy, materials, and manufacturing techniques!"[7]

Yet all was not as well as it seemed. A peculiar thing had happened back in 1950: C.D. Howe had ordered production of the Avro Jetliner stopped after the first aircraft was completed. One of the outstanding aeronautical achievements of its day, the one and only Jetliner broke records with every flight. Robert Rummel, chief engineer for Trans World Airlines in the United States, described the pioneer plane: "The Jetliner, the first jet transport produced in North America, was an advanced, medium-range, 450-mph plane that first flew an amazing eight years before Boeing's 707. This extraordinary achievement is all the more remarkable considering that it was the first product of a new company in a country not dominant in the development or construction of aircraft. The design, developed by A.V. Roe Canada (AVRO), was conspicuously ahead of any competitive transport."[8]

Then, one Saturday early in February 1957, after eight years of flying, the Jetliner came in for a routine check. The following Monday morning, the staff found the craft cut in two. It was sold for scrap. In 1959, Fred Smye, at the time the president and general manager of Avro Aircraft, said: "It had exceeded every specification and if it had gone ahead would be selling around the world today."[9] A few days after the Jetliner was destroyed, the *Saturday Evening Post* of February 16, 1957, carried a two-page centrefold advertisement of the new Boeing "Jetliner," the 707, proudly describing it as "America's first Jetliner, the only American jet airliner flying today."[10]

Now, on the morning of February 20, 1959, at 9:30, Prime Minister John Diefenbaker was in the House of Commons to deliver a statement on "one facet of the national defence" of Canada. "The government," he went on, "has carefully examined and re-examined the probable need for the Arrow aircraft and Iroquois engine known as the CF-105 ... The conclusion arrived at is that the development of the [Arrow] aircraft and Iroquois engine should be terminated now."[11]

The shocked employees heard the news first from a reporter. A telegram from Ottawa ordered Avro to "cease and desist as of receipt of this telex on all government contracts and acknowledge that you are so proceeding." And over the public address system, 14,528 employees were told their services would no longer be needed. They were laid off immediately. Ordered by Raymond O'Hurley, minister of defence production, to "cut up the Arrow and destroy ... all material associated with it," Smye refused. O'Hurley replied: "If you don't do it, we'll send the army in to do it."[12] Teams of men with cutting torches came into the factories and cut the completed Arrows into scrap. The blowtorches didn't stop until the "obscene destruction of millions of dollars worth of finished and almost-finished planes, of tools, jigs, fixtures and masses of expensive production and test equipment" was complete.[13] Some of the employees who had built the aircraft were seen to "stand and cry as grown men seldom cry" as they watched the torches "melt down and cut to pieces the magnificent airplanes which they had spent seven years of their lives designing, creating and building."[14] Operating manuals, blueprints, records, drawings and thick volumes of specifications data were collected and destroyed.

The mutilated scraps of the most advanced engine and airplane in the world were delivered under tight security to a Toronto scrapyard, along with the tools that produced them. Afterwards, a government official said tersely, referring to the Arrow, "Forget it! *It never existed.* Get that into your heads."[15]

Some 650 major sub-contracts were cancelled. The Arrow's demise affected the livelihood of nearly 100,000 Canadians and the fate of dozens of industries. Some historians, commentators and government members, using wildly distorted figures, have cited high production costs as one reason for the Arrow's cancellation. The total spent on the Iroquois engine and development of the Arrow, including the finished aircraft, was approximately $300 million. Another $200 million would have been required to complete them, after which each Arrow would have cost the government $3.7 million, roughly the price of a contemporary, less sophisticated U.S. plane. And the money, technology, jobs and talent would have remained in Canada. (The *Financial Post* estimated that at least 65 percent of the total cost of the Arrow program came back directly to the government in taxes.) The Arrow, in the words of Edith Kay Shaw, an aviation-engineering technologist who worked on the Avro Jetliner, the CF-100 and the Arrow, "represented one of the greatest bargains in aircraft ever offered," to say nothing of the tens of thousands of jobs created and dozens of domestic spinoff industries in everything from plastic to design.[16]

WHY WAS THE Arrow cancelled? The official reason given by the government was that the missile age had dawned and manned jetfighter aircraft, including the Arrow, had become obsolete. Accordingly, the new American Bomarc missile system was to be purchased, and because Canada could not afford both the Arrow and the Bomarc, the Arrow had to go. Behind-the-scenes pressure from the United States for Canada to buy the Bomarc — a system that was untried, unproven and would eventually prove useless — was direct and effective. In a meeting between the Canadian defence minister, George Pearkes, and the U.S. secretary of state for defence, Neil McElroy, the Canadian government asked what would happen if Canada refused to buy the Bomarc. The Canadians were told that "the consequence would be ... the emplacement of at least one more Bomarc squadron in the U.S., south of the Great Lakes."[17] Because the Bomarc had a limited range of 250 miles, this would mean, in the event of war against incoming Soviet missiles from the north, the certainty of nuclear holocaust above Canada's most densely populated regions. Consequently, the Canadian government decided to purchase the Bomarcs, put them further north in Canada, and terminate the Arrow.

Within two months of the Arrow's cancellation, Canadians were told that fighter aircraft to intercept Soviet bombers were still necessary after all. Ten months later, General Lawrence Kuter of the United States, commander-in-chief of the North American Air Defense agreement (NORAD), requested that Canada equip itself with supersonic fighters such as the American F-101B. In 1961, Canada purchased sixty-six of these dated aircraft — in no way comparable to the Arrow — from the United States. Two decades later Canada would spend roughly $5 *billion* ($30 million per plane) purchasing the American F-18A, an aircraft still inferior to the Arrow.

As for the Bomarc missile system, admitted by the Americans themselves to be entirely for the defence of the American Strategic Air Command and not for Canada, it turned out to be an expensive dud that became obsolete before it was installed.

A significant but little-known fact is that the Arrow was the only aircraft in the world capable of downing the new, top-secret

U-2 spy plane developed by the U.S. Central Intelligence Agency (CIA), which in the late 1950s was overflying countries around the globe. The U-2 flew at an altitude of 70,000 feet, unreachable by any existing interceptor but well within the Arrow's range. In 1960, Defence Minister Pearkes admitted the U-2 was overflying Canada and that without interceptor aircraft, Canada was powerless to police its own skies against such an intruder.

Judith Robinson of the Toronto *Telegram*, on February 10, 1959, wrote that Canada's role from the point of view of U.S. defence planners was to "provide for the defence of the United States three things: a narrow margin of time, distant early warning signals, and rocket bases. Just those three things. Manned supersonic fighters based in Canada have no place in U.S. defence plans."[18]

The New York *Times* carried a report stating: "Canada has had the dubious privilege of being first in learning the economic and political implications of U.S. domination in weapons ... the result is ... no real defence ... a disappearing Canadian Air Force and aircraft industry; and a fearfully ill-equipped Army ... Why? Because . . . [Canada has] conformed to U.S. concepts, doctrines and weapons."[19]

In 1717, the manufacturing of beaver hats was begun in Montreal. Four finished hats were turned out every day. Then came the order directly from the king of France to kill the industry. There was to be no competition from the colony for French hatmakers. Colonies "are established solely for the utility of the country that forms them," Louis XIV said.[20] Two and a half centuries later, instead of from Versailles the pressure came from Washington.

The Avro Jetliner was destroyed to allow the Americans to introduce their Boeing Jetliner, eight years after the Canadian Jetliner had first flown. Just as the Mark II was about to fly, and in all likelihood bring the world's speed record to Canada, thirty-seven supersonic aircraft were scrapped. To make sure no new aircraft would rise from the cuttings of the blowtorches, a free-trade agreement in defence supplies, the Canada-U.S. Defence Production Sharing Agreement of 1959, was signed. That agreement integrated the defence industries of the two countries. Canada agreed to rely on the United States for defence technology, and has never again tried to be self-reliant in the aerospace and defence industries. Instead of producing its own aircraft, Canadian industry was reoriented to produce parts for U.S. contractors. Shortly before the Arrow's cancellation, Canada joined NORAD, which integrated the air defence of the two countries under a 'joint' command headquartered in Colorado. In the future, Defence Minister Pearkes said, the United States would supply jet interceptor defence if Canada should require it. The operation of these two agreements ensures that Canada does not create and produce high-tech military aircraft. The very country that has invaded Canada repeatedly, and has been by far its most dangerous and sustained threat over the centuries, now "looks after" Canada's defence.

Canada went on to spend billions of dollars on civilian and military aircraft from American firms, aircraft less suited to its needs and climate. The "Canadian" defence industry today consists mainly of subsidiaries of American corporations. These subsidiary firms are encouraged to station scouts in the United States to catch word of pending U.S. contracts. They can then make a bid to produce U.S. weapons.

With the cancellation of the Arrow, thousands of the highly skilled engineers, designers and aerospace workers, some gathered with great difficulty from all over the world, who for ten years had refused repeated offers from U.S. firms to leave Canada, were thrown out of work and now had little choice. Twenty-six of Avro's top engineers, including Jim Chamberlin from British Columbia, Avro's chief of design, were sent by the Canadian government to NASA, where their skills played a crucial role in landing an American on the moon. Chamberlin was later described by NASA management as "probably one of the most brilliant men ever to work with NASA."[21] Highly skilled Avro engineers made their contributions in almost all fields of aviation and technology throughout the Western world, not only with NASA but also with Boeing of Seattle, RCA in Massachusetts, Hawker-Siddeley of England, Fokker of Holland, and the European Space Agency.

With an eight-year lead on the United States in civilian jetliner technology and the Avro Arrow, the Canadian aerospace industry could have taken on the best in the world. It would also have been competition for U.S. corporations. Instead, Avro scrambled for whatever business it could find, at one point landing a contract to produce pots and pans. In 1962, Avro sold what remained of its gutted operations to de Havilland, leaving a wealth of concepts, ideas and designs that, over the next three decades, were used by leading British and American firms. And the myth began to be fostered that Canada did not have the skills, capabilities or resources to build world-class industries on its own.

Polish-born Janusz Zurakowski, the decorated fighter pilot who test flew the Arrow, wrote: "Canada, by creating its own industry, could have satisfied most defence requirements — but not the American industrialists who wanted the market." He added: "Governments and torches can destroy an aircraft, but they cannot destroy hope, and aspiration ... in the hearts of the people, the dream lives on."[22]

If the Jetliner and the Arrow had gone ahead, they, like the CF-100, would have been purchased by other countries. American industrialist Howard Hughes was interested in producing the Jetliner in the United States, and several American companies wished to order the aircraft from Avro. An American company had signed a contract with Avro to produce the Iroquois under licence — the first contract of its kind signed by the United States with a Canadian company. France had approached Avro about purchasing 300 Iroquois engines for use in its Mirage jet fighter. Both the United States and Britain were interested in the Arrow because they had nothing comparable.

The technology, the research and the talent, as well as the money since spent on foreign aircraft, both military and commercial, would have remained in Canada. A dynamic aerospace industry would have established itself as one of the major engines driving Canada's economy. Equally significant, Canada would have had the capability to patrol and defend its own borders and airspace against incursion by all intruders. If the Arrow had flown with Iroquois engines, it almost certainly would have broken world records for both speed and altitude. Had the Canadian public seen that happen, cancellation of the Arrow would have been impossible. Perhaps that is why the blowtorches came in before the Mark IIs could lift off the ground.

The Arrow was not cancelled because it was costly or obsolete or defective. It was, in the words of electronics engineer and Arrow researcher Palmiro Campagna, "erased from existence, because it was too damn good!"[23]

14

We Were Fighting
for Canada

IN 1939, CANADA HAD thirty-eight ocean-going merchant
ships; six years later, the fleet was ten times greater and Canada
had the third-largest merchant navy in the Western world. By the
end of 1945, Canada, with 500 ships employing 20,000 men, stood
fourth among the ship-owning nations of the world.

Both high-seas and Great Lakes seamen were part of Canada's
merchant navy, and 8000 of them were members of the Canadian
Seamen's Union (CSU). The CSU, a Canadian union without U.S.
ties, was organized by Canadians themselves. It was born on the
Great Lakes in the 1930s Depression, when a sailor's lot was little
different from that of a slave. During the war, the CSU organized
ocean-going seamen and won, without a strike, improvements in
living accommodations — mattresses, proper food, cutlery, water
provisions and the like — as well as better wages and hours. A highly
effective union, the CSU in 1946 fought and, in one of the most
dramatic strikes in the history of the labour movement, won the
eight-hour day. This in an industry where the 84-hour week had
been the norm. By 1947, with more than 12,000 members, the CSU
was the largest purely Canadian affiliate of the Trades and Labour
Congress (TLC), forerunner of today's Canadian Labour Congress
(CLC).

The American Federation of Labour (AFL), which already
controlled a good number of unions in Canada, decided at its 1944
convention that the Seafarers' International Union (SIU) of the
United States, with virtually no members in Canada, would
henceforth have jurisdiction over all "seamen and fishermen in
all waters of North America and Canada."[1] Further, it demanded
that the Canadian TLC end any recognition of the Canadian

121

Seamen's Union and recognize only the U.S. affiliate.*

Shocked by the illegal action of the AFL, the head of the TLC, Percy Bengough, rejected the demand, saying: "Members of unions cannot just be taken out of one union and put into another like cattle taken out of one stall and moved into the next."[2] In keeping with the growing anti-communist hysteria of the era in the United States, the AFL responded by charging that the CSU was a "communist" union and then established itself as a kangaroo court to try the TLC. The AFL claimed it had created the TLC. However, although the Canadian labour organization was founded about the same time as the AFL, it was certainly not at the AFL's insistence. Indeed, the TLC had a national predecessor, the Canadian Labour Union, founded in 1873, that predated the American organization by thirteen years. At the union trial held in the United States in February 1949 without notice to the TLC, the AFL announced it had found a "shocking picture of the influence wielded by the communists in Canada over the affairs of TLC."[3]

It was not only the Canadian union that the U.S. government and its allies in the AFL wanted to eliminate. They wanted to get rid of the Canadian fleet so that Canada's overseas trade would go in U.S. ships, provide American jobs and be under U.S. control. Standing in the way was the CSU, whose number-one demand was preservation of the Canadian fleet of ships so that Canada could maintain "some measure of independence in its foreign trade."[4]

Mackenzie King and C.D. Howe did not want a peacetime Canadian fleet. They planned to direct most of Canada's trade to the United States, an arrangement that did not require many ships. As well, government supporters from business were calling for the privatization of the merchant fleet. Howe announced the plan to sell off the fleet, even though there existed a serious world shortage of shipping, and even though most maritime nations were building up their shipping and allied industries.

The sailors saw their fight for a Canadian merchant fleet as part of the fight for Canadian independence. As Joe Grabek, a Canadian seaman, put it: "We wanted to maintain a fleet under the Canadian

---

* American unions operating in Canada call themselves "international." In reality, they are not international — they have no British, Finnish, Chinese or French members. They are American unions, headquartered and controlled in the United States, with branches in Canada.

flag ... Look at the jobs that are lost in the shipyards, maintenance, the seamen. Not only that, but Canada is paying through the nose to foreign shipowners to carry her cargo. As a trading nation, we should have a fleet to carry our goods . . . We were fighting for Canada ... We would not sell out to the U.S. like our government did."[5] It was also the fight of a Canadian union to exist in a Canadian industry against an American union that had unilaterally declared Canada was its jurisdiction.

By 1949, the Canadian government's sale of the fleet was well under way at fire-sale prices. Canadian ships were sold to American or Greek companies that would immediately dismiss the Canadian crew, take down the Canadian flag, run up a Panamanian, Liberian or other "flag of convenience," and hire another crew, usually from a third-world country, for starvation wages and in appalling working conditions.

During the Second World War, Canada had escorted 25,343 merchant-ship voyages across the submarine-infested North Atlantic. More than ninety Canadian ships were sunk, most of them merchant ships, and more than 6000 sailors were killed or wounded. Yet the ships never stopped; 90,000 tons of war supplies were delivered every day of the war. Rear Admiral L.W. Murray, commander of the Canadian Naval Escort Force in the Western Atlantic, said: "Make no mistake, the real victors in the battle of the Atlantic were not the navies or air forces but the Allied merchant seamen."[6]

There had been no U.S. protection for Canadian ships on the North Atlantic, and the seamen on board had developed a "spirit of independence from things American."[7] They were now called "communists," and the Canadian docks would soon run red with the blood of the men who had braved German U-boats for five years all across the Atlantic.

The man sent to destroy them drove north from San Francisco early in 1949, behind the wheel of a white Cadillac. Harold Chamberlain Banks's assignment was to break the Canadian Seamen's Union by any means necessary, and to do so he was sent to Montreal by a combination of American union, business and government interests, with expert backing and apparently unlimited funds. On St. James Street in Montreal, Banks built the most expensive union headquarters in Canada. Entry involved passing a gauntlet of locked doors and the menacing scrutiny of strong-arm men. Banks's huge desk and swivel chair were mounted on a raised concrete platform, while the legs of chairs for visitors were cut to six inches. At his fingertips was a brass console with an intercom to monitor every room in the building. The private elevator to Banks's third-floor office could be stopped between floors, giving enforcers adequate time with visitors who had displeased Banks. After the beatings, they would be dumped out at street level.

Within a few months of his arrival, Banks, backed by some of the press, the RCMP and the Canadian government, boasted: "I will soon be in the dubious position of being the top labor man in all of Canada."[8]

The SIU, a U.S. union that lacked not only membership but also legal status in Canada, had been trying to sign up sailors in Canada for a year without success. Then, representatives of the owner-members of the Canadian Shipping Association went secretly to San Francisco and signed an agreement with the president of the SIU. It included contracts with the government-owned Canadian National Steamships, already legally under contract with the Canadian Seamen's Union. If the contracts were allowed to stand, it would mean the death of the CSU and the delivery of all remaining Canadian seamen into the hands of a U.S. union that none of them had joined — and that was known to have links to organized crime in the United States.

The CSU responded by calling a strike, which began in Halifax. On April 8, 1949, at 3 a.m., a special train carrying 200 strikebreakers, including sixty SIU members flown in from the United States, pulled onto the Halifax docks, under the protection of 100 armed officers of the Canadian National Railways Police and the RCMP. Banks's strongmen attacked the CSU picketers with sawed-off axe handles and shotguns, while officers on board the ships turned steam hoses against the strikers. The fight went on for hours and left eight CSU members lying wounded and bleeding on the dock. In the wake of this vicious assault against a greatly outnumbered group of legal picketers, the federal government promised an investigation into how sixty American SIU members were granted entry into Canada and put on board three ships owned by the Canadian government. The investigation never took place.

Instead, much of the media joined in an all-out attack on the Canadian seamen. Under assault by American unions backed by the Canadian government and the RCMP, the CSU mounted a battle that in the end involved fourteen countries on four continents and hundreds of thousands of sailors. Some 50,000 dockers in London stopped work when asked to load a Canadian ship manned by strikebreakers. The work stoppage in support of the Canadian strike lasted seventy-four days, spreading to other British cities and leading to the declaration of a state of emergency and the call-out of 35,000 troops in the United Kingdom.

In a speech given two years later to an SIU convention in San Francisco, Banks explained: "The . . . Seafarers' International Union of North America and the Sailors' Union of the Pacific gave all-out aid, morally, financially and physically, particularly [union official Morris] Weisberger came into Halifax with a group of experts and fought a battle that they will remember. They brought in specialists in certain fields. They brought in men who knew their business when it came to drawing up transcripts for radio broadcasts, they brought in experts in public relations and they brought in broad-shouldered boys — in fact, a complete setup."[9]

By using a blacklist, Banks soon controlled the bargaining rights of almost every Canadian merchant seaman. Before Banks arrived in Canada, the shippers had used a "do not ship" list to keep union organizers off their ships. When Banks arrived, the list included the names of about eighty sailors. He took over the list himself — for "Commie agitators, epileptics, sleepwalkers, perverts, drunks and thieves," as he explained.[10] By 1956, the list contained 6000 names. By 1964, 10,000 sailors had been deprived of their livelihoods. Nearly every active member of the CSU was on the blacklist, and there was never a trial of any kind. Everyone who disagreed with Hal Banks was considered a "communist" whose name was quickly added to the growing list. When short of funds, Banks would add another batch of names to the "do not ship" list and bring into the SIU a group of new members with their large initiation fees.

For fifteen years, Banks reigned over the Canadian waterfront, helped by other American unions, especially the International Longshoremen's Association and the International Brotherhood of Teamsters. Under the threat from its fourteen American affiliates to withdraw, the Trades and Labour Congress of Canada, which had initially challenged the SIU, buckled under and expelled the CSU. The union members, deprived of the right to work, saw their lives in ruins.

Banks ordered ships employing members of the Canadian union to be boycotted in American cities. "We are going to keep communists from Canada from entering American ports," he declared.[11] The RCMP took up positions along the St. Lawrence Seaway to protect SIU ships, and escorted strikebreakers replacing CSU members. From his office fortress, Banks came close to fulfilling his boast of controlling "everything that floats" in Canada.[12]

Banks lived a life of unbridled luxury and corruption. His personal fleet of speedboats, Cadillacs and cabin cruisers was paid for by union funds, as were his liquor, his cigarettes and his prostitutes (listed under the expense heading, "female companionship"). The "union" also paid for his large house in Point Claire, and for the luxury apartment where he was rumoured to entertain VIPs, shipowners, MPs and Cabinet ministers with pornographic movies and prostitutes — while cameras worked steadily behind two-way mirrors, providing blackmail material.

Bribes to at least one reporter and a police officer, and contributions to the campaigns of half a dozen Montreal MPs, were all paid for by the SIU, as were the new, always white, Cadillacs — thirty-three in all — that Banks drove. The Canadian district of the SIU never held a union convention. Banks never ran for any kind of office. Once, to demonstrate how his "union" was run, Banks told a visitor: "I am going to make a motion that I raise my salary from $12,000 to $20,000 a year." Then he stood up and said. "I second the motion." And then he sat back down behind his enormous desk, saying: "Accepted."[13]

For Banks, women occupied a position even below that of "commies and epileptics." Each of his wives fled from repeated beatings. Women would be invited onto his boat, where they had the choice of submitting to Banks or swimming to shore.

Approached in his Montreal office by a sailor's wife whose husband had been injured and whose family was penniless, the distraught woman asked if the union's welfare plan could help her. Banks laughed, saying: "You just want to get f****d." The woman ran from the building, Banks's laughter echoing in her ears. On another occasion, the wife of a union member was reportedly raped in front of her husband in Banks's office.[14]

By pressing a button, Banks could get Ottawa or Washington — and nobody in power put Hal Banks on hold. John Schlesinger, one of Banks's highly paid lawyers, confessed afterwards: "Sometimes it horrified me to think that a man could have that much power."[15]

Captain Henry Walsh of the Canadian Merchant Service Guild refused to sign over his union of ships officers to Banks. Banks called him into his office and outlined his choices: (1) Walsh could sign over his union and receive a big office, a large salary and a nonexistent workload; (2) he could have the "pavement treatment," in which the victim's legs are raised onto a curb and jumped upon by a hired goon, breaking the bones; or (3) Walsh could "simply disappear."[16]

Walsh refused the big office and refused to cave in. In a dark parking lot in Owen Sound, Ontario, in August 1957, the five-foot, four-inch Walsh received the standard beating by three large men, one of them Banks's personal bodyguard, a professional boxer from the United States. Walsh's teeth were kicked out, and he was smashed onto the pavement. He would never again take a step without pain. Seven years later, as a result of that beating and following a courageous battle by Walsh, by Harry Crowe, research director of the Canadian Brotherhood of Railway and Transport Workers, and by others, Banks's downfall would begin.

In August 1960, the SIU was finally expelled from the CLC, and two years later, as the result of pressure from Canadian unions, an inquiry into the activities of Hal Banks and the SIU, headed by Thomas G. Norris of the B.C. court of appeal, was at last begun.

Central Intelligence Agency (CIA) agent Edwin Wilson was sent up from the United States to defend Banks. He was helped by Ed Mackin, another American, also the recipient of CIA funding, who took the stand as the main witness for Banks. The head of the American Federation of Labor-Congress of Industrial Organizations (AFL-CIO), George Meany, and the U.S. secretary of labor, William Wirtz, condemned Canada for acting like a totalitarian state and called upon all AFL-CIO-affiliated unions to back the SIU in its battle for "free trade unionism" in Canada.[17]

The inquiry heard horrific evidence of women attacked in their homes and of men beaten senseless. Judge Norris wrote in the inquiry's report: "It is very difficult for me to understand how in this state of our so-called civilization, things of this sort could happen in Canada ... Witnesses came to give evidence still bearing the marks of beatings — some were crippled or marked for life."[18] Morris Marrinan, a sailor whose life Banks had ruined through the blacklist, courageously testified that Banks was a "noted bully and a most outstanding tyrant" who had caused "untold sufferings, hardships and misery to Canadian Flag Seamen."[19]

In May 1964, Banks was sentenced to five years for the beating of Henry Walsh. Two weeks later, out of jail on bail, he drove his Cadillac across the border, unchallenged. Before long, Banks's loyal vice-president, Red McLaughlin, took over as SIU president. In 1968, the SIU was readmitted to the CLC. When McLaughlin moved on to the

International Labour Organization in Geneva in 1973, Banks's former bodyguard, Roman "Shotgun" Gralewicz — "one of Banks's goons," Judge Norris had called him — took over the top job.[20]

When Canada asked for Banks's extradition from New York, a lower-court judge ordered his return. Banks's lawyers, in a rare move, bypassed the appeals courts and went directly to the U.S. secretary of state, Dean Rusk. Rusk's legal advisors unanimously said there was no choice but to send Banks back, it had been 130 years since a secretary of state had refused an extradition request from Canada, and no case could be found of a lower-court ruling being overturned by the secretary of state. But Rusk overruled them all, on account of "the unique facts of this case." Banks lived out his life in San Francisco, where he died in 1985.[21]

How this convicted criminal entered Canada remains uninvestigated. When a judge turned down Banks's request for landed immigrant status, the Canadian government gave it to him by order-in-council. How a man who had been in court for murder, burglary, child-stealing, assault causing bodily harm, possession of a sawed-off shotgun, intimidation, and defamatory libel received Canadian landed-immigrant status still remains a mystery. More than fifty files on the case at the Department of Immigration remain "too private" and are closed to the public.[22]

On the May morning in 1964 when Banks drove back to the United States, the once proud Canadian fleet, which had employed more than 15,000, consisted of two ships. The Canadian shipbuilding industry, in which more than 40,000 people had worked, was dead. The exports of Canada, the nation with the longest coastline in the world, were shipped on foreign vessels. They still are, and the remaining seamen in Canada are still represented by the Seafarer's International Union. In contrast, the United States prohibits foreigners, or foreign-owned companies, from engaging in or acquiring control of companies involved in either fresh-water or coastal shipping, dredging or salvage. American companies must use ships made and serviced in the U.S.A.

15

"You Pissed on My Rug"

JOHN DIEFENBAKER'S COMPLIANCE in killing the Avro Arrow, purchasing Bomarc missiles, joining NORAD and signing the Defence Production Sharing Agreement was not enough to satisfy Washington for long.

On January 1, 1959, Fidel Castro's revolutionaries took power in Havana, Cuba. They had fought their way down from the mountains and overthrown the corrupt and brutal dictatorship of Fulgencio Batista. A few months later, in April, as a guest of the American Society of Newspaper Editors, Castro made a triumphant visit to Washington. His presence created major traffic jams, with people shouting "Viva, Castro!" and "Hey, Fidel!" He laid wreaths at Lincoln's and Jefferson's monuments, told the American press that he opposed communism, and declared he would not expropriate U.S. property. Some of the most powerful men in the United States, however, were not shouting "Viva, Castro!" They decided to get rid of the bearded, smiling 32-year-old; he was, as Vice-President Richard Nixon said after meeting the Cuban leader, too "anti-American." Planning began at CIA headquarters for a covert military operation to invade Cuba and to overthrow Castro's young government.[1]

Two years later, on April 13, 1961, the United States launched its invasion of Cuba, using planes, tanks and ships. In an attempt to portray the invasion as an internal Cuban matter, most of the soldiers involved were Cuban exiles. However, the entire operation was conceived, organized, financed and commanded by the U.S. government. Fidel Castro's forces fought back. Three days of heavy fighting saw the defeat of the Americans and the capture of almost 1200 of their soldiers.

The following year, on October 22, 1962, President John F. Kennedy announced to the world that Soviet ships were bringing nuclear missiles to Cuba. The United States mounted a naval blockade of the island and drew a line in the ocean beyond which the Soviets could not cross. For a week, "the world held its breath" as the Soviet ships approached the American destroyers.[2] The United States placed its military on red alert, the final stage before releasing missiles. The Soviet ships failed, by mistake it turned out, to get a halt order in time from Moscow, and they crossed the line. The U.S. joint chiefs of staff met and voted for a nuclear first strike against the Soviet Union. Washington demanded Canada put its military on red alert and support it publicly.

Diefenbaker refused to be stampeded. Speaking to the Canadian people, he declared: "What people all over the world want tonight and will want is a full and complete understanding of what is taking place in Cuba." Pointing to the Soviet statement that the missiles were of "an entirely defensive nature" for the purposes of preventing a repeat American invasion of Cuba, Diefenbaker asked that the matter be referred to the United Nations immediately. "The only sure way that the world can secure the facts would be through an independent inspection," Diefenbaker announced. The Liberals supported Diefenbaker and so did the NDP, whose leader, Tommy Douglas, referring to the American double standard, said: "We have only the statements of the Americans ... Before we get too excited we should remember that for fifteen years the Western powers have been ringing the Soviet Union with missiles and air bases."[3]

In a dramatic example of how the new "joint decision-making" of NORAD would work, the Canadian armed forces went on red alert at U.S. command, overriding the express opposition of their commander-in-chief, the Canadian prime minister.

Diefenbaker's resistance to the U.S. military plans for Cuba made the demise of his government a major goal of the Kennedy administration. In January 1963, the U.S. government demanded that Canada equip its recently purchased Bomarc missiles with U.S. nuclear warheads. Diefenbaker hesitated, and on January 30 the U.S. government issued a press release that "brutally assaulted the prime minister for his indecision."[4] Diefenbaker took the unprecedented step of recalling the Canadian ambassador from Washington. Speaking carefully, the prime minister said: "This action on the part of the department of state of the United States is unprecedented, and I weigh my words when I say that it constitutes unjustified interference in Canadian affairs."[5] Washington responded by repeating its demand that Canada acquire nuclear arms.

Hoping to win the coming election, the leader of the Liberal Party, Lester B. Pearson, did a turnabout of his own position and announced he would accept nuclear warheads. Referring to Pearson's Nobel prize for peace, a professor at the University of Montreal, Pierre Trudeau, called him the "de-frocked prince of peace."[6] In a tumultuous debate in the House, Social Credit leader Robert Thompson reminded Diefenbaker that "the United States is our friend whether we like it or not."[7] The issue was forced to a vote, which the government lost, and then to an election. Six of Diefenbaker's Cabinet ministers deserted him, including his defence minister, Douglas Harkness. From south of the border, *Newsweek* magazine opened the election campaign with a cover story that featured a front-page photo of a demonic-looking Diefenbaker and ridiculed him as a "sick and maniacal" character, guilty of uttering "shrill cries of anti-Americanism."[8]

Kennedy not only loaned his personal pollster, Lou Harris, and his 500 poll-takers to direct Pearson's campaign, but also telephoned Pearson with campaign advice. Once, trying to reach Pearson on the campaign trail, the president phoned a Legion hall in Edmonton. Pearson, in terror that the janitor who answered the phone would go public, told Kennedy not to call that way again; if Diefenbaker, and worse, the Canadian public, found out, it would mean the end of his campaign.

A spellbinding orator, Diefenbaker, the "old lion," barnstormed across the country, virtually alone. The late George Grant, noted conservative nationalist, said afterwards: "The full power of the Canadian ruling class, the American government and the military were brought against him."[9] And Diefenbaker himself would say: "It's me against the Americans ... Everybody is against me, everybody but the people." And: "We are a power, not a puppet ... I want Canada to be in control of Canadian soil. Now if that's an offence I want the people of Canada to say so." The United States had stayed neutral in the First World War until 1917, he pointed out, and in World War Two until the end of 1941: "We don't need any lessons as to what Canada should do after that record of service."[10]

At the beginning of the campaign, Pearson stood twenty points ahead in the polls, and a majority Liberal government seemed certain. But by election night, Diefenbaker had "snatched a moral victory from the gaping jaws of defeat"; only 250,000 voters had abandoned the Conservatives.[11] It was, nevertheless, sufficient to give the Liberals a minority win. "So Diefenbaker went down, and the nuclear warheads went in."[12] The nuclear weapons remained until Trudeau's government phased them out, the last one in 1984.

In the White House Situation Room, officials were jubilant. McGeorge Bundy, national security advisor to Kennedy, exuberantly wrote that he had "knocked over the Diefenbaker government."[13]

Meeting Pearson after Kennedy's assassination, the new president, Lyndon Johnson, called the Canadian prime minister "my best friend."[14] Before very long, "the best friends" would run into problems over a place called Vietnam.

IN MAY 1954, the Vietnamese army, in a battle that reverberated around the world, had decisively defeated the French and ended eighty years of French control over Vietnam, a small country in Southeast Asia. The United States, which had equipped and financed the French in Vietnam since the late 1940s, then moved in and took over the war. By 1962, the U.S. military had 11,000 men in Vietnam; by 1964 the number was 23,000 and rising rapidly. The Vietnam War became a "war of example" for the rest of the world.[15] General William Westmoreland explained: "We are fighting the war in Vietnam to show that guerrilla warfare does not pay."[16] President Johnson said: "I intend to teach those slant-eyed yellow bastards a lesson."[17] Like the Canadian sailors of the 1940s and 1950s, the Vietnamese farmers were labelled "communists."

President Dwight Eisenhower had explained the matter differently and somewhat more directly in a speech in 1953: "Now let us assume that we lost Indochina [Vietnam, Laos and Cambodia] ... the tin and tungsten that we so greatly value from that area would cease coming ... so when the United States votes 400 million dollars to help that war, we are not voting a give-away program. We are voting for the cheapest way that we can to prevent the occurrence of something that would be of a most terrible significance to the United States of America, our security, our power and ability to get certain things we need from the riches of the Indochinese territory and from Southeast Asia."[18]

By mid-1969, the United States had 630,000 soldiers directly involved in the Vietnam War plus mercenary troops from Taiwan, Thailand and South Korea. Asians fighting Asians was a paying proposition. The United States could conscript South Korean young men, send them to Vietnam and maintain them on the battlefield for $1.25 per day per soldier, much less than the $50 for a U.S. soldier and far less politically damaging to the American administration. In addition, the United States, through its surrogate government in South Vietnam, had drafted more than one million Vietnamese soldiers into the war. Still, the United States was unable to "nail the coon skins to the wall," as President Johnson put it.[19] "We're going to bomb them back into the Stone Age," said General Curtis "Killer" Lemay, former head of the U.S. Strategic Air Command. "We must," he said, "be willing to continue our bombing until we've destroyed every work of man in North Vietnam if this is what it takes to win the war."[20] The U.S. war in Vietnam became, in the words of French philosopher Jean-Paul Sartre, one of "total genocide ... perpetrated in Vietnam not against the Vietnamese alone, but against humanity."[21]

Vietnam is about the size of Finland and is half the size of the province of Alberta. Its neighbouring countries, Laos and Cambodia, are even smaller. From 1963 to 1975, the United States dropped 10 million tons of bombs on the three countries — four times the total dropped in all theatres of the Second World War. The most extensive premeditated ecological catastrophe in the history of the planet was created by the U.S. Air Force. In a program code-named "Operation Hades" after the Greek god of death, millions of gallons of Agent Orange, the powerful herbicide 2,4-D mixed with 2,4,5-T at ten times regular strength, were sprayed over the forests, fields and crops of Vietnam. "Only We Can Prevent Forests" was the slogan of the flyers "putting in a burn."[22] More than two million Vietnamese were directly contaminated by Agent Orange. Over 335,000 tons of napalm, a flaming, searing jelly that ignites everything it touches, were dumped on Vietnam. Internationally outlawed cluster bomb units (CBU 55s) were used. When CBU 55s explode, they take all the oxygen out of an area and choke the people to death without leaving visible injuries. White phosphorus, which burns until it reaches bone, was also employed, as were innumerable other anti-personnel weapons. A March 1966 article in *Aviation Week* explained:

> The pellets from anti-personnel bombs are designed to cause irregular and hard-to-cure wounds. This serves two functions. First, it means that instead of a single man dead and withdrawn from military production, six to ten people (as well as facilities and supplies) must care for him. Secondly, the sufferings of a badly wounded victim tend to have a greater demoralizing effect on the remaining population than the dead. Thus, such weapons "build a

deterrent capability into conventional ordnance." That is, they have a "separate and distinguishable psychological impact ... apart from the actual destruction which they caused."[23]

An American woman who had adopted three Vietnamese children under the Foster Parents Plan went to Vietnam to see for herself. These are her words:

Before I went to Saigon, I had heard and read that napalm melts the flesh, and I thought that's nonsense, because I can put a roast in the oven and the fat will melt but the meat stays there. Well, I went and saw these children burned by napalm, and it is absolutely true. The chemical reaction of this napalm does melt the flesh, and the flesh runs right down their faces onto their chests and it sits there and it grows there ... These children can't turn their heads, they were so thick with flesh ... And when gangrene sets in, they cut off their hands or fingers or their feet; the only thing they cannot cut off is their head.[24]

The Phoenix Program, run by the CIA under director William Colby, set up a body quota system, with prize money of $11,000 for a live Viet Cong (slang for Vietnamese communist, VC) and half that for a dead one. The program had 100,000 victims. "Death is our business and business is good" was the slogan painted on the helicopters.[25] An officer of the First Brigade of the 101st Airborne division told a reporter: "When we kill a pregnant woman, we count it as two VC — one soldier and one cadet."[26]

Still, the war was not being won. The WHAM (Winning Hearts and Minds) Program set up the most refined torture techniques in the world, combining medieval methods with the latest medical and psychiatric discoveries. The "water cure" involved putting cloth over the mouth and nose and pouring water on the cloth until the victim was forced to breathe water into the lungs. The "field telephone treatment" involved the application of escalating doses of electric shock applied to the victim's genitals. The "dowel treatment" consisted of driving a sharpened wooden peg into the ear little by little as the interrogation went on. K. Barton Osborn, a U.S. intelligence expert in Vietnam from 1966 to 1969, stated later: "I never knew an individual to be detained as a VC suspect who ever lived through an interrogation." The motto of the U.S.-trained Saigon police was, "If they are innocent beat them until they become guilty."[27]

Every conceivable kind of terror was employed. The United States began to use biological weapons, nerve agents and poison gas. The people of Vietnam were forced to live underground in thousands of miles of tunnels to avoid the rain of bombs and chemicals from airplanes flying so high they could not be seen. An American diplomat summarized his country's efforts in Vietnam, one of the oldest civilizations in the world, thus: "To make progress in this country, it is necessary to level everything. The inhabitants must go back to zero, lose their traditional culture, for it blocks everything."[28]

To express something of the widespread Canadian and international opposition to the daily horror as the world's most powerful nation unleashed its full arsenal of weapons on a small third-world country that did not even have an air force, Lester Pearson made a speech in Philadelphia in April 1965. In the mildest way, he questioned "Operation Rolling Thunder," the massive continuous U.S. bombing campaign. Lyndon Johnson promptly called Pearson to Camp David, where for over an hour he "bellowed at Pearson." Following that, "the president of the United States grabbed him by the shirt collar, twisted it and lifted the shaken prime minister by the neck," and said, "You pissed on my rug!" The stunned Canadian observers were told by a humiliated Pearson not to breathe a word about it back in Canada. Later, Pearson wrote a letter thanking Lyndon Johnson for "speaking to me so frankly."[29] And the Canadian government continued its role in Southeast Asia as "the Butcher's Helper" — to quote Claire Culhane, a Canadian hospital administrator and eyewitness — supplying chemicals, weapons and ammunition.[30]

The Vietnam War was the longest, perhaps most costly war in U.S. history, with expenditure estimates ranging from $200 billion to over $400 billion. Three million U.S. soldiers fought there. Both Johnson and his successor, Richard Nixon, and Nixon's security advisor, Henry Kissinger, repeatedly contemplated using nuclear weapons. Only a fear of a response in kind from China and the Soviet Union prevented their use.

In the end, on April 30, 1975, the last of the U.S. military fled in helicopters from the roof of the U.S. embassy in Saigon, abandoning millions of dollars of weapons, helicopters, tanks and other equipment, thousands of CIA operatives, more than five hundred thousand prostitutes and drug addicts in Saigon alone, over eight million refugees and orphans, hundreds of thousands of wounded, deformed and chemically damaged Vietnamese, the world's greatest

136 THE FIGHT FOR CANADA

demand for artificial limbs, and 150,000 tons of unexploded bombs in the fields and forests. More than 10,000 Vietnamese, mostly farmers and their families, died in the years following 1975, when their ploughs inadvertently hit these hidden bombs containing delayed-action fuses.

Approximately six million died in Vietnam, Cambodia and Laos, and countless others were maimed and wounded as the result of American military aggression. For its war crimes in Southeast Asia, the United States has never paid. The men responsible remain free and powerful — often interviewed respectfully by the Canadian media. Henry Kissinger is still "a jet-setting superstar ... guarded by a phalanx of private bodyguards," with an estimated annual income of over $2 million.[31] Richard Nixon remained an influential figure in the U.S. until his death. William Colby was asked for his views on "Arab terrorism." Ronald Reagan, as president, said: "Vietnam was our most glorious cause."

How was it possible that one of the poorest countries in the world — Vietnam ranks in the bottom twenty of world nations, with a per-capita daily income of less than one dollar (U.S.) — with a population at the height of the war of 35 million, was able to defeat the most powerful nation the world has ever seen? In 1985, McGeorge Bundy, who in 1963 had become President Johnson's national security advisor, answered: "The skill, courage, and determination of the Vietnamese was a factor we were unable to offset by all the means at our disposal."[32]

Part Two

The Fight of
Our Lives

These photographs capture a glimpse of the intensity of the 1988 Free Trade election campaign, with Prime Minister Brian Mulroney *(above)* confronted in a familiar scene by angry demonstrators, and John Turner *(below)* being urged, shortly after the election, to continue the fight against the FTA on behalf of the majority of voters. (PHOTOS: THE *GLOBE AND MAIL*; CANAPRESS)

16

The Rabid Nationalist

THE YEAR 1980 SAW the first major attempt by a Canadian government to re-establish control of an essential but foreign-controlled industry. Foreign corporations, mostly American, accounted for 82 percent of Canadian oil production; since 1947, they had taken over more than 300 Canadian oil companies. The federal government received less than 10 percent of the revenue from the Canadian oil industry, while the provinces and the oil companies took in 90 percent. The president of the U.S. National Coal Association went so far as to tell the American Senate in 1971: "Our government considers Canada our own for energy purposes."[1]

Responding to this situation, the government of Pierre Elliott Trudeau announced in October 1980 the National Energy Program (NEP), with a goal of 50 percent Canadian ownership of the industry by 1990. Under the program, Petro-Canada, the only Canadian company in the top ten oil companies operating in Canada, would make one or two major takeovers and would have the right, without compensation, to a 25 percent interest in each oil and gas development on Crown lands, on behalf of the Canadian public. It was a modest proposal. Most oil-producing countries have gone much further. Statoil in Norway takes a half-interest in any development on lands it does not already own, and the British National Oil Company had the right to 51 percent.

Canada's intention to hold its domestic gas and oil prices permanently lower than world levels would give Canadian industry a real chance to compete with the United States for the first time since John A. Macdonald's National Policy. Also, with more of the oil companies' profits diverted to the federal government, revenue would be available to develop Canadian industry.

American oil companies, outraged, condemned the 50 percent Canadian ownership target as "nationalist and anti-American."[2]

Both the American government and U.S. oil companies denounced the 25 percent Canadian government share as expropriation without compensation. (Not explained was how the Canadian government could expropriate something it already owned.) Although the U.S. mining industry was 95 percent American controlled and its oil and gas industry 82 percent domestically controlled, Pierre Trudeau was accused of "rabid nationalism" and "fanning the flames of anti-Americanism" in Canada.[3] A delegation of American officials flew to Ottawa to express their anger and disappointment.

"If the U.S. allows Canada to get away with its new policies, what about Mexico?" asked an American official. Another official, recalling the U.S.-backed coup in Chile in 1973, outlined a plan to topple the government by "destabilizing the industrial base" in Ontario and Quebec.[4]

Bowing to U.S. pressure, Ottawa announced in May 1981 two concessions: Canada would pay for the 25 percent share in existing oil projects, and the NEP would be amended so Canadian companies would not have preference over foreign companies in bidding on mega-projects.

Still, the rhetoric from Washington escalated. Myer Rashish, a senior State Department official in Ronald Reagan's government, publicly warned Canada that "relationships are sliding dangerously towards crisis." Treasury secretary Donald Regan flew to Ottawa and requested a guarantee that no other industries would be Canadianized, no "son of NEP" created. Canada complied. Finance Minister Allan MacEachen's budget of November 12 announced: "The special measures being employed to achieve more Canadian ownership and control of the oil and gas industry are not ... appropriate for other sectors."[5]

In 1970, a three-party standing committee of the House of Commons had released the Wahn Report, which recommended 51 percent domestic ownership of Canadian industry as a way of dealing with overwhelming foreign ownership and a crippling flow of capital and profits out of Canada. In the 1980 Speech from the Throne, the Trudeau government announced its intention to Canadianize other industries by strengthening the Foreign Investment Review Agency (FIRA). This agency had been established in 1973 to screen and control foreign investment — a practice common to all industrialized nations — by negotiating with foreign corporations to increase the benefits for Canada in terms of employment, use of Canadian materials, commitment to export, and pledges to do research in Canada. But now, in response to Washington's outcry over the NEP, the government retracted the promises made to strengthen FIRA.

Using threats and bluster, the United States had derailed the repatriation of Canada's economy. Bolstered by this success, U.S. trade representative William Brock wrote to the Canadian government and demanded a further eight changes. Washington not only demanded amendments to existing FIRA legislation that it had not complained about before, but also insisted on a complete gutting of the rest of the NEP — including an end to the 50 percent Canadian ownership goal.

The Trudeau government decided enough was enough and dug in its heels. Calling the letter "strange and excessive," Canada refused Washington's demands and proceeded with the NEP.[6] The United States backed off, a frustrated U.S. official admitting that, as for retaliation, "anything we've come across so far would hurt us more than them."[7]

Even according to polls conducted by oil companies in April 1981, 84 percent of Canadians wholeheartedly supported Canadianization and wanted the government to go even further. As one journalist noted: "Everyone hated the NEP, that is except the people."[8] By the end of 1984, in spite of plummeting oil prices, the NEP was achieving its goal: Canadian ownership of the industry had risen dramatically, to over 40 percent. The federal government's share of revenues from the oil and gas industry, 8.8 percent in 1979, was now 26 percent, while the oil companies' share had dropped from 43 to 37 percent. Canada, which had imported over one million barrels of oil a day in 1978, was now almost self-sufficient. According to one commentator, Canada had "re-established the right to interfere in its own affairs."[9]

Macdonald's National Policy had a long and costly birth, which paid off handsomely; the National Energy Program, however, would be killed in its infancy, its architects leaving the Canadian political stage before the policy could fully prove its potential.

The NEP frightened some powerful Americans. The goal of 51 percent Canadian ownership was unthinkable to them, even though the United States owns 97 percent of its own economy and a large part of Canada's, while less than one-half of one percent of the U.S. economy is Canadian controlled.

In response, the Americans would attempt once again, as in 1891,

1911 and 1948, a free-trade agreement. This time, however, it would go beyond anything ever before proposed.

IN HIS SUCCESSFUL 1980 campaign for the White House, Ronald Reagan had announced his goal of a free-trade zone from Tierra del Fuego to the Arctic Circle. Soon Washington's plans would be boosted by a prime minister in Ottawa willing to throw away the hard-earned right to Canadian independence.

By 1983, the Americans already had their plan, their man and a number of prominent Canadians willing to play along. In that year, the U.S. ambassador to Canada, Paul Robinson, invited Sam Hughes, head of the Canadian Chamber of Commerce, to his exclusive Rockcliffe Park residence in Ottawa. The United States, he said, had decided to enter into free-trade agreements with selected countries. The first was to be Israel; Washington wanted Canada to be next. Thomas d'Aquino, chairman of the Business Council on National Issues — the lobbying arm of 150 major corporations, many American-owned — was the next guest at Robinson's home, followed by Roy Phillips, president of the Canadian Manufacturers' Association.

These steps taken, Robinson was told by his boss in Washington, Special Trade Representative William Brock, to back off — that to be successful, the approach for free trade must be seen as coming from Canada. If Canadians realized that the push was from the United States, they would react unfavourably.

In an exceptionally candid speech in 1990, Robinson recalled with satisfaction: "I'm pleased to say I did play a principal role in the re-initiating of the free trade agreement which I know is controversial in Canada. It's not controversial in the United States — we thought it was a good idea ... I thought it was a 10-year project. As it turned out to be, it was a 5-year project ... We knew that if this was regarded as a purely American attempt to, say, quote, gobble up Canada, close quote, which we were all aware of ... that we'd be doomed to failure, and that what we really should do is try to interest Canadians..."

Even the terminology had been decided in the United States. "We were afraid," Robinson said in an interview, "to call it free trade, so we referred to it as 'freer trade,' which was kind of silly."[10] As if on command, most of the Canadian media began referring to freer trade. Newspaper articles, commentaries, even letters to the editor were carefully scrutinized, and "free" was replaced by "freer."

Meanwhile, in 1983, the leader of the Conservatives, Joe Clark, was under attack from within his own party by a man named Brian Mulroney. One hundred years earlier, the Liberal Party had been the vehicle for the Americans' plans; this time it would be the party of John A. Macdonald himself. Dalton Camp, former president of the Progressive Conservatives, confirmed in an interview during the 1983 Conservative leadership campaign that foreign money was backing Mulroney's attempt to unseat Joe Clark. "Obviously the money was not coming from inside the country," Camp told a reporter. "I'm not sure right now I want to get into any great detail on it. But it's not anything I would raise if I didn't know what I was talking about ... It's not money raised in nickels and dimes and dollars from supporters of the Conservative party ... It costs money to fly people around the country and put them in hotel suites and install a very sophisticated communications system — a bunker operation."[11]

By the fall of 1984, Mulroney had overthrown Clark, and the Conservatives, advocating an end to patronage and promoting "change," had gained power. Free trade with the United States had not been an issue in the election campaign. Earlier, however, when campaigning for the leadership of the party in June 1983, Mulroney had declared his position on the issue in unmistakable language: "Free trade was decided on in an election in 1911. It affects Canadian sovereignty and we will have none of it, not during leadership campaigns or at any other time." And to the *Globe and Mail*, the same month, he had asserted: "This country could not survive with a policy of unfettered free trade."[12]

Except for John Crosbie, all the other contenders for the Conservative leadership in 1983 had also firmly opposed free trade. "It's silly," proclaimed David Crombie. "Canada must improve relations and trade with the United States, of course. But our natural destiny is to become a global leader, not America's weak sister." Michael Wilson, soon to be one of the architects of the agreement, was unequivocal: "Bilateral free trade with the United States is simplistic, and naive. It would only serve to further diminish our ability to compete internationally."

And Joe Clark was adamant: "Unrestrained free trade with the United States raises the possibility that thousands of jobs could be lost in such critical industries as textiles, furniture and footwear.

Before we jump on the bandwagon of continentalism, we should strengthen our industrial structure so that we are more competitive."[13]

Although Mulroney had been explicit about his opposition to free trade, eight days after he was elected prime minister he held his first press conference, not in Canada in front of the Canadian news media, but in Washington, at Ronald Reagan's side. There he pledged Canada to closer ties with the United States.

By the time of the Canada-U.S. "Shamrock Summit" in Quebec City in March 1985, all of Mulroney's professed opposition to free trade had disappeared. Reagan and Mulroney signed a declaration on trade, which instructed their trade ministers "to chart all possible ways to reduce and eliminate existing barriers to trade."[14] This declaration, abruptly classified "secret" by the Department of External Affairs, disappeared from public view. The summit closed with the spectacle of the president of the United States and Brian Mulroney, on national television, singing together "When Irish Eyes Are Smiling."

Canada was once again headed down the road to free trade with the United States, or as John A. Macdonald had described it, "down the slippery slope to annexation." Officials in the United States were jubilant. William Merkin, deputy assistant in the Office of the U.S. Trade Representative, said: "We want to come up with the broadest possible concept."[15]

IN THE BACKGROUND, a number of factors had been at work. In November 1982, a Royal Commission chaired by Donald Macdonald, a one-time Liberal Cabinet minister, had been appointed by the Trudeau government to look into Canada's economic future. The commission was widely condemned for its generous budget, with Macdonald drawing $800 per day ($925 on the road). After Mulroney's election, many Liberal appointments were terminated. On September 7, 1984, three days after the election, Macdonald wrote to Mulroney: "My first words are those of congratulations on an historical electoral success." Macdonald expected that Mulroney would be "reviewing a number of ongoing activities and assessing options" and "felt that it would be appropriate to offer ... a current report on the Royal Commission's work." Instead of terminating Macdonald's appointment, as was widely expected, Mulroney, on November 2, 1984, replied: "[P]ursuant to that meeting [with the

Minister of Finance, Michael Wilson], I wish to confirm the Government's views on how the Commission should complete its mandate."[16] Shortly thereafter, one year before the Commission was due to report — and before it had even completed its fact-finding hearings — Macdonald announced in Harriman, New York, that he was in favour of a comprehensive free-trade agreement. "Leap of Faith, Canada Must Act on Free Trade, Macdonald Says," read the *Globe and Mail* headline on November 19, 1984.

Keeping Macdonald on the government payroll had paid off handsomely. Mulroney had succeeded in lending an aura of bipartisan support to something he had no mandate from the Canadian people to pursue. (Two years later, Macdonald, along with the ex-premier of Alberta, Peter Lougheed, would co-chair the big-business lobby group Canadian Alliance for Trade and Job Opportunities, leading the fight for free trade. After the 1988 election, Macdonald was appointed by Mulroney as high commissioner to London, England.)

In mid-May 1985, the premiers of the four western provinces — Howard Pawley of Manitoba, Grant Devine of Saskatchewan, Alberta's Peter Lougheed and Bill Bennett from British Columbia — met in Grande Prairie, Alberta, and, seemingly out of the blue, issued a communiqué calling for "a comprehensive common market arrangement,"* with the United States.[17] Peter Lougheed, the promoter of the concept, flanked by his chief backer, Grant Devine, told reporters afterwards that the term "common market" was used because it was better understood than free trade and helped to dispel the idea Canada would be giving up its sovereignty. Lougheed said he would press the prime minister to make a proposal to President Reagan by September. It was a virtual replay of 1887, but this time there was no John A. Macdonald in Ottawa to resist their plans.

A cabal of economists led by Richard Lipsey, then of Queen's University at Kingston, began issuing predictions of dramatic economic growth under free trade. Some of these rosy computer-driven studies went so far as to project a 7 percent increase in gross national product if Canada entered a free-trade agreement with the United States.

---

* Common market: A free-trade agreement that involves the free movement not only of goods and capital, but also of labour. It goes beyond a conventional free-trade area in that its members adopt a common external tariff on the goods of all other countries.

On September 5, 1985, two months ahead of schedule, the
Macdonald Commission made public its huge $20 million report —
its major recommendation a comprehensive free-trade agreement
with the United States. Three weeks later, Mulroney announced he
was beginning talks with the United States on free trade.

From their very beginnings, the free-trade talks were shrouded
in secrecy. On September 20, 1985, a document was leaked to the
Toronto *Star*. There in black-and-white was spelled out the
government's plan on how to push forward on an unsuspecting
public the most sweeping program in Canadian history for economic
union with the United States. The document, entitled
"Communications Strategy for Canada-U.S. Bilateral Trade
Initiative," was prepared by a task force in the Prime Minister's Office
that included Bill Fox, then press secretary to Mulroney, Peter Daniel,
director general of communications with the Finance Department,
and pollsters from Decima Research. It stated:

> It is likely that the higher the profile the issue attains, the lower the
> degree of public approval will be ... The strategy should rely less on
> educating the general public, than on getting across the message
> that the trade initiative is a good idea. In other words, a selling job ...
>
> The name of the initiative will be an important communication
> symbol. The more process oriented it seems and the less it stimulates
> fears of mass changes in the trade relationship with the United States,
> the easier it will be to manage the public debate ...
>
> Sampling Canadian public opinion on the issue of free trade is
> not unlike canvassing children for their views on world peace: the
> question determines the response ...
>
> The majority of Canadians do not understand fully what is meant
> by the terms free trade, freer trade or enhanced trade. The popular
> interpretation of free trade appears to be keyed to the word "free." It
> is something for nothing — a short-cut to economic prosperity. It is
> bigger markets for Canadian products, more jobs, more of everything.
> It is ... having your cake and eating it too ... [18]

Many of the most powerful Cabinet ministers, including the prime
minister, were on record as having stated that free trade would
devastate the Canadian economy and affect Canada's sovereignty.
Internal government studies showed that 500,000 jobs could be lost.
Mr. Mulroney was well aware that Canadians had rejected free trade
in the past. Perhaps for these reasons the leaked government strategy

repeatedly emphasized the need to camouflage the effects of free trade and to prevent open debate. Without open debate and an informed public, democracy cannot exist. Yet the document called for the prime minister and government members to tell Canadians the government was entering the negotiations only to see "what is possible," not to commit itself to an agreement; to talk only about how an agreement would "save jobs ... and create jobs"; and to emphasize that an agreement would "secure, enhance and enshrine access to the U.S. market." Outlined was a plan to target and discredit opposition MPs who raised concerns about the negotiations and to "monitor" and then "divide and neutralize" those Canadians who would oppose free trade, because of "the possibility of compromised sovereignty" and "continental integration." The revealing document continued:

> The public support generated should be recognized as extremely soft and likely to evaporate rapidly if the debate is allowed to get out of control so as to erode the central focus of the message. At the same time a substantial majority of the public may be willing to leave the issue in the hands of the government and other interested groups if the government maintains communications control of the situation. Benign neglect from a majority of Canadians may be the realistic outcome of a well executed communications program. In these circumstances it appears that the best strategy for the government is to adopt a low profile approach to the general public while dealing with the specific concerns of interest groups on an individual basis ...
>
> It may be appropriate, in some cases, to pursue a tactic of divide and neutralize as opposed to co-opting where opposition or confusion exists on the issue. Where support exists, efforts should be pursued to enlist in promoting the initiative. Groups willing to be counted should be clearly identified and amplified to a level that would serve to support the notion of a national consensus and act as a counterbalance to the opposition. Not all organizations that support the initiative, however, can afford to do so publicly; their wishes should be respected ... [19]

"To stand still is to slide backwards" was to be the theme of the prime minister's carefully planned speeches "insuring that a positive, confident tone is projected — a sense of real opportunity for Canadians in all regions to advance their own best interests."

And, because "[f]ear will be manifest in intense lobbies by those concerned with sovereignty, cultural issues and job losses," providing special staff to monitor the formation of any coordinated action by opponents of free trade, "is crucial to the communications exercise."[20]

In essence, the document said: If Canadians were to learn what free trade meant, they would oppose it. Therefore, the government would do everything in its power to mislead and prevent the public from discovering what was at stake until it was too late. And it would attempt to divide and neutralize those Canadians who did learn about it.

In early November 1985, another secret document was leaked. The 29-page memorandum, prepared by External Affairs at the Cabinet's request, was entitled "Canadian Sovereignty." It outlined "a sweeping program to reassure Canadians that the nation's basic sovereignty is not under threat." The paper began:

> Canadian sovereignty is not at risk. No country, in particular the United States, poses any serious risk to our sovereignty in the forms in which sovereignty is most often understood ...
>
> But for largely historical reasons, Canadians have a special preoccupation with sovereignty, which can produce a particularly vigorous reaction when a sovereignty-related issue arises to touch a nerve in the body politic ... and there is an accumulation of such issues to be dealt with now ...
>
> The Canada-U.S. trade negotiations are a central element of the government's program for economic renewal, and to be successful those negotiations may require trade-offs between different policy objectives ...
>
> A challenge in the next 12 months will be to convince Canadians that the objective of trade negotiations with the United States is to secure net economic benefits for Canada ...
>
> [A] special effort will be required to ensure that sovereignty is seen to be a principal objective of Canadian domestic and foreign policy.[21]

The plan called for a far-reaching publicity campaign, involving Cabinet ministers, the prime minister and even the Governor General, "to reassure Canadians that the government is actively engaged in protecting Canadian sovereignty and promoting Canadian independence, and that co-operation with the United

States and other countries will strengthen, not weaken, our national identity."[22]

The document proposed that measures be designed to demonstrate that "Canadians are a strong and confident people and can embark on new ventures without fear of losing their identity in the process." A new "Sovereignty Group" of government departments and agencies was called for to develop programs to promote policy. In addition, "a good deal could be accomplished through packaging existing policies to play up their sovereignty dimensions and through drawing attention to international events where Canada can be seen as an important and independent player."[23]

"Sovereignty messages" were to be "included routinely" in speeches by the prime minister and Cabinet ministers. The document recommended whipping up a kind of false and shallow patriotism at Vancouver's Expo '86 and the Calgary Olympics in an attempt to get Canadians to forget about the free-trade issue. It concluded optimistically: "Handled with care it [this program] will encourage Canadians to deal with their American neighbors with confidence and in a spirit of co-operation."[24]

The delivery of the second-largest nation in the world to a foreign power was under way, with all the government and public relations manoeuvering necessary — including the spending of billions of dollars of taxpayers' money — to deceive Canadians for as long as it would take to get the job done. On November 8, 1985, Mulroney announced the formation of a special Trade Negotiations Office (TNO), outside the Department of External Affairs, reporting to and controlled directly by himself. It would handle the talks with the United States.

No expense was spared: $800,000 for decorating the office, $1 million per year for rental, and a staff of 84 with a $10 million annual budget. The man appointed to its head was Simon Reisman.

17

The Most Critical Date on this Continent

FROM THE AUTHOR'S JOURNAL — OCTOBER 1, 2 AND 3, 1987

THURSDAY, OCTOBER 1
7:40 A.M.
(Reviewing the previous week)

ON SEPTEMBER 23, Simon Reisman leaves the negotiations, returns to Ottawa from Washington. He goes on the "Journal," says the talks are dead, over, that he "pulled the plug." The Americans were not giving Canada anything. The radio, television and newspapers are full of post-mortems.

Allan Fotheringham [syndicated columnist] on CBC's "As It Happens" says he knew months ago that free trade was failing, that it was "never on." He took Peter Murphy [chief U.S. free-trade negotiator] home from a party a couple of months ago in Washington, and Murphy told him there would be no deal.

Everyone, even anti-free traders, seems to have swallowed the line; they give interviews saying, "Don't worry — it's over." Marjaleena Repo [co-founder and national organizer of Citizens Concerned About Free Trade (CCAFT)] disagrees: "I don't believe it for a minute; it's all window dressing."

We give interviews saying that we don't believe the talks are over. A lone voice in the wilderness, ours gets almost no press coverage.

The CBC drops all pretense at balanced coverage. John Crispo [business professor and free-trade promoter] appears on the "Journal" unopposed. "Journal" [host] Barbara Frum falls all over herself when Crispo declares that without free trade, the U.S. will clobber us with so many trade actions we won't know what hit us.

150

Next morning Crispo is featured on CTV's "Canada A.M." Almost frothing at the mouth, he predicts dire consequences if we "lose this chance." A few days ago, CBC's "Sunday Morning" carried an item on free trade — interviewed Albertans who've worked for American companies all their lives, who told us they love Americans and can't see any difference between them and Canadians. The report flagrantly pushed free trade, suggesting Western Canadians will be completely disillusioned with Canada if it is rejected. Last night, CBC-TV news featured a clip on the Israel-U.S. free-trade agreement, saying it has been great for Israeli business and exports. All resemblance of objective analysis has been stripped from the CBC; even mentioning opposition to free trade has become taboo.

At a time when you can almost feel the fear and opposition of people across Canada, the media is pouring on the coal — goading, pushing the government to get back to the table. The news is all couched in terms of "optimistic," "pessimistic," "good sign," "gloom." "Good news means the possibility of a deal; "gloomy" means we might not get one.

9:20 P.M.

Pat Carney [Minister of International Trade] and Michael Wilson [Finance Minister] leave Washington after a 2 1/2-hour meeting with James Baker [U.S. Treasury Secretary] and Clayton Yeutter [U.S. Trade Representative]. They say nothing. Press reports that their faces are "glum." "Bad" news. Announcement that Mulroney is calling the ten premiers to Ottawa tomorrow. Nobody knows why — [B.C. Premier] Vander Zalm says he is "confident" a free-trade deal can be worked out. [Saskatchewan Premier] Devine says the Conservatives might take some political heat for it but Canada needs a free-trade deal and should do what is right! [Royal Commission chairman] Donald Macdonald is interviewed; he is "disappointed." The interviewer is very sympathetic — asks Macdonald what Canada has lost by not getting a free-trade agreement.

The phone keeps ringing. From Prince Albert: "It's all a ploy, they'll go ahead with it." From Saskatoon: "Knowing the talks are still going on is like a death sentence for Canada." From Moose Jaw: "It's like waiting for a pardon."

Gary [Daniels; farmworker] walks into the house, says: "Lots of tension, eh? You'll know by Sunday if all your work in fighting it has paid off."

U.S. Senator Richard Lugar says that the date of signing the FTA will be "the most critical date on this continent and perhaps in the Western Hemisphere."[1]

10:30 P.M.

Turning on the 10 o'clock news. Stomach in knots. Too tense to eat supper. Top of the news, [CBC anchor] Knowlton Nash practically shouting with excitement, satisfaction? "The free trade talks are back on!" Picture of Simon Reisman getting into a limousine and heading back to Washington. "We're still in business." Sudden jolt back to earth. All the media hype falling into place. The talks were never off.

FRIDAY, OCTOBER 2
11:30 P.M.

Mulroney has the premiers in Ottawa. They come out of the meeting like sheep. Mulroney tells the press that all the premiers support him. "The premiers believe we are defending the national interest with vigour and with skill." Not one disagrees. There is no opposition here. We were right about the premiers: they will not stand in the way.

Dad [Ralph Orchard; retired farmer] calls. Says he went to hear Roy Romanow [Saskatchewan NDP leader] speak. Romanow made almost no mention of free trade, so he asked in the question period if the NDP had a plan to fight free trade. "No," Romanow replied, "by Monday [October 5] everyone will feel a lot better — these talks will have fallen apart and be all over."

The line-up of pro-free traders on the "Journal" goes on and on. Tonight, Donald Macdonald is the guest. Even the interviewer seems jumpy, asks if there was "cause for concern" doing such a big deal in such a rush with 24 hours left to the deadline. "Oh no, not at all," Macdonald gushes. For almost ten days no opposition to free trade has been allowed on CBC television. It's as if it didn't exist. All the plugs are pulled out to inundate the public with reports that say nothing about what is really going on.

SATURDAY, OCTOBER 3
11 A.M.

Media full of reports of the "problems" left to be overcome, the "tough negotiating" ahead, the "barriers to be swept aside," "major hurdles" yet. It's all phony. The deal is done — it will be announced. They have no intention of turning aside now.

This morning Steven Langdon [NDP trade critic] is on television saying there are "hooks" in the free trade package. He doesn't think the "people of Canada will accept it." Marjaleena [Repo] asks: "How are they going to get a chance to accept or reject it?"

News reports give us hour-by-hour quotes from Carney, Wilson, Devine or Mulroney. The rape of Canada is on, and the press is describing it excitedly in minute detail. The nation, forced to watch and listen, doesn't hear one word of horror or outrage. At most, an opposition member or a premier is "skeptical" about it. Any opposition is unmentionable.

10:30 P.M.
I'm on the phone. Marjaleena is shouting: "They've done a deal, they've done a deal!" Another phone rings; "Quick turn on the television. Murphy is talking!"

Across the country, radio and television programs are interrupted for special reports. It's the Americans who tell us what's happened. James Baker: "It's a comprehensive deal." Clayton Yeutter, smiling, complimenting Canada on the "good effort the negotiating teams from both sides" did.

I recall Tommy Douglas saying that when a Yankee calls you a tough bargainer, he's just taken you to the cleaners.

[Journalist] Mike Duffy is interviewing Peter Murphy. Practically glowing with his catch, Duffy explains that Murphy wanted to give Canadians this interview because he had said "no comment" for so long during the negotiations. Duffy seems almost falling at Murphy's feet.

Norman [Beach, farmer, from Swift Current] calls: "So they gave up everything to the Yanks ..." There is a long silence on the line. "Mulroney... is not a Canadian, really ..."

DURING THE NIGHT I keep waking up — search the television and radio channels for news. None.

Finally at 6 a.m. a report. In the middle of the night Mulroney announced that they've signed a comprehensive free-trade agreement giving us "access to the richest, most dynamic market in the world" that "will bring added prosperity to all regions of Canada."

18

Crusaders for the Deal

ON PARLIAMENT HILL in Ottawa, October 5, 1987, Prime Minister Mulroney announced:

> I am pleased to inform the House that we have concluded an agreement in principle for a comprehensive trade agreement between Canada and the United States of America ... the largest trading agreement ever entered into between two sovereign nations ... This is a good deal, a good deal for Canada and a deal that is good for all Canadians. It is also a fair deal, which means that it brings benefits and progress to our partner, the United States of America ... Mr. Speaker, this Agreement will expand our access to the world's largest, richest and most dynamic markets ... The result will be lasting jobs and sustained prosperity ... We have set a course for a stronger, a more united, and a more prosperous Canada.[1]

From across the floor, John Turner, former finance minister, former prime minister and now leader of the opposition, replied: "What the Prime Minister has given us today is an absolute fraud ... He has now become the architect of the yielding in the most massive way possible of our sovereignty as an independent nation."[2] The leader of the New Democratic Party, Edward Broadbent, concurred: "I can tell you that for the first time in the history of Canada, we have a man who is prime minister who has, without even being asked, volunteered Canada to be the 51st state in the United States ... in the last 48 hours his Government entered into an agreement with the U.S. for which it had no mandate. The long-range implications are that Canada, an independent nation able to set its own priorities, would go down the drain."[3]

What was actually in the Free Trade Agreement (FTA)? What was it that the government tried so hard to hide, spent so much money to sell and eventually would impose against the will of the majority of Canadians? To begin to understand the FTA, six basic documents are needed:

1. the actual text of the FTA,
2. the implementing legislation in Canada,
3. the implementing legislation in the United States,
4. the *Standard Industrial Classification* (4th edition, 1980),
5. the tariff schedule of Canada,
6. the tariff schedule of the United States.*

Investment: Open Season

INVESTMENT WAS NOT going to be part of the free-trade negotiations, promised the Canadian government. And according to Simon Reisman, investment was not even within "my terms of reference."[4]

Yet, on the very first page of chapter 1 of the FTA, investment is listed as a key component of the deal. At the heart of the agreement is "national treatment," which means that henceforth, by law, American investors, citizens and corporations shall be treated in Canada as if they were Canadians. No level of government in Canada can any longer favour Canadian citizens and companies in any way, through government contracts, grants, taxation policies or other programs. American companies have the right to exactly the same treatment as Canadian companies.

Furthermore, article 1602 of the investment chapter states that no government in Canada — federal, provincial or local — can any longer screen, regulate or prevent any new American investment coming into the country. Canada is already the most foreign-dominated of any industrialized country in the world: 100 percent of the tobacco industry, 98 percent of the rubber industry, 92 percent of the automotive industry, 84 percent of transportation, 78 percent of the electrical apparatus industry, 78 percent of the petroleum and coal industry, 76 percent of the chemical industry and 75 percent of heavy manufacturing are foreign, largely American, owned. In contrast, the foreign ownership of the United States's economy is

---

* This chapter, a lay guide to the contents of the FTA, is based on the speech delivered by the author across Canada in 1987-88. All figures refer to this time period.

only 3 percent; of Britain's, 3 percent; Japan's less than 2 percent; and France's, 3 percent.

The high level of foreign domination in Canada is an intolerable situation for any sovereign country. More than $35 billion flows annually out of Canada in interest, dividends and "service charges" between subsidiary corporations and their head offices. These service charges are a tool of convenience for an American corporation wishing to show no profit in its Canadian subsidiary for tax or other reasons; it will charge that branch plant hugely inflated prices for supplies or services, thereby transferring all profits across the border. This $35 billion that hemorrhages out of Canada each year, the bulk of it to the United States, is the approximate amount of the annual federal deficit.

What the government and media call "investment" is, in reality, ownership and control. High levels of foreign investment mean foreign control, pure and simple.

In the first eight years of the Mulroney government, more than 4000 Canadian companies worth $100 billion were taken over by foreign corporations — most of them American. De Havilland Aircraft, a world-class aircraft-manufacturing firm built with millions of taxpayers' dollars, was given to Boeing of Seattle in 1986 for less than the value of the suburban Toronto real estate on which it stood. The United States has strict laws that prevent the ownership of hydro-electric utilities by investors out of state, let alone outside of that country. Yet in 1987, an important utility, the West Kootenay Power and Light Company in British Columbia, was delivered to Missouri owners — with all its dams and water rights — in spite of massive local opposition. And in the same year, Dome Petroleum, the largest holder of oil and gas lands in Canada, established with hundreds of millions of taxpayers' dollars, was handed over lock, stock and barrel to Amoco of Chicago. And now, under article 1607.3 (aside from a few limited exceptions), Canada cannot block the takeovers of any existing Canadian corporation with a value of less than $150 million — which means 90 percent of the corporations in Canada.

The Act implementing the FTA amends section 14 of the *Investment Canada Act* to read:

(i) Every reference in those provisions to "Canadian" shall be read and construed as a reference to "American."

(ii) Every reference in those provisions to "non-Canadian" shall be read and construed as a reference to "non-Canadian, other than an American."

(iii) Every reference in those provisions to "Canadian-controlled" shall be read and construed as a reference to "American-controlled."

(iv) The reference in subparagraph 27(d)(i) to "Canada" shall be read and construed as a reference to "the United States."

It effectively bestows Canadian citizenship on American corporations and investors. They are now free to come to Canada, exercising their "right of establishment," and set up operations, buy out competitors, merge or sell-out to whom they please, charge prices of their choosing, and transfer all profits back to the United States. There is an express provision, article 1606, of the FTA prohibiting any government restrictions on the transfer of "any profits ... including dividends; any royalties, fees, interest and other earnings ... any proceeds from the sale of all or part of an investment out of Canada.

Article 1603 forbids any performance requirements. The Foreign Investment Review Agency used to be able to require an American company coming to Canada to purchase a certain amount of local materials, to hire a specified number of local people, to do research and development in Canada, or to sell a certain percentage of its shares to Canadians. Now, American companies can hire whom they please, including their own citizens, and purchase all supplies and services from the United States if they so choose.

The United States wanted investment included in the FTA not as a tool for increasing trade between Canadian and American companies, as Canadians were so often told. Rather, it wished to remove any restrictions against buying Canadian companies and resources, so that more of the trade between the two countries would be done by American corporations operating on both sides of the border. Already, about two-thirds of the trade between Canada and the United States is trade within corporations (intracorporate trade): Esso, Cargill, General Motors, Ford, IBM, Chrysler and the other big American corporations trading Canadian resources south to their parents and then selling the finished product back into Canada. They would like to see the border between Canada and the United States erased so that there would be absolute freedom for them to move resources, products and profits back and forth at will.

Energy: One-Way Sharing

November 17, 1988, Toronto. CFRB Radio: The Andy Barrie Show.

Andy Barrie: Good morning, and welcome to the Andy Barrie show. We are going to be talking to Simon Reisman, our chief negotiator in the free-trade arrangements with the United States ...

I'd say some people would suggest, Mr. Reisman, hearing your voice on Tory radio commercials right now, seeing you accusing the Leader of the Opposition of being a traitor, that you've become partisan ...

Simon Reisman: ... I am partisan, as you have said, about the free-trade area. I'm partisan, I'm passionate, I believe it. I think we have got a good agreement for Canada, and of course I don't want to see it fail. It won't fail. It will succeed. And it will do great things for the Canadian people ...

Barrie: But we know about the leaked document from the PMO [Prime Minister's Office] that said that the Canadian people are going to be asked to feel good about the free-trade deal and not going to be given concrete information about it. John Crosbie even admitted on my program that the government waited too late to realize that we were not going to be waltzed around on free trade ... and when we wanted facts from Simon Reisman, we got you calling free-trade opponents "Liars, like the Nazis," and now lately you have been calling John Turner a "traitor." People say that if this guy so passionately believes in free trade, why is it necessary for him to attack his enemies in so ugly a way?

Reisman: ... about my personality, look, yeah, I'm pretty strong. You know, I was in the army for four years. In the army you learn to do things in a pretty straightforward way. You kill and if you are not good at it, you get killed. And I played tough.

Barrie: And when you were in the army, traitors were people lined up against a wall and shot.

Reisman: ... Look, I have taken more abuse than I've dished out. But when I get abused I will dish it out in kind ... Would I ever sell out

Canada? The things that I have done have kept this country prosperous and in good form and I resent things and I'm going to fight back ... And if you, Andy, want me to be a mollycoddle; Simon Reisman is not a mollycoddle ...

Barrie: We have on the telephone ... a man who has already been a guest on this show; he is David Orchard, the national chairman of Citizens Concerned About Free Trade ...

David Orchard: Mr. Reisman has signed a deal which delivers control of Canada to the United States and he has the gall to call those who oppose it traitors ... Mr. Reisman talked about energy and said we made no new commitments under this deal ... Under this deal we agree to give the Americans the same proportion of any good that they have been taking from us, including all forms of energy, and if there is a shortage we have to give the Americans the same proportion of any good they've been taking from us [over the previous three years].

Reisman: It isn't a supply commitment. It's just that if you have an emergency, that you won't cut off your best customer without a dime, so Mr. Orchard has not told you the truth about what the agreement contains in the matter of energy.

DESPITE SIMON REISMAN'S assurances, the energy section of the FTA, chapter 9, gives the United States sweeping new rights to all forms of Canadian energy — petroleum, natural gas, uranium, electrical energy and coal, and all the products of each. Articles 408, 409 and 904 furthermore state that even if Canada faces a shortage of "any good" exported to the United States, including all forms of energy, no matter how it's caused — even if it comes from the Americans starting a war in the Middle East — Canada must share its resources with the United States. The Americans are entitled to the same proportion of any Canadian resource they have been taking, as averaged over the three years prior to the shortage.

The Americans now take roughly 40 percent of Canada's oil. If there is a shortage, a likely scenario in the foreseeable future, Canada is obligated under this deal to provide the United States with 40 percent of its total supply, whether or not there is enough to serve Canadians. The resources are to be delivered without disrupting "normal channels of supply," even if supplies to Canadians are disrupted or indeed terminated. Further, articles 408, 409, 903 and 904 state Canada cannot, through any government policy, charge the Americans more than Canadians for "any good," including energy. This sharing is essentially a one-way street. Although these provisions are reciprocal, the fact is that Canada imports only 3 percent of its oil from the United States (and even less of other key resources); in contrast, the United States imports 50 percent of its oil. This reality is of critical significance because Canada's total known reserves of oil make up, according to one estimate, less than one year of U.S. consumption.

Low-cost energy and ample natural resources were Canada's tools with which to compete — its one major set of advantages over the United States. The U.S. has a more hospitable climate, a bigger population and easier transportation links — but Canada has energy and resources. It is impossible, for example, for the Canadian agriculture sector, with its shorter growing season and harsher climate, to compete with the long growing season in California. Because of such disadvantages for agriculture and Canadian industry in general, cheaper energy and resources were the instruments needed to make Canada a major industrial nation in the world economy — and they have now been given to the Americans. By these provisions, Canada has cut its throat in terms of ever becoming a major industrial power that can compete with the United States.

Since 1907, Canada has had regulations governing the exports of natural gas companies. After 1959, these companies had to show that there was a 25-year reserve supply of gas in the ground for future Canadian use, before exports were allowed. Under article 905(2), that requirement is now abolished. The companies no longer have to leave 25 years or 25 days; they don't even have to leave one day of reserve Canadian energy in the ground for future generations — it can now all be exported.

Article 905(2) also eliminates Canada's "Least Cost Alternative Test," a requirement that meant corporations could not sell hydroelectricity or other energy to the United States for substantially less than what their customer would have paid from an alternative source in the U.S. The situation is that often companies in Canada sell their products to their American parent corporations; for example, Esso delivering Canadian energy to Exxon in the United States. Canada's fight has been to force companies to charge a reasonable price and to pay a fair royalty for the Canadian energy they export. Canada would then receive a decent return from its resources. This is what the Trudeau government began to do under the National Energy Program. A key instrument applied by the NEP was an export tax on all oil shipments to the United States. Export taxes are now explicitly prohibited on all goods by article 408 of the FTA. For good measure, the prohibition is repeated in article 903 for "any energy good." So companies can charge their head offices as little as they like for Canadian energy. Although massive amounts of oil are being pumped daily to the United States at far below the replacement cost, the Canadian government is getting practically nothing in return. The oil industry is now receiving roughly 70 percent of the revenue, while the Canadian government is getting less than 5 percent.

The government spokespeople counter by saying that at least we got secure access to the United States markets: the Americans have committed themselves to buying Canadian energy. But the market access wasn't the problem. The United States needs Canada's energy because its own supplies are rapidly dwindling. In the summer of 1992, the number of oil rigs operating in the United States was the lowest on record. Official U.S. oil reserves are estimated by some sources to be only nine years, and natural gas reserves seven years.

Furthermore, the United States has not committed itself to buying from Canada. Under this agreement, Canada is obliged to allow the Americans access to a constant proportion of Canadian energy, even during a shortage, but the Americans are not obliged to buy at any time. If cheaper prices or better terms are available elsewhere, the Americans are not bound by this agreement to purchase energy from Canada. On the one hand, because the United States is Canada's main customer, in a depressed market the price of Canadian resource exports will drop to match the lowest prices available to the U.S. from anywhere in the world. On the other hand, if a shortage occurs and world energy prices go up, the people in the Yukon, Newfoundland, Alberta, Nova Scotia and British Columbia are going to have to match that price or else freeze in the dark.

The question is often asked: who are the Canadian winners under this deal? The answer is: the uranium industry. In the words of the chairman and chief executive officer of Eldorado Nuclear, L.G. Bonar, in 1987, the FTA amounted to a "Bill of Rights" for his industry.[5] In Saskatchewan's north, new uranium mines are being developed on the strength of this deal. As a "bonus," Canada not only will keep the waste from the mines, but will face intense pressure to accept nuclear waste as well. U.S. standards for waste disposal are, in many cases, stricter than in Canada, so American corporations are eager to export their waste. The U.S. Department of Energy has put $30 million into developing a site in Canada for storing radioactive waste from the United States.* Many states have passed laws prohibiting the storage of nuclear waste; they want it sent north to Canada. Article 901(2)(c) allows for free cross-border flow of depleted uranium, radioactive residues, plutonium or its products, thorium or its products, and spent fuel cartridges of nuclear reactors.

One of the strongest promoters of free trade has been the government-and industry-financed C.D. Howe Institute. Its vice-president, Edward Carmichael, was candid: "The most important benefit of free trade to Canada's oil and gas industry is the protection it provides against foolish Canadian energy policies ... Export controls, export taxes, and minimum export prices will be ruled out. This means that Canadian governments will not be able to intervene to set export prices above domestic energy prices as the federal government did after 1973 and in the National Energy Program of 1980."[6]

Energy minister Pat Carney in Calgary, July 6, 1988, gloated: "Critics say the problem with the free-trade agreement is that under its terms Canada can never impose another National Energy Program on the country. The critics are right. That was our objective in these negotiations."[7]

The Canadian government is actually bragging that it has handed control of Canada's oil and gas reserves to a foreign country, and has done so to prevent any future Canadian government from creating energy and resource policies in the national interest. Influential Americans were not slow to react. "When we got such a great deal on energy, we were crusaders for the deal," enthused director R.K. Morris of the U.S. National Association of Manufacturers.[8] The pleasure of U.S. business is easy to understand; a study released by the Manitoba government in 1988 showed that if the FTA had been in place from 1979 to 1982, Canadians would have paid $76 billion more for energy than they did, and most of it to

---

* In reply to an expression of concern by Manitoba residents about drilling at Lac du Bonnet, Pat Carney, then minister of Energy, wrote to the town council of Gimli: "As regards the disposal of waste from other countries in Canada, such a project could offer considerable commercial benefits ... AECL [Atomic Energy of Canada Ltd.] would be remiss not to consider the possibilities of such a project." (Walter Robbins, "Hewers of Wood, Storers of Poison; Is U.S. Nuclear Waste Bound for Canada?" *This Magazine,* October, 1987.)

American corporations. David Yager, publisher of the oil magazine *Roughneck,* summed it up: "We can't have a made-in-Canada price. That's what the free trade agreement is all about."[9]

Article 906 of the agreement specifically allows the continuation of Canadian government subsidies to American oil companies for exploration and development (This is one kind of Canadian government subsidy that Washington has no problem with.) When the oil is found, however, the taxpayers who funded its discovery are prohibited from receiving lower prices than Americans get; nor can Canada apply minimum export prices to cover the replacement costs of more expensive new oil. Thus, Canadians are subsidizing U.S. consumers, including U.S. motorists who fill their tanks with Canadian gas at cheaper prices than Canadians must pay themselves.

The deal goes beyond anything to do with free trade in energy — Canada and the United States essentially had that already. Rather, the FTA provides for forced trade of Canada's precious finite resources during a shortage.

Banking and Finance: Rockefeller's Dream

November 17, 1988, Toronto. CFRB Radio: The Andy Barrie Show.

David Orchard: We've agreed to change twelve of our banking laws to allow the Americans to take over our banks and financial institutions lock, stock and barrel.

Andy Barrie: Mr. Orchard, hold it. Hold it. Come back. He's [Simon Reisman] stomping out of the studio...

Orchard: Well, he can stomp out of the studio, but his bluster doesn't bother me. I'm talking about the facts ... why did we agree to change twelve of our banking laws ... while the Americans don't agree to change one of their banking laws under this deal?

Simon Reisman: ... We have a commitment from the United States, in this agreement, that if and when the *Glass-Steagall Act* is amended, that Canada will automatically get any and all privileges that are given to their own banks. There is no other country in the world that's got that. On the business of Americans being able to buy

Canadian banks, that is a complete misrepresentation because we have provided a right for Americans in respect to banking that we now have with respect to Canadians and the same restrictions that apply to Canadians, apply to them. No single Canadian or no group of Canadians that are related, may own more than ten percent of a bank, and that applies firmly to Americans, as well as to Canadians. So the notion of an American grabbing control of a Canadian bank is a falsehood. Now I heard Mr. Orchard debate with Gordon Ritchie, who was the second in command in my organization. Do you know that I almost had a fit, because he, Orchard, made an error in every statement. And Gordon Ritchie, who is a gentleman, much more a gentleman than I am, because I'll fight back, so Gordon sat there telling the truth, doing it gently and kindly and Orchard, this same man, told a lie in every sentence he utters, and I want the Canadian people to know that Orchard is a fake. He knows nothing about trade, he's distorted this agreement, he is a self-proclaimed expert. What credentials has he ever had? I negotiated GATT, I negotiated the Auto Pact, I negotiated this agreement. I worked for forty years in this business. I think that Mr. Orchard is a fake. He's a plant, he's a fake ...

Barrie: Who planted him?

Reisman: You did. And when he came onto this program and you said he would ask a question and he made a speech for five minutes, I think that's bad faith. That is bad faith, sir.

Barrie: You've had five minutes to respond to his [Orchard's] ninety seconds on the air.

Orchard: ... He has not answered the question.

Reisman: [Shouting] The man is a fake ... and you have allowed him to abuse this program ... You've allowed him to abuse this program. You brought me in, not him, he's had his hour.

Orchard: If you can't handle the heat ...

Barrie: Mr. Reisman, listen, everybody is either going to be a traitor, or a plant or disloyal to Canada. I am really sorry...

Reisman: I didn't say that. You have broken faith ...

Barrie: I want to take a break, and I hope you will cool off. Have a drink of water...

PRIOR TO THE FTA, under the *Canadian Banking Act* no federally licensed banks or financial institutions (trust companies, insurance companies, loan companies, investment companies), including the big five Canadian banks, could be more than 25 percent foreign owned. This Act, and other regulations, have kept the banking sector mainly Canadian owned. (This legislation — strongly opposed by the U.S. State Department — was introduced by Finance Minister Walter Gordon in 1964, after he was visited in Ottawa by David Rockefeller, who informed him that Rockefeller's bank, Chase-Manhattan, was planning to acquire control of the Toronto-Dominion Bank.)

Under article 1703 of the FTA, American banks and financial institutions have been given a blanket exemption from the operation of these laws. Article 1703.1 states, simply and bluntly: "United States persons ... shall not be subject to restrictions that limit foreign ownership of Canadian-controlled financial institutions." American citizens and institutions can now take over every federally licensed financial institution in Canada, including all of Canada's banks. (The one restriction remaining applies to both Canadian and American institutions and states that a single shareholder is restricted to a 10 percent share.)

Foreign banks operating in Canada, known as schedule B banks, such as Lloyds, were not allowed under Canadian banking regulations to control more than 16 percent of the total domestic banking assets in Canada. Under the FTA, American banks are no longer restricted to 16 percent of Canadian banking business. They can do as much business in Canada as they want. The laws enacted over the years to protect Canadian financial institutions have been amended to exempt American financial institutions. The Act implementing the Free Trade Agreement amends the *Bank Act*, the *Loan Companies Act*, the *Trust Companies Act* and the *Insurance Companies Act* in key sections to read: "any reference therein to a non-resident shall be read as a reference to a non-resident other than a non-resident who is a United States resident."

Canadian banks are not even given the pretense of equal treatment in the United States. Canada agrees in article 1703 to change *twelve* of its banking laws to allow U.S. banks to take over

Canadian institutions. In the United States, banking is regulated by each state, and more than forty states have laws limiting foreign ownership of their banks. The United States agreed to make only a single minor regulatory change, allowing Canadian government-backed stocks and bonds, in some circumstances, to be sold by banks in the U.S. Canada is only given an assurance, in article 1702, that Canadian banks in the U.S. won't be treated any worse in the future than they were as of October 4, 1987, and a promise that, if the U.S. amends its fifty-year-old federal banking legislation (the *Glass-Steagall Act*), Canadian financial institutions will receive the same treatment under those amendments as U.S. institutions. The catch is that no date is given for these changes, nor is any assurance, or even indication given that there will be changes made at all.

By the financial services chapter of the FTA, Canada gave up control of its economic base. If the country loses control of its financial institutions, it will mean one more nail in the coffin — as far as Canadian independence is concerned. Once these institutions are American controlled, they will owe their allegiance not to Canada, but to the United States.

On the very day of the election, November 21, 1988, the Mulroney Cabinet passed an order-in-council. In violation of existing Canadian law it gave the giant American Express Company the right to operate as a bank in Canada, even though Amex did not meet the Canadian legal requirement that it exist as a bank in its home country before receiving a licence to operate in Canada. "What other bloody country in the world would permit that?" asked Bank of Nova Scotia chairman, Cedric Ritchie.[10] The board of American Express included Henry Kissinger and chairman James D. Robinson III, who had been a key promoter of the FTA. He had his reward for a job well done.

Services: "The Most Favourable Treatment"

A COUNTRY'S ECONOMY is usually seen as having three major sectors: (1) the primary sector, which comprises industries such as mining, forestry and agriculture; (2) the secondary sector, which includes construction, processing and manufacturing; and (3) the services sector, which covers everything else and in all industrialized nations has become the major employer. Service industries include everything from data processing to automobile repair shops, from tourism, entertainment, insurance and health services to shipping, trucking, utilities, banking and financial industries. In Canada, 70 percent of the jobs are in the services sector; it accounts for $220 billion worth of Canada's gross domestic product. (GDP is the sum of goods and services produced in the country.) Some 87 percent of women who work outside the home work in the services industries.

The services chapter of the FTA gives the Americans national treatment in a whole long list of industries. That is, American companies have the right to be treated as if they were Canadian.

The agreement was drafted in a way designed to create the impression that most services were not affected; the services chapter lists most of the industries involved by code numbers only. In order to find out which industries are included, one needs to go to the *Standard Industrial Classification* (4th edition, 1980), a separate, often hard-to-find book available only in some libraries, and look up the numbers to identify the industries covered. The list extends for more than one hundred typewritten pages. More than 150 industries are there, including all forms of insurance, printing and publishing, real estate, accounting, advertising, architectural services, engineering, agricultural services, postal and courier services, all construction and building trades — some fifteen pages for the construction industry alone — data processing and computer services. (William Loewen, chief executive officer of Comcheq and head of the Canadian. Independent Computer Services Association, has stated that 350,000 Canadian jobs are being lost in the data-processing industry alone because companies are free to do their data processing in the United States or wherever it is cheapest for them.) The list goes on: wholesale trade in the food, beverage, drug and tobacco industries; the metals, hardware, plumbing, heating and building materials industries; household goods industries; and the machinery, equipment and supplies industries. Accommodations, the food and beverage services industrics, tourism, education services (including business schools, vocational schools, forestry technology and engineering schools, fishery colleges and schools of fine arts) are also included.

Health and social services are listed under code number 866. The government repeatedly vowed that health and social services were not affected. Yet the agreement specifically includes the management of general hospitals, extended-care hospitals, psychiatric institutions, children's hospitals, homes for emotionally disturbed children, foster homes, halfway houses, home-care services (including home nursing), public health clinics, medical laboratories, community health services (including out-patient services), dental health clinics, and the offices of physicians, surgeons, dentists, cardiologists, gynecologists, psychiatrists, nurses (both registered and practical) and social workers. This is only a partial listing.

What this enormous list of services means is that all governments in Canada lose the right to restrict U.S. companies or to favour Canadian companies in those 150-plus fields. U.S. corporations now have by law the same rights as Canadian citizens. American businesses have the right in all these areas to set up in Canada, called "right of establishment," and then to get "national treatment," which prevents Canadian governments from, among other things, giving preference to Canadian companies or insisting on any local sourcing or local content guarantees from American corporations. In fact, articles 502 and 1402 state American corporations are to receive "the most favourable treatment" that is given in each province to that province's own companies and citizens. It means, for instance, that in British Columbia the provincial government must treat American corporations as if they were British Columbian. B.C. may still discriminate against firms from Ontario, Saskatchewan, Quebec or any other province, but it cannot discriminate against those from the United States. It is the same for each province and for the territories.

Thus, American companies, in industries covering 70 percent of the jobs in Canada, now have more favourable treatment in each province than firms from the rest of Canada.

Agriculture: "Not on the Table"

AGRICULTURE IS ONE of the biggest industries in Canada. It is by far the largest in each of the three Prairie provinces, and is significant in most of the others.

The public was told over and over again that agriculture was not going to be included in the deal. Early in the negotiations, Agriculture Minister John Wise assured farmers that "agriculture is not on the table." When it became obvious from press leaks that agriculture was very much on the table, he admitted that agriculture may be on the table, but claimed that farm marketing boards were not. When the actual agreement appeared, agriculture was the longest chapter, some fifty-five pages, and it is a nightmare for

Canadian agriculture. The McLeod Young Weir firm of accountants, in a study of the agreement, named wheat, oats and barley producers, food processors and fruit and vegetable producers as "losers" under the FTA.[11] Article 705 allows the free flow of wheat, oats and barley and all products thereof — including bakery products — across the border, whenever the level of government support for these products becomes equal in each country. Allowing American grain into Canada immediately acts to drive down the price of Canadian wheat, barley and oats to the U.S. level.

Cargill Grain of Minneapolis, Minnesota, had a remarkable position in the free-trade negotiations. The chief negotiator for agriculture on the U.S. side was Daniel Amstutz, undersecretary for agriculture in the United States and formerly chief executive officer for Cargill Investor Services. Advising the Canadian government on agriculture policy was David Gilmore, vice-president of Cargill Grain Canada. Thus, Cargill, the largest grain company in the world, had its interests represented on both sides of the negotiating table, and it got, not surprisingly, exactly what it wanted — the weakening of the Canadian Wheat Board and the removal of its power to control American grain coming into Canada.

The government told farmers to expect a big new market for grain south of the border. But the United States produces ten times more grain than Canada, and it is dumping it at cut-rate prices around the world. Under this deal, American grain will be able to flow north into Canada, undermining Canadian grading and cleanliness standards — which are much higher than those in the United States — and also, more significantly, threatening to destroy Canada's entire orderly grain-marketing system.* Cargill is many times larger than any of the Canadian grain companies. It can afford to pay farmers a few cents more per bushel of grain, until the Canadian companies are driven out of business. The result will be the return — with a vengeance — of the private, or open, market system, notorious for its low and wildly fluctuating prices. This is what Prairie farmers fought long and hard against in the 1920s and 1930s when they formed the giant cooperative wheat pools and marched in the streets of Regina to force the government to set up the Canadian

---

* Orderly marketing system refers to the fact that all wheat for export from Western Canada must be sold through the Canadian Wheat Board rather than by private grain companies, as is the case in the United States. This removes a large element of speculation from the market, because all farmers get paid the same amount for their grain, regardless of when it is delivered.

Wheat Board (CWB). The CWB, accountable to the public through its government-appointed commissioners and farmer-elected advisory board, became the sole marketing agent for Prairie wheat, oats and barley for export.

Trade barriers come in two kinds: tariff and non-tariff. Prior to the FTA, if a Canadian baker wanted to import a bushel of wheat from the United States, a tariff, or duty, of 12 cents would be charged to bring it across the border. In addition to paying this duty, the baker was required to obtain an import licence from the Canadian Wheat Board. This was a non-tariff barrier.

Because Canada produces roughly five times more wheat than it can use, the CWB usually refused to grant licences to import wheat into Canada for milling purposes.

Canada is the world's largest producer of high-protein wheat for export. American companies often require high-protein wheat for blending with their lower quality wheats for export. For U.S. corporations to gain unfettered access to the Canadian grain industry, the historic power of the CWB to prevent cross-border trade in grain had to be removed. The FTA did just that. Owing in part to the existence of the CWB, regarded as the "most powerful and prestigious" marketing board in the world, the Canadian grain industry has remained 70 percent domestically controlled.[12] But now, under the FTA, American grain companies that operate on both sides of the border, and around the world, have a tremendous advantage over Canadian grain companies that operate only in Canada. American companies can move grain back and forth across the border easily. If they want to move high-protein Canadian wheat south, and blend it with their lower quality wheat and sell it to their foreign customers (including Canada's traditional customers), they can do that. If they wish to import U.S. grain into Canada, they can do that, too. Not only is the tariff being removed, but also, much more significantly, the power of the Canadian grain industry to regulate the flow of grain across the border (the non-tariff barrier) no longer exists; article 705(1) eliminates Canada's import licence requirements.

The *Western Grain Transportation Act* is based on the historic Crow's Nest Pass agreement of 1897, whereby the Canadian Pacific Railway, in return for huge subsidies of cash and land, agreed to lowered rates (Crow rate) — "in perpetuity" — to move Prairie grain to port. In the FTA, this Act is referred to as a subsidy, which is to be abolished on all shipments of agricultural products to the United

States. In the long run, without the protection of the *Western Grain Transportation Act,* instead of sending Prairie grain west to Vancouver or Prince Rupert, east to Thunder Bay, Toronto and Montreal, or north to Churchill, as is done today, it would be cheaper to ship wheat south down through the Mississippi River system and out the Gulf of Mexico — exactly where the big American grain companies want to take it and where they have the barges, elevators and fleets of ships to handle it. The largest grain-handling facility in the world, at Thunder Bay, would become redundant, and the jobs of those who depend on it for their living would become obsolete. The port of Churchill would die.

Article 708 reads: "the Parties shall seek an open border policy with respect to trade in agricultural, food, beverage and certain related goods." Accordingly, the agriculture chapter of the agreement contains more than one hundred commitments to harmonize Canadian standards, regulations and procedures with those of the United States. Included is everything from allowable pesticide residue levels, food additives and food inspection standards to packaging and labelling requirements. "Harmonize" in the agreement is defined as "making identical." Because of the dominance of American products in Canada in everything from veterinarian drugs to fertilizers, pesticides, other chemicals and food additives, American standards and practices will prevail over Canada's generally higher safety and health regulations. For example, annex 708.1, schedule 7, binds Canada to harmonize pesticide standards with the United States. In licensing pesticides, the United States uses a risk-benefit approach, which weighs damaging health effects against the economic loss that may be suffered if an application for registration is denied; Canada's criteria for registration is based solely on health safety.

Hog producers were promised bigger markets and higher prices. Yet more hogs are slaughtered in Iowa than in all of Canada, and the U.S. industry has the capacity to look after its own market as well as Canada's. In poultry, two companies, Cargill Foods and Cal-Maine Foods, have more birds than all the poultry producers of Canada combined. These big integrated operations in the United States, which own everything from the trucking companies through to the hatcheries, can flood the Canadian poultry market.

In beef, Canada essentially has had free trade with the United States for years. Now, under this deal, the government gives up the right permanently to stop the flow of American products, including cheap U.S. corn-fed meats, over the border into Canada.

The deal also spells big trouble for Canada's vulnerable fruit and vegetable industry. Canada has a shorter growing season than the fruit and vegetable regions of the United States, a colder climate and greater transportation problems. The removal of even the very limited protection provided by tariffs puts this whole industry in jeopardy.

The food-processing industry, one of the biggest industries in Canada, is already 80 percent American owned. According to the head of the Grocery Products Manufacturers' Association, George Fleischmann, an open border will make it impossible for the Canadian operations to compete. They have to pay higher prices for dairy, poultry and some other farm products because Canada has marketing boards, which provide producers a half-decent return. American producers have no such protection, so processors in the United States are able to buy cheaper farm products. In order to survive, the few Canadian food processors left are going to have to expand their operations in the United States instead of in Canada, leave Canada entirely or get out of business.

The Auto Pact: "Extreme Jeopardy"

THE CANADA-U.S. Automotive Products Trade Agreement, or Auto Pact, negotiated by Simon Reisman in 1965, is a conditional, or managed, free-trade agreement covering motor vehicles, and some auto parts. It essentially provides that for every car the big three American auto producers sell in the Canadian market, they are compelled to assemble one in Canada, using a certain proportion of Canadian content. In order to qualify for this tariff-free trade, the companies must meet the Canadian content conditions. If they start bringing in vehicles from the United States and selling more than they produce in Canada, they have to pay tariffs on the ones brought over the border. The tariff was 9.2 percent. The threat of having to pay that tariff has ensured the manufacturers produce cars in Canada.

The Americans have complained for years about the regulations in the Auto Pact. They don't like being forced to do business in Canada. But Canadians were repeatedly promised that the Auto Pact would not be in the FTA. Pat Carney, as minister for international trade, stood up in the House of Commons, thumped her desk for emphasis and declared that the Auto Pact was not on the table in the free-trade negotiations.

Yet article 401 of the FTA abolishes all tariffs. There will no longer be any penalty to force these companies to produce vehicles in Canada. The Auto Pact remains on paper, but the enforcement mechanism is gone. If the big three wish to produce in Canada — that is, if they can get enough grants or subsidies from the Canadian government and get satisfactory wage settlements from Canadian workers, and if the Canadian dollar is low enough — they will continue to do so. If not, they will simply move their operations to the United States or to Mexico, together with the jobs that previously belonged to Canadians.

Prior to the FTA, the Auto Pact had a 60 percent Canadian content requirement for automobiles assembled in Canada. Under annex 301.2 of this agreement, the Canadian content rule is abolished and replaced with a 50 percent North American content rule — which means that the whole 50 percent can now come from the United States.

Today the automotive industry in Canada is well over 90 percent foreign owned. Canada is the only major car market in the world without its own car. Canadians assemble cars designed in the United States, where the thinking, research, planning and development are done. Canadians were told in 1965, and are still being told today, by government, media, and academic and industry spokespersons, that Canada is "too small" to have its own auto industry. In fact, Canada is a large market — 1.4 million cars and trucks with a value of $19 billion are sold annually. How Sweden, South Korea, Japan, Germany, France and other countries can produce and market their own successful automobiles is apparently a mystery. The Canadian government goes on bended knees to these countries, some barely the size of a single Canadian province, with far fewer resources and a smaller domestic market than Canada, begging them to establish an assembly plant here and offering huge handouts of public money for them to do so.

In the 1930s, Japan passed legislation encouraging the big American auto companies to leave. That is when Datsun, Nissan and Toyota took over. Today they beat the Americans at their own game. Brazil insists on 100 percent domestic content in their automotive industry.

The Americans know that Canadians are perfectly capable of developing and building a Canadian car, a Canadian truck, and a Canadian automotive industry in the same way Avro set in motion a domestic aerospace industry in the 1950s. With an integrated North American automobile market locked into place by the FTA, that can't happen. Under its terms, even the branch-plant automobile industry in Canada is in extreme jeopardy.

Secure Access: Peddling an Illusion

PRIME MINISTER MULRONEY repeatedly and adamantly guaranteed Canadians that the main purpose of the FTA was to get secure access to the U.S. market for Canadian exports. He told the New York *Times* on April 3, 1987: "There are several vital conditions [the trade agreement] would have to meet. Most important among these is that Canada must be permanently exempt from the United States' fair-trading laws." Throughout the 1980s, the Americans had taken action against imports of Canadian lumber, hogs, groundfish, shakes and shingles, and potash. A free-trade agreement would stop that from happening, confident promoters declared.

A paragraph from section 201 of the 1974 U.S. *Trade Act* gives an example of how sweeping American trade law is. It provides that if imports into the United States have expanded significantly over the previous five years and are causing injury to American corporations, those imports can be blocked. Section 337 of the 1930 *Tariff Act* states: "[A]ny unfair act in the import of articles into the United States that causes injury or the threat of injury to American establishments or prevents the establishment of similar industries in the United States is unlawful." And if that isn't enough, there is a catch-all provision that allows the U.S. president to counter the trade practices of any other country if he simply finds their practices to be "unjustifiable, unreasonable, or burden or restrict U.S. commerce in any way."

But Canada did not get secure access to the U.S. market or exemption from any U.S. trade laws in the FTA. Instead of removing the softwood lumber tariff of 15 percent, the agreement permanently enshrined it in article 2009. In fact, the United States did not back off on any of its trade actions. Hogs, steel, plywood and all other U.S. trade rulings against Canada were made permanent under article 1904(2) of the agreement. Far from offering Canada an exemption from American trade law, the FTA, under article 1902, states: "Each Party reserves the right to apply its antidumping law and countervailing duty law to goods imported from the territory of the other Party." *(Dumping* is the sale of a product in a foreign country for less than the price charged for it in its domestic market. Corporations do this to get rid of excess production or to cut into a new market or simply to increase exports. If a producer of a similar product in the foreign country objects, an *anti-dumping duty,* equal to the difference between the dumped price and the price charged at home, can be imposed on the offending imports. *Countervailing duties* are duties imposed on a product if it is deemed to have been produced in its country of origin with the help of subsidies. Only the U.S. frequently uses countervailing duties and it is the only country to have done so against Canada.)

In the FTA, the United States retains all its trade law — intact — and in article 1902(2) expressly reserves the right to make U.S. trade laws even tougher if it so chooses. Article 2002 permits the United States to place a blanket tax on all imports from Canada any time it feels it needs to protect its dollar. This is exactly what Richard Nixon did in 1971, when he slapped a 10 percent surcharge on all products entering the country.

One of the reasons repeatedly given for negotiating the FTA was to gain exemption from a 1200-page "Omnibus" trade bill the United States was about to pass, which would hurt Canadian exports. The *Omnibus Trade and Competitiveness Act* was passed in August 1988, seven months after President Reagan and Prime Minister Mulroney had signed the FTA. By its terms, Washington can take action against any country that trades "unfairly," the definition of unfair to rest entirely with the United States. Canada received no exemption whatsoever; in fact, the Act states that it takes precedence over the Canada-U.S. FTA, allowing the United States to act against imports any time it chooses.

What Canada got, with great fanfare, in article 1904 was the right to appeal to a panel certain trade rulings by the United States. But this five-member panel — two Canadians, two Americans, a fifth member selected by lot — has no power to enforce any of its rulings, and it is restricted to deciding, in all the cases brought before it involving U.S. action against Canadian exports, whether the United States has applied its own laws correctly!

Under this dispute settlement panel, Canada forgoes the right to take countervailing and anti-dumping disputes with the United States to the General Agreement on Tariffs and Trade (GATT), an organization of ninety-seven countries from around the globe. Founded in 1947, the GATT was, until now, the main contract Canada had for governing trade among itself, the United States and the other member countries. The GATT panel on trade disputes is much more impartial: if two countries are involved in a dispute, their nationals do not sit on the panel for that case, leaving representatives from other neutral countries to rule on the dispute.

The agreement gives the impression in article 1801(2) that Canada can choose to take a dispute either to the GATT panel or to the Canada-U.S. panel, and the Canadian government stated over and over again that Canada-U.S. disputes can still go to the GATT. That is not true according to Mel Clark, deputy head negotiator for Canada at the Tokyo round of GATT negotiations. Clark testified in 1988:

> Article 1801, paragraph 1 makes it clear that the option of referring a complaint to the GATT panel does not apply to countervailing and dumping cases. More important is the 1949 GATT decision that "the determination of rights and obligations between governments arising under a bilateral trade agreement is not a matter within the competence of the contracting parties." During the intervening 39 years, the GATT has not established a panel to examine a dispute arising out of a bilateral agreement. The situation therefore is that Canada could not refer a countervailing and dumping case to GATT under any circumstances. Nor is it likely that GATT would establish a panel to examine a complaint involving other bilateral agreement rights and obligations until the 1949 decision is changed and the prospects of GATT making such a change are not good. Article 1801, paragraph 2 is an illusion.[13]

Under the GATT, the legality of a countervailing or anti-dumping duty is decided on the basis of GATT law. Under the FTA, U.S. law has replaced GATT law. In addition, GATT rules cannot be changed without agreement among the member countries; in contrast, the FTA allows the United States to change its trade law unilaterally, including its countervailing duty law. Article 104 states unequivocally that the FTA overrides all other bilateral and multilateral agreements to which Canada and the United States belong. This, of course, includes the GATT.

So Canada has cut itself out of the GATT and the world community, as far as anti-dumping and countervailing trade disputes with the United States are concerned. Over the years Canada has had good results from the GATT, in cases against the United States, it has lost only one. Now Canada is much worse off; having signed the FTA, it is one-on-one with the Americans.

Water Is in the Deal

THE CANADIAN GOVERNMENT repeatedly denied that water was in the FTA. In May 1988, International Trade Minister John Crosbie proclaimed: "Water is not even the subject of a provision of the U.S.-Canada Free Trade Agreement." By July 8 of that year, he clarified the government's position: "All that the FTA provides for the record is the elimination of tariffs on the export of bottled water." On July 21, Mr. Crosbie explained that tariff item 22.01 in the FTA "refers to water under the 'Beverages, Spirits and Vinegar' chapter."[14]

Water is, in fact, clearly listed in the agreement. Article 711 of the agriculture chapter states: "agricultural goods means all goods classified [under specific code numbers]." One of the numbers listed is tariff heading 22.01, which in the tariff schedules (a legal part of the FTA) of both Canada and the United States reads: "waters, including natural or artificial mineral waters and aerated waters ... ice and snow." Any good so listed is covered by all the provisions of the agreement, including the national treatment commitment contained in article 105 and the commitment to proportional sharing contained in article 409.

Furthermore, article 408 says that the agreement covers "any good." Article 201, the General Definitions article, states that "For purposes of this Agreement ... goods of a Party means domestic products as these are understood in the *General Agreement on Tariffs and Trade.*" Water has been included for years in the schedules to the GATT. This means that if Canada ships water to the United States, water will be subject to the same provisions as all other goods. Even if Canada itself faces a shortage, it will be obligated to supply to the United States the same proportion of its total supply that the Americans were taking over the previous three years, and, because all export taxes, duties and charges are prohibited, at prices no greater than those charged to Canadians. But more significantly, the FTA has given the United States national treatment rights to all Canadian waters, thereby giving it substantial new rights to Canada's water.

The provinces constitutionally have large jurisdiction over all natural resources, including water. If a province made a deal with the United States, how would the federal government stop it? Before the FTA, the federal government could have simply applied an export tax at a high enough rate to kill any export of Canadian water. Now, however, article 408 of the FTA prohibits export taxes, thereby depriving the federal government of the means to halt water exports.

THE CONNECTION BETWEEN water diversions and the Free Trade Agreement has been made clear by no less an authority than Canada's chief free-trade negotiator, Simon Reisman. Prior to that appointment, Reisman was an advisor to the Great Recycling and Northern Development (GRAND) project, a huge scheme to dam and dyke twenty rivers that flow into James Bay and send them down into the United States.

In April 1985, Reisman openly described his connection with the large water diversion project:

> ... What has become known as the Grand Canal Project would entail the conversion of James Bay from a salt-water body to a fresh-water lake by means of a sea-level dyke across the mouth of the bay. The fresh water pouring into James Bay from some twenty rivers would be fed into the Great Lakes-St. Lawrence water basin through the Grand Canal system, which would consist of a series of canals, dams, pumping stations, and underground water tunnels and make use of northern rivers as well as the Ottawa and the French river systems ...
>
> I am personally associated with the ongoing work of the company...
>
> Let me give you some idea of the dimensions of this project. It would move into Lake Huron an amount of fresh water equivalent to twice the present flow of the Great Lakes system. Once in the Great Lakes, it would be available to stabilize water levels in that system. The bulk of the water would be available for transfer through a North American grid to Western Canada and to the midwestern and other parts of the United States where fresh water is becoming increasingly scarce ...
>
> The magnitude of the Grand Canal Project would be some five times the size of the Apollo moon-landing project, roughly $100 billion in current dollars. It would take ten years to construct and put into operation.
>
> The urgent need for fresh water in the United States would, I believe, make that country an eager and receptive partner ...
>
> I believe that this project could provide the key to a free trade agreement with the United States containing terms and conditions that would meet many of the Canadian concerns about transition and stability ...
>
> Do we have the flexibility to approach this subject with open minds, free from preconceived ideas and the prejudices of the past?

Do we have the courage and the imagination — yes, the audacity — to take on these two big projects, free trade and fresh-water sharing, at the same time?

I have personally suggested these ideas to leaders in government and business on both sides of the border, and I have been greatly heartened by the initial response. Americans are fully aware how sensitive both issues are in the Canadian scheme of things and would not take the initiative. Any proposals would have to come from Canada ...[15]

Shortly after making this speech, Reisman was appointed by Mulroney as the chief free-trade negotiator for Canada.

On June 28, 1988, Representative Fred Grandy of Iowa spoke for many others when he said: "I think one of the reasons the United States wants to negotiate a free trade agreement with Canada is because Canada has the water resources that this country is eventually going to need."[16]

In 1983, Mulroney announced his support for the Grand Canal project. In 1985, after an interview in the United States with the prime minister, *Fortune* magazine reported: "Mulroney is so ready for the leap that he is prepared to sell some of his country's abundant fresh water — a shocking thought in Canada, and one most previous Canadian political leaders wouldn't have entertained for a moment ... But Mulroney seems to invite offers. If a proposition makes economic sense and would help relations between the countries, he says, 'Why not?' "[17]

Native People: Bound by Every Article

THE IMPACT OF THE FTA on Native people in Canada has not been adequately understood or sufficiently discussed. In article 103 of the agreement, Canada and the United States have agreed to "ensure that all necessary measures are taken in order to give effect to its provisions, including their observance ... by state, provincial and local governments." As a result, reserve and band-level governments — increasingly important local governments — are bound by every article of the FTA, including the resource commitments to the United States in articles 408, 409, 903 and 904. The agreement ends any hope Native people have for authentic self-government with control of their resources.

Chief Konrad Sioui, vice-chief of the Quebec region of the Assembly of First Nations, in testimony to the Parliamentary Committee on Free Trade, explained the implications of the FTA for Aboriginal people in Canada:

> The final outcome of this deal will, of course, mean that the aboriginal rights we have struggled for so long to achieve will be meaningless ... The effect will be to transfer the ownership of Canada to the United States. In recounting the foregoing it is not my intention to convey the impression that the aboriginal people do not believe in trade. Certainly we believe in trade. We were in fact trading with Indians, between aboriginal nations, long before the arrival of the Europeans. What I want to impress on this committee and all Canadians, Mr. Chairman, however, is that it is a fundamental duty of all citizens of this country to decide whether we will govern trade or be governed by trade. This is the crux of the matter. It has nothing at all to do with the mindless breath-baiting free trade advocates whose main message is that we are Canadians and we are tough and we can compete against anyone in the world and we are going to prove it by signing a free trade agreement with the U.S. This phony macho message might make the big boys in the Canadian Manufacturers' Association feel good but does it make any sense? Of course it does not. The CMA's counterpart in Japan with the toughest trading laws of any industrialized nation howl with laughter when they hear gibberish like this. If Canadian manufacturers are such competitors why, we must ask, is our manufacturing industry so heavily dominated by foreign trans-national corporations who send the profits from their Canadian operations to foreign owners? All of this raises an interesting question. Who is the fight for free trade to be fought against? The answer is one the committee must take into account because the fight for a Canada-U.S. free trade deal is being waged by the government of Canada against the citizens of Canada. Nothing else can explain the panic-stricken attack against those who question the deal ... What we have to ask is what is going on? Is it no longer tolerable to raise serious questions about the future of our country? Is the deal so ill-conceived that the government has to try and sell it like a package of soap?[18]

The resource-sharing commitments of the FTA are particularly significant for Natives, but so also are the provisions regarding services, investment, agriculture, water and national treatment. The environmental damage as a result of the agreement will be monumental — as forests are clear-cut to send pulp and paper to the United States, uranium mines proliferate, and demands increase to send Canadian water and energy south. A great deal of that destruction will take place on Native lands. In addition, Native communities already reeling under extreme unemployment rates — 90 percent in some areas — will be particularly hard hit by the prohibition against local sourcing and content requirements.

The federal government is promising Canada's first nations greater control over their land and their futures through self-government. This is an empty promise. The nasty surprise for Native people is that the resources on or under Indian lands have been committed by the FTA to the United States of America.

Other Nasty Surprises

THE FREE TRADE AGREEMENT contains 140 articles, and the above examples by no means cover all of them. Other articles contain additional unpleasant surprises for Canadians.

- Article 2010, called Monopolies, states that if national or provincial programs are introduced in Canada, for example an auto insurance scheme such as is found in British Columbia and Saskatchewan, the government would be required to give advance notice to the United States, to "engage in consultations" if Washington asked for them, and to be prepared to modify the program in order to eliminate any adverse effect or loss of business — real or potential — to American companies. This last requirement includes being prepared to compensate American corporations affected by the program's implementation. A graphic example of this reality was seen in 1991, when the Ontario government backed down on its 1990 election promise and scrapped a long-standing NDP commitment to introduce a provincial auto-insurance plan after learning that State Farm, the largest U.S. auto insurance company, claimed that under the FTA $1.3 billion would be owed by Ontario as compensation to U.S. auto-insurance companies.
- Article 401 provides for the elimination of tariffs on all goods by 1998. Before the FTA, Canada's tariffs were, on average, three times higher than those of the United States. The equal elimination

of each country's tariffs thus amounts to a threefold advantage to the U.S.

- Purchasing by governments in Canada has been a way of supporting Canadian industry. Chapter 13 of the FTA, Government Procurement, changes all that. Articles 1304 and 1305 provide that on all contracts over U.S. $25,000 (with some limited exceptions), the Canadian government shall accord to U.S. companies "treatment no less favourable than the most favourable treatment accorded to its own goods," and it agrees to award contracts that "are free of preferences in any form in favour of its own goods." Purchases by all levels of government in Canada amount to over $75 billion annually, or about 20 percent of the economy. With lower wages, cheaper overhead and larger volume runs, U.S. companies will be able to undercut and outbid Canadian firms supplying their own government in Ottawa. As with many other parts of the agreement, there is no pretense of equality. The Canadian government proportionately opens up far more of its market to U.S. bidding than does the U.S. to Canadians. By excluding military procurement, the largest industry in the United States, the Americans have kept intact one of their major methods of stimulating regional development — the allocating of defence contracts. In contrast, Canadian governments have given up their power to purchase from domestic companies, traditionally an instrument of regional development in Canada.

- Chapter 6, Technical Standards, states: " ... each Party shall make compatible its standards-related measures and procedures for product approval with those of the other Party." This provision includes a commitment to harmonize their respective technical regulatory requirements and inspection procedures covering, among other things, testing facilities, inspection agencies and certification bodies. The repercussions are serious for Canada's sovereignty in terms of its ability to set and enforce national standards of its own choosing.

- Article 2011, called Nullification and Impairment, provides that if either country considers that "any measure" taken by the other, "whether or not such a measure conflicts with the provisions of this agreement," reduces any benefit the other might have "reasonably expected," "directly or indirectly" from the agreement, the other country may demand consultations; if not satisfied, that country may challenge the action before the Canada-U.S. Trade Commission dispute panels set up in chapter 18 of the FTA. These chapter 18 panels can be invoked "whenever a Party considers that an actual or proposed measure of the other Party is or would be inconsistent with the obligations of this Agreement." This sweeping provision gives the United States the ammunition to challenge Canada on virtually any social and economic policy it doesn't like. In effect, Washington has achieved a veto over future Canadian policy decisions. Technically, this measure is reciprocal, but Canada's ability to impose its will on Washington is, in this regard, nonexistent.

- Chapter 15, Temporary Entry for Business Persons, allows movement across the border of a long list of professions and personnel, including teachers, dentists, nurses, veterinarians, architects, engineers, scientists, librarians, social workers, psychologists, journalists, lawyers and thirty-three other occupational categories. Americans falling into these categories, as well as into a far-reaching grouping of anyone "engaged in the trade of goods and services or in investment activities," are to be allowed entry into Canada for unspecified lengths of time without the usual immigration requirements or prior-approval procedure. Again, this measure is reciprocal, but the difference in population size makes Canadians ten times more vulnerable to being swamped with American competition.

Culture: Not Exempted

CULTURE, CANADIANS WERE assured, was exempt from the Free Trade Agreement. To prove it, the government pointed to article 2005.1, which states: "Cultural industries are exempt from the provisions of this Agreement, except as specifically provided in Article 401 (Tariff Elimination), paragraph 4 of Article 1607 (divesture of an indirect acquisition) and Articles 2006 and 2007 of this Chapter." The very next sentence, article 2005.2, however, nullifies this supposed exemption. It reads: "Notwithstanding any other provision of this Agreement, a party may take measures of equivalent commercial effect in response to actions that would have been inconsistent with this Agreement but for Paragraph 1." This provision means that if a government takes any action to promote or protect cultural industries in a way that alters U.S. control of these industries in Canada, the Americans have the legal right to estimate their losses from the measure, and then take action of equal value against another Canadian industry *without even having to go through the dispute settlement panel.* If, for example, Canada took steps to increase Canadian films' access to theatres, or to increase Canadian content on television, the United States would have the right to retaliate against any other Canadian industry it chose, be it lumber, steel, pork, fish or automobiles.

This "exemption" casts in stone the existing U.S. control of Canada's creative expression by granting the United States the specific right of retaliation should Canada ever move to reduce the almost total American domination of Canadian cultural life. It means U.S. interests have achieved a veto over future federal and provincial cultural programs.

Some 96 percent of the videos and 85 percent of compact discs, records and tapes sold in Canada are foreign. Under the FTA, tariffs on cassettes, films and recordings are to be removed, foreshadowing severe difficulties for the sound recording manufacturing industry in Canada. Roughly 80 percent of the magazines and books on Canadian store shelves and 95 percent of the drama on Canadian television screens are non-Canadian — primarily American. The U.S. government has long understood the power of culture, and particularly film: if you can control a nation's dreams, its resources will soon follow. For seventy-five years, unrestricted trade in motion pictures has existed between Canada and the United States, with the result that 97 percent of the movies shown in Canada are foreign (essentially American). Some 97 percent of film revenues leave the country, with all but a fraction going to the United States. Many Canadian movie-goers have never seen a Canadian film on the big screen. Why? Not because Canadians don't make good films — they have won awards around the world. Simply, they are not shown in Canada because American chains own the film distribution networks and many of the theatres.

Canadian artists and film producers were promised by Joe Clark, then minister of external affairs, a "big new market" under free trade. The problem is that these film producers are locked out of their own Canadian market, which is controlled from Hollywood. The idea of Canadian film producers being able to go up against Hollywood for access to the U.S. market is like a small entrepreneur building a car in a back garage and trying to compete against GM.

One commentator has aptly described the Canadian experience with free trade and culture: "No country in the world probably is more completely committed to the practice of free flow in its culture and no country is more completely its victim."[19]

19

Everything We Wanted

IT WASN'T EASY to get a copy of the signed Free Trade Agreement. In post offices and supermarkets around the country, the government placed the *Canada-U.S. Trade Agreement in Brief.* Produced by the Department of External Affairs, the booklet contained none of the text of the FTA, but consisted of glowing explanations of how wonderful the Free Trade Agreement would be for Canada. "Prices will drop," the text proclaimed. "And, above all, it will lead to the creation of hundreds of thousands of new jobs."

Old-age pensioners and people who receive family allowances were sent a little blue-and-white form, from the minister of international trade, asking if the recipient wanted more information about free trade. It said: "Please indicate document(s) requested: *Agreement in Brief, Overview, Regional Pamphlets or Issue Pamphlets.*" None of these documents contained any text from the Free Trade Agreement, but the praise for it continued. "Minutes before midnight on October 3, 1987," begins the *Overview,* "Canada and the United States agreed ... to conclude what will be the largest commercial accord in history, with major economic benefits for both countries." Under the heading "A Good Deal for All of Canada," Canadians were told: "The Agreement will promote growth. It will mean a significant increase in jobs for Canadians - as many as 350,000 new jobs between now and 1995 ... "

The government started distributing another document, *The Canada-U.S. Free Trade Agreement: A Synopsis.* Saskatchewan's premier, Grant Devine, for instance, held fifty town-hall meetings around that province to promote the FTA, and he handed out the *Synopsis.* Published by the federal Department of External Affairs, the sixty-page synopsis purports to be a summary of the agreement, but in fact is made up of interpretations extolling the "benefits" of the FTA. Canadians who thought they had a copy of the agreement entered a world of Alice in Wonderland when they began reading:

> Saskatchewan thrives on its exports and the Agreement has benefits for all industries ... Manitoba industry, especially manufacturers, will find new opportunities ... Clothing manufacturers ... will find their coats more competitive in the U.S. ... For British Columbia's fisheries, the Agreement will . . . improve British Columbia's competitive edge in U.S. markets ... The Agreement provides prodigious opportunity to Alberta ... No part of Canada has more to gain from the Agreement than Ontario ... The phaseout of tariffs over the next decade will benefit manufacturing in Ontario ... Ontario farmers ... will benefit from better access to the U.S. market ...
>
> The deal on agriculture is a good one for Quebecers ... There will also be new opportunities for Quebec industry to sell to U.S. federal government agencies ... By gaining more secure and enhanced access to the largest market in the world, Atlantic Canadians will be able to realize their potential ... Michelin Tires ... the biggest private employer in the province [Nova Scotia], will benefit ... Tariff elimination will offer scope for the fishing industry ... to expand its processing capacity. National Sea, the largest fish company in Canada, has already stated that this opportunity could lead to 400 new jobs ... The removal of the tariff ... will provide Newfoundlanders with opportunities for manufacturing.

At government offices, citizens were handed the *Synopsis* and told: "That's got the details in it right there." Several newspapers featured the *Synopsis* and told their readers it was a summary of the FTA. Calls to members of Parliament requesting the actual text of the agreement were met with a variety of responses: "We don't have any." "We can't get any." "There's no such thing." "The MPs will only get a few." "It's not available to the public." In a typical example, a caller was told by the office of his member of Parliament, then federal justice minister, Ray Hnatyshyn, that "the document is not for public consumption." When pressed, the offer was made of a private viewing of the agreement in Mr. Hnatyshyn's office on condition that it not be removed from the premises.

Those who did get their hands on the actual agreement found a 300-page document of twenty-one chapters. The introduction declares: "The agreement meets the test of fairness and of mutual advantage. It is a win-win agreement." At the beginning of each chapter is a one- to six-page "explanation." As in the *Synopsis,* these introductions play fast and loose with the truth. For example, the explanation that opens chapter 7, Agriculture, states: "Canada's farmers will make real gains." For chapter 9, Energy: 'This chapter ... will secure Canada's access to the United States market for energy goods." And the introduction to chapter 19, Dispute Settlement, concludes: "Canadian firms will have not only more open access, but also more secure and more predictable access. At the same time, Canada's capacity to pursue regional development and social welfare programs remains unimpaired. Indeed, it has been strengthened." To which Judge Maxwell Cohen, one-time chairman of the Canada-U.S. International Joint Commission, responded: "There is not a word in chapter 19 that makes this hyperbolic hope a reality."[1]

The text itself is written in complicated language, virtually impossible for a person without specialized training to understand. Three weeks after its release, on January 1, 1988, the legal text of the agreement, almost totally unseen and unknown to Canadians, was signed by Mulroney and Reagan - just hours before the American-imposed "fast track" deadline.

Because most Canadians did not have access to either the FTA or the documents necessary to make sense of it, the government was able to exploit the public hunger for information. More than $25 million of public money was spent producing and circulating booklets, pamphlets and materials like the Synopsis, the *FTA in Brief* and other articles of a similar nature. One example was a booklet produced and distributed by External Affairs to Canadian elementary schools for use in grades 3, 4 and 5. Entitled *Canada: Our Place in the World,* it opens with a message from Pat Carney, minister of international trade. The "notes to the teacher" section sets out the aims and objectives of the book: "Students learn that the Canadian climate and our desire for certain products make us dependent on non-Canadian goods and imported materials." Is the Canadian government attempting to make the point, one is tempted to ask, that Canada's climate makes us dependent on American aircraft and films?

In "student activities," beside an illustration of a smiling beaver saying "Let's Trade," the students are asked: "Which country is Canada's main trading partner? What have the governments of the two countries done to try to make trading easier? Ask exporters, local and national business and exporters groups for their opinion about freer trade with the United States." And: "Write a song, poem or play about products and services that are either imported or exported by companies in your community."

In the section "International Investment," the students are asked: "If a foreign company invests in a Canadian company, what are the advantages to the foreign company, the Canadian company, the employees of the Canadian company? Make a mural to show your knowledge." And: "What are the advantages to the foreign company, the Canadian municipality, Canadian workers, Canadian buyers, provincial and federal governments when a foreign company builds a factory in a Canadian town?"

This educational exercise does not ask students any questions about disadvantages.

IN CONTRAST TO the vague and desperate claims from the Canadian government that both sides "won," many of the U.S. announcements were clear and to the point. Immediately after the signing on October 3, 1987, Clayton Yeutter, U.S. trade representative, let fall his observation: "We've signed a stunning new trade pact with Canada. The Canadians don't understand what they've signed. In twenty years, they will be sucked into the U.S. economy."[2]

Confidential briefing papers prepared for Treasury Secretary James Baker and Trade Representative Yeutter were leaked and published in the United States. These papers contained the American government's internal assessment of its achievements:

> We have achieved a major liberalization of the investment climate in Canada and imbedded it permanently so that in the future Canada's investment policies cannot retrogress to the old policies of the NEP and FIRA ... The vast bulk of U.S. direct investment in Canada now will go forward with no Canadian government interference whatsoever.
>
> There is broad agreement to assure the freest possible bilateral trade in energy, including nondiscriminatory access for the United States to Canadian energy supplies ...

The briefing paper concludes: "Essentially, in the text we got everything that we wanted."[3]

The Hearst newspaper chain was delighted, just as it was in 1911.

Editor-in-chief William Randolph Hearst Jr. wrote from New York that the agreement was

> a bright new feather in the president's achievement cap ... The momentous move toward uniting the two countries economically is very gratifying to me. For more than a decade, my Pop urged in his newspapers that Canada become part of the U.S. ... In the past, it was Canadian liberals who urged free trade with us. This time, it was a conservative government led by Mulroney who has been called the most pro-American prime minister in Canada's history. At the risk of his political career, he worked for 16 months with an American conservative president to forge the free trade agreement.[4]

IN CANADA, TWO citizens organizations, the Council of Canadians (first led by publisher Mel Hurtig and later by Maude Barlow) and Citizens Concerned About Free Trade, both founded in 1985, were distributing information about the agreement to a hungry public. The Canadian Labour Congress issued a prediction, soon to more than prove itself, that the FTA would cost Canadians one million jobs. 1984 polls had shown 78 percent support for free trade, but the Conservatives knew, of course, that this support was not based on knowledge of the agreement which had not yet been negotiated. Government pollster Allan Gregg labelled the support "nonbrainer," based only on a vague concept of something free, which could evaporate quickly.[5]

The government knew that its only hope was to prevent the contents of the FTA from becoming accessible to, and understood by, the public. Debate was cut off by the government majority in the House. Cabinet ministers were ordered not to debate the agreement in public. A long-arranged debate in Vancouver, between John Crosbie, then federal minister of transport, and Michael Walker of the Fraser Institute versus MP Sheila Copps and this writer, was abruptly cancelled by the Prime Minister's Office on December 2, 1987, one day before the event. Sharon Lund, a Vancouver member of Citizens Concerned About Free Trade heard that John Crosbie was in Vancouver and scheduled as the guest on that city's CKNW open-line radio show. After dialling for almost an hour, she got through: "Mr. Crosbie," she asked, "why have you pulled out of the debate tonight? You are going across the country saying the deal is good but you won't face the public. Are you scared?" Crosbie, caught, declared that he would attend. As the hour approached, a large red helicopter landed on the lawn in front of Simon Fraser University, and Crosbie and entourage swept into the hall. What followed was a no-holds-barred event, the largest free-trade debate to take place in B.C.

Soon afterwards, government ministers, from the prime minister down, refused to debate the agreement. Instead, they would make vague and general claims, one more preposterous than the next, often uncritically repeated by the media. John Crosbie, as international trade minister, declared: "The Canada-U.S. FTA does nothing but promise to create more wealth for Canadians so that we can have more and better social programs." Charles Mayer, minister responsible for the Canadian Wheat Board, claimed: "The FTA will mean access to the huge U.S. market without giving anything in return."[6] The prime minister announced: "What free trade is going to do is give Canada more money so we can do more for all of you."[7]

Government members, many academics and most of the media acted as if the agreement dealt only with removal of tariffs. The other twenty chapters of the document, its most significant part by far, were treated as if they did not exist. A wave of advertising swept the country promoting the agreement as making Canada stronger, providing jobs and making goods cheaper. Virtually all the media jumped on the bandwagon, the Toronto *Star* and the Edmonton *Journal* the only two major newspapers taking an editorial position against the deal. Most provincial governments and the bulk of academic economists joined the rush.

The government not only avoided debate in open forums, but also launched a strategy of attacking those who raised questions. Pat Carney, Crosbie's predecessor as minister of international trade, regularly referred to opponents of the deal as "wimps." To Finance Minister Michael Wilson they were "weak-willed and narrow of vision." Prime Minister Mulroney denounced the free-trade opposition as, among other things, "anti-NATO Reds," "bomb throwers" and "kneecappers."[8] Simon Reisman went even further, labelling free-trade opponents "Nazis," who used Goebbels' own technique of "the Big Lie."

At the same time, the government stuck carefully to its plan to "divide and neutralize" its free-trade opponents. Mel Hurtig, head of the Council of Canadians, had spoken across Canada against the FTA. While attending a spring 1987 demonstration in Ottawa, when

Ronald Reagan was there for a summit, Hurtig returned unexpectedly to his hotel. Upon opening his door, he discovered a U.S. Secret Service agent standing in his room. When confronted by Hurtig, the agent claimed he had permission from hotel management to be there. The hotel denied any knowledge of the man.

Less than a month later, on May 7, 1987, during a visit to Saskatoon by the prime minister, Citizens Concerned About Free Trade mounted a demonstration against the free-trade talks featuring a large banner which read. "No Ratification Without A General Election." As the prime minister approached, this writer called out: "Mr Mulroney, you have no mandate to negotiate a free-trade agreement with the United States," and was promptly detained by plainclothes policemen, placed in an unmarked black car, driven to another location and held for 25 minutes. Prior to an interrogation in the car, the arresting officer said, "We know you. You are the instigator of this opposition to free trade."

Due to the persistence of a handful of reporters, the story was carried across the country. It was raised on Parliament Hill by two NDP members of parliament who referred to the matter as "a serious violation of a citizen's right to free speech," and said: "The incident is part of the government's policy of insult and intimidation of opponents of free trade." They called upon the Minister of Justice, Ray Hnatyshyn, "to launch an immediate investigation into the action of the RCMP"*

No investigation was held into the incident. Instead, eighteen months later after holding almost one hundred volunteer-organized public information meetings across Canada, featuring a full explanation of the history and contents of the FTA, Citizens Concerned About Free Trade was the surprised subject of a leaked internal RCMP memo. The memo contained a head-and-shoulders photograph. Across the bottom in large letters were the words: "David Orchard – Citizens Concerned About Free Trade." The text read:

David Hugh ORCHARD (DB: 1950 JUN 28)
FPS - Nil (No criminal record)
Male Caucasian; 6'0"; 180 lbs; brown hair; hazel eyes;
single; wears glasses.

---

* For a fuller account of the arrest and aftermath see: Peggy Smith, "How free are we to oppose free trade?" *Prairie Messenger,* August 31, 1987.

ADDRESS: Box 192, Borden, Saskatchewan.

ALIASES: Nil

VEHICLES: 1976 Red GMC truck, licence FYJ 675;

1977 Brown Olds 88, licence JSX 297

Subject is a member of the "Free Trade" and "Anti-Nuclear" movements in Saskatoon. He is a manipulative, argumentative, scheming and self-centred individual, interested in only personal recognition and gain. He hates authority of any description and could become violent if confronted when he is excited about an issue/event. ORCHARD has had numerous confrontations with police in Saskatoon, the most recent of which was on the Prime Minister's visit in July 1987,* and is well known to them and our members alike.[9]

The shocked people at the Citizens Concerned About Free Trade office who received the document recognized a professional disinformation campaign to discredit the anti-free-trade movement and intimidate its members. They considered this an ominous new development in the government's attempt to pursue a free trade agreement at any cost.

---

* Apparently refers to May, 1987 incident.

20

The Sale of Canada Act

THE ACT TO IMPLEMENT the *Free Trade Agreement between Canada and the United States of America* was introduced into the House of Commons on May 24, 1988. Once passed, this legislation would give legal effect to the FTA in Canada. The proposed Act covered more than 120 pages and made major amendments to twenty-seven federal statutes governing the country: the *Broadcasting Act, Bank Act, Canadian Wheat Board Act, Copyright Act, Canada Grain Act, Customs Act, Excise Tax Act, Export and Import Permits Act, Federal Court Act, Income Tax Act, Investment Canada Act, Department of Agriculture Act, Importation of Intoxicating Liquors Act, Loan Companies Act, Meat Import Act, Meat Inspection Act, National Energy Board Act, Seeds Act, Standards Council of Canada Act, Statistics Act, Trust Companies Act, Investment Companies Act, Canadian and British Insurance Companies Act, Customs Tariffs Act, Special Import Measures Act, Canadian International Trade Tribunal Act and Western Grain Transportation Act.*

On the U.S. side, the implementing legislation covered fewer than fifty pages and made amendments, almost all of a minor nature, to fewer than half as many acts as in Canada.

Paragraph 8(2) of the Canadian *Implementing Act* stated: "No person shall, in the purported performance of duties or functions under any law of Canada, do any act, exercise any power or carry on any practice that is inconsistent with or contravenes this Act or any regulation made under this Act, or the [Free Trade] Agreement."

In other words, every citizen of Canada was bound by the terms and conditions of the FTA.

Further, paragraph 8(1) stated that in the case of any inconsistency or conflict between any provision of the Free Trade Agreement and any Canadian law, the Free Trade Agreement is to take precedence over any other Act of Parliament. Thus, the FTA would override any

Act of Parliament in Canada — past, present and future. In contrast, the implementing legislation in the U.S. Congress stated right at the beginning: "In the event of a conflict between a U.S. statute and a provision of the Free Trade Agreement, U.S. law shall prevail."

The government announced it would allow only five days of debate on second reading of the legislation before imposing closure to force its passage through Parliament. Closure is a rarely used device to curtail debate by overriding the usual rules of Parliament. (The use of it four times in 1956 led to the toppling of St. Laurent's government amid opposition cries of "dictatorship" in the famous Trans-Canada pipeline debate.) Yet between 1987 and 1991, the Conservatives under Brian Mulroney used closure nineteen times, more than the total number it had been used since its introduction in 1913.

In the Commons John Turner, leader of the official opposition, rose to deliver his reaction. Turner's detailed and passionate speech on the Free Trade Agreement foreshadowed the coming election battle:

> Mr. Speaker, we are here today to discuss one of the most devastating pieces of legislation ever brought before the House of Commons ... a Bill which will finish Canada as we know it and replace it with a Canada that will become nothing more than a colony of the United States.
>
> This Bill ... is to supersede any other Act of Parliament, past or future. It has almost the authority of a constitutional provision ... Not only that, we find that Canadians can be fined, even imprisoned, for contravening American law, present and future, laws we haven't even seen yet ...
>
> Why are we now being forced to give hasty approval to legislation which represents the largest sell-out of our sovereignty since we became a nation in 1867? Why? ...
>
> In spite of its title and the Government's definitions, this agreement is not free trade ... We have yielded control over investment ... this legislation turns 242 million Americans into Canadians for the purposes of the *Investment Canada Act* ...
>
> Mr. Speaker, we have given up control over our capital markets ... The *Bank Act* is amended. From now on, Americans will no longer be non-residents of Canada under Section 109.1 ...
>
> This deal sells out our energy, the life-blood of this country ... That means that we as Canadians ... cannot charge a higher price to

Americans than we charge for domestic consumers, nor can we give a specific preferential rate to our own consumers, nor can we set our own surpluses, nor can we set our reserves, nor can we protect our self-sufficiency in the future ... The National Energy Board becomes nothing more than a monitoring agency ... With this agreement, it is Washington that is taking control of our country's energy resources ...

The Government and the Minister have denied that water is included in the deal ... The truth is that water is included in this deal just as surely as I have this glass of water in my hand ...

When you read this agreement we have become a storehouse, a reservoir for the U.S. ... The U.S. gets a guaranteed proportion of our country. What is theirs remains theirs, what is ours becomes theirs.

Is it any wonder that the President of the United States is happy with this deal? ... He got access to all our resources and did not have to yield anything in return. No wonder he called this the fulfillment of the American dream.

Ever since the American Revolution and the Declaration of Independence the Americans have looked to Canada as part of their manifest destiny ... what the Americans were not able to take by force of arms in 1812-14, they have taken by virtue of this agreement while not firing a shot ...

The fulfilment of the American Dream! Fifty-four Forty, or Fight! Manifest Destiny! A United States of America that will go down past the Rio Grande and right up to Alaska and the Arctic frontier. It is a dream come true for Americans. At long last they found a Government in Ottawa dumb enough, stupid enough, patsies so craven in the face of American demands that they just caved in to every request made of them.

I say to the people of Canada that this is not a trade deal. This is "the *Sale of Canada Act* ..."

We who oppose this deal are painted by the Prime Minister as being afraid or timid, of having no confidence in our future and no confidence in Canada. That Prime Minister is dead wrong. We do have confidence in this country ... The difference is that for us our future is not a continental future. Our future is a Canadian future ...

In 1867, the Fathers of Confederation established this House of Commons ... They gave this Chamber the responsibility to build a great sovereign independent nation ... If this legislation is allowed to pass, it will be said that in 1988 this House abdicated that role set for us by the founders of our country, that we surrendered that responsibility and abandoned our sovereignty. As a nation, we cannot allow that to happen.[1]

Eventually, the government made some minor changes in the free-trade implementing legislation, including the removal of section 8. Its initial presence there, however, revealed the intentions of the Canadian government. These changes in the implementing legislation did not in any way alter the FTA itself, which, by virtue of article 103, supersedes domestic legislation.

After the legislation was forced by the government majority through the House, only the opposition-controlled Senate stood between the FTA and its passage into law. Allan MacEachen, the leader of the Liberals in the Senate, declared they would pass the FTA as an ordinary piece of legislation. Citizens Concerned About Free Trade (CCAFT) responded by organizing a nationwide letterwriting and phone-in campaign to convince the Senate to block the deal. There was widespread skepticism that the Senate, which had rarely blocked any bill, would stop the most far-reaching document in Canadian history. CCAFT went ahead nevertheless and made public a toll-free number to the Senate. The results were dramatic, with citizens from across the country phoning, faxing and visiting their senators in unprecedented numbers. On July 20, 1988, Liberal leader John Turner made his historic announcement that the Senate would indeed block passage of the FTA implementing legislation until a general election had "let the people decide."

21

It Is Manifest Destiny

THE GOVERNMENT WAS in a tough position. Without any mandate from the voters, Mulroney had signed a vast agreement with the U.S. president that would change Canada forever. The government called it a free-trade agreement, but it contained whole chapters that had nothing to do with trade and included many areas that the government had expressly promised would not be on the table. Now it faced an election over the document. What to do? Mulroney's inner circle decided to stick to the game plan contained in its leaked secret document — never to discuss the contents of the agreement, but rather to do a "selling job." Thus, the government and its academic and corporate supporters avoided any mention of the specific contents of the agreement and instead promoted a number of myths and, in some cases, outright lies. A case in point: the full-page ads that appeared in newspapers across Canada, stating, "Free Trade Will Make Canada Stronger: Don't be deceived by political showmanship, scare tactics and bombastic humbug. Free trade means: more prosperity, more take-home pay, more employment, more pension money, more money for social services, more money to protect the environment, more regional development."

But the entire FTA is built on myths and falsehoods. They begin in the preamble of the agreement, where its purpose is defined as "to strengthen the competitiveness of the United States and Canadian firms in global markets." The myth is "competitiveness," because a foreign-owned branch-plant economy cannot compete with its foreign owners.

Can GM of Canada compete around the world with GM of Detroit? Can Ford of Canada whip Ford USA? Can IBM (Canada) produce and market a better computer than its parent in the United States? Can Dow (Canada) beat out Dow of Michigan in markets and innovation? Can Imperial Oil take on its parent company Exxon in the battle for North American or world markets? Can John Deere (Canada) produce and distribute a better implement than John Deere of Illinois? Can Boeing Canada build and market an aircraft in competition with Boeing USA?

The bulk of Canadian manufacturing has been taken over by American companies. Most branch plants are not even allowed by their parents to export into the United States. Further, many subsidiaries in Canada are expressly prohibited by licence from their parent from exporting anywhere, thereby limiting the Canadian branch to the domestic market. Branch plants do not do the research and development that is necessary to compete. It is done by the head office. This is the reason why Canada has the lowest level of research and development in the industrialized world.

Canadian branch plants don't buy most of their materials in Canada — they import them from the United States, usually from the parent company, in order to increase its sales. A branch plant is not set up to compete with its parent, or to provide employment or national pride. Its purpose in Canada has always been to increase exports from the U.S. parent and to provide jobs and, more particularly, increase profits in the United States. A telling sign of a branch's powerlessness is revealed in the limits placed on its budget. A court case revealed that the president of Mobil Canada could not make a charitable donation or even approve club memberships without approval from his head office, never mind drill an oil well. These executives aren't making decisions in Canada. The decisions are made by the parent office in the United States.

The government, its academics, university professors and media commentators tell Canadians ad nauseam that they aren't "competitive enough." But in reality, true competition can come only when Canada builds its own industries — an automobile industry, an aviation industry, a film industry, a merchant navy, and all the other industries an independent nation requires. Canada has the resources, the population and the capital. All that is lacking is the political will at the centre to create, and then defend, the conditions for Canadian industry to succeed.

The FTA, instead of fostering competition, has made real competition impossible. It has tied Canada into a straitjacket and shackled it with leg irons. It means Canada cannot use the tools other industrial nations — Japan, the United States, Germany, Sweden, France, Britain — have used, namely government policy and protection, and restrictions on foreign ownership, to build its industries into world-class players.

Canadians were informed over and over again that their market is too small — our "little shrivelled" market, as John Crosbie regularly put it. In fact, Canada is the largest market in the world for American goods. The province of Ontario alone buys more from the United States than does any country in the world, including Japan. Canada is a huge market for the United States, and a huge market by any standards. Free-trade promoters claimed Canadians were going to have access to that "big, dynamic market" in the United States. That is not the main problem for Canada. Canada's fight is to gain control of *its own lost markets* so that Canadians can serve their own domestic market. There is no such thing as secure access to another country's market. Canada's access to the United States can be ended at any time by a stroke of the president's pen or a whim of the U.S. Congress, free-trade treaty or no free-trade treaty. But in chasing this fantasy of secure access — which it did not get — the Canadian government gave up the only secure market any nation has: its own internal market. Why should Canadian movie producers, for example, start chasing a huge, new market in the United States when what they first and foremost need is access to more than 3 percent of the screen time in their own country?

It is the controls on foreign ownership that are important, not a country's size. Japan is 5 percent of Canada's physical size and has 5 percent of Canada's resources, but it outproduces in key industries the United States of America. Sweden, with eight million people, one-third Canada's population, has a land size that could fit inside the Yukon. It is not "too small" to have a major automotive industry that exports around the world. The significant difference is that Sweden, like Japan, has had strict controls on the amount of foreign ownership it allows into the country. As a result, both Sweden and Japan own most of their own economies. If Canada owned its own economy and talked about free trade with a country whose economy was closer in size to its own, that would be a different story. Instead, Canada has entered into a massive free-trade agreement with a country ten times bigger, a country that already owns much of Canada. That's where the problem lies.

Another myth used to mislead Canadians was that the European Economic Community (EEC) has free trade, and it's been great for its members; therefore, it will be good for Canada. There are many differences, however, between the EEC and the Canada-U.S. free-trade area. The European Economic Community was formed as a defensive arrangement to counterbalance the power of the United States. In significant areas, for example services and resource sharing, the FTA goes beyond what the European common market has in place after thirty years. Also, no one country dominates the others the way the United States dominates Canada. Germany does not own Britain or France; they are of a much more similar size and balance each other off. The EEC members have safety in numbers. They have well-established cultures reaching back a thousand years, as well as language barriers that protect those cultures, something that most of Canada does not have with the United States.

Canadians were reminded that they were a trading nation and told that the FTA would increase Canada's trade. But while there may be more intracorporate transfers across the border between GM of Canada and GM of Detroit, between IBM of Canada and IBM of New York, genuine arm's-length trade will actually decrease. Canada will have less trade with other countries as it becomes more and more tied to the United States. The Canadian standard of living will drop as workers find themselves competing with the wages of Mexico and the southern states.

Canadian farmers already have a good deal of experience with what happens under free trade. Since 1944, Canada has had free trade with the United States in farm machinery. Cheaper farm machinery was not the result. What happened instead is that Canada lost its largest manufacturing industry: major farm equipment manufacturing. Massey Harris, later Massey Ferguson, Canada's greatest multinational, once led the world in farm-machinery technology. Today a shell of its former self, it is U.S. owned and has moved its head office to Buffalo. Versatile Tractor of Winnipeg once had 25 percent of the North American market for four-wheel drive tractors. It has since been sold to Ford-New Holland of Pennsylvania. The forces of free trade have irresistibly taken Canada's major farm machinery industry and transferred it south of the border, where the bigger markets are, and now American corporations ship their farm equipment into Canada.

Virtual free trade in beef has existed for many years between the United States and Canada. When the price in the United States is a couple of cents per pound higher, the cattle trucks take Canadian beef south of the border, drop it off there, and drive down the price to the American farmer. When the Canadian price is a little higher, the trucks come over the line with American beef and drive down the Canadian price. That's how free trade works in this case.

Another myth advanced, with great repetition, is that foreign investment is good for Canada and provides jobs for Canadians, and that it doesn't matter who owns the country. Economists told Canadians not to be "scared" to compete, that a global flow of capital benefits everyone. It was quite something to see these individuals — almost all securely tenured university professors who don't compete with anyone for their generous monthly pay cheque, courtesy of the taxpayers — lecture farmers, fishers, factory workers, secretaries and business people. Increased American competition would be good for them, these academics said, and a reality they should learn to adjust to. A fatal flaw in the argument of these economists was their refusal to grapple with or even acknowledge the issue of foreign investment, which means foreign ownership and foreign control. Classical free trade between two nations, each owning its economy, might be possible and beneficial to each. Free trade between two nations, one already largely owned by the other, is another matter. Free trade in these circumstances is impossible.

Again, American corporations don't invest in Canada to provide Canadians with jobs; they are here to increase their profits, sales and employment at home. In the period 1978-85, almost 900,000 new jobs were created in Canada by *Canadian-controlled companies,* while foreign companies decreased their employment in Canada. A study by University of Alberta economists T.L. Powrie and M.A. Gormley, "The Contribution of Foreign Capital to Canadian Economic Growth," showed that if no outside capital at all had entered Canada between 1950 and 1976, at worst the Canadian standard of living would have been 98.7 percent of its actual level. This study did not even deal with branch-plant neglect of export opportunities or certain other aspects of foreign investment that damage the Canadian economy.

It is foreign ownership that lies at the very root of Canada's economic problems. If the economy were not faced with a huge drain of profits and opportunities to the United States, the standard of living and quality of life of the vast majority of Canadians would be substantially higher.

Another myth consisted of rewriting the history of free-trade agreements elsewhere in the world. Canadians were urged "not to worry," that historically, under free-trade agreements, the smaller partner usually comes out the winner. The record, however, shows just the opposite.

THE U.S. ARMY INVADED Puerto Rico July 25, 1898. Puerto Rico was then governed under U.S. military occupation for two years while U.S. legislators debated its future. On April 2, 1900, Senator Bate of Tennessee asked the Senate: "What is to become of the Philippines and Puerto Rico? Are they to become States with representation here from those countries, from that heterogeneous mass of mongrels that make up their citizenship? That is objectionable to the people of this country, as it ought to be."

Senator Joseph Foraker of Ohio responded that Puerto Rico and other territories were indispensable because: "We have reached the point in the development of our resources and the multiplication of our industries where we are not only supplying our home demands, but are producing a large surplus ... Our greatest present and prospective commercial need is for markets abroad. We cannot find them in the countries of Europe. Their demand upon us is limited. They strive to supply themselves and to compete with us in the markets of the world."[1]

Foraker came up with a solution: not statehood, and not territories (a step towards statehood). They should be "possessions." The *Foraker Act*, passed in 1900, provided for a government to be appointed by the U.S. president, with Washington retaining the right of veto over any Puerto Rican legislation. Puerto Rican males with a certain income level were allowed to vote for a "resident commissioner" who could sit in the U.S. House of Representatives with a voice, but no vote. And the *Foraker Act* imposed free trade between the United States and Puerto Rico.

In 1917 it was time to update the *Foraker Act* — there had been efforts by Puerto Ricans to obtain their independence. In the debate over the successor to the *Foraker Act*, called the *Jones Act*, Congressman Cooper of Wisconsin said: "We are never to give up Puerto Rico for, now that we have completed the Panama Canal, the retention of the island becomes very important to the safety of the Canal, and in that way to the safety of the nation itself. It helps to make the Gulf of Mexico an American lake."[2]

The *Jones Act* came up with a solution to quash Puerto Rican nationalism. It imposed U.S. citizenship on Puerto Ricans, but kept in place most of the provisions of the *Foraker Act*, including the U.S. veto and the authority of the U.S. Congress to legislate over all Puerto

Rican matters not purely of a local nature. Although denied full U.S. constitutional rights and still denied any vote in the U.S. Congress, Puerto Ricans would be taxed and drafted into the U.S. Army. The *Jones Act* passed in February 1917. Four months later, President Woodrow Wilson ordered the registration and recruitment of Puerto Rican men from ages 21 to 31 into the U.S. armed forces, where they were sent to the European war that the United States had just entered. Puerto Ricans who renounced U.S. citizenship and attempted to retain their Puerto Rican citizenship were divested of all political rights. The great Puerto Rican orator and independence fighter, José de Diego, described the *Jones Act*:

> Never was anything like this seen before, in ... international law, in the democratic nations of the world: one million, two hundred thousand human beings, who by law of the Congress of a Republic — which seems more like an order from the times of the Low Empire — are deprived of their national citizenship, but ... are obliged to carry all the burdens of the state and to render military tribute to the dominating nation ... Puerto Ricans, who for a crime unknown as yet in universal law — love of their own citizenship — are reduced to the condition of foreigners in their own country, are exiled from their land ... *No* must be and is the only word which will preserve the liberty and dignity of the peoples in servitude.[3]

By 1931, the United States was taking 95 percent of Puerto Rico's exports and providing 90 percent of its imports. Political leader Luis Muñoz Marín said in 1929 that Puerto Rico had become "a land of beggars and millionaires, of flattering statistics and distressing realities. More and more it becomes a factory worked by peons, fought over by lawyers, bossed by absent industrialists, and clerked by politicians. It is now Uncle Sam's second largest sweatshop."[4]

By 1980 the island was the largest per capita export market of the United States and its fourth-largest customer overall. Today, Puerto Rico exists as a political, cultural and economic colony of the United States. The United States controls all aspects of Puerto Rico's defence, foreign policy, and even its postage and currency. Its youth have been drafted for, and have fought in numerous U.S. wars, including the Second World War, Vietnam and the Gulf War, where they have died in disproportionately higher numbers than Americans who can vote in U.S. elections.

The *Jones Act*, which remains in effect today, stipulates Puerto Rico can have no role in negotiating U.S. trade treaties, even though it is bound by them. Thus, at the beginning of the Canada-U.S. FTA, Puerto Rico is listed as a customs territory of the United States of America and bound by its terms. Canada has a free-trade agreement with a country that had no say in the matter whatsoever.

THE HAWAIIAN KINGDOM was a monarchy throughout the 1800s. After 1840 it had a written constitution and was recognized as an independent country both by the United States and by the European powers. In the early 1880s, the American whaling fleets began wintering in Hawaii. U.S. traders and adventurers followed the earlier arrival of New England missionaries.

In 1876, Hawaii signed a ten-year free-trade agreement with the United States, to gain secure access to the U.S. market for its sugar. Ten years later, Hawaii was dependent on the U.S. market and desperate to renew the pact. The Americans agreed to renew on condition that they receive exclusive rights to Pearl Harbor and a commitment that Hawaii never sign a trade agreement with any other country. With these conditions secured, the treaty was renewed for a further ten years. In 1890, the United States allowed sugar from all countries to enter duty free, and it announced a two-cent preference for U.S. growers. The Hawaiian economy began to suffer. Annexation would end the discrimination against Hawaiian products, said some of the American growers who by now controlled most of Hawaii's sugar production.

American businessmen and lawyers staged a revolt in 1893 and were backed by U.S. troops, who landed from the American cruiser *USS Boston*. Hawaii's Queen Liliuokalani fought back under the rallying cry "Hawaii for Hawaiians," but she was overthrown. The U.S. minister in Honolulu, John Stevens, hoisted the American flag and wrote his State Department: "The Hawaiian pear is now fully ripe, and this is the golden hour for the United States to pluck it."[5] A delegation of "Hawaiians" from the new government — four Americans and one Englishman — rushed to Washington and asked for annexation. Within a month, a "hastily drawn, hastily signed and hastily submitted" treaty of annexation was on the floor of the U.S. Senate.[6] The new government, under Sanford Dole, proclaimed a republic and was immediately recognized by the United States.

U.S. President Grover Cleveland, troubled by the blatant and clearly illegal action, withdrew the treaty of annexation and sent a commission of inquiry to Hawaii. The commission found the evidence of what had happened "so damning as measurably to dampen the annexation craze in America."[7] Cleveland gave instructions for the deposed queen to be put back on the throne if she promised to deal leniently with the Americans who had overthrown her government. The queen's calm reply was that she would first have their heads and then their property.

The Americans in control in Hawaii refused to give an inch. A new president, William McKinley, soon replaced Cleveland, and the annexation treaty proceeded. When the Japanese protested that annexation would upset the status quo in the Pacific and put in danger Japanese residents in Hawaii, the State Department replied that annexation was the logical conclusion to seventy years of U.S. association with Hawaii.

In 1898, the American Congress, by a joint resolution, simply annexed Hawaii. The Hawaiians were never given a vote on whether or not they wanted to become a part of the United States, because, as President McKinley explained: "We need Hawaii just as much and a great deal more than we did California. It is manifest destiny." On the passing of the resolution, McKinley mused: "Annexation is not change; it is consummation."[8]

The American representatives travelled to Hawaii, and in 1898, in a heart-wrenching scene, the Hawaiian flag was lowered for the last time and the American flag raised. The United States thereafter governed Hawaii as a territory. Hawaiians were forced to pay U.S taxes, yet they lacked representation in Congress. Some began to demand statehood. Others attempted to revive the fight for independence. In 1959, Hawaii was finally made a state.

THE UNITED STATES signed a free-trade agreement with Israel in 1984. The Israeli communications minister said after the signing that the Israeli economy had become totally dependent on U.S. good will. "We have very little maneuvering room nor the power to say no to specific requests from the United States," he said. Under the terms of the treaty, Israel had to discuss with the United States any new industrial measures it wished to take and, after 1990, obtain U.S. consent before introducing any new industrial policies of its own. In 1987, the Israeli trade minister approached the

Americans to reopen the deal because Israel was having so many problems with it. The U.S. reply came from Kelly Winkler, spokesman for Clayton Yeutter's office. "We believe the agreement is running well and there aren't any sticking points that we particularly want to discuss."

In October 1987, Pinhas Dror, the Israeli embassy's top trade official in Washington, commented on the Canada-U.S. Free Trade Agreement: "All in all, if someone puts together what Canada gave up and what the United States gave up, my own personal opinion is that the Canadians gave up 100 times more."[9]

22

Closure on Christmas Eve

ON NOVEMBER 21, 1988, in a historic election viewed by the nation as a referendum on the Canada-U.S. Free Trade Agreement, the pro-free-trade Conservatives received 43 percent of the vote. A full 57 percent of the voters cast their ballots against Mulroney; 53.5 percent voted for political parties opposed to the FTA.

In only 85 ridings of the 295 across the country did the Conservatives receive a majority of votes. In Saskatchewan, 62 percent voted against them, in Ontario 59 percent, in the Northwest Territories 69 percent. In only two provinces, Alberta and Quebec, was the vote in favour of free trade greater than the vote of those opposed. Even Quebec, pounded by more pro-free-trade propaganda than any other part of Canada, and with both provincial parties — the Liberals and the Parti Québécois — working for Mulroney, voted 44 percent against Mulroney.

In the election of 1891, free trade was defeated 52 percent against to 47 percent in favour. In 1911 it was defeated 51.2 percent to 47.8 percent. In 1988, the most decisive rejection of free trade took place in our history — over 1.2 million more voted against it than for it. This, despite massive intervention by U.S. corporations in the election and widespread electoral abuse, including the denial of the vote to an "unusually large" number of people, according to a damning report by Jean-Marc Hamel, Canada's chief electoral officer.[1] The total estimate of government and corporate spending to promote the FTA exceeded $56 million.

Shortly after the election, in a highly unusual Christmas sitting, the House of Commons was recalled to deal with a single piece of business: the passing of the free-trade legislation in time to meet the January 1, 1989, implementation deadline. As John Crosbie said: "The Government does not propose to start a new relationship with the United States by asking it to do us a favour"

207

by extending the deadline.[2]

Against the expressed will of the majority of the population, the Conservatives rammed the FTA, their economic union bill, through the House of Commons by repeatedly using closure and riding roughshod over every rule that stood in their way. Ed Broadbent, the leader of the NDP, told the House he "was shocked that immediately following the election ... the first act of the Government should be in fact to tear up the rule book of Parliament."[3] On December 15, 1988, Liberal leader John Turner, his blue eyes blazing, pointed his finger at the prime minister across the floor and delivered a scorching analysis of the election:

> We were winning the election and then two things happened. I believe that all Canadians and the House had better come to grips with it. There was the unprecedented intervention of big business with millions of dollars in an advertising campaign in support of the deal ... They could not attack the message because the message was winning, so they attacked the messenger ... they mounted an unprecedented personal attack on my character, on my sincerity, and on my competence ... It was nothing short of the Americanization of Canadian politics, as the Government wants to Americanize everything else in this country ... It was the most vicious campaign in Canadian history ... In this campaign through the tactics of the Government, we saw democracy stripped of its majesty ... I say to the prime minister that you have a tarnished mandate, a sullied victory. You bought an election and you sold out the country ... we are now about to be absorbed remorselessly into the American orbit ...[4]

Finally, in the small hours of Christmas Eve, the free-trade legislation was forced through the House. The majority of Canadians, who had voted against the FTA, were stunned and angry. How could this happen in a country that calls itself democratic?

NINETEEN EIGHTY-EIGHT WAS CANADA'S first free-trade election to involve three national political parties — and the two main opposition parties fought each other as if it were an ordinary election instead of a referendum on the country's future. Mulroney won the election only because the opposition parties split the anti-free-trade vote. If the Liberals and the NDP had run a joint campaign in defence of Canada by not running candidates against each other, the Conservatives would not have taken a single seat in Saskatchewan and would have won only two seats in B.C. In all of Atlantic Canada, one seat would have gone to the Conservatives. In Ontario, eight seats out of ninety-nine would have gone to Mulroney, instead of the forty-six he received. The day after the election, the opposition parties would have been sitting on the governing side of the House — John Turner as prime minister, Ed Broadbent as deputy prime minister — and together they would have had 210 seats. The Conservatives would have been in opposition, the free-trade deal buried and Mulroney gone into oblivion. This scenario would have been a more accurate reflection of the will of Canadians.

But instead, the opposition parties attacked each other in the election, split the anti-free-trade vote and let Mulroney come up the middle for a majority of seats in Canada's archaic and deeply flawed voting system.

It further helped the pro-free-trade forces that, at a crucial moment in the election campaign, the NDP turned its attack on John Turner instead of Brian Mulroney. The NDP had earlier, in July 1988, also slammed the Senate, which in response to widespread public demand had blocked passage of the free-trade bill to give Canadians a vote on the biggest issue in the history of the country, something Mulroney had no intention of doing. The Senate was "undemocratic" to block legislation from the House of Commons, the NDP said,[5] even though the same NDP eleven months earlier had asked the Senate to block the Drug Patent bill and eighteen months later would ask the same Senate to block a newly introduced goods and services tax, the GST. It turns out that the NDP election campaign, which had systematically downplayed the free-trade issue, was guided throughout by an American pollster, Fingerhut/Madison Opinion Research of Washington, D.C. (pollster for both the American Federation of Labor and the Democratic Party). Interviewed after the election, president Vic Fingerhut defended his advice to the NDP to downplay the free-trade issue, saying that Canadians were not interested in talking about sovereignty during an election campaign. At the same time, he was advising the Democrats that trade issues have an "incredible potency."[6]

On November 22, the day after the election, NDP leader Ed Broadbent declared that the fight against the FTA was over, that

Brian Mulroney "has been given a clear mandate" to proceed with
it, and that it would be "churlish and inappropriate" for the NDP
to stand in his way. "The agreement with all of its faults has been
approved by the people. It would not be appropriate to oppose it
now," he told the nation.[7] The NDP's repeated campaign promise
to fight harder than the Liberals against the FTA had suddenly
vanished, along with the hopes of millions of Canadians. (Within
a matter of months, Mulroney appointed Broadbent to head the
new International Center for Human Rights and Democratic
Development, with a $15 million budget and a personal annual
salary of over $100,000. This centre had been approved in
principle just prior to the election.)

A few hours later, Liberal leader John Turner stepped to the
microphones and threw in the towel. "The cause of my life," he
had told voters only days earlier, was to defeat the FTA. Now his
words were: "The people have decided. So, having stated our case,
we'll let matters proceed."[8]

In fact, even after November 21, 1988, it would not have been
too late to stop the free-trade bill. If, after Mulroney forced it
through the House in December, John Turner and Ed Broadbent
had joined forces to ask the Senate once again to block the FTA
on behalf of the majority of Canadians, and if Canada's labour
union leadership had supported this call by mobilizing thousands
of members outside the Parliament buildings the day of the Senate
vote, the fight against the FTA, instead of ending, would have
gained new momentum.

The Senate had the power, the right and the duty to conduct
full-scale national public hearings, giving Canadians, the
majority of whom still did not know what was in the agreement,
a chance to discover what the FTA contained. The most sweeping,
far-reaching, economic integration pact in Canadian history, and
perhaps between two countries anywhere in the world, had been
forced through the House of Commons by an unprecedented
reliance on closure. No public hearings had been held on the
final text. Instead of organizing those hearings, which would have
provided the delay necessary to mobilize further against the
agreement, the Liberal Party leadership suffered a failure of nerve.
Canadians witnessed the abject spectacle of the Liberal senators,
shortly before New Year's Eve, lacking the strength to lift their
arms to vote as the bill transferring control of Canada to
Washington passed without a single opposition vote. They

abstained. Simply by casting their votes in opposition, the Liberal majority could have prevented its passage.

By giving up the day after the election and by conceding Mulroney had a mandate for the FTA, the Liberals and New Democrats betrayed the electors who voted for them. In essence, their behaviour enabled Brian Mulroney to deliver Canada to the United States. The worst blow for many was not the rather transparent fact that Mr. Mulroney and his American backers had "bought an election," but that both opposition parties, who had promised to fight, collapsed at a crucial moment. The majority of Canadians were left with no voice in Canada's national Parliament on the most important issue facing the country.

23

The First Four Years

Jobs, Jobs, Jobs

FROM 1985 TO 1988, Prime Minister Mulroney promised continually that the FTA would create "new wealth and new jobs" for Canada — he predicted 500,000 new jobs.[1] Instead, in the first three years of free trade, 1.4 million jobs disappeared. More than 500,000 manufacturing jobs were wiped out — over 24 percent of the entire manufacturing sector — and the numbers continued to climb. Plant closures continued relentlessly, the casualties including some of the best known manufacturers in Canada: Inglis, Gillette, Northern Telecom, Burlington Carpet, Campbell's Soup, Canada Packers, Fleck Manufacturing, Midas Muffler, Allied Chemicals, Colgate, Kellogg's. Most involved not temporary layoffs, but permanent job losses in the manufacturing sector, the engine of a nation's economy. Archie McLean, vice-president of McCain's Foods, in 1990 testified to the Senate Committee on Foreign Affairs that free trade would cost 100,000 to 150,000 jobs in the Canadian agri-food industry alone. In one six-month period of 1990, ninety-seven Ontario plants closed their doors or scaled down production; in the first seven months of 1992, at least eighty-six plants shut down permanently. By May 1992, over 28 percent of Ontario's manufacturing sector had disappeared in just over three years. Some free-trade promoters rushed to blame the "global recession" and announced the FTA was not responsible; others fell uncharacteristically silent. The Canadian government told anyone who would listen that, contrary to public misconception, free trade was actually helping Canada cope with the recession. The facts speak otherwise. In the first four years of the FTA, the United States lost 6 percent of its manufacturing base; Canada, at over 24 percent, lost four times this amount of its manufacturing sector. By September 1992, Canada had the highest number of unemployed in its history, while companies were moving in record numbers to the United States and to the Mexican Maquiladoras. *

As early as July 1989, the U.S. magazine *Business Week,* in an article entitled "The Trade Pact Is Turning into a One-Way Street — So Far," reported: "Canadian executives are rushing across the border to set up manufacturing bases in what they see as a more hospitable climate ... Rather than doing east-west business across tremendous distances, Canadian companies are looking south ... Canada's integration into a continental-scale economy is accelerating."[2] B.C. millionaire Jim Pattison said: "We're taking everything we've got and pushing into the United States ... I keep telling our people to forget the border — it doesn't exist anymore."[3] Frank Stronach of Magna International, who had been an energetic opponent of the FTA and joined John Turner's anti-free-trade campaign as a Liberal candidate, explained in 1990 that some of the financial problems of his company, the largest auto-parts producer in Canada, had to do with being too good a corporate citizen; he had not relocated factories quickly enough into Mexico and the United States.

More than twenty U.S. states have opened offices in Canada, advising companies how to move south and offering incentives for them to do so. Some of these inducements include lower interest rates; lower gas and electricity rates; paid travel costs between Canada and the United States for training; tax credits of up to $2000 for each new job created; training costs for employees; and lower employer costs for employee benefits, workers' compensation and unemployment insurance. Several states such as Alabama, Arizona, Florida, Louisiana, South Carolina, Tennessee and Mississippi have no minimum wage; others have a minimum hourly wage as low as $1.60. Mississippi offers industrial wages as low as $3.85 per hour, with one week of unpaid holidays per year and three paid statutory holidays. It doesn't snow in Mississippi, and a plant can be constructed for less than half the cost of building one in Canada.

Canadian truckers, forced to compete directly with U.S. fleets using cheaper fuel, better tax write-offs and lower-priced equipment, are

---

* Maquiladoras: In 1965, the United States and Mexico set up the Border Industrialization Program, designating a 20-kilometre strip south of the U.S.-Mexican border as a special free-trade zone, known as "Maquiladoras," where American or other foreign companies could bring in their parts and components, assemble them with Mexican labour and then re-export the finished product to the United States without payment of duties on either side, apart from a small value-added tax paid to Mexico.

being driven out of business. Furniture plants, swamped by U.S. imports, are going broke or moving to the United States. As a result of the first FTA Dispute Settlement Panel ruling, American processors can now buy B.C. fish right off the boats of Canadian fishermen for processing in the United States. Previously, the fish had to be landed in Canada. The entire fish-processing industry in B.C., involving 5000 jobs and the livelihood of coastal communities from Vancouver to Prince Rupert, is at risk. Prior to the election, Gordon Cummings of National Sea Products promoted free trade across Atlantic Canada, promising that his company would expand its operations if the public voted for free trade. Instead, massive plant closings by fish companies have included National Sea.

Gordon Ritchie, Canada's deputy chief free-trade negotiator, admitted in 1990 that the deluge of promises about jobs made prior to the election was false. "The free-trade agreement will not be a major creator of jobs," Ritchie said. "That was a specious claim made in the middle of an election campaign."[4]

Complete Nonsense

ONE WEEK BEFORE the 1988 election, Prime Minister Brian Mulroney dramatically vowed to Canadians: "Never would I sign an accord that would have the effect of threatening my own mother's old-age pension and social benefits. Not now, not ever. You have my commitment as prime minister of Canada and as a son whose mother counts on her pension and her medicare. I would never sign a treaty that would jeopardize social programs." Two weeks earlier, Finance Minister Michael Wilson proclaimed indignantly: "John Turner ... said he [Mulroney] has agreed to let the Americans have a say in the future of our social programs such as unemployment insurance and medicare. I say to Mr. Turner that is a lie."

Simon Reisman was categorical: "There is no threat of any kind to our medicare, old-age pensions or other social programs."[5] And John Crosbie was vehement, even the suggestion that his government would make cuts to the unemployment insurance program after the election was "complete nonsense ... You're damned right ... absolutely no."[6]

Almost immediately following the election, $3.3 billion was slashed from the unemployment insurance (UI) system, and all federal contributions ended, thus removing any financial incentive for the federal government to reduce unemployment. These fundamental changes, along with the 1993 amendments to deny benefits to anyone who quits his or her job without what the government deems "just cause," brought Canada's UI program more in line with American practice, which covers only 30 percent of the unemployed as compared with 80 percent in Canada. The U.S. unemployment insurance system has no government contributions, and the Americans had complained that Canadian federal contributions were an unfair subsidy to Canadian companies.

As for medicare, the federal government, by Bill C-96, passed in 1986 and amended in 1989, is essentially getting out of the program. By or soon after the year 2000, medicare's funding and direction will be largely left to the mercy of the provinces. Ottawa will no longer be able to use its funding clout to enforce national standards or, as an example, act as it did in the early 1980s to stop extra billing. Provinces have responded to these funding cutbacks by closing hospital beds and privatizing some health services. As these cutbacks progress, more services covered by medicare will be dropped, becoming available only through American medical insurance companies.

There is no universal medicare in the United States, and 37 million Americans have no health insurance at all. In Canada, 80 percent of the unemployed are entitled to unemployment insurance, and all receive medicare; in contrast, 70 percent of the U.S. unemployed have neither. It costs a U.S. automotive employer almost $9000 per employee for medical insurance benefits. In Canada, medicare means the same employer pays perhaps $2000 per employee.

As trade expert Mel Clark explains: "The FTA provisions combine to establish a high risk that sooner or later U.S. companies will initiate countervail actions against Canadian exports by alleging that Medicare grants a subsidy. Such actions will accelerate the privatization of Medicare just as the threat of U.S. countervailing duties was a reason — possibly the dominant reason — why the Mulroney government stopped contributing to Unemployment Insurance ... The FTA will result in the Americanization and privatization of medicare."[7] In June 1992, three and a half years into the Free Trade Agreement, Newfoundland's minister of health, Chris Decker, said: "I've resigned myself to the fact we will have 10 or 12 balkanized health-care systems in the country."[8]

Monique Bégin, former minister of health, summed it up: "Free trade is a direct threat to one of the five basic conditions of medicare ... If a hospital is run by an American business for profit, who in the hospital will protect universality, accessibility and comprehensiveness? ... Free trade will ... reinforce the various segments of Canadian society, including some provincial governments, which would prefer to see medicine privatized as much as possible. All too soon, Canadians will have a two class health-care system: one for those who can afford it, another for the rest."[9]

Expected Fewer Hassles

THE GOVERNMENT PROMISED secure, unrestricted access to the U.S. market if Canada entered this deal. Instead, Canada has faced more U.S. trade harassment since 1989 than before the deal was signed. Steel, durum wheat, fish, lobsters, softwood lumber, shingles, raspberries, ice cream, yogurt, beer and other exports have faced U.S. trade actions. Potatoes and meat have been held up at the border, and automobiles, magnesium and sugar have been targeted. Prior to the FTA, 90 percent of Canada's lumber exports to the United States were duty free. Now, B.C. and Quebec exports to the United States face charges of about 20 percent, and Prairie exports, over 6 percent.

Free-trade promoters repeatedly claimed that disputes would be settled much more quickly if Canada signed the FTA. The GATT dispute-settlement process, they complained, was too slow. In practice, pork, Canada's biggest agri-food export to the United States, was tied up for over two years by American countervail action. After spending millions of dollars in legal fees, the industry succeeded only in restoring the situation that existed before the free-trade deal was in place. The final ruling took twenty-eight months — more than twice as long as the average period for a GATT dispute ruling (nine to twelve months) and far more expensive to the industry — yet it was touted by the government as a "major victory" for the FTA.

The FTA makes Canadian exports much more open to U.S. harassment, not less. Section 409 of the U.S. implementing legislation authorizes the president to take steps to attain "increased and more effective discipline on those Canadian Government (including provincial) subsidies having the most significant adverse impact on United States producers." The section goes on to invite any U.S. industry, or any entity, "including a trade association, firm, certified or recognized union, or group of workers, that is representative of a United States industry," which believes it faces, or "is likely to face," subsidized competition from Canada, to file a petition for investigation and action by U.S. authorities against Canada. This clause makes it easier for any U.S. industry to take a trade action against Canada than against any other GATT country. Under GATT rules, section 409 would be illegal.

However, under the FTA, U.S. trade actions against Canada are now governed by U.S. law instead of by the GATT. The Americans are free to change their trade law at will, and have already done so to Canada's detriment on two occasions since the FTA was signed. All the dispute panel can do when American countervailing and anti-dumping actions are brought against Canada is to determine whether the United States applied its own law correctly. Furthermore, legal fees for a Canadian company to get a FTA panel ruling can exceed $10 million. There are no such charges under the GATT, because the Department of External Affairs fights these cases on behalf of a Canadian industry.

All these factors put increased pressure on Canadian companies simply to relocate to the United States to avoid the threat of harassment. So much for the repeated promises by Mr. Mulroney and the rest of his government that Canada would have tariff-free trade and secure access to the biggest, richest market in the world.

Don Mazankowski, as minister of agriculture, acknowledged these developments in a moment of candor, February 9, 1990: "With the advent of the trade agreement with the United States we expected fewer hassles, not more."[10]

Cheaper Goods

A NATIONWIDE ADVERTSING blitz guaranteed Canadians that they could expect cheaper goods and services with free trade. There would be, the government pledged, "about $800" in "average annual savings" for middle-income families. "The cost of establishing and furnishing a home will decline by as much as $8000."[11] Pre-election government brochures featured pictures of smiling shoppers pushing shopping carts overflowing with consumer goods at lower prices.

Instead, after the election prices rose, and shortly after the FTA came into force the government imposed a goods and services tax (GST) of 7 percent on most transactions in the country.

There were two main reasons for the GST. First, the federal government had to replace the billions of dollars lost in revenue with the phase out of tariffs under free trade. By the time the free-trade deal is fully implemented in 1998, this loss of tariff revenue to the

Canadian government will, according to retired judge Marjorie Montgomery Bowker, amount to $24 billion. Secondly, the previously existing manufacturers' sales tax (MST), a tax at the manufacturer's level since 1924, was a slight disadvantage to Canadian companies when compared against American manufacturers. To keep any companies operating domestically under the FTA, Canadian corporate taxation cannot diverge significantly from that in the United States. So the MST was replaced by a tax on the general public, who cannot move across the border quite as easily. According to a conservative estimate the GST annually transfers more than $4 billion in taxes directly from corporations to the backs of consumers. And once a province adds its sales tax on top of the GST (a tax on a tax), as five provinces now do, the disposable income of Canadians is cut by an average of 5 to 7 percent. That's as long as the GST stays at 7 percent. So much for the promise of cheaper goods and services.

Some "cheaper goods" are instead being bought in the United States. Cross-border shopping — which was up 400 percent in the first year of free trade in B.C.'s lower mainland — has devastated businesses in Vancouver, Thunder Bay, Windsor and hundreds of other municipalities within driving distance of the border. The Canadian Federation of Independent Business, an organization that promoted the FTA, in June 1992 released a survey estimating that cross-border shopping was costing the Canadian economy $10.4 billion a year and about 250,000 full-time and part-time jobs. The efforts to stem this drain have failed because no attempt has dealt with the underlying cause, namely the FTA. Cross-border shopping eased somewhat in early 1993, only because a fall in the Canadian dollar made it less attractive.

Beating the Americans

CANADIAN COMPANIES WILL flourish with free access to the huge, rich market in the United States, free-trade proponents prophesied. Consolidated Bathurst, the pulp and paper giant, was repeatedly cited as an example of a Canadian company that would benefit from free trade, and Robert Campeau and the Reichmanns were held up as model Canadian entrepreneurs who knew how to beat the Americans at their own game. This was something all Canadians could aspire to under free trade. They just had to shed their timidity, fear of competition, and inferiority complex, and seize the once-in-a-lifetime opportunity being extended to them. As John Crosbie blustered in December 1987: "We can move into the U.S., which is the biggest free market in the world and we can compete in it and we can win! ... We don't think there is an American in the world who can beat us."[12]

Less than three years later, Mr Campeau was apologizing to his shareholders for the bankruptcy of his companies, Consolidated Bathurst was owned by Stone of Chicago, and the Reichmanns would soon be applying to the courts for bankruptcy protection. Takeovers of Canadian companies, mostly by U.S. corporations, in the first year of free trade were up 400 percent. They have continued unabated. Personal and business bankruptcies — another index of the economic climate — rose to record levels. As employment vanished, more than one million Canadian adults and children turned to food banks to feed themselves.

Some of the above problems were, of course, due to the recession, but Canada's recession was free-trade driven. Unlike previous economic downturns, Canada entered this recession before the United States, and was hit much harder. Previous recessions, such as 1982, ended when temporarily shut-down plants recalled workers and recommenced production; permanently closed plants that have moved to the United States can do neither.

Some select companies are doing well under the FTA — those that have either diverted operations to the United States and those who have found a niche for themselves in the U.S. market — but they are the exception rather than the rule. The larger point is that Canadian workers, industry and technology have the potential to be something far greater than supplicants to fill niches in the United States.

Canada Gains a Trade Deficit

ADVOCATES OF FREE TRADE said the agreement would increase trade, making Canada and Canadians richer. When the trade talks started, Canada had a trade surplus with the United States of $20 billion in goods; that is, it sold the U.S. $20 billion more in goods (lumber, automobiles, steel, oil, etc.) each year than it bought from them. With the introduction of free trade, this surplus dropped dramatically, while the Canadian deficit in services (tourism, transportation charges, management fees, etc.) soared. In 1989, the first year of free trade, Canada's trade performance was the worst in its history. By 1992, its trade surplus in goods with the United States had dropped 50 percent from 1987, while its deficit in services had risen to the point that Canada's overall trade balance with the world had plunged from a surplus before the FTA, to a serious deficit.

Recently, the Canadian government has pointed to an increase in exports to the United States as proof that the FTA is working. Incredibly, defenders of the FTA don't refer to the much greater increase in imports from the United States that occurred at the same time. Yet it's the balance that counts.

As John L. Orr, former assistant deputy minister in the then federal Department of Industry explained in a 1992 analysis of the FTA: "the true criterion of trade performance must be the trade balance rather than export growth alone." Referring to Canada's total world trade, Orr wrote:

> [A]lthough cumulative exports of goods and services for the first three years of Free Trade increased by $47.1 billion (compared with the preceding three year period), imports grew by $77.6 billion over the same period. Thus the principal accomplishment of the FTA has been to expand imports at a rate almost 65% greater than that of exports, resulting in a cumulative trade deficit of $30.5 billion since January 1989 ...
>
> The drastic reversal of Canada's trade balance from surplus to deficit was directly reflected by a progressive decline in total employment and a corresponding rise in unemployment ...
>
> Correspondingly, Canada's Gross Domestic Product declined from a growth rate of +4.7% in 1988 to a negative growth of -1.5% in 1991.[13]

Orr concludes: "By every measure, Free Trade with the U.S. has had a negative impact on the Canadian economy in every year since its inception ... Undoubtedly, the FTA has greatly worsened the impact of the global recession in Canada."

At about the same time, an *Interim Assessment* by the U.S. Department of Commerce in 1992 called the FTA "one of the truly bright spots on the economic horizon," which, it continued, "has allowed American exporters to make important gains in the Canadian market ... The strong growth in exports to Canada since the inception of the CFTA [Canada-U.S. Free Trade Agreement] has important ramifications for the American economy, especially job creation.

According to one Department of Commerce formula, U.S. exports to Canada may have accounted for almost two million jobs in 1991. This includes 28,000 jobs created between 1990 and 1991, job growth which has softened the impact of the recession on the U.S. economy."[14]

It is hardly a triumph for the FTA that, to pay for growing American imports, Canada is shipping immense and increasing amounts of raw materials across the border at fire-sale prices.

Resource Grab

THE AMERICANS HAVE moved quickly to sign up Canadian resources at bargain-basement prices. Ninety percent of Canada's Arctic gas is now under contract to American corporations, and the implications are staggering. During a shortage in Canada, the Americans, under articles 409 and 904 of the FTA, have the right to take the same proportion of any "good," including all forms of energy, that they were taking before the shortage. If they increase their take of Canada's total supply of natural gas to 90 percent for three years and then a shortage developed, Canadians would have the right to the remaining 10 percent.

Canadian energy and resources have been signed away so completely that within a very short time Canadians could be begging for access to their own supplies. Instead of Canadian self-sufficiency, the catch phrase has become "North American" self-sufficiency, with Canada's needs ranking far down the ladder. Given that the United States imports 50 percent of its petroleum requirements, Canada will help increase U.S. self-sufficiency, and at prices so low that precious Canadian resources will be squandered in record time, instead of being conserved for future use in a climate that makes them vital.

A string of pulp and paper mills, many to serve the U.S. market, are already in operation, or in the planning and construction stage, across Saskatchewan and Alberta. These mills will have the capacity to clear-cut every tree in the northern half of these provinces, and yet most have gone ahead without any effective environmental impact assessment. The consequences are devastating for ecology and wildlife, and for the lives of northerners. At the moment of writing, a Native blockade, the longest in Canadian history, is under way north of Meadow Lake to stop clear-cutting of what remains of Saskatchewan's best forest. A viable way of life is being destroyed, and the local population is being increasingly driven onto welfare rolls in the city — all to deliver pulp to the Scott Paper Company in the United States to be made into toilet paper for the American market.

Adjacent to the northern Saskatchewan logging site, in May 1992 a group of hunters from New Jersey slaughtered black bear. In preparation for their visit, the American owner of the nearby fishing lodge had put out bait during the winter, to accustom the bears to coming around. With the arrival of the hunters, the animals were trapped and then shot. According to local Native hunters, 125 bears were killed for "sport" by a single hunting party in a previous year.

This mindless destruction of the wildlife and the forest is an outrage. The animals and the forest of the North are necessary to provide a decent living for the local Native inhabitants and are the treasured heritage of all Canadians; they are not a part of Canada to be sacrificed as blood sport for wealthy foreign thrill-seekers.

The proportional-sharing provisions of article 409 of the FTA apply to pulp and paper just as to oil and gas. Once these mills are operational, the United States can insist it continue to receive the same proportion of Canada's forest until all that remains are millions of acres of clear-cut devastation.

Water: "Squeamish Canadians"

MEANWHILE, AMERICAN PRESSURE is increasing for Canadian water. Water is one of Canada's most precious resources. Contrary to a common perception, Canada is not overendowed with water; it possesses 7 percent of the earth's land mass and 9 percent of its supply of renewable water. For years, powerful interests in the United States, among them the North American Water and Power Alliance (NAWAPA), a gigantic water-diversion project drawn up by Ralph Parsons, a Los Angeles engineering firm, to take Canadian waters south, have lobbied for vast water-diversion plans. A continent-wide series of dams and canals could redirect some of Canada's major rivers south, to satisfy the United States's fresh-water desires. With the FTA, these dreams have been brought a step closer to realization. Along with many existing dams, the recently constructed Old Man River dam in Alberta and the Rafferty-Alameda dams in Saskatchewan are placed in locations that will make possible the wholesale diversion of fresh water from Canada to the United States. The Old Man River dam can control the flow of mountain-fed water into the South Saskatchewan River, where it can be drawn off at the existing Diefenbaker dam, fed into the Qu'Appelle River, and then transferred to the Souris by a short canal or by pipe. Once in the Souris Valley, it flows naturally south across the border into North Dakota, from where it is easily transferable to the water-hungry southern states via the Missouri River system.

The size and structure of the Rafferty dam — built on a tiny stream without any secure source of water, and still dry some years after its construction — make little sense, except as part of a large water-diversion scheme such as the NAWAPA. General A.G.L. McNaughton, chairman of the Canadian section of the International Joint Commission from 1950 to 1962 and the man who fought valiantly against the sell-out of Canadian interests in the Columbia River Treaty signed in 1961, defined water exports as "a means of allowing the United States to develop beyond the limit of its resources on the basis of those belonging to another country."[15]

About the NAWAPA, McNaughton had this to say in 1967:

[This is] a monstrous concept, not only in terms of physical magnitude, but also in another and more sinister sense, in that the promoters would displace Canadian sovereignty over the national waters of Canada, and substitute therefore a diabolic thesis that *all* waters of North America become a shared resource, of which most will be drawn off for the benefit of the midwest and southwest regions of the United States, where existing desert areas will be made to bloom at the expense of development in Canada.[16]

Momentum is growing to revive the NAWAPA. In May 1992, in an interview in the Vancouver Sun, Francis Dale, formerly president Nixon's ambassador to the United Nations and now president of NAWAPA, said some Canadians are "squeamish" over the idea of water diversion. Dale, in Vancouver to promote the NAWAPA plan, told another interviewer that he was only asking Canadian governments to take a "non-emotional, scientific, detached look at this concept." He understood Canadian fears about giving up control of their water supplies, he explained, but that water does not belong to provinces, states or communities. Therefore, he said, B.C.'s water must be considered a "continental right" to be shared by the two countries.[17]

With more than 600 dams and sixty major diversions, Canada already diverts more water than the United States and the former Soviet Union combined. The social and ecological cost of these dams and diversions, in terms of environmental damage and human dislocation, is only beginning to be understood. Canada must not fall into the trap of supplying water to the United States. Once the United States depends on Canada for its water, that tap cannot be turned off without risking an invasion to force continued compliance.

Agriculture Endangered

PREMIERS DEVINE OF Saskatchewan, Getty of Alberta, Vander Zalm of B.C. and Bourassa of Quebec joined the federal government in promising that free trade would be good for agriculture and good for farmers.

Three years later, almost 20 percent of the farmers in Saskatchewan were facing foreclosure. Another 10 percent were in trouble — one out of every three farms in Canada's most agricultural province. Instead of the promised secure access to the American market, since the implementation of the FTA, Canadian agricultural products have faced a long list of U.S. trade actions. In response to the devastated agricultural economy, large protest rallies have been held across the Prairies. At these rallies, subsidized grain grown in Europe is often targeted as the source of Canadian farmers' problems.

But it is not European farmers, fighting for their own survival, who are to blame for the problems of Canadian agriculture. Rather it is the U. S. government, which in direct violation of a commitment made in article 701(4) of the FTA is using an Export Enhancement Program to give cash to its grain exporters to allow them to sell to foreign countries at lower prices. This highly subsidized grain is being sold to traditional customers of Canada, including Russia, Algeria and Egypt. A Philadelphia-based forecasting company (WEFA Group), in a 1992 analysis of the Export Enhancement Program, showed that these U.S. subsidies had cost Canadian farmers $1.5 billion in lost income between 1985 and 1991, and estimated they will lose the same amount again over the next three years.

Equally significant, the two-price system for wheat, in which domestic millers paid a higher price to Canadian farmers for wheat destined for Canadian consumption than for wheat for export, was one of the first casualties of the FTA. That change meant an annual income loss of over $400 million for wheat producers alone (the amount that Saskatchewan's Premier Grant Devine, a staunch promoter of the FTA, begged for, and received, from Ottawa as emergency assistance for farmers in the spring of 1990 — and his successor, Roy Romanow, continued to beg for annually).

Under the FTA, Canada, which produces some of the world's highest quality wheat — far more than it can consume domestically — has seen cheaper U.S. wheat flow into the country while Canadian grain sells for prices that, when inflation is considered, are the lowest in the country's history. Many American wheat fields are closer than Canada's to the flour mills in Ontario and Quebec, and the simple threat of bringing U.S. grain into the country has in many cases been sufficient to drive down the price of Canadian grain. By 1990, the Canadian Wheat Board, previously the sole marketing agency for Prairie wheat, oats and barley, had oats removed from its control. In early 1993, the government moved to do the same with barley.

Hog-processing companies, which promoted free trade vigorously before the election, promising expansion if the deal was passed and threatening layoffs if it wasn't, are closing or cutting back. Dairy and poultry producers are facing the virtual certainty that the restrictions on imports, which enable their marketing boards to function, will be lost, just as yogurt and ice cream quotas were dropped, allowing an influx of cheaper American products.

Conditions in the fruit and vegetable industry are, if anything, even more grim. Already 90 percent of the fresh vegetables sold in Canada come from the United States. And while American fruit pours across the border, Canadian producers are forced to pull out their trees and grape vines for lack of a market. The state of Washington, for example, using Canadian water courtesy of the Columbia River Treaty, has tripled its apple production since 1980. Canadian producers, whose return for apples is now a fraction of their cost of production, annually see over 100,000 tonnes of apples, mostly from the United States, freely enter Canada.

Deprived under the FTA of even seasonal tariff protection, both the producing and processing ends of the fruit and vegetable industry face extinction. Large U.S. companies, like Dole, control the market for produce, capitalizing on California's twelve-month growing season. The U.S. companies can afford to dump produce into Canada during its four-month growing season at prices below the cost of production. They eliminate their Canadian competitors and then, once the Canadian season is over, recoup their losses by raising prices. As a result, Canadian producers are driven out of business.

In 1991, lettuce producers in B.C. ploughed under 1.8 million heads — the equivalent of 75,000 cases of lettuce. They could not be sold because of the amount of American lettuce dumped into B.C. at prices far below the U.S. cost of production. In 1988, B.C. onion producers had obtained an anti-dumping ruling that the United States cannot send onions into B.C. at less than $5.38 for fifty pounds. George Rush, manager of the Cloverdale Lettuce and Vegetable Co-operative in B.C., tells the story; "To circumvent the ruling, U.S. shippers said to Canadian distributors, 'Buy at $5.38, and after the season is over we will give you and your family an all-expenses paid tour of Disneyland'; or 'Buy our onions at $5.38 and we'll give you broccoli for less.' In some cases, the U.S. shippers opened bank accounts in the U.S. where they deposited the kick-backs — the difference between $5.38 and the real, much lower, selling price. Then the Canadian importer would collect the money at the end of the season."

Referring to the temporary return to seasonal tariffs of 15 percent (provided for in the first twenty years of the FTA, when produce prices are depressed to a certain level), Rush commented: "The snap-back provisions [of the FTA] which were supposed to work are totally useless. We tried to impose them last year [1991] but you have to prove the production of Canadian lettuce hasn't gone up. This couldn't be done until the season was over. By then the damage was done ... They did impose a snap-back tariff on lettuce in 1992, but the U.S. price was so low that the 6 percent snap-back [i.e., to 15 percent] amounted to one cent per head. It was a joke."[18]

Canada is facing the systematic destruction of its ability to be self-sufficient in food. Iran, a major wheat producer, became a net importer of wheat under the rule of the American-imposed Shah. South Vietnam, home of the Mekong Delta, rice basket of the world, became an importer of U.S. rice during its occupation by the Americans. Canada is now following suit. Although perfectly capable of feeding itself many times over, it is becoming food-dependent on the United States.

Eugene Whelan, former federal minister of agriculture for almost twelve years, has predicted that under the FTA the entire Canadian food-processing industry — one of the largest employers in Canada — as well as the vegetable industry and dairy and poultry production, will disappear. Canada has a harsh climate, which means higher costs to processors. The government promised a "level playing field" under free trade; however, instead of recognizing the reality of climate, which is the biggest agricultural non-tariff barrier of all, federal Cabinet ministers called Canadians "wimps" if they couldn't compete with the producers of California, Hawaii and Florida and their 365-day growing season. Bringing Mexico into the FTA will put Canadian fruit and vegetable producers up against even cheaper food produced by large American-owned farms in Mexico. Such farms exploit Mexican labour at four dollars per day — a situation impossible for Canadian producers to compete against. Canada's self-sufficiency in food, something countries for very good reasons spend billions to achieve, is, like that in energy, being thrown to the four winds.

Investment and the Dollar

FREE TRADE WILL bring more investment to Canada and that will help the economy grow, or so the promise went.

Instead, U.S. branch plants are pulling out of Canada and a flood of Canadian investment is going south, buying or building plants in the United States and, increasingly, in Mexico.

What form of U.S. Investment is coming to Canada? Takeovers — almost entirely. New businesses aren't starting up. Nor is U.S. investment helping the Canadian economy. Over 90 percent of foreign investment from 1985 to 1992 was in the form of takeovers of Canadian companies. Ironically, 90 percent of these takeovers are financed with Canadian dollars from Canadian banks. The usual result is decreased employment and economic activity in Canada.

Prior to the 1988 election, pro-free-trade economists assured Canadians that the dollar would be the "safety valve" if Canada got into trouble under the FTA. The value of the dollar would fall if Canadian companies couldn't compete, thereby making exports cheaper; the U.S. would then buy more, thus alleviating any stress from the FTA, they argued. In public meetings and debates across Canada since 1985, this writer predicted that under free trade the dollar would not fall, but would be forced upwards to 85 cents or even higher, and Canada would face an influx of American products.

By simply forcing the Canadian dollar up, the U.S. could nullify any benefits Canada would receive from lowered tariffs. U.S. corporate interests, acting on their own or in concert with the U.S. government, have the power to hold the Canadian dollar high until Canadian manufacturers are forced out of business and no longer pose a threat to U.S. production. Then the dollar can be allowed to fall, making Canadian resources cheap for Americans to buy. When the dollar was trading at 69 to 70 cents, such predictions were greeted with incredulity. However, after the signing of the FTA, the Canadian dollar began a spectacular climb in relation to U.S. currency.

By August 1990 the dollar reached 88 cents (U.S.). Faced with this reality, the Canadian Exporters' Association (CEA), vociferous proponent of the deal, seemed suddenly sobered: "It has totally wiped out most of the advantages of the free-trade deal," said CEA spokesman Clem Srour in December 1989, referring to the high dollar. The CEA estimates that each one-cent rise in the dollar costs its members approximately $1.3 billion in lost exports. Free trade negotiator Gordon Ritchie admitted in March, 1990 that the dollar's rise had cost more jobs than the FTA had produced: "The adverse impact of movement of the Canadian dollar is 20 times the (positive) impact of tariff reduction," he acknowledged.[19] The Canadian Manufacturers' Association, which before the 1988 election maintained it could compete under free trade and win, announced that manufacturers must have a 77-cent dollar for the Canadian manufacturing industry to survive and compete.

This 18-cent rise in the dollar was equivalent to a 25 percent tariff on all Canadian exports. Before the FTA, the average tariff on all Canadian exports to the United States was less than one percent. In 1992, the dollar began to drop; by then, damage to Canada's industrial base was severe.

Trade Deal Only?

THIS AGREEMENT WAS just a commercial arrangement that would have no effect on foreign policy or sovereignty, Mr. Mulroney and his government told the public.

In 1989, shortly after the FTA was passed, Canada joined the Organization of American States (OAS). For Christmas of that year, the world watched the invasion and bombing of Panama, a tiny member nation, by the United States. The head of state of Panama, General Manuel Noriega, was labelled a drug runner by the president of the United States. Captured by U.S. troops, he was brought to Florida in chains to face trial in an American court. Noriega was forced to pose with a number around his neck, and the resulting "mug shot" was distributed to media around the world. A few months later, U.S. prosecutors admitted that they could not find evidence of drug-running. The kilograms of "cocaine" found in General Noriega's residence, and shown to the world as evidence by U.S. television networks, turned out to be powdered corn meal. To ensure a conviction, Noriega and his defence lawyers were repeatedly prohibited during his trial from introducing any evidence relating to the role of U.S. President George Bush (former head of the CIA) and the U.S. government in Panamanian affairs.

The government of Canada — which had just signed the OAS charter, expressly prohibiting intervention in or invasion of any member state — gave whole-hearted support to the U.S. invasion, one of only three countries in the world to do so. General Noriega was a "thug," Brian Mulroney declared, as if that settled it. By supporting this violation of international law, Canada suffered a serious loss of credibility in Latin America and is increasingly seen as a puppet of the United States.

The real reason for the invasion had less to do with cocaine or corn meal than with Noriega's refusal to capitulate to the United States on the right of his country to control its strategically important Canal Zone. So the Americans invaded, and swore in a new — and compliant — Panamanian government in the compound of an American military base. This happened just ten days before increased control of the canal was to be transferred to Panama under the terms of the 1977 treaty signed by Panama and former U.S. president Jimmy Carter — a treaty neither the Reagan nor the Bush administration was willing to honour. This episode is the latest chapter in a long and brutal history of U.S. involvement in Panama ever since Theodore Roosevelt used military force to seize the area from Colombia in 1903.

The demise of an independent Canadian foreign policy was glaringly revealed by the contrast between Mulroney's support for the American invasion of Panama and his condemnation and subsequent action in response to Iraq's invasion of Kuwait just one year later.

In late 1990, amid a barrage of media and government propaganda, Canadian armed forces went to war against Iraq, where they operated under direct U.S. command. In fact, the announcement of Canada's military participation in this U.S. mobilization was first made from Washington by James Baker, U.S. secretary of state, two hours before the prime minister of Canada's announcement from Ottawa.

Although the Gulf War was sold to Canadians as a United Nations operation, then UN secretary general Perez de Cuellar himself set the record straight: "The victory of the allied, or coalition, countries over Iraq is not at all a victory for the United Nations, because the war was not its war. It was not a United Nations war. General Schwarzkopf was not wearing a blue helmet."[20]

This was a war to give the United States control of Arab oil, from where much of the wealth of the seven major British and American oil companies has come, and which is also the energy source of its major industrial competitors, Europe and Japan.

The price tag, according to the former U.S. attorney-general, Ramsay Clark, was between 150,000 and 300,000 dead in Iraq — 90 percent civilian. Tonnes of depleted uranium ammunition was fired into Iraq by the U.S. Since the end of the war, more than 100,000 infants have died from leukemia, malnutrition, dysentery and other effects of the bombing and ongoing blockade of Iraq. (In January 1993, the U.S. began bombing Iraq again. On the evening of January 17, it unleashed, according to media reports, 40 cruise missiles on Baghdad, the country's capital, with more bombing in the days and years to follow.)

Canada's minister of external affairs, Joe Clark, said early in the war that the reason Canadian forces were in the Gulf was that Canada would not stand for the invasion of small countries by powerful ones. In the last 200 years, the United States has invaded smaller countries more than 300 times. This record, as we have seen, includes repeated invasions of its neighbours. From Mexico, it took half a country's entire territory. From Canada, it took a chunk of New Brunswick and a piece of the Yukon, and now it challenges Canada's sovereignty over waters of the Northwest Passage and boundaries off Georges Bank in the east, and Dixon Entrance in the west. A partial list of U.S. invasions and interventions in the past four decades includes many small countries, including Iran, Guatemala, the Dominican Republic, Cuba, Laos, Cambodia, Vietnam, Chile, Lebanon, Nicaragua, Libya, Grenada and Panama.

The reaction of Joe Clark and Brian Mulroney to recent American invasions has not been to call for sanctions against the United States or to advocate the bombing of Washington in retaliation, but rather to applaud the U.S. actions.

In the Persian Gulf, Canada, an oil-exporting nation, went to war to protect U.S. oil interests and to help keep oil prices low for U.S. consumers. Similarly, the Mulroney government supported the U.S. bombing of Libya in 1986, which killed president Moammar Khadafy's four-year-old daughter. The U.S. government claimed the bombing of the Libyan capital was "in retaliation" for Libyan involvement in the bombing of a German discotheque. (It turned out Libya had nothing to do with the discotheque incident.) The more fundamental reason for the American attack was that Libya claimed the Gulf of Sidra as its territorial water. Its claim rested on the same legal principle by which Canada claims the waters of the Northwest Passage. In both cases, the United States insists the waters are international. The Canadian government, by supporting the U.S. attack against Libya, seriously damaged its own claim to sovereignty in the Canadian North, to say nothing of the morality of supporting what the United States admitted to be an outright assassination attempt against the head of state of a foreign country in peacetime.

The almost total U.S. control of Canadian foreign policy stems directly from American control of Canada's economy; when a country is owned by another, its freedom and independence are gone.

From his retirement Pierre Elliot Trudeau, in 1990, broke his silence on the internal and external dangers he saw facing his country:

"Calling it national reconciliation, Prime Minister Mulroney has in fact been dismantling Canada for the benefit of the provinces. And under the noble pretext of satisfying Quebec he has been fostering exactly the kind of dualism that is the stuff of the separatists fondest dreams: an exclusively English-speaking Canada alongside an exclusively French-speaking Quebec.

Worse still, the commendable goal of promoting freer trade has led to a montrous swindle, under which the Canadian government has ceded to the United States of America a large slice of the country's sovereignty over its economy and natural resources in exchange for advantages we already had, or were going to obtain in a few years anyway through the normal operation of the GATT.

Alas, by now it is clear that, barring a sharp and unlikely change of course, our Great Helmsman is indeed steering Canada toward peace and reconciliation — the kind to be found in the graveyards of the deep."

24

Prying Open Mexico

AS SEEN IN CHAPTER 4, the United States seized by force all of
Mexico's territory north of the Rio Grande and Gila rivers. By 1910,
the United States owned more of Mexico than did all other foreign
nations combined, and most of the 15 million Mexicans were
reduced to poverty-stricken peonage. (A peon had no legal rights;
was usually paid in scrip, which was worthless except at the
landowner's store; and lived his life in debt to the owner. At death,
under Mexican law, the parents' debts transferred to their children.)
Some 800 landowners owned more than 90 percent of rural land,
while 10 million peasants were landless. And at the very bottom of
the ladder were the Indians. Safe for tourists and extremely profitable
for foreign businessmen, "Mexico had become a mother to aliens
and a stepmother to her own citizens."[1]

The Great Revolution, which began in late 1910, viewed foreign
ownership as a key issue. When Francisco Madero, father of the
Mexican Revolution, took power, overthrowing the thirty-year
dictatorship of Porfirio Diaz, the U.S. government openly intervened.
Madero's assassination was planned in the U.S. embassy and carried
out in February 1913. Soon known as the "pact of the embassy," the
assassination of Madero and his vice-president shook all of Mexico.
Said Mexican congressman Luis Manuel Rojas: "I accuse Mr. Henry
Lane Wilson, the ambassador of the United States in Mexico of the
moral responsibility for the death of Francisco I. Madero and José
Maria Pino Suárez."[2]

One year later, U.S. troops invaded the country. U.S. business,
including the newspaper empire of William Randolph Hearst, whose
Mexican ranch was larger than Rhode Island, heartily approved.
Some American sailors had entered a prohibited wharf area in the
Mexican seaport of Tampico. Briefly arrested by Mexican authorities,
they were released with a full written apology. The apology was not

enough, said American admiral Henry Mayo, who demanded the Mexican authorities raise the American flag and honour it with a 21-gun salute. When Mexico refused, President Woodrow Wilson, backed by a standing ovation in a joint session of Congress, ordered the entire American Atlantic Fleet to Tampico. The city of Veracruz was bombarded, resulting in hundreds of Mexican casualties, and then occupied for seven months by several thousand American troops. Violent anti-American demonstrations broke out across Mexico. The statue of George Washington in Mexico City was knocked over and smashed, and American flags and businesses were burned and looted by crowds chanting "death to the gringos." The Mexican government, the revolution still in progress, issued a call for united action to expel "the pigs of Yanquilandia."[3] American citizens were forced to huddle behind locked doors.

In 1916, American troops invaded again. Some 12,000 of them crossed from New Mexico, ostensibly to capture Mexican revolutionary leader Francisco "Pancho" Villa, but with the larger goal of thwarting the revolution itself. Ten months later, empty handed and distracted by the First World War, the United States was forced to turn its attention on Germany.

One of the most famous leaders of the Mexican Revolution was Emiliano Zapata, a quiet farmer of Native ancestry, under whose slogan, "land and liberty," thousands of the humble people of Mexico fought. Zapata's guerrilla army, made up mostly of farmers of Indian origin, fought in bands of 30 to 300, seizing its weapons from the enemy. In its ranks and among its leaders were women soldiers *(soldadas)*.

Although Zapata was assassinated in 1919, the influence of the Zapatistas continues to this day. The constitution of revolutionary Mexico was, in 1917, the first in the world to recognize workers' rights to unions, an eight-hour day and a minimum wage. It established the peasant's right to own land and took national control over natural resources. Women were entitled to the same pay as men for the same work; and foreigners, except in certain controlled situations, were not allowed to own land.

With the end of the war in Europe, the United States once again turned the full force of its attention onto the Mexican Revolution, with a campaign of intimidation and threats of invasion. The U.S. oil companies maintained their own private armies in Mexico and refused to allow enforcement of the new constitution. New York congressman Fiorello LaGuardia warned Mexicans that intervention could be avoided only if they "put out the present administration." The New York *Times* directed Mexico to "undo the mischief" of the constitutional provisions dealing with foreign ownership.[4] The rights for labour contained in the new constitution angered the powerful U.S. mining companies, who idled their mines in protest, throwing thousands out of work.

Under sustained U.S. interference, many of the revolution's aims were not realized until the 1930s when, under General Lázaro Cárdenas, the Mexican Federation of Workers and the national peasant federation joined forces to set up the Partido Revolucionario Institucional (PRI).

After winning the presidency, Cárdenas and his government expropriated the American and British oil companies and implemented a land redistribution program to peasants, the most widespread such action in Mexico's history. The oil companies responded with a barrage of economic warfare, boycotts, blacklists and anti-government propaganda, but in the end they were forced to settle their claims on Mexico's terms. Cárdenas emerged as the most popular president in Mexican history. March 18, the date in 1938 of the expropriation, is celebrated to this day as an official national holiday (Day of the Oil Expropriation).

During the next three decades, Mexico sharply reduced the level of foreign control of the economy while at the same time maintaining impressive national economic growth rates. Airlines, railroads, phone and electric companies, and the petroleum industry, all were nationalized. This development laid the groundwork for growth that gave Mexico fifty years of stability and made it the only Latin American country other than Costa Rica to escape military dictatorship. At the same time, Mexico pursued a foreign policy independent of the United States and, like Canada, maintained trade and diplomatic links with Cuba despite stiff U.S. opposition.

In the 1980s, much of this picture began to change. The PRI, in power fifty years, had grown increasingly corrupt, and the falling world price of oil hit Mexico hard. The government incurred large foreign debts and embarked on a massive sell-off of public assets. In 1987, Cuauhtémoc Cárdenas, the son of Lázaro, launched a campaign to reform the party, but was unceremoniously rejected by its leadership. The new head of the PRI was a Harvard-trained economist, Carlos Salinas de Gortari.

Cárdenas left the party and set to work to form a new coalition. In the 1988 election, four opposition parties formed an alliance and, to avoid splitting the vote, withdrew all their presidential candidates and backed Cárdenas. Cárdenas and his coalition stood four-square against free trade with the United States and for a resurrection of the principles of the Mexican Revolution. Sabotage, intimidation and murder characterized the Mexican election campaign of 1988. Four days before the July vote, a close advisor of Cárdenas was shot to death along with his assistant as they worked on establishing an independent network to count the votes.

By 7 p.m. election night, the government knew Salinas had lost the election. The results were being transmitted by secret code to the government's computers before being released. One of the opposition parties, Partido de Acción Nacional (PAN), cracked the code and learned the outcome. At that point, the government-controlled Federal Commission of Elections shut down the computers and stopped broadcasting the results. It took more than a week for the government to produce doctored figures to justify Salinas's claim to victory.

In what Cárdenas called the "technical equivalent of a coup d'état," the election had been stolen from the Mexican voters. Full ballot boxes from areas supporting the opposition were found floating in rivers; 20,000 missing votes were discovered under a pile of ashes outside the city of Chilpancingo, and others were dumped out of helicopters over Coyuca. The official published ballot total was very low, despite an extraordinarily high voter turnout. The newspaper *El Norte* found error rates of 36 to 49 percent in voter registration in Monterrey. In Juárez, fraudulent voter registration included the registering of two-year-olds, and a government official in Mexico City had seventy-two people registered at his house, where only four people lived. In some rural areas, with the paramilitary organization Antorcha Campesina keeping polling observers away, over 99 percent of the vote was "won" by Salinas. In Guerrero, when the opposition was able to count 80.5 percent of the votes from copies of official tally sheets, Cárdenas received 359,369 votes, and Salinas 90,796. When the official count was released, however, Cárdenas had 182,874, Salinas 309,202.[5]

Spontaneous demonstrations — the largest in Mexico's history — erupted. Public opinion polls showed that 90 percent of the population believed Salinas had not been elected. Still, his claim to the presidency was recognized and instantly backed by the United States and big business organizations in Mexico. Those who continued to resist this "electoral coup" were jailed or worse. By early

1990, 60 journalists and opposition figures had been murdered. By 1992, the number was 140 and still rising.

IN 1987, THE UNITED STATES had signed a trade agreement with Mexico. It was only three pages long and did not include any commitments for Mexico to change its domestic laws or banking or energy regulations. It was basically an arrangement for Mexicans and Americans to consult with each other if they had a trade dispute. During negotiations with the United States, Mexico asked for the inclusion in the agreement of an American promise not to use military intervention to enforce any trade dispute. The United States refused.

The United States wanted an end to Mexico's rules restricting foreign ownership. Unlike the Canadian government, however, Mexico in 1987 was not prepared to change its constitution or repeal its restrictions. The Mexicans also had a regulation that prohibited selling more than 50 percent of their energy supplies to one customer. Mexico already shipped close to 50 percent of its oil to the United States; unlike Canada, it was not willing to tie itself even more tightly to one market. Because Mexico was not prepared to cave in to U.S. demands, and because the United States would not sign the promise not to use military intervention, no free-trade agreement was signed. The disappointed Americans observed in their confidential briefing notes: "The political climate in Mexico is not ready for a market-based energy trade arrangement at this time; the degree of government involvement in Mexico's energy sector has always been very large and is considered essential by many elements within Mexico."[6]

In a remarkable parallel to the Canadian experience, shortly after being placed in power in 1988, the new pro-American president, Carlos Salinas, like Brian Mulroney in 1984, announced he would be entering talks for a free-trade deal with the United States — something Mexicans had always resisted.

During the 1988 Canadian election, the Mulroney government promised that Mexican goods would not, under any circumstances, be able to come into Canada as part of the FTA. Two years later, the same government was at the table with the United States and Mexico, negotiating free trade for all of North America. The reason given by the Canadian government for its about-face was that it had to protect its "gains" under the Canada-U.S. FTA. Canadians, however, had been told these were exclusive and unique to Canada.

In March 1990, Brian Mulroney went to Mexico and, in a speech widely covered in the Mexican press, said Canada's free-trade deal with the United States had created more than 200,000 jobs in Canada and improved the Canadian economy dramatically. This speech played a key role in the effort to sell free trade to a Mexican public suspicious of its government's promises, but lacking the facts to refute them. President Salinas, using Mulroney's figures, spoke across Mexico. Mulroney would not have been able to get away with such a statement in Canada, where not even the Conservatives could deny the economy was in a recession. Instead, the Mexican people, who knew as little about free trade as Canadians did when it was sprung upon them, were being fed, courtesy of Canada's prime minister, the same kind of hype and misinformation Canadians got before the 1988 election.

WHAT HAS EMERGED from the negotiations is the North American Free Trade Agreement (NAFTA), an immensely long, complicated agreement (1100 pages plus tariff schedules). Boiled down, it extends the FTA to include Mexico, and in some areas it takes the FTA provisions even further in a direction opposed to Canadian interests.

Trucking, rail and bus services (land transportation), excluded from the FTA, are in NAFTA with full national treatment, meaning each of these industries will be under even greater pressure from the U.S. carriers. Canadian ownership and content regulations are prohibited, as they are in the FTA; it would be impossible, for example, to insist that Canadian grain or other products be transported across Canada or out of Canadian ports, or that transportation companies be Canadian owned.

All the energy provisions of the FTA are reproduced in NAFTA, but there is one surprise. Mexico is exempted from the infamous proportional-sharing clauses that oblige Canada to export to the United States the same proportion of its resources as over the previous three years, even in conditions of shortage. At the negotiations, instead of allying with Mexico to extricate itself from these destructive provisions, the Canadian government joined with the United States to demand Mexico sign the same terms. "Even as late as ... July, 1992," stated the Canadian Centre for Policy

Alternatives, "Canada's Ambassador to Mexico, David Winfield, was still insisting that Canada wanted Mexico to accept the proportional sharing clause."[7]

The services chapter of NAFTA carries the FTA even further and states in article 1205: "A Party shall not require a service provider of another Party to establish or maintain a representative office, branch or any form of enterprise, or to be resident, in its territory as a condition for the provision of a cross-border service." This means that U.S. or Mexican companies are free to operate across the border into Canada without establishing an office or other presence in Canada and can avoid any obligations, including taxes, to Canada. A Canadian seeking to sue such a company would be unable to do so in his or her own country.

Article 1210 states that within two years each country "shall eliminate any citizenship or permanent residency requirements for the licensing and certification of professional service providers in its territory." This means professions governed by federal and provincial laws (lawyers, for example), which now have Canadian citizenship as a membership requirement, suddenly face a new world; competition from American professionals who will be treated as Canadians. And while Canada agreed to open all of its engineers to this section, Mexico excluded all its engineers except civil engineers.

Telecommunications is expanded to include all long-distance services and gives U.S. companies access to Canadian networks and services on "reasonable and non-discriminating terms and conditions." "In short, if NAFTA is implemented," says one analysis, "it will be open season on the Canadian telecommunications industry ... Powerful foreign telecommunications companies will be free to pursue their private interests in this country and Canadians will be powerless to apply the policies that are needed to ensure that companies operating here meet this country's telecommunication needs."[8]

The financial services chapter is extended to include provincially licensed institutions such as trust, loan and mortgage companies. The definition of financial services is substantially widened in article 1417 to include "any service of a financial nature including insurance" as well as "any service incidental or auxiliary to a service of a financial nature." Article 1404.5 gives American and Mexican financial institutions operating in Canada the right to "transfer and process information outside" Canadian territory. This provision not only means lost data-processing jobs. It will allow, with the full approval of the law, confidential information — about Canadians — to be stored in the United States.

Chapter 15, "Competition Policy, Monopolies and State Enterprises," spells out drastic controls on all Crown corporations, including provincial ones, in Canada. Henceforth, it decrees, Crown corporations must act "solely in accordance with commercial considerations" (article 1502.3b), which are defined as "consistent with normal business practices of privately-held enterprises in the relevant business or industry." Most of Canada's Crown corporations — the CBC, CN, Petro-Canada, Canada Post and many others — were set up precisely to serve needs not being met by private corporations. As an example, many cities in Canada would not have received air service without the establishment of Air Canada. In addition, article 1502.3d prohibits Crown corporations from using the revenue from their monopoly operations to provide public services in another field if it would "adversely affect" an American or Mexican investor.

Then, in an abrupt change of direction after more than one thousand pages of unrelenting pursuit of open borders, NAFTA contains a new chapter, entitled "Intellectual Property." "Intellectual property," which refers to the ownership of knowledge and information, includes the regulation of patents, copyrights, trademarks and industrial designs. In this field, the Americans have very definite ideas about borders. Protection is suddenly no longer a dirty word, but an important concept indeed.

The Canadian government recently amended Canada's drug patent law to give foreign corporations twenty years of monopoly protection before Canadian manufacturers of generic drugs can begin producing a new drug. Not only will this legislation cripple the generic drug manufacturing industry in Canada, but Canadians, and their health-care system, can now expect to pay additional costs, estimated at from $550 million to $1 billion, in increased drug prices over the next eight years — most of it to American pharmaceutical giants. NAFTA's article 1709 requires these changes to Canada's drug patent legislation.

Article 1709 also obliges each country to "provide for the protection of plant varieties through patents." This requirement will have tremendous repercussions for agriculture. Indeed, a farmer planting seed from his own crop would be making an unauthorized reproduction of a patented item, and could be required to pay royalties to the company who had originally patented that seed. At present, large U.S. chemical companies are actively working to develop seeds that will actually depend upon the herbicides, pesticides or fertilizers that they produce. The long-term implications of corporate control over plant genetic stock as well as the effects of ever-increasing pesticide use are frightening to contemplate. Further, many countries and organizations have opposed allowing private corporations to patent forms of plant, animal or human life, arguing that they should be the common property of all humanity. Perhaps for that reason, this chapter of NAFTA contains nine pages of enforcement measures, including criminal charges for those who may contravene its provisions.

In a blatant attempt to impose American foreign policy on both Canada and Mexico, article 1211, "Denial of Benefits," states that the United States can deny the benefits of the agreement to a company operating in Canada or Mexico but owned by a country that does not have diplomatic relations with the United States.

Chapter 20 sets up a permanent Free Trade Commission to act as the governing body of this continental free-trade area. Not elected by any of the citizens of Canada, Mexico or the United States, this body is given sweeping powers to "supervise the implementation" of the agreement, to oversee its "further elaboration," to "supervise the work of all committees" set up by the agreement, and to "consider any other matter that may affect the operation of this Agreement." All new government measures in Canada must conform to NAFTA; by article 1206.1b, "any non-conforming measure" of provincial legislation must be itemized and submitted to the commission within two years.

One of the revealing things about NAFTA is that Mexico succeeded in protecting parts of its economy and resources that Canada in 1988, with a far stronger bargaining hand, did not. This provides remarkable confirmation that there was in reality no government acting in Canada's interests at the table, either in the FTA or the NAFTA negotiations, but rather an administration calling itself Canadian, but acting more like an arm ofthe U.S. State Department. Not only in energy and in areas of government ownership, but also, for example, in culture, Mexico achieved an exemption. Although Canada utterly failed to achieve any change from the cultural provisions of the FTA, Mexico reserved the right to use 30 percent of its theatre time for Mexican films.

Unlike the FTA, NAFTA contains an accession clause, under which other countries may join. The United States does not intend to stop with Mexico. In October 1992, then presidential candidate Bill Clinton said: "If we can make this agreement work with Canada and Mexico, then we can reach down into the other market-oriented economies of Central and South America to expand even further."[9] In this zone, the United States will have unrivalled supremacy and control, something it is not able to achieve through the General Agreement on Tariffs and Trade, which includes other nations capable of challenging its power.

Other countries can be added to the NAFTA, with or without Canada's approval, in much the same way that Puerto Rico since 1900 has been denied any role in the negotiation of U.S. trade treaties. Unlike Puerto Rico, however, by article 2205(2) Canada has the right to remove itself both from this agreement and from any future agreement involving another country.

A section of the confidential 1987 document, "Appraisal of the U.S.-Canada Pact," prepared for then Treasury Secretary James Baker and U.S. trade representative Clayton Yeutter and subsequently leaked, reads: "The broad U.S. objective in these talks was to freeze as well as to extend as much as possible, the substantial liberalization of the Canadian investment climate that the Mulroney government has already put in place. The freeze is essential to help U.S. direct investors because future Canadian governments must be prevented from retrogressing to the highly unsatisfactory policy regime from just a few years ago."[10] In April 1991, a confidential memo from the U.S. ambassador to Mexico, John Negroponte, was also leaked. It contains a remarkably similar expression of intent towards Mexico: "The FTA can be seen as an instrument to promote, consolidate and guarantee continued policies of economic reform in Mexico beyond the Salinas administration. I think it's reasonable to suppose that the FTA negotiations themselves will be a useful lever in prying open the Mexican economy even further. For example, I think we can reasonably expect the foreign investment law to change as a result of FTA talks."[11]

The average hourly wage in the Maquiladora free-trade zones is forty to sixty cents. That is where U.S., Japanese and Canadian corporations are going — more than 1500 of them since 1978. Half a million Mexicans work in the Maquiladoras, many living in tar-paper shacks without electricity, drinking water or sewage facilities. Given a choice of setting up a plant in Canada and paying wages of eight, ten or fifteen dollars an hour, vacation pay, social benefits, and health and education taxes, or going to Mexico, paying 60 cents an hour with virtually no benefits or union protection, and simply shipping the product north, it's not hard to see where business will go. Some 70 percent of the television sets sold in the United States now come from the Maquiladoras. One U.S. company promoting the Maquiladoras explains that by relocating from Canada or the United States, a corporation can cut its production costs in half and save up to $25,000 per year per employee.

In December 1992, Puerto Rican governor Pedro Rosselló said that under NAFTA "Puerto Rico can no longer compete on the basis of cheap wages. Even though salaries here are half those on the American mainland, on average they are four times Mexican wages. In any industry that depends on cheap labour, we are going to be at a disadvantage."[12]

There are 20 million unemployed or underemployed in Mexico — almost twice the entire labour force of Canada. As Bram Garber, the chairman of Canada's largest carpet manufacturer, Peerless Carpets, put it: "A free-trade agreement with Mexico would finish off whatever secondary manufacturing industries are able to survive the apparent disastrous FTA with the United States."[13]

The creation of a North American free-trade zone is designed to lock Canada more securely into American control and make abrogation of the Canada-U.S. FTA even more difficult. Cheap Canadian resources and cheap Mexican labour, both U.S. controlled, are what the North American free-trade deal is all about. Domestic Mexican industries will be hurt in the same way as Canadian companies because, under NAFTA, large American corporations operating in all three countries will have a tremendous advantage over those based in only Canada or Mexico.

As in every free-trade area, the pressure in a North American free-trade zone will be for a common currency. This currency will not be the Mexican peso or the Canadian dollar. Governor George Sinner of North Dakota expressed this sentiment most directly when he said he would like to see the Canadian dollar at par with the U.S. dollar, and to see Washington's picture on it. With free trade in place, he said, a common currency is inevitable; it was time for Canada to be done with the fiction of two separate economies.

On December 17, 1992, upon signing the NAFTA in Washington, George Bush invoked the name of the great liberator Simón Bolívar, who fought his whole life *against* foreign control of South America and to whom six countries, including the one bearing his name, owe their freedom from colonial rule. Implying Bolívar would approve, Bush said: "Today ... we take another giant step toward [creating] an America united in heart, subject to one law and guided by the torch of liberty."[14]

What all this means is that Canada and the countries of Latin America are being returned to colonial status, this time to provide cheap resources and labour in order to put U.S. business back on top in their competition with Japan and Europe.

Free trade with the United States is not an expression of outward-looking internationalism, as Canadians are repeatedly told. Rather, it is the code word for continental integration. Opposing it is not provincialism or isolationism. Rather, with roughly 80 percent of Canada's trade already with the United States, it is the Canadians fighting against the Free Trade Agreement who are advocating a true internationalism through diversification of Canada's economy out from under the control of one nation and trading throughout the world.

In 1992, the U.S. Federal Reserve Board published figures that the "top 1 per cent of Americans (834,000 households) had more total net worth ($5.7 trillion) than the bottom 90 per cent (84 million households), which had about $4.8 trillion.[15] NAFTA is about to make the top one percent a good deal richer."

If NAFTA is to be stopped, it will not, as some are hoping, be done by Bill Clinton's White House. And the people of Mexico, labouring under "the perfect dictatorship," have had their freedom of action temporarily restricted. If "manifest destiny" is to be stopped, it will have to be done where it has been done before: in 1690, at the great rock of Quebec; in 1775, under the battlements of that same city; in 1812, on the battlefields of Queenston Heights and Châteauguay; in 1864, in Charlottetown; in 1870, on the plains south of Winnipeg; in 1871, in British Columbia; and in 1949, in Newfoundland. When the chips were down, Canadians have never failed the test of history. The chips are down today.

25

"We Don't Scare Easily"

CONTROL OF CANADA has increasingly passed out of the hands of Canadians into those of U.S. corporations and of the U.S. government. How did this happen? As we have seen, American money and advisors had backed Mr. Mulroney since at least the early 1980s. After gaining the leadership of the Progressive Conservative Party in 1983, Mulroney and his supporters took steps to attain power nationally. Prior to 1984, the Conservatives had little strength in Quebec, so Brian Mulroney made a deal with the ruling Parti Québécois (PQ) — if they would support him, he would reopen the constitutional question, which had been dormant since 1982. Soon afterwards, known separatists were taken into positions of influence and power in the Conservative Party and Cabinet, the most prominent being Lucien Bouchard — PQ member since 1976, a campaigner on the Yes side in the 1980 referendum on Quebec sovereignty, and the chief negotiator for the PQ in its negotiations with the public service in 1982-83. (Bouchard, first appointed as the Conservatives' ambassador to France, was later elected in the 1988 Lac-Saint-Jean by-election, with the aid of a pledge of $163 million in federal spending to the riding.) In the 1984 federal election, the PQ electoral machine was placed at Mulroney's disposal, with highly successful results. Then, when the PQ lost power in the fall of 1985, Mulroney reached an accommodation with the new Liberal premier, Robert Bourassa, who would soon receive his five demands — and then some — on the Constitution.* Shortly thereafter, Bourassa abruptly reversed his publicly declared opposition

---

* Quebec's five demands: (1) a veto on constitutional amendments, (2) limitation of federal spending power, (3) a role in appointments to the Supreme Court, (4) a greater role in immigration, (5) the recognition of Quebec as a distinct society.

to free trade with the United States. The result in the 1988 federal election was that both provincial parties in Quebec supported the federal Conservatives.

What emerged from this alliance between the Conservatives and the separatist forces in Quebec was the Meech Lake Accord, an amendment to the Constitution of Canada. It was conceived and drawn up by the prime minister and the ten provincial premiers, without any public input, in the spring of 1987. After two all-night bargaining sessions, April 30 and June 3, they emerged, signed the accord and announced that not one comma could be changed.

The Meech Lake Accord would have changed the Constitution by giving the provincial premiers sweeping new powers unheard of in any federal state in the world, including the power to choose the judges of the Supreme Court of Canada and the authority to select the members of the upper house of Parliament, the Senate. It gave the provinces the right not only to pull out of national cost-shared programs, but as well to set up their own programs and receive compensation from the federal government for doing so. In addition, each premier received the power of absolute veto over any future constitutional change involving the Senate, the Supreme Court, the establishment of new provinces and a number of other matters.

The Yukon and the Northwest Territories, 40 percent of Canada's entire land mass and the last remaining area where Native people are still the majority, would, under Meech Lake, have had to receive permission from each provincial premier before becoming provinces, something none of the existing provinces had had to do. This process would have included approval by Manitoba, Saskatchewan, Alberta and B.C., provinces that may well prefer to see their own borders extended to the high Arctic to double their size and secure the bountiful resources of the North.

The Meech Lake Accord called for "not less than two" federal-provincial conferences every year — for eternity. This provision would have created and enshrined in the Constitution a new, most powerful level of government in Canada, consisting of an exclusive club of the eleven first ministers, free to operate behind closed doors, with no annoying opposition benches or reporters to face, and totally unreachable by the public. Small wonder that for three years Canadians saw provincial premiers using every device to convince the public of both the necessity of Meech Lake and their own stature as statesmen.

246 THE FIGHT FOR CANADA

IT WAS OVER THE issue of the power of the states that the United States fought a long and bloody civil war. John A. Macdonald was adamant, when negotiating the *British North America Act* in 1867, that the mistake of excessive decentralization not be repeated in Canada's Constitution. The "fatal error" of the American Constitution, Macdonald argued — giving too much power to the states — must be avoided at all costs. The other framers of the *BNA Act* agreed. They deliberately created a Confederation with a strong and supreme central government, and subordinate provincial governments with carefully defined and limited powers.

Beginning in 1887, provincial premiers began in an organized manner to demand more powers for themselves. Prime ministers from John A. Macdonald to Mackenzie King, Louis St. Laurent, John Diefenbaker, Lester Pearson and Pierre Trudeau resisted these endless provincial demands for ever-greater powers. The centrifugal forces in a country as far-flung as Canada are such that without a strong central government the nation will be unable to resist the pull of the United States. Nevertheless, over the years the provinces have succeeded — through court challenges, constant demands, organized action and threats — in increasing their jurisdiction to the point that the power of the Canadian provinces now exceeds that of the American states. The constant push for increased provincial power at the expense of the federal government came to a head in 1987 at Meech Lake when, for the first time at a federal-provincial conference, the federal government did not resist. One of the premiers, Manitoba's Howard Pawley, expressed astonishment that no one appeared to represent the central government. "Mulroney never once defended the national government's powers," he reported after signing the accord.[1]

Meech Lake was a naked power grab by the premiers of the English-speaking provinces riding in on the coattails of Quebec. Publicly, Canadians were told the accord's purpose was to deal with legitimate concerns of Quebecers about the survival of the French language and culture. Instead, it gave large, new powers to all the provinces including the English-speaking ones, whose language was not threatened.

Premiers who had built their careers attacking Quebec now expected the public to believe they supported Meech Lake for the sake of national unity and the love of French-speaking Canada. The purpose of the Meech Lake Accord was to bring Quebec into the constitutional family, the Western premiers declared solemnly and repeatedly, with David Peterson of Ontario nodding and premiers John Buchanan of Nova Scotia and Frank McKenna of New Brunswick standing firmly at his side. Seldom if ever mentioned was that each received the same powers granted the premier of Quebec. It was no wonder Mulroney received the support he needed from the premiers on free trade; that Bourassa's Liberal machine worked for the Conservatives and against the federal Liberal Party; and that David Peterson suddenly forgot to fight free trade, though a large majority in Ontario had returned him to power in 1987 on his promise to do so.

Meech Lake represented a massive victory for provincialism and a severe blow to the central power of the Canadian government. Yet after its signing, both Liberal leader John Turner and NDP leader Ed Broadbent crossed the floor of the House of Commons and shook Brian Mulroney's hand in congratulations. However, it had yet to pass through each provincial legislature to become law.

It was left to Pierre Trudeau, retired prime minister of Canada, to provide the intellectual and moral leadership to oppose Meech Lake, with only a handful of the Liberal Party joining his fight. In a front-page article in the Toronto *Star*, entitled "Say Goodbye to the Dream of One Canada," Trudeau wrote that provincial governments would now have the real power, an absolute right of veto over Parliament through their control of the Senate and "supreme judicial power" through their right to select Supreme Court judges:

> [S]ince 1982, Canada had its Constitution, including a charter which was binding on the provinces as well as the federal government. From then on, the advantage was on the Canadian government's side ... the federation was set to last a thousand years! ... Alas, one eventuality had not been foreseen: that one day the government of Canada might fall into the hands of a wimp. It has now happened. And the Right Honorable Brian Mulroney, PC, MP, with the complicity of 10 provincial premiers, has already entered history as the author of a constitutional document which — if it is accepted by the people and their legislators — will render the Canadian state totally impotent.
>
> That would destine it, given the dynamics of power, to be governed eventually by eunuchs.[2]

Every provincial premier, most politicians, and literally dozens of media commentators leapt to dismiss Trudeau as "the voice of the past," "shrill," "confrontational," "embittered," a "radical centralist," "irrelevant," and "pathetic."

Trudeau, and those who stood with him, were viciously attacked by the rest of the Liberal Party, led by leadership aspirants Sheila Copps and Paul Martin. The NDP leadership — Ed Broadbent, Lorne Nystrom, the late Pauline Jewett and others — joined Copps and Martin in denouncing Trudeau and promoting Mulroney's position on Meech Lake from 1987 right up to the death of the accord. Even after the accord had been killed in Manitoba through the efforts of Native MLA Elijah Harper, NDP leader Audrey McLaughlin declared on national radio and television that her party was not opposed to the "principles of Meech Lake," only to the process.

The media's role in promoting and fuelling the Meech Lake crisis was revealing. Day after day and night after night, Canadians were barraged with propaganda from television, radio and newspapers. English-speaking Canadians were warned that without Meech Lake, Canada would break up and Quebec would separate. The unending message from virtually every media outlet in Quebec was that all opposition to Meech Lake was a rejection of, and an expression of hatred towards, Quebec. Radio-Canada (French-language CBC TV) repeatedly aired across Quebec the powerful image of a handful of bigots at an anti-French demonstration in Brockville, Ontario, wiping their feet on the Quebec flag — as if that reflected the views of the whole country outside of Quebec.

A document leaked from David Peterson's office prior to the final federal-provincial conference on Meech Lake outlined a strategy to use the media, especially the CBC, to fuel a sense of national crisis and to undermine the credibility of opponents of Meech Lake. This strategy, remarkably like that used on the free-trade issue, was fully realized. Manitoba Liberal leader Sharon Carstairs, an original and articulate opponent of Meech Lake, was asked point blank on national television by CBC journalist Barbara Frum how it felt to be responsible for the breakup of Canada. Joe Clark, then minister for external affairs, told the country that if the Meech Lake Accord were rejected, Canada would see the rise of FLQ (Front de libération du Québec) violence in Quebec. English Canada must choose between Quebec and Newfoundland (whose premier, Clyde Wells, opposed the deal), insisted then federal minister of the environment, Lucien Bouchard. Brian Mulroney told Quebecers over and over that if

Meech Lake failed, English Canada was saying "no to Quebec." The Alliance for the Preservation of English in Canada (APEC) organized anti-French resolutions in Ontario cities and the foot-wiping incident in Brockville. APEC is an offshoot of and receives funding from the American extremist organization U.S. English, which mobilizes against demands by Spanish-speaking Americans. APEC's mentor, J.V. Andrew, author of the rabidly anti-French *Bilingual Today, French Tomorrow*, a book that advocates the splitting of Canada into two countries, declared to the television cameras that "Canada needs the French fact like we need the AIDS virus." Meanwhile, the separatist movement in Quebec had a heyday — quoting the latest voice of racism from English Canada and asking why Quebec had to take these insults any longer when it could go its own way.

Finally on June 12, 1990, Elijah Harper, the sole Native member of the Manitoba Legislative Assembly, backed by the Assembly of Manitoba Chiefs, succeeded in blocking passage of the accord through the legislature. For eleven days Harper, holding a single eagle feather and shaking his head No, used rules of procedure to stop the accord. Support swelled from across the country from Native and non-Native alike until, in a dramatic finale on June 23, 1990, the deadline for ratification by all the provinces ran out. At 7:40 that night, the government in Ottawa bitterly announced that Meech Lake was dead. Clyde Wells was left merely to perform the symbolic act of adjourning Newfoundland's legislature without a vote.

Contrary to repeated high-level predictions, with the defeat of Meech Lake the dollar did not fall, nor was the economy affected in any detectible way. Within a month, however, the true agenda of the premiers quickly re-emerged when, at the end of July 1990, the four Western premiers set up a common front, dropped all talk of loving Canada or Quebec, called for the power to veto federal spending and to levy a regional income tax, resumed attacks on "Central Canada" and made their usual demands for massive new powers. The premier of Saskatchewan, who two months before had said he was "hugging" Quebec, now stated that Quebec was like a "runaway horse" which needed to be brought under control, given "a good whipping" and "put in the barn."[3]

A multimillion-dollar commission was soon set up under the chairmanship of Keith Spicer, whose purpose, Canadians were informed, was to hear what the citizens thought the country needed constitutionally. When even Spicer, appointed by Mulroney and a supporter of both free trade and Meech Lake, was forced to admit

250 THE FIGHT FOR CANADA

that the main message his commission was hearing was that Canadians wanted a strong central government and the power to impeach Brian Mulroney, his $20 million report was buried.

A new process was began. Amid much media fanfare, carefully hand-picked groups of "ordinary citizens" were gathered by the government to "discuss the new Constitution" and give an aura of citizens' participation to Ottawa's unrelenting plan for constitutional changes. Closer examination revealed that many of the so-called ordinary Canadians involved in the major forums were on the government payroll one way or the other and were previous supporters of Meech Lake. (Yves Fortier, Mulroney's appointee as Canada's ambassador to the United Nations, was listed at one of the Atlantic meetings as an "ordinary" Canadian. Peter Lougheed, long-time Conservative premier of Alberta and Mulroney supporter, co-chaired meetings in the West.) In January 1991, the Quebec Liberal Party's *Allaire* report was released, calling for a referendum on full Quebec sovereignty within a year and a half unless the federal government agreed to a virtually complete decentralization of power, leaving Ottawa with jurisdiction only in defence, customs and tariffs, currency and equalization payments.

Fifteen months after the demise of the Meech Lake Accord, the Conservatives, in September 1991, introduced Meech Lake II, another, much larger proposal to amend the Constitution. Entitled *Shaping Canada's Future Together,* this document proposed twenty-eight changes to the Constitution. The proposal, which would have transferred many of the powers of the central government to the provinces and weakened Charter of Rights and Freedoms protection for individual citizens, was heralded as the new Constitution that would save Canada from breaking up. The spectacle of Mulroney, Clark, Wilson and the other architects of the FTA cloaking themselves in the mantle of Canada's saviour was too much for most Canadians to swallow. As with the Meech Lake Accord, the media and the opposition parties immediately began to promote the document. The Constitution must be amended, Canadians were again told. The status quo was not working; sweeping changes were necessary if Canada was to survive.

The Canadian house was on fire. While it burned out of control, its citizens were being asked to sit in the living room, along with the arsonists who set the fire, and discuss future furniture arrangements. An example: In the constitutional proposals, Canadians were asked to debate — in all earnestness — giving the

Senate "a mandate to ratify appointments to the National Energy Board." Chapter 9 of the FTA, however, gives the United States such sweeping control over Canada's energy that the board has been reduced to a rubber stamp for the massive exportation of Canadian resources at rock-bottom prices.

The opposition parties, and dozens of groups who once claimed to oppose the government's agenda, eagerly participated in this constitutional diversion, while the greater danger — both to Quebec and the rest of Canada — of assimilation into the United States through the FTA and NAFTA, went virtually unchallenged. The Liberals and NDP, by agreeing to talk Constitution, fell straight into Mulroney's arms. These parties, trembling in fear of the separatists in the West and in Quebec, could simply have refused to go along. The most discredited government in Canadian history — the very one responsible for creating the crisis in Canada — had no mandate, credibility or legitimacy to rewrite the supreme law of the land.

Yet on August 20, 1992, the latest "make-or-break the nation" constitutional accord, soon to be known as the Charlottetown Accord (in reality, Meech Lake III), was announced from Ottawa. Those who opposed the package, Brian Mulroney immediately declared, were "enemies of Canada." Joe Clark warned that "the day of judgement is at hand." Thus, the nation was put on notice of further threats to come — by the very men who had delivered Canada to the United States under the FTA and who were at that moment upgrading that sale under NAFTA. Meanwhile, the Charlottetown text had yet to be seen by the Canadian public.

Seizing on complaints that Meech Lake I had been negotiated by men (anything to avoid criticism of its content), the government placed some women in the forefront of the process for Meech Lake III. Rosemarie Kuptana of the Inuit Tapirisat emerged from the final Ottawa negotiations to tell Canadians that she was one of the "Mothers of Confederation." She explained that her nurturing abilities had helped the new Constitution emerge, because when Clyde Wells — the one potentially serious critic in the room — felt isolated and withdrew, she had been able to draw him back into the process.

In a calculated attempt to play on the symbolism of the original Charlottetown conference of 1864 that had led to Confederation, the 1992 conference adjourned to Charlottetown, Prince Edward Island, for the final announcement. In the same spot that John A. Macdonald had fought *against* large provincial powers, *against* equal representation in the Senate from each province, and *for* a strong central government, the jubilant first ministers announced an "unprecedented" agreement to make the most wide-reaching constitutional amendments in Canadian history, which would do precisely the opposite.

The Charlottetown Accord went well beyond Meech Lake I in devolving federal powers to the provinces. The provinces were henceforth to have exclusive jurisdiction over forestry, recreation, tourism, mining, housing, municipal and urban affairs, culture, and job training. Control over immigration and regional development was to follow. Members of the Supreme Court were to be chosen from lists drawn up by the provincial governments. Apparently, there was to be no more Canadian culture; henceforth, the provincial governments "may exclusively make laws in relation to culture in the province." A new "elected" Senate was created. This Senate, when in conflict with a newly expanded House of Commons (thirty-six more members from Ontario and Quebec), would sit in a joint session — and be easily swamped. On closer examination, it turned out the new Senate could be elected either directly by the people or "indirectly" by the provincial governments; the method of selection was to be decided by each provincial government. The Quebec government promptly announced its legislature would appoint the senators from that province. As in the original Meech Lake Accord, each province also received the right to pull out of national cost-shared programs, and to set up their own programs and receive federal funds for doing so. There would be no new national programs in Mulroney's new Canada. The abhorrent "notwithstanding" clause (section 33 of the *BNA Act*), which allows Ottawa and each province to override an individual's basic legal rights, as contained in the Charter — forced into the Constitution in 1981 by power-hungry Western premiers — was not abolished. That clause was given also to the new Native elite — the so-called "third order" of government — who would be able to use it to override the rights of grassroots Natives, whenever the "third order" saw fit.

To top it off, each province received the right of veto over any further changes to national institutions, including the Senate, the House of Commons, and the role of the Supreme Court — thus casting in stone the self-serving document intended to be the prime minister's new election platform.

And what of her Majesty's loyal opposition, those elected and paid to oppose? As with Meech Lake I, they marched in lock-step with the Mulroney government. The Liberals, in their ongoing rush to betray the legacy of Pierre Trudeau, and the NDP, a party that has regularly professed its commitment to national programs, both joined the Mulroney government to promote the accord. The "new" premiers elected after the death of Meech Lake, Mike Harcourt, Roy Romanow and Bob Rae, the ink scarcely dry on their election promises to fight the "Mulroney agenda," now sang with the prime minister in exactly the same key as Bill Vander Zalm, Grant Devine and David Peterson before them and with precisely the same lack of mandate from the electorate to change the Constitution. Some Native leaders, who in 1990 declared they were opposing Meech Lake to save the country, now emerged, reincarnated as salespeople for Brian Mulroney's "renewed" Canada. These leaders received large new powers for themselves, including a whole new level of separate aboriginal government, without a hint of checks and balances, without any system of accountability to rank-and-file Natives, and with the power to override the Charter of Rights and Freedoms whenever ordinary Indians questioned this new, Canadian version of apartheid.

Like the Meech Lake Accord, these constitutional amendments would have undone not only the work of the original fathers of Confederation, but also the efforts of all those who have resisted provincial demands over the years. These constitutional changes would have balkanized the country, leaving ten provincial fiefdoms even more susceptible to manipulation by the United States. The accord would have drastically weakened the east-west links of Canada and, in concert with the FTA, would have allowed the north-south pull to grow even stronger.

Eighteenth-century Poland gave to each noble the veto power over decisions in its parliament. The resulting paralysis led ultimately to Poland's absorption by Prussia, Russia and Austria. Canada, locked into the economic embrace of the most powerful nation ever known, was facing the destruction of its existing Constitution.

Against this backdrop, on September 3, 1992, the prime minister announced that a national non-binding referendum on the accord would be held October 26. Public opinion polls showed the accord would pass with majority support. Virtually the entire Canadian political establishment outside Quebec (where both the PQ and Bloc Québécois opposed the accord for not giving enough power to that province) joined the rush to support Charlottetown. Many of the same cast of individuals who had promoted Meech Lake and the free-trade agreement crossed the country, threatening the population and predicting dire consequences if they did not vote Yes. A No vote would lead to the end of Canada, warned the prime minister. Joe Clark, now minister of constitutional affairs, invoked the spectacle of Canada becoming a Beirut or Yugoslavia with rejection of the accord. In the midst of the campaign, the Royal Bank released a study predicting the loss of $4000 for each Canadian and an exodus of one million people to the United States if Quebec separated. Now minister of fisheries, John Crosbie warned Atlantic Canada that its transfer payments would cease if Canada broke up. Former allies in the fight against free trade joined the government's campaign. The Canadian Labour Congress spent thousands of dollars of workers' dues to run ads supporting the Yes side.

To counteract the anti-native thrust of the Meech Lake Accord and the exclusion of all Native participation in its development, four carefully selected and federally funded Native organizations were invited to negotiations leading to the Charlottetown Accord: the Assembly of First Nations (AFN), led by Ovide Mercredi; the Inuit Tapirisat, under Rosemarie Kuptana; the Native Council of Canada (NCC), headed by Ron George; and the Métis National Council of Yvon Dumont. These Native spokespersons played a central role in the federal government's strategy to sell the accord to a suspicious population; they were wined, dined and flown across the country at public expense — as were all the accord's promoters — to repeated press conferences and highly publicized assemblies. Barely a speech or comment by a premier or federal cabinet minister did not invoke the name of Ovide Mercredi or one of the other Native leaders as an example of how the accord would right the historic wrongs perpetrated against the first nations. The genuine desire of the majority of Canadians to improve the Native condition and to correct past and current injustice was exploited relentlessly as the key to a Yes vote.

Other Native organizations, however, quickly came out against the accord. The Native Women's Association of Canada (NWAC) fired a shot across the bow of the Yes campaign with a powerfully worded press release declaring the Charlottetown Accord would "deny basic political rights to all Indians both on and off the reserves ... All of our human rights are thrown out the window along with the dirty water of colonialism." The document concluded: "We are also asking all Canadians ... to join with us ... and to vote No in the referendum."[4]

Confidential government briefing notes, made public by NWAC in its court action to stop the accord, revealed the government did not intend to release the final text of the accord before the October 26 vote. The public outcry forced the government to hastily put together and release in October a draft legal text. But it became clear that the government had reserved the right to make further changes after the vote, and that the voters were being asked to give the politicians a blank cheque. The Union of B.C. Indian Chiefs released its analysis of the accord, which concluded: "Kim Campbell, the Minister of Justice, has not delivered the legal text of the Accord for us to see before the referendum. She says, 'Trust me!'... we have no good reason to trust Kim Campbell or Brian Mulroney ... Take it slow, VOTE 'NO!'"[5]

An ad hoc organization, Canada for all Canadians, was set up in Ottawa and was joined by Citizens Concerned About Free Trade to hold press conferences and public meetings, and to produce and circulate literature about the dangers in the accord. Provincial Liberal Party leaders Sharon Carstairs in Manitoba and Gordon Wilson in B.C. publicly broke with their party's national position and delivered passionate and reasoned warnings on the contents of the accord. Polls showed support rapidly beginning to slip. The Reform Party and the National Action Committee on the Status of Women each launched a high-profile opposition to the document. In Quebec, the Parti Québécois and the Bloc Québécois mounted a polished campaign to defeat the accord, for reasons of their own.

What is wrong, people asked, with Canada's existing Constitution? Had it not served the country for 125 years, with updates, usually minor, introduced as needed? Constitutional amendments were necessary, Canadians were endlessly told, because Quebec had been "left out" of the Constitution in 1982. A look back, however, reveals that in 1981, seventy-three of Quebec's seventy-five MPs had voted for the repatriated Constitution. And in Quebec's legislature, on December 1, 1981, thirty-eight members of the Liberal Party had voted against a PQ resolution condemning the plan to repatriate the Constitution. The 1982 Constitution was rejected only by the PQ government, whose stated reason for being was to take Quebec out of Canada. Premier René Lévesque could hardly sign a constitutional arrangement that would have the opposite effect. Polls in Quebec in 1982 indicated high support for the constitutional package.

Nor was there any demand in Quebec for further major constitutional change when Mulroney came to power in 1984.

Through the 1990s, polls have consistently shown that less than 10 percent of Quebecers view the Constitution as a national priority.

It appeared that Canadians were experiencing an orchestrated campaign to create a diversion from the destruction of the Canadian economy and the transfer of its sovereignty to the United States under the FTA and its off-spring, the NAFTA — the real new Constitution of Canada. They were also witnessing a drive to secure the re-election of Prime Minister Brian Mulroney and his party. Had a constitutional crisis been deliberately created to destabilize the Canadian federation?

Once again it remained for Pierre Trudeau, by now eight years out of office, to provide the "official" opposition. In a lecture delivered on October 1, 1992, at a packed Montreal restaurant, with reporters practically fighting for seats, Trudeau said: "Unfortunately, high-level politicians and even high-level bankers want us to believe that voting YES is a 'yes to Canada' while NO is a 'no to Canada'. This is a lie that must be exposed." He concluded his analysis: "They have made a mess, and this mess deserves a big NO." After the speech, at the first press conference he had given in more than eight years, Trudeau continued: "Canada is already the most decentralized country in the world, of all the ... industrialized countries ... and here they come along with a further massive decentralization of power ... it is a crippling blow to the Canada that we know and love." A reporter asked: "How do you respond to criticism ... that yours is the voice from the past, that you're out of touch?" To which Trudeau, 72, replied: "Well, Pythagoras is a man from the past, but two and two are still four."

Lifting his chin in his trademark expression of contempt, Trudeau delivered a warning directly to the "doddering fools," as he called them, who'd written the accord: "You're trying to scare us into voting Yes to a Constitution that is bad for Canada, and we don't scare easily."[6]

The lecture and press conference, widely reported throughout the country and broadcast live across Quebec, provided the turning point in the campaign. A most unequal battle had suddenly become less one-sided. Politicians and pundits filled the airwaves and newspaper columns with outrage and indignation. As earlier, after his critique of Meech Lake, Trudeau was attacked by almost everyone who mattered in Canadian political, media and social circles; everyone except the people who discussed the issues he'd raised and went out in droves to purchase his article, "Say 'No' to Blackmail," in an all-time best-selling issue of *Maclean's* magazine. An instant book containing the transcript of his October 1 speech also became an overnight bestseller.

On October 26, a majority in Nova Scotia, Quebec, Manitoba, Saskatchewan, Alberta, British Columbia and the Yukon gave a resounding No to the assorted elites — political, business, labour, media and Native — who had bullied, threatened and smooth-talked, while spending nearly half a billion dollars of taxpayers' money to accomplish their goals: to decentralize Canada radically and to give politicians more, power to use against the citizens. Overall, 54.4 percent of Canadians voted No, and 44.6 percent Yes in a most unequally funded campaign. In most of Canada, the No campaign was paid for by the citizens themselves, out of their own pockets. The referendum had allowed only the Yes side access to public money, other than in Quebec, where public funding was available to both sides, equally. For the first time in a long while, the "little people" were able to give a collective swift kick to the behinds of the ruling elites.

A bitter Ovide Mercredi, chief of the Assembly of First Nations, and a vengeful Ron George of the Native Council of Canada, told the media on the night of October 26 that Canadians, in voting No, had rejected Native people. Less than forty-eight hours later, the count of votes on reserves came in: an even higher percentage of Native than non-Native voters had rejected the accord. Both men were forced to retract their statements.

After Charlottetown

THE DAY AFTER THE accord was defeated, the sky did not fall in over Canada and the dollar remained steady. The civil war in Yugoslavia appeared, if anything, more remote for Canada than the week before. For five long years, Canadians had been barraged with a form of psychological warfare, had been threatened repeatedly with the breakup of their country if they did not give in to the blackmail to weaken the Canadian Constitution. The politicians who had been threatening Canadians fell suddenly silent. With startling speed, the media began to act as if nothing had happened.

Since 1987, the separatist forces in Quebec had been on the march, unable to quite believe the golden opportunity Mr. Mulroney had handed them. In 1984-85, the Parti Québécois was broken and demoralized. Lévesque, refusing to advocate independence in the forthcoming provincial election, had called federalism "le beau risque" (a risk worth taking). The PQ finance minister, Jacques Parizeau, had split with Lévesque and, with several other indépendantistes, quit the party in disagreement. Five years later, they were heading the PQ and driving the agenda of Quebec and much of the rest of Canada. Lucien Bouchard had left his federal Cabinet post to lead a group of federal MPs called the Bloc Québécois (BQ), which campaigns openly for Quebec's separation while its members of Parliament continue to receive a federal paycheque. According to both parties, independence will solve the problems of Quebec by, among other things, reversing historical humiliation at the hands of the British on the Plains of Abraham (the American role in the conquest is ignored in separatist history). Such a solution has an emotional appeal, particularly potent to young Quebecers who see the French version of the national anthem booed at Toronto's SkyDome; who listen as anti-French quotations from the Reform Party, the Confederation of Regions Party, or APEC (Alliance for the Preservation of English in Canada) are read by PQ leaders; and who have not been able to hear a political leader in Quebec speak for Canada and in defence of federalism.

But what will the realities of an independent Quebec be? For example, what currency will it use? Few Quebecers want to take a chance on forming an unknown and inevitably weak Quebec currency; most would prefer to keep the Canadian dollar. This option may not be possible after a prolonged and bitter separation. That leaves the third option — the U.S. dollar — against which all illusions of independence evaporate.

Independence is a myth when the economy is foreign owned, be it Quebec's or Canada's. The economy of Quebec, with its dependence on hydro-electric exports to the United States, is particularly vulnerable to U.S. control. The PQ supported free trade because, as Parizeau put it, it saw it as a blow that would weaken Confederation and give Quebec the chance to escape from Canadian oppression by forging even stronger ties to the United States. In addition to being dangerously naive and short-sighted politically, this view has proved economically erroneous.

The damage to Quebec from the FTA is as great as, if not greater than, the damage to any other part of Canada. Quebec agriculture, particularly poultry, egg and dairy producers are at risk. Auto-parts companies, as well as power-intensive industries including Quebec's steel industry, are under American pressure. Both the PQ and the Liberal governments in Quebec have relied on a policy of using cheap hydro-electric power to increase manufacturing in the province. The United States has declared these hydro rates to be subsidies. In the summer of 1992, the United States levied a punishing duty of 53 percent on imports of magnesium from Norsk Hydro's Quebec plant, citing subsidized power rates the company received from Hydro Quebec and a grant from the government for anti-pollution equipment. This decision strikes at the root of Quebec's industrial policy. Norsk, according to the Montreal *Gazette*, "ended up renegotiating its power contract to satisfy U.S. authorities."[7] Quebec's large aluminum companies could be the next targets of U.S. duties. All industries wanting to avoid such harassment will tend simply to locate in the United States, where they can buy Quebec's power under the terms of the FTA at the same price as Quebec's companies and not have to worry about any U.S. trade actions.

The PQ will soon discover that the FTA strips all governments — provincial as well as federal — of the powers they have used to advance Quebec's interests. But the party, at the head of a population inundated with images of racism and rejection from English Canadians and fuelled by constant reminders of the historical "humiliation" of the conquest of 1759, is prepared to take Quebec even further into the U.S. embrace.

Meanwhile, the Reform Party has emerged in the West as a third opposition force. Although promising "reform" and a "new" Canada, it is essentially an attempt to re-create a national Social Credit Party based on pro-American and anti-Quebec sentiments. Its promise of change, while alluring to a population sick to death of existing politicians, is similar to the 1935 promise Social Credit made to Albertans of a monthly twenty-five dollars per person. In the depths of the Depression, this promise got Ernest Manning (Reform Party leader Preston Manning's father), William Aberhart and their party elected, but no one ever received the twenty-five dollars. The Reform Party's position on Quebec would lead to the splitting of the country, denying as it does the existence and rights of French Canadians as a founding people of Canada. (The same criticism applies to the Confederation of Regions Party, based in New Brunswick, whose brand of anti-French and anti-Quebec politics is as virulent as that of the Reform Party.)

The Reform Party supported the FTA before and during the 1988 election, and it still does today. The deadly combination of its pro-free-trade and anti-Quebec positions makes this party — along with the PQ in Quebec — an advocate of Canada's disintegration. When push comes to shove, the Reform Party will drop its rhetoric about "grassroots change" and attempt an alliance with the federal Conservatives, with whom, in spite of their opposition to the Charlottetown Accord for other reasons, they agree on the major issues of greater provincial powers constitutionally and free trade with the United States. Preston Manning has promised U.S. business groups to be an even "better U.S. ally" than Mulroney. The late Stan Waters, Reform Party senator, urged selling Canadian water to the United States. Not surprisingly, American influence reaches the highest levels of the Reform Party. Thomas Flanagan, previously its director of research and now senior advisor on policy, is a former American, infamous for his attacks on the Métis of Western Canada; American Frank Luntz, formerly Ronald Reagan's pollster, has been hired to assist the party.

A separate Quebec faces two options: incorporation into the United States — the Louisiana option; or existence as a marginal colony — the Puerto Rico option. In either case, the survival of the French language and culture will be far more threatened than within Canada. Equally, with Quebec gone, the rest of Canada will have a much harder time resisting assimilation into the United States.

As we have seen from history, only if Quebec and the rest of Canada stand together will both English and French Canada have the best chance to resist the power of the United States. The invasion of 1775 and the War of 1812-14 were only two examples of the kind of French-English — and aboriginal — cooperation that saved Canada.

Henri Bourassa, the great Canadian nationalist* leader of Quebec in the early decades of this century, argued that the only way for Canada to survive was to build a Canadian patriotism: "le Canada pour les Canadiens" (Canada for Canadians). English Canadians, he said, could win French Canadians to Canadian patriotism only by accepting the right of French culture to co-exist with English

---

* "Nationalist" in Quebec has come to mean a person advocating sovereignty for Quebec; by contrast, Henri Bourassa was a Canadian nationalist who vehemently opposed even the idea of Quebec's separation and who fought to prevent the Americanization of Canada.

culture all across Canada. The whole of Canada, he said, could be liberated from foreign domination if Canadians stopped fighting each other. "Those who are searching for the destruction of the French language are the worst violators of the Canadian constitution," he said. And "those who put shackles on the propagation of the language from one end of Canada to the other are, some without knowing it, others perhaps knowing it, the surest agents of destruction of ... the unity of Canadian confederation, and the most efficient instruments which the Americans could employ to absorb the Canadian confederation gradually."

It was not the French who threatened the national unity of Canada, Henri Bourassa said. The threat, rather, was the "slow but sure penetration of Americanism into all phases of our national, political and social life." Two national languages and two different cultures, far from being an obstacle to the progress of Canada, constituted its most powerful factor, Canada's greatest national asset and one of the strongest ways of resisting sure conquest "by American ideas, by American mentality, by American morals, by American pronunciation, by the American fashion of seeing, feeling and acting in everyday life." Bourassa wrote in 1915:

> I wish to show that there is, for the whole Canadian nation, for Anglo-Protestants as for French-Canadian Catholics, a marked advantage and even a strict *necessity* to preserve the French language and to favour its expansion to all parts of Confederation ... [The American] power to absorb us is not counterbalanced here, as it is in Belgium, in Holland, or in Switzerland, by the rival influence of another great nation. [But Canada has] one real and durable force with which to oppose it, the presence of a considerable ethnic group, speaking a different language, with other traditions and other ideals than those of the American people.[8]

Henri Bourassa's position is just as valid today; all that needs to be added is a recognition of aboriginal rights.

The most effective way to undermine the separatist forces in Quebec would be for Quebecers to be made to feel at home and *welcome* all across Canada by making Canada a truly bilingual nation. Right now, despite the anomaly of its sign laws, Quebec is the only effectively bilingual province in Canada. If Quebecers received the same services, treatment and respect in the rest of Canada that English-speaking Canadians receive in Quebec, the separatist movement in that province would be significantly reduced. If the only place Quebecers can feel truly at home in Canada is inside Quebec, then the PQ is on the road to victory. And Canada — French and English — is on the way to assimilation by the United States.

One cannot truly grasp the full sweep of Canadian history and culture without a knowledge of its languages. Making Canada functionally bilingual could be done for a fraction of the cost estimates being bandied about by opponents of the French language. Teaching French and English from grade one on in every school across the country would be the way to start. By high school graduation, students could be functionally literate in both languages. Rapid expansion of student exchange programs between Quebec and English Canada should be encouraged, not eliminated, as is being done. It would do wonders to break the dangerous isolation that currently exists between Quebec and the rest of the country, and would introduce young people to the realities of each other's language, culture and common history. As Trudeau put it in his 1962 essay, "New Treason of the Intellectuals": "Had English-speaking Canadians applied themselves to learning French with a quarter the diligence they have shown in refusing to do so, Canada would have been effectively bilingual long ago."[9]

It's time to stop fighting centuries-old European wars in Canada. People are no more English in "English Canada" than Quebecers are "French." The fact that Wolfe's forces had a lucky break on the Plains of Abraham and won a fifteen-minute battle cannot forever drive Canada's national agenda. What English-speaking Canada can do — what it must do — is challenge the existence of anti-French sentiment wherever it raises its head. Without Quebec's crucial and founding role in Canadian history, there would be no Canada. Awareness of this reality does not mean kowtowing to the separatist ideology with its dangerous naiveté about the power of the United States; it means recognizing the reality of the French-Canadian contribution to all of Canada, including the West. The first European language spoken at Fort Edmonton (now Alberta's capital) was French. Without that language, and without the men and women who spoke it and fought for it, all of Canada would be part of the USA.

WHICH BRINGS us to those people who spoke the first languages — not only at Edmonton, but throughout Canada.

Canadians of English, French and all other backgrounds are systematically deprived — by the educational system, the political system, the media, and the social barriers in general — of meaningful information about the history, culture and daily reality of Aboriginal people. As a result, a profound ignorance prevails in Canada about the Native population.

For more than three centuries, governments — French, British and Canadian — often forcibly removed Native leaders from their communities, executing some and jailing others. In Regina in 1885, the great Cree statesman Poundmaker was tried and convicted for nothing more than an effective, and restrained, defense of his people against a sudden and unprovoked attack on sleeping men, women and children by the Canadian army. The powerful Big Bear was similarly convicted, his crime being to refuse to sign away the land for a reserve. "What can that mean, I and my family will have a reserve of one square mile?" Big Bear had asked Governor Morris, who had come to impose a treaty on the Cree. "Who can receive land? From whom would he receive it?"[10] Both Indian leaders were released from Manitoba's Stony Mountain penitentiary to make their way back to Saskatchewan — five hundred miles, on foot — only when it was certain they were dying.

In 1876, Canada passed the *Indian Act*. That act introduced a chief and council system with formidable control over the daily lives of reserve Indians, including, as time went by, decisions over who gets housing, telephones and even jobs. These chiefs and councils are not accountable to the Indians they are supposed to serve, but are instead accountable to the federal minister of Indian affairs and responsible for carrying out the federal government's Native policies. After 1885, a pass system was instituted, under which Indians on reserves in the West by law had to obtain a pass — even to go to town. To break the will of Indian people, the government has used starvation, residential schools and missionaries. Social and cultural ceremonies, including traditional dances and the potlatch, were forbidden. Native children were punished for speaking their own language. In a further attempt to divide and conquer, Natives were sorted into various categories — status, non-status or Métis — each with different rights. Small wonder that the South African government, when planning to set up its apartheid system, sent a delegation to Canada to study the reserve system as a model. Until as late as 1960, Native Canadians were denied the right to vote. Jails still are disproportionately full of the nation's first peoples.

As a relatively new development, since the late 1960s the federal and provincial governments have been financing national and provincial Native organizations that have no accountability to grassroots Indians. Ottawa and the provinces negotiate with these organizations as if they were genuine Indian governments. Two centuries ago, Tecumseh fought hard against the "peace" chiefs for selling out Indian land they did not own. In many cases, these artificial organizations are their modern-day counterparts. As an example, Roland Crowe, the chief of the Saskatchewan Federation of Indian Nations, in a highly publicized ceremony with Mulroney during the referendum campaign, signed the Framework Land Entitlement Agreement, which would extinguish Native water and mineral rights across the province in return for $450 million. Crowe publicly advocates the continuation and expansion of uranium mining in northern Saskatchewan, defends the practice of clear-cutting the northern forest, supports the campaign to build a nuclear reactor in the province, and is lobbying for the establishment of Native-controlled Las Vegas-style gambling casinos. None of these policies has been endorsed by the province's grassroots Natives, who do not even have the right to vote for, or against, Crowe.

In spite of lack of information, the majority of Canadians have a powerful desire to see justice done to Indian people, but it is a desire that can be easily manipulated. Thus, during the Charlottetown referendum, many Canadians gave great credibility to statements by non-accountable Native leaders, even after, for example, Ovide Mercredi declared his alliance with Joe Clark: "We ... smoked this peace pipe together";[11] or after Bill Wilson of British Columbia, political secretary to the Assembly of First Nations and strong promoter of the accord, claimed he did not need to be accountable to anyone, "nor would I submit to a democratic election. I'm a hereditary chief who has proven himself for 30,000 years ..."[12]

"Self-government," however, cannot be imposed on ordinary Indians by the federal government and by the Native leaders allied with it, as the accord attempted to do. Genuine changes to the status quo must emerge from the efforts of women and men dealing with the realities that exist in their lives on reserves and in urban centres across Canada. The self-government provisions of the Charlottetown Accord were a blatant attempt by the premiers and the federal government to wash their hands of the Indian "problem." Saskatchewan's minister of justice, Bob Mitchell, in defending the accord was candid about this intent: "We turned to the Aboriginal people [and told them] here, have your governments back. You can't possibly do worse than we did ... so, have at it."[13]

This attempt to transfer power from one set of irresponsible white hands to a set of equally unaccountable, albeit Native, hands, was rejected by Native and non-Native voters alike. According to Manitoba Métis leader Jean Allard, head of the oldest Métis organization in Manitoba, La Société de Saint-Joseph de Manitoba, which was founded in 1887 and has never accepted government funding, the Charlottetown Accord would have created a "system of tin-pot dictators in banana republics" whose residents would be completely cut off from Canadian society and who, if they attempted to challenge those dictators, would be denied the protection of the Charter of Rights and Freedoms. [14]

Most Native voters had little desire to see brown hands "have at" them without having a say, and ongoing control, over those hands. "No one," writes Native commentator Michael Doxtater, "knew what Charlottetown meant, and no one was taking any politician's word on it either. Especially politicians from the Assembly of First Nations and its 550 band council chiefs, who were making a power-play for control of $5-billion in Native Affairs funding. This would have come at the expense of treaties and native rights. All because these 'leaders' don't know their own people."[15]

Eileen Linklater, a member of the Peter Ballantyne band in northern Saskatchewan, mother of four and one of the leaders in the fight to stop ratification of the $450-million Framework Land Entitlement Agreement, said in an interview shortly after band members had come out in force to block the entry of Roland Crowe and his officials onto their reserve in November 1992:

> The government is buying our leaders to manipulate our people. What the government wants, specifically from the Peter Ballantyne Band Cree Nation, is the water, our mineral rights and the forestry. The reason why they want the water is they have made a deal with the USA and it connects with the Free Trade Agreement. There are two dams that are waiting right now to be filled, the Rafferty and the Alameda, and then they'll divert the water to the States. They're going to start from Lake Athabasca, coming down the Reindeer River, Churchill River and go through our rivers. And there won't be anything left [for the people]. On all the reserves I've been to, the only people that benefit from the funding we get from the government are the chosen few. For jobs, for housing, for everything. The leadership always favour the ones that help them, the family, friends and people who help make things go through for them. And

as for the rest, they don't bother with them. And that's exactly what's going to happen with that Framework Agreement.

Graham Linklater, local band councillor and husband to Eileen, was succinct: "The way I look at it, our leaders these days, a majority of them, are totally bought off by the federal government. And, the federal government is bought off by the U.S.A. And I don't agree with that at all."[16]

The results of the referendum showed that 62 percent of the reserve residents who voted had repudiated their own "leaders," revealing that these organizations are, if possible, even further removed from their constituency than the provincial and federal governments are from theirs.

As in the past, when alliances between Native, French- and English-speaking Canadians kept the Americans at bay, similar alliances must be forged today between non-Native Canadians fighting their non-representative leaders and Native people fighting theirs. Across Canada, grassroots Indians, often in open conflict with their own government-supported leaders, are on the front lines in the fight against diversion of rivers, clear-cutting of forests, the destruction of Canada's environment and the loss of sovereignty over its water. Instead of a sense of guilt that can be manipulated by selected leaders, Canadians who are serious about building such an alliance must work to allow the voices, thoughts and experiences of grassroots Indians to emerge. Just as English-speaking Canadians must act to integrate the French language and Quebec history and culture into mainstream Canadian life, so too must the fight be waged to have Native history, culture and languages permeate our educational and social system in a way we have never before seen.

Those who came to Canada after 1867 came to a nation that was already formed, one whose borders had already been defended in blood by its founding peoples. The rights, languages and respect due those founders — aboriginal, French and English — are not to be toyed with and belittled by those who came subsequently. When this is understood and put into practice, Canada will have less trouble resisting the power of the empire to the south.

Part Three

Awakening the Giant

26

"You Know We'll Abrogate"

ON FEBRUARY 24, 1993, Brian Mulroney announced that he was resigning as prime minister; the writing had been on the wall since the defeat of the Charlottetown constitutional referendum. Across the country there was an immediate outpouring of feeling: joy, relief — and anger at his legacy. A cartoon appeared in major newspapers showing a fallen Mulroney lying in the snow with a bullet hole squarely between the eyes, a silent Trudeau walking away holstering his gun. From south of the border, ex-President George Bush issued a statement of regret saying Prime Minister Mulroney was a good friend of the United States.

Attempting to distance itself from the Mulroney image, the Conservative Party chose a woman from Western Canada, a relative newcomer to the party, Kim Campbell, as its new leader. She called an election for late October, 1993. Before Mulroney's departure, however, his government introduced into the House of Commons the sweeping NAFTA implementing legislation changing twenty-nine Canadian federal statutes.

Following the 1988 election, the Liberal Party had replaced John Turner as leader of the party with Jean Chrétien, a long-time high-profile member from Shawinigan, Quebec, and former senior cabinet minister in the Trudeau government. A few years earlier, Mr. Chrétien had published his bestselling autobiography entitled *Straight from the Heart,* in which he set out his position on free trade:

> Some people say that the only way for Canada to avoid being hurt by American protectionism is to guarantee Canadian access to the U.S. market by free trade. My concern is whether Canada could survive politically or whether the logical result wouldn't be the integration of the two countries ... Without safeguards or defences we probably would be clobbered, because the Americans would be able to do whatever

they want. Those who argue that free trade is our only hope and perhaps inevitable have either given up on the idea of a unique and independent Canada or haven't thought about the consequences ...[1]

Under Mr. Chrétien, the official Liberal Party policy on free trade was that "if the Free Trade Agreement cannot be renegotiated, the Government of Canada exercise its right under the Agreement to end the Agreement." In May 1992, the party introduced a motion in the House calling for abrogation of the FTA "unless the Agreement has been successfully renegotiated in a manner satisfactory to Canadian interests."[2]

As the 1993 election campaign got underway, the Liberal Party released its Red Book of election promises, which described the free trade agreements as "flawed" and "an energy giveaway," and stated:

A Liberal government will renegotiate both the FTA and NAFTA to obtain: a subsidies code; an anti-dumping code; a more effective dispute resolution mechanism; and the same energy protection as Mexico.

Each of the promises would be honoured, candidates from the leader down vowed repeatedly, holding up the book as their pledge, in campaign stops across the country. Speaking to an audience in Toronto shortly before polling day, Jean Chrétien stated, "If we can't renegotiate, you know we'll abrogate."

Meanwhile, NAFTA had passed the Mexican Senate, and debate was underway in the U.S. Congress. It appeared the vote would be close, as Bill Clinton was having trouble getting enough members of his own party to vote for it. Debate raged across the United States. Billionaire presidential candidate Ross Perot had campaigned hard against ratification, and Ralph Nader's Public Citizen, the U.S. labour movement, and many citizens' organizations were fighting it. Polls showed a majority of Americans opposed to NAFTA.

Four days before the election, U.S. Ambassador James Blanchard flew to Quebec City to meet Chrétien's chief of staff, Jean Pelletier. Washington, he said, was worried. If Canada insisted on renegotiation, NAFTA would be dead in the U.S. Congress. "This is really sensitive, but I'll confide in you," Blanchard told Pelletier:

Your new government will have the life-and-death power to kill NAFTA, in an instant. And you can kill it without anyone ever knowing you killed it. You can kill NAFTA if, the day after the election, Jean Chrétien says that he's hoping to renegotiate it. If he says that, it's dead, because Congress will say they're not going to vote on it until they see the new deal and they'll walk away from it. If you want to kill NAFTA without leaving any fingerprints, I'm telling you now, as a fellow politician, you have a perfect way to do it. But I hope you won't ... the important thing is that, no matter how many times you're asked, no matter how many different ways, on election night or in the days that follow, we would really appreciate that you not use the word 'renegotiate'. You can say you want to consult with us, you can say you have some concerns you want to discuss, but don't suggest renegotiating the agreement or it's finished.[3]

On election night, October 25, 1993, the Conservative Party was hurled from office in the most sweeping repudiation of a political party in a Western democracy — reduced from 159 seats in the House of Commons to 2, losing even its official status as a party. The Liberals had achieved a majority government.

The political eyes of North America turned to Canada's new prime minister. The newly elected Liberal Party held in its hands the power to kill what it had dubbed "the Sale of Canada Act" and undo the Mulroney legacy it had campaigned against for eight years.

An ominous silence emanated from Ottawa.

On November 17,1993, NAFTA passed by a narrow vote of 234 — 200 in the U.S. House of Representatives. The next day Jean Chrétien and Bill Clinton met in Seattle. The U.S. ambassador Blanchard picks up the story:

The meeting had already been plotted in some detail. Originally we wanted to announce that we had a deal on NAFTA, but that would have made it look as though Chrétien had flown to the United States and immediately capitulated. Instead, the president would raise the subject, the prime minister would respond with his concerns, and they would agree to pass the file over to their trade officials. Then, if it all worked out according to plan, the Canadian cabinet would approve NAFTA in a few weeks and the government would proclaim it.

Two weeks later the Liberals issued the following statement:

Talking Points on NAFTA Improvements

- In an historic breakthrough, Canada has won the significant improvements it sought in NAFTA, and is prepared to implement the agreement on January 1, 1994.

- Jean Chrétien has stood firm. He has consistently stated his requirements for changes to NAFTA. Critics said the U.S. wouldn't even discuss changes. They said it couldn't be done. They were wrong.

- For the first time in a long time, a Canadian government has stood up for Canada's interests in dealing with the Americans.

- Tough bargaining by Canada has won us the bulk of the changes we sought. This is a good deal for Canada — a far better deal than the Tories negotiated. It's a good deal for all three countries.

- Canada has always been and always will be a trading nation. In the new global marketplace, protectionism is passé.

During the last week of 1993 the Chrétien government ratified NAFTA without changing a single word and kept the FTA in place exactly as negotiated between the Mulroney and Reagan administrations. Abruptly, Liberal members who had for six years condemned "the Mulroney sell-outs" began to praise the agreements they had just campaigned against. Summing up the U.S. ambassador said, "Chrétien did everything humanly possible to help us get NAFTA through."[4]

For years afterward, prominent Liberal ministers continued to maintain they had secured "changes" to NAFTA. In order to be binding any change would have required ratification by the Mexican Congress, the U.S. Congress and the Canadian Parliament. None was. On January 1, 1994, NAFTA — as originally initialled by George Bush, Carlos Salinas and Brian Mulroney — took effect.

Having adopted the central plank of the Mulroney government, the new Liberal regime rapidly embraced virtually every major policy of the previous government — including the Goods and Services Tax it had also campaigned against — and set about escalating their thrust. Deputy ministers and department heads from the Mulroney era were left in place along with their policies.

During the election the Liberals had campaigned against the Conservatives' focusing "obsessively" on the deficit, as the Red Book put it. In power, Liberal ministers suddenly began to condemn government spending in apocalyptic terms. The new finance minister, Paul Martin, vowed dramatically to "break the back" of the deficit, "come hell or high water." Cuts to government programs begun by the Conservatives were not reversed but increased. Whole government departments were slashed beyond recognition. The debt and deficit became a kind of mantra invoked by the government to justify its withdrawal from wide spheres of economic and social activity, simply turning them over to "the marketplace," which for Canada often simply means U.S. ownership.

As for the "debt crisis," Canada's total debt was less (on a comparative basis) in the 1990s than in the years following the Second World War. The bulk of the debt came from high interest rates paid by both federal and provincial governments to domestic and foreign banks — a situation which could be largely remedied by simply doing government borrowing where necessary from the Bank of Canada, rather than from foreign banks. (The precedent for this practice was set during the Second World War, when Canada used the Bank of Canada to double the size of the economy in just six years — without borrowing a cent abroad.) Any interest earned by the Bank of Canada, a publicly owned institution, returns to Canadians. Instead, under an ideology that government must "stand aside," billions of citizens' hard-earned tax dollars were handed annually to foreign and domestic banks enjoying record profits, while Canadians were bombarded ceaselessly with the message that they must lower their expectations and tighten their belts because "the cupboard is bare."

Meanwhile, the wave of takeovers from south of the border continued unabated across the Canadian economy. By 1998, more than 6000 Canadian companies had been taken over since the FTA — most by American corporations. U.S. investors are snapping up Canadian hotel properties at a feverish pace and are completely dominating the hotel investment market, the *Globe and Mail* reported. Virtually the entire flour milling industry moved from Canadian to American hands in the space of 18 months. U.S. grain companies threaten the Canadian Wheat Board. Canadian Pacific put the American flag on its logo and sold its Sherbrooke-Saint John line to a U.S. company. By 1995, only one of the top ten advertising agencies in Canada — a $10 billion industry — was Canadian.[5] Even the famous Bauer Skate Company in Ontario was taken over by Nike, closed down, and production was transferred offshore. Exclusive promotional rights to the RCMP and all of its symbols were given to Disney Corporation. When students at a Vancouver high school, in early 1998, called the RCMP seeking a scarlet uniform to use in a play they were told they must first get permission from Disney Corporation in the United States. In a crowning gesture of colonial fawning, Canada Post even issued a stamp bearing the Disney name and logo.

27

The Great Canadian Train Robbery

IN APRIL 1993, Conservative finance minister Don Mazankowski had announced, "Since 1984, the government has privatized or dissolved thirty-nine Crown enterprises and other holdings." In opposition and during the 1993 election campaign the Liberals had condemned the Mulroney privatizations. Less than a week before the October 1993 election, opposition leader Jean Chrétien had attacked the Conservatives' "tolerance of rail line abandonments and consideration for the privatization of CN Rail."

Then in 1995, 16 months after the election, Paul Martin, the new Liberal finance minister, rose in the House of Commons and stated: "Today we are announcing that the Minister of Transport will initiate steps this year to sell CN."[1] Refusing to use the word privatization, apparently for fear of public reaction, the government introduced what it called the *CN Commercialization Act*.

The history of CN had actually begun in 1836 when Canada's first railway, the Champlain and St. Lawrence, began operations. In 1856, the Grand Trunk, which George-Étienne Cartier had been instrumental in building, linked Toronto and Montreal. By 1860, the Grand Trunk was the longest railway in the world. By 1917 Canada had three national railways and numerous smaller ones, but many were facing bankruptcy including the Grand Trunk itself, long the dominant railway in Ontario and Quebec, now surviving on government handouts. It became clear the country could not sustain three national railways. The Borden government decided, against loud and bitter opposition from the large financial interests and much of the press, to nationalize, with compensation, all the major railways except the CPR, which was still financially solvent. "If the public does the financing, the public should enjoy the ultimate reward," the Conservative minister of finance, Thomas White, told the House.[2]

Canadian Northern, the Grand Trunk, Grand Trunk Pacific, National Transcontinental, and the Intercolonial, along with over 200 affiliated railway, shipping and telegraph companies, including the historic Champlain and St. Lawrence, were amalgamated into one system — Canadian National — incorporating five major railways and over 30,000 kilometres of track.

The new president, Henry Thornton, set up Canadian National's headquarters in the Grand Trunk building in Montreal, with the goal, he said, "to make our railway, the People's Railway, of real service to the people of Canada."[3]

CN ran medical, dental, and school cars — people across the North attended its "schools on wheels" — and created one of the best passenger services in the world. Tourists crossed the Atlantic for the experience of riding CN's "landliners," fancy sleeping cars named after Canadian cities, across the Prairies and through the Rockies. Farmers could, and did, set their watches by CN trains. Unique among the world's railways, CN pioneered a radio service which broadcast concerts, plays about Canadian history, and hockey games to its passengers on the first radio network in North America. It became the foundation of the Canadian Broadcasting Corporation. Later CN founded the airline which evolved into Air Canada.

Thanks to the painstaking work of the great engineer Sandford Fleming, appointed by John A. Macdonald's government to survey a trans-Canada rail route and pass through the mountains, CN possesses the easiest grades through the Rockies of any North American railway.

But now in 1995, the Liberals had decided that CN would be sold. Key Americans would be brought in to do the job. First, a Chicago management consultant firm was hired, which recommended "brutal surgery" for CN. Then, in the months leading up to the announcement of the sale, a barrage of media stories appeared: CN was "a lunking over-regulated bureaucratic giant," "a Crown-owned basket case," "the national nightmare," "fat," "bloated," "inefficient," "debt-ridden," "a subsidy-consuming behemoth," a "white elephant," "a pig," even "a pig with lipstick," which had received "boxcars of subsidies."[4]

The party which had come to power promising to end "the Mulroney sell-outs" was about to transfer into foreign hands Canada's great national railway — its roots going back over 150 years.

"The National dream of iron horses, steel rails and steam is dead," declared the minister of transport, Doug Young, announcing CN's sale. "Today, Canadians see medicare, old age security, education and other social programs as the essential goals of government."[5]

Goldman Sachs of New York was awarded the contract as global coordinator of the sale and lead manager internationally.

U.S. investors do not like to buy into partnerships with government, it was reported, so the Canadian government eliminated all foreign ownership restrictions on the sale. The Conservatives had sold parts of Air Canada and Petro-Canada, but under the Liberals there would be "no more half-hearted, hand-wringing, cautious Canadian privatizations," declared a senior bureaucrat in charge of the sale.[6]

Private investors would object to CN's debt load of roughly $1 billion — so the government decided to have the taxpayers absorb it before the sale.

The Crow's Nest Pass freight rates, called by John Diefenbaker "the Magna Carta of the western farmer," had been guaranteed to farmers "in perpetuity" on shipments of grain to port. To make CN more attractive for sale, the government simply abolished the historic 1897 Crow rate* and passed legislation making it easier for railways to abandon lines. In the space of a year, freight rates for Saskatchewan farmers to ship their grain soared 300 percent adding on average $15,000 a year in increased costs per western grain farm.

On November 17, 1995, the longest railway in North America was put on the market — at a fraction of its value. The stock market went into a frenzy. "The demand for Canadian National Railways shares swept the Canadian and U.S. stock markets like wild fire yesterday as traders burned up the phones trying to fill orders," reported the *Globe and Mail*.[7] In a week, 65 percent of the shares were foreign owned, mostly in U.S. hands. Within a year the share price had risen more than 100 percent. By 1998 it had quadrupled, giving investors a 400 percent return — achieved on the work and vision of Cartier and Macdonald and the blood, sweat and tears of hundreds of thousands of Canadians who had built and financed the great railway.

After the sale was completed, it turned out that CN had made a profit in all but two of the past seventeen years. A world leader in information technology with double-track capacity from sea to sea carrying the continent's best balanced mix of freight, CN was the continent's only truly transcontinental railway. "CN has the benefits of the ports of Halifax and Vancouver, two of the deepest and most

---

*   Crow rate. A reduced freight rate for transporting grain. As specified in the 1897 Crow's Nest Pass Agreement and revisions, the railways, in return for large subsidies of public land and cash, agreed to lowered rates "in perpetuity" to move Prairie grain to port.

efficient natural harbours on the continent ... a double-track core system in Ontario and Quebec that thrusts itself into the U.S. market all the way to Chicago," pointed out one informed observer. With excellent rolling stock and almost 30,000 kilometres of track, almost all in good shape, CN was "physically and strategically this continent's best railway."[8]

At the sale of the biggest and oldest of Canada's Crown corporations, the finance minister, Paul Martin, and the minister of transport, Doug Young, posed for the cameras with broad smiles, holding a mock cheque for $2.1 billion.

Slightly over a year later, the Association of American Railroads gave CN's president, Paul Tellier, its "Right Hand Man" award. The U.S. magazine, *Railway Age* of January 1997, presented him with its "Railroader of the Year" citation, praising his role in selling the company.

In 1997 all of the rail lines of northern Manitoba and the Port of Churchill itself were sold by CN and the Canadian government to Omnitrax of Denver, for a reported price of $1. Shortly thereafter, CN sold two more lines in Saskatchewan to Omnitrax. At about the same time, the Liberal Party received large donations from many of the banks and brokerage companies that had handled the CN sale and that had received millions of dollars in fees for doing so.

At the same time the government was preparing to sell Canada's national railway in New York, the October 30, 1995, Quebec referendum campaign was underway. Quebec premier Jacques Parizeau had made no secret of his intention in the event of a Yes vote to pass a unilateral declaration of independence and appeal for international recognition.

The same federal government systematically dismantling the social, economic, cultural and rail links necessary to hold the country together now declared it was for "national unity." How could a government embarked on a campaign of selling off the national infrastructure (CN had been one of Montreal's largest industries) convince Quebecers, or anyone else, that Canada could or should survive? The nation watched transfixed. The Reform Party leapt into the void, releasing its "proposals to modernize and decentralize" the nation. Its Agenda for a New Confederation called for a massive weakening of the power of the federal government, stating: "We propose measures which will assert the autonomy of all provinces." Natural resources, manpower training, culture, housing, tourism, and sport and recreation were to become exclusive provincial jurisdictions.

The judges of the Supreme Court and the directors of the Bank of Canada were to be chosen by the provincial premiers. Thenceforth, "Ottawa will play a cooperative role rather than a dominating role" in Reform's new Canada.

Meanwhile, Lucien Bouchard, now leader of the official opposition in Ottawa, nevertheless campaigned non-stop across Quebec for the Yes side in highly charged rallies. Quebec had been humiliated, he repeated over and over.

Bouchard's arguments went virtually unanswered from the federal side; he had the stage almost to himself.

On October 30, the voting was heavy. As the votes were counted that night the streets of Montreal were almost deserted. By 10 p.m., with 80 percent of the vote counted, it was still too close to call. Finally the tally stood at 49.43 percent yes, 50.57 percent no, and Premier Parizeau began to speak. "We are beaten, it's true. But by what? By money and the ethnic vote," he declared. Fifteen hours later he announced his resignation. The prominent Quebec playwright, René-Daniel Dubois, gave a full-page interview to *Le Monde,* in which he described the sovereignty movement as "a vast, empty exercise in emotional blackmail, devoid of critical thought and antagonistic toward it."[9] The referendum was an attempted suicide that failed, he said, lashing out as well at the federal government: "I think we have only one party here. But we have two factions. The purpose of both is the same: to become Americans. One group thinks we will get a better price if we sell along with the rest of Canada and the other says, 'No, if we can sell ourselves alone, we'll get better revenue!' And I disagree with both sides. I don't wish to be American."[10]

After the referendum, other premiers rushed to explain what the vote meant. Quebecers want constitutional change, the Western premiers announced. The days of a strong central government are over, pronounced B.C.'s Mike Harcourt. Alberta's Ralph Klein declared: "What Quebec wants to achieve is what all provinces want to achieve and that is the restoration of our constitutional authority." Daniel Johnson, opposition leader in Quebec, said that now "everyone in Quebec can join the Liberals to embark on a role of decentralization of the constitution."

The federal government over the next three years proceeded to do exactly that, transferring, or agreeing to transfer, to the provinces control over manpower training, immigration, tourism, mining, forestry, recreation, social housing and virtually the entire field of environmental protection. The Charlottetown Accord, voted down by both French- and English-speaking Canada, was being implemented anyhow. Somehow the public was supposed to believe that dismantling the federal government and giving greater powers to the provinces would appease the separatists, improve the economy and help Canada survive. Meanwhile, a post-referendum poll in Quebec found that only 16 percent of Quebecers thought constitutional change should be Canada's top priority. Nevertheless in 1997 the premiers gathered in Calgary and announced a new proposal called the Calgary Framework — and again in Saskatoon in 1998 calling it a "social-union agreement" — where they demanded as the price for constitutional peace the transfer of even more powers away from the central government to the provinces.

For the vast majority of Canadians — French- and English-speaking — the discontent in Canada is not constitutional; the problems the country faces are not constitutional. Therefore, tinkering with the Constitution will not solve them. What is needed is a national vision and the will to implement it. This means building a genuinely Canadian economy with employment, pride and dignity for all. What is required is the political foresight and backbone to make Canada an economic and cultural force as well — creating and building, for example, a Canadian car, a fully-fledged Canadian aerospace industry, and a Canadian motion picture industry, and rebuilding a merchant marine fleet — so essential to a seafaring nation — to carry our products around the world. Rather than clearcutting our forests, exporting unprocessed lumber, raw logs and increasing quantities of precious non-renewable natural resources — which means exporting jobs and our future security — we should be building world-class industries here based on the sustainable use of our nation's assets.

Instead, at this critical moment, the Canadian government was escalating its policy of transferring its constitutional power to the provincial premiers and control of Canada's economy and its resources to foreign ownership.

28

10 Years After

IN 1995, SHORTLY AFTER the government announced its intention to sell CN Rail, the Liberals began negotiating behind closed doors in Paris to expand the investment section of NAFTA into a new agreement called the Multilateral Agreement on Investment (MAI). These negotiations were kept secret until early 1997, when a draft text of the MAI was leaked and made public by citizens' organizations.

The 140-page proposed MAI text extended the investment chapter of NAFTA to all 29 countries of the Organization for Economic Cooperation and Development (OECD), with a few key changes. Both the FTA and NAFTA have a clause stating that any country can, at any time, give the others six months' notice and then withdraw; the MAI, however, had a 20-year lock-in period. A country could not give notice to withdraw for five years, and then, even after it had withdrawn, the provisions of the agreement would "continue to apply for a period of fifteen years." In other words, the agreement proposed to bind future governments for two decades, no matter what had been their election platforms or the wishes of the population. In fact, India's former GATT negotiator, Bhagirath Lal Das, wrote a comprehensive critique at the early stages of MAI negotiations, warning that the treaty "will give investors total rights without responsibilities."

In Chapter 11 of NAFTA, for the first time in a multilateral trade agreement, foreign corporations were given the right to sue national governments directly, for any law, regulation or program which causes them "loss or damage" and which they feel breaches NAFTA's rules. (Under previous trade agreements and under the GATT, only governments could challenge other governments' laws or practices and disputes are adjudicated by neutral third countries.) These NAFTA lawsuits against Canada — which can take aim at any federal, provincial or municipal policy — are heard not in Canadian courts, using Canadian law, but by special tribunals operating behind closed doors, outside the country. Their decisions are based not on Canadian law, but on NAFTA's rules. There is no right of appeal.

The first NAFTA lawsuits are proceeding. Ethyl Corporation of Virginia makes a gasoline additive called MMT, which has been declared a health hazard in the United States and banned in California since 1978. In opposition Jean Chrétien had called MMT "an insidious neurotoxin" with "truly horrific effects" and demanded a Canadian ban on "a substance that threatens the health of millions of Canadians, particularly our children."[1] In 1996, the Canadian government passed legislation barring the importation and transportation of MMT, and Ethyl responded with a $347 million NAFTA lawsuit against the Canadian government. The government declared it would defend its legislation vigorously, citing "Canada's sovereign right" to protect Canadians' health and "to preserve the environment."[2]

In July of 1998 in a sudden and dramatic move, the Canadian government announced it was withdrawing its MMT ban, issued a written apology to Ethyl stating "MMT poses no health risk," and paid Ethyl almost $20 million for its legal costs and for lost profits. In return Ethyl agreed to withdraw its lawsuit. This stunning development revealed that NAFTA gives U.S. corporations the power not only to undermine Canada's laws, but to actually reverse them, in this case, with compensation! Writing from Atlanta's Emory University, Dr. Howard Frumkin summed up the episode: "A U.S. company hammered Canada with the NAFTA club, and Canada had to back down. This was a triumph for the Ethyl Corp. and a few gasoline refiners — but a sad day for science, public health, the environment, consumers and Canadian sovereignty."[3]

A second NAFTA lawsuit involves the Metalclad corporation of California, which purchased a toxic waste dump in the Mexican state of San Luis Potosi. The residents of the area demonstrated, with machetes in their hands, and forced the site to close down. Metalclad is now suing the Mexican government for $97 million (U.S.).

In late summer of 1998, the S.D. Myers corporation of the U.S. launched a NAFTA lawsuit against Canada regarding a law on highly toxic PCBs, and not long afterwards Time Inc. threatened to do likewise if Canada did not abandon proposed legislation concerning advertising in foreign-owned publications.

The NAFTA right of foreign corporations to sue national governments was reproduced in the MAI and extended to all the corporations from the 29 OECD countries. Because only foreign corporations (not domestic ones) are given the right to sue the

Canadian government under NAFTA (and the proposed MAI), foreign corporations now have greater rights in Canada than Canadian citizens, or Canadian companies. This right to sue is a powerful and indefensible lever over public policy given to foreign companies with no responsibility or accountability to Canadian citizens.

The proposed MAI also contained sections called "Standstill" and "Rollback." Standstill required, as did NAFTA, that each government list all its laws and programs that do not conform with the MAI; and then, again as in NAFTA, each government was prohibited from passing any new laws that are "non-conforming." The rollback section called for each government to "roll-back" or "phase-out" over time all of its laws and programs that were "non-conforming."

Canada now maintains restrictions on the foreign ownership of its banks (except as regards American citizens), media, and in some provinces, farmland and oceanfront property. The existence of the CBC, the Canadian Wheat Board, medicare and public education are all "non-conforming measures" which would be subject to phase-out under the sweeping rollback section.

The government responded that it would list reservations which would "protect" existing Canadian regulations and institutions. But it was precisely to these reservations that the rollback section was designed to apply.

As the contents of the MAI became publicly known, a furor of opposition developed around the world. The French government withdrew from negotiations and in April 1998, the other negotiating governments announced they were going to take a temporary break in negotiations, presumably to allow the opposition to die down. The head of the OECD, Canadian Donald Johnston, made it clear in June 1998 that he intended to resume the negotiations and achieve agreement as soon as possible.

The wording and arguments used by the Liberal government to defend the MAI were virtually identical to those previously used by the Mulroney government promoting the FTA and NAFTA — which the Liberals had attacked for so long.

On December 11, 1997, Sergio Marchi, the minister of international trade, whose government had achieved power campaigning against NAFTA, announced, "Our mandate is to replicate NAFTA, no more, no less." The government argued that the MAI would simply extend the FTA and NAFTA and that those agreements were good for Canada.

What, then, ten years after the Canada-U.S. FTA, was the government "replicating"? At the time of entering the FTA, Canada's unemployment rate was roughly equal to the U.S. rate and had been for years. By 1997 it was double the U.S. rate. Throughout the decade following the passage of the FTA, Canada experienced its longest period of sustained high unemployment and its worst social conditions since the 1930s. People were begging on the streets of cities across the country in a way not seen since the Great Depression. Personal and business bankruptcies reached record levels year after year after the FTA was passed.

The promise of increased prosperity from free trade, with more secure, higher-paying jobs, remains unfulfilled. A 1998 job survey from Statistics Canada revealed that the top ten categories of employment in Canada were not the secure high-tech jobs forecast to flow from free trade. Rather, they were (for men): truck drivers, retail sales, janitors, retail trade managers, farmers, sales reps, motor mechanics, material handlers, carpenters and construction trade labourers; (for women): retail sales, secretaries, cashiers, registered nurses, account clerks, elementary teachers, food service, general office clerks, babysitters and receptionists.

The survey found that working-at-home, being self-employed, and part-time work categories were growing by leaps and bounds while full-time jobs were vanishing.

Instead of rising, wages, and our standard of living, have fallen since the FTA. A dramatic example was the extraction by Maple Leaf Foods of a 45 percent wage rollback from its workers in early 1998. The president of the company, Michael McCain, cited NAFTA in explaining the cut. Wages of $6.00 an hour for meat-packing are common in the United States, and the industry makes extensive use of illegal immigrants. These are the standards that Canadian companies such as Maple Leaf must compete directly against under the FTA. The promise of richer social programs as a result of increased prosperity from free trade stands revealed as perhaps the greatest fraud, since virtually every public program in the country has been downsized or cut under the FTA. Canada's universal medicare system is under unprecedented assault as private U.S. health corporations move in under the terms of the FTA.

Government and academic promoters of free trade with the United States point to increased exports as proof the FTA and NAFTA are working. But Canadian exports are high because of a low dollar, and because the U.S. economy is expanding faster than Canada's, not because of the FTA. The average tariff on all our exports to the U.S. prior to the FTA was 1 percent and falling. Hardly a barrier to trade. In the first half decade of the FTA not only did Canada lose a quarter of its manufacturing jobs, the industrial heartland collapsed and commercial real estate values in Toronto plummeted by two-thirds.

In the six years before the FTA the Canadian gross domestic product grew by $260 billion; in the six years after, by $106 billion — less than half the previous rate of growth. In 1988 it grew by $54 billion; in 1991 by $5 billion — one-tenth as much — the direct result of the free trade induced recession. Instead of recognizing the FTA as the cause of reduced revenue, governments of every stripe are cutting, slashing, downsizing, offloading and blaming each other for lack of funds. Had Canada continued growing at the rate it had in the half decade prior to the FTA the budget deficit would have disappeared in the early 1990s — without cutting expenditures. And unemployment would be under 3 percent. Instead, the entire national infrastructure is under siege. U.S. ownership is at an all-time high and sweeping Americanization is affecting all aspects of Canadian society.

While north-south trade between Canada and the United States is up dramatically (most of it between U.S. corporations and their subsidiaries in Canada), east-west trade across Canada is down sharply. As the trade links between Canada's far-flung regions are cut, so too are the already far too limited social, cultural and economic contacts, increasing the pressure for political disintegration. Speaking to a joint session of the Maine legislature during his 1998 "American spring" tour of the United States, Lucien Bouchard, now premier of Quebec, said: "Those of us who believe that Quebec should become an independent country were at the forefront of the trade liberalization movement. And a good decision it was ... In the last five years, the United States has become our first trading partner, and conversely, Quebec now stands as one of the U.S.'s top trading partners. In fact, our trade with your country weighs more than the total of our commercial exchanges with Canada."[4] Why, he concludes, does Quebec need to remain part of Canada?

Part of the increased trade is the escalating sale of raw energy across the border — at fire sale prices. The "energy giveaway" condemned in the Liberals' Red Book escalated under their administration. Between 1992 and 1997, the United States boosted its yearly take of Canadian natural gas by over 50 percent. By 1998 the United States was taking over half of Canada's annual oil and gas production while our reserves rapidly dwindled.

According to National Energy Board figures, as exports deplete our reserves, the cost of natural gas to consumers will increase dramatically, and by 2012, at the current rate of extraction, Canada's entire known gas reserves will be extinct. Yet huge new gas pipeline projects for export are forging ahead, including the Alliance proposal to build the continent's largest pipeline — from Fort St. John, B.C., to Chicago. This pipeline alone would increase Canada's exports of natural gas by 10 percent.

At a time when cutbacks to education have Alberta's parents putting on bake sales to purchase basic necessities for their schools, the royalties the Alberta government is receiving on the petroleum going to the United States out of the giant Athabaska tar sands of northern Alberta range from 0 to 1 percent. It takes approximately twelve barrels of water to produce each barrel of petroleum from the tar sands, and this water is given free to the oil companies by Alberta. The water is worth more than Alberta is receiving back in royalties!

Shortly after the Liberals ratified NAFTA, a series of conferences were held in Canada and the United States on further continental union under NAFTA. At the November 1994 *Conference on the Next Stages of North American Economic Integration* in Montreal, attended by prominent political, academic and financial figures from the three countries, a paper was presented calling for Canada and Mexico to become the 13th and 14th federal reserve districts of the U.S. federal reserve system and recommending the phase-out of the Bank of Canada and adoption of the U.S. dollar as the common currency for the NAFTA region. By 1998, prominent voices in both Canada and the United States, including the Wall Street Journal and leading Quebec separatists, were calling openly for a common North American currency. With the loss of its currency Canada would be unable to pursue fiscal policies of its own and would cease to be an independent nation.

And what about the promise that NAFTA would be good for Mexico, raising its standard of living at last to first world status? Since NAFTA's signing, Mexico's unemployment rate has doubled, the peso is worth half its former value and prices have risen roughly 100 percent. The ongoing revolt in Chiapas — begun in response to the imposition of NAFTA — was timed to begin January 1, 1994, at NAFTA's implementation. NAFTA, said its leaders, was "a death sentence for the indigenous people of Mexico."

In July 1998, the C.D. Howe Institute of Canada, the government and corporate think tank that had promoted the free trade agreements relentlessly for over a decade, released a study concluding that in "cases with major stakes for the Canadian economy," Canada "may be better off simply not using the [NAFTA] Chapter 19 process, and taking disputes to the WTO." The study reviews the track record of settling disputes at the GATT-World Trade Organization and recommends that "Canada should consider using the dispute settlement process of the World Trade Organization instead of that of the North American Free Trade Agreement (NAFTA) to oppose any future U.S. countervail action against Canadian lumber or in any other complex subsidy case."

The C.D. Howe Institute appeared to discover, with surprise, what opponents of the Canada-U.S. FTA had maintained for over a decade. Under the heading "The Multilateral Alternative," the study states:

> Despite persistent criticism that the GATT multilateral dispute process was slow and not legally rigorous, it worked well to resolve most trade disagreements ... 88% of the disputes put before it between 1948 and 1989 were successfully resolved ...

> Canada was successful against the United States in seven out of eight legal actions to which both countries were parties, a remarkable record that indicates a multilateral process can do much to redress a power imbalance between large and middle-sized international trade partners."[5]

With even its most ardent promoters drawing conclusions about what was cited as the crowning achievement, the very raison d'être, of the free trade agreement with the United States — its dispute settlement mechanism — what reason remains for Canada to stay in the agreements that are doing so much damage and costing the nation its sovereignty?

29

The Sleeping Giant

ONE OF THE MOST IMPORTANT rights a nation has is the control over its economy in general and its trade in particular. This was the issue over which the American Revolution was fought in 1775. With the Canada-U.S. Free Trade Agreement, Canada has lost that control. The FTA has given the United States the kind of control over the Canadian economy it was only previously able to secure by military intervention, in countries such as Grenada, Panama and Puerto Rico. What John Turner described as "the Sale of Canada Act" and Pierre Trudeau called a "monstrous swindle" was not a free-trade deal at all; it was the return of Canada to colonial status. Shortly before his death in 1994, the chief U.S. negotiator for the FTA, Peter Murphy, gave an interview to a Canadian journalist. "We didn't enter the agreement over tariffs," he told her. "The Canadian agreement is a political one — to make sure you don't go back to those policies like the National Energy Policy ... It wasn't that Mulroney aggressively needed prodding. It was a future prime minister we were worried about."[1] This point was understood by the U.S. economic forecaster Marvin Cetron, author of the 1990 U.S. bestseller, *American Renaissance: Our Life at the Turn of the 21st Century*, which features on its cover an American flag with fifty-five stars. "The extra stars of the American flag," Cetron wrote, "represent the state-to-be of Puerto Rico and the four states to our north."[2]

Is the U.S. empire in decline? Cetron asks. No, he replies, and goes on to explain:

> One of the most important factors in America's future prosperity was decided not in Washington, but north of the border. When Canada's voters went to the polls in November 1988, to elect a Prime Minister, the decisive issue in their minds was the historic free-trade agreement with the United States...

287

Once the free-trade agreement with the United States takes full effect, the next logical step will be to accept politically what has already happened economically — the integration of Canada into the United States ... And fulfilling a Canadian nationalist's worst nightmare, Canada may — if not by the year 2000, then soon thereafter — become the fifty-second through the fifty-fifth states of the United States. Canada's western provinces — Alberta, Manitoba, Saskatchewan, British Columbia, the Yukon Territory, and the Northwest Territories — will be compacted into two states; Ontario and the eastern provinces — Newfoundland, Nova Scotia, New Brunswick, and Prince Edward Island — will combine into two more ... Quebec will at last receive its wish and become an independent nation, if in name only. Economically, it will remain wholly dependent on its neighbors for survival.

In fact, incorporation of most of Canada into the United States will do neither nation any great good beyond, perhaps, the psychological benefit of recognizing reality. The 1988 free-trade agreement will accomplish far more. Though Canada's population represents a relatively small market compared with Japan, France, or Germany, the guarantee of unrestricted access to both Canada's people and its raw materials will give American manufacturers a safe haven from which to support their other trading ventures.[3]

For Canadians to regain control of their country, the free-trade deal must be abrogated. As Canadian trade expert Mel Clark has put it: "There are only two options: cancel the Agreement or accept it and become Americans."[4]

Cancellation of the agreement can be done quite simply. The last clause of the FTA, article 2106 (or in NAFTA, article 2205), states that any country can, at any time, give the other(s) six months' notice to cancel the agreement.

In order for Canada to avoid losing its sovereignty as a nation, this clause must be invoked. Government spokespersons have responded to the call for abrogation with familiar predictions of economic catastrophe for Canada. But, in fact, with cancellation, the rules governing Canada's trade with the United States would automatically and immediately return to those of the GATT, which for decades gave Canada better protection from U.S. harassment than the FTA now provides. The first Canada-U.S. free-trade agreement, the Reciprocity Treaty of 1854, was cancelled in 1866 by the United States. Canada not only survived, but was pushed to step dramatically into nationhood.

But globalization, we are told, is inevitable. It is time to make the best of it. In fact, a reaction against globalization is sweeping the world. Polls in all three NAFTA countries have repeatedly shown majority opposition. In the fall of 1997 Bill Clinton introduced into the U.S. Congress his proposal for fast-track authority to negotiate the MAI and an extension of NAFTA to South America. But he was unable to get a majority of his own party to support him, and was forced to withdraw the measure. Ralph Nader's Trade Watch and other citizens' organizations teamed up with the labour movement, led by the Teamsters Union, to mobilize. Their campaign was a highly significant victory. In Europe, especially in France, opposition to the MAI was rapid and effective.

The proponents of globalization maintain there is no alternative, that the clock cannot be turned back. This claim does not stand up to scrutiny. Switzerland has quite successfully remained out of the European Union. It enjoys an unemployment rate half that of the EU, and far lower than Canada's.

Norway has twice voted to stay out of the European Union, most recently in a 1994 referendum. During the referendum campaign most of Norway's major political parties and the majority of its press promoted the agreement and warned that if Norway stayed out its unemployment rate would rise and its standard of living would fall; Norway would become isolated, its economy the sick man of Europe. Nevertheless, Norwegians voted No. Today Norway has no debt, no deficit and no downsizing. Its unemployment rate — 2.5 percent — is the lowest in Europe, its economy the fastest growing. There are no visible signs of poverty in Norwegian cities. Norway has free universal health care and free dental care for everyone under 19; it pays 42 weeks of maternity leave and extends retirement pay to homemakers. Norway has recently lowered its retirement age from 67 to 64, and its unions are pressing to lower it to 62 with full pension. Norway has not sold its resources to foreign hands — its publicly owned oil company contributes in a major way the revenues necessary to maintain some of the richest social programs in the world. Norway is living proof that a nation, with one-seventh of Canada's population at that, can use its resources to provide a high standard of living and virtually full employment for its people.

Japan is another striking example of a nation rejecting the policies of free trade and foreign ownership and achieving dramatic results.

In 1950, Canada and Japan had the same size economy. Now, on a per capita basis, Japan outproduces the United States and has, since 1950, bypassed the size of Canada's economy several times over. How did a small country with few resources accomplish this feat? Like Switzerland and Norway, it follows a government policy to foster and protect key industries. In 1939, Japan passed legislation — protectionist legislation — which resulted in Ford, GM and Chrysler leaving that country. In 1941, Japanese-owned manufacturing companies produced fewer than 1100 cars. By 1950, Japan was producing about 32,000 motor vehicles a year, far behind Canada, which produced almost 400,000 vehicles that year. The United States was then producing more than eight million vehicles, 75 percent of total world production.

The U.S. auto giants fought furiously to get back into Japan, and the pro-free trade economists in Japan condemned their government, saying the battle was hopeless. The president of the Bank of Japan said, "It is meaningless to try to build an automotive industry in Japan. This is the age of the international division of labour and Japan would best rely on the United States for motor vehicles." However, the Japanese government persevered; it refused to allow the U.S. industry back and imposed strict quotas limiting imports of foreign cars and trucks to just 5 percent of Japan's output. Japan does not allow foreign takeovers of its key industries.

The whole world knows the result. In 1988, Japan manufactured 12,699,803 vehicles, outproducing the United States. This is just one example of how economic nationalism can co-exist with a global economy.

Canada's performance during the Second World War is another example of what this nation can do without foreign capital. In 1939, Canada had a gross national product (GNP) of about $5 billion and an unemployment rate of 11 percent. Six years later, the unemployment rate was 1.4 percent and the GNP had doubled. Not only did Canada not use foreign capital to achieve these results but, during the same period, it gave substantial aid to Britain for its war effort. This dramatic development was a result of active federal government intervention in the economy against the advice of the economists of the time who insisted vehemently that it could not, and should not, be done.

Today we are constantly told Canada is "too small," that we must abandon our independence and integrate our country into the U.S. market to succeed.

Yet, in size, Canada is the world's second largest country; in terms of population it has more people than most of the world's nations, more people in fact than Britain had when it ruled a global empire. Canada has everything needed to give all Canadians meaningful work and a good standard of living. It has the resources, skills, population and more geography than the United States. Countries a fraction of Canada's size design and build their own automobiles; Canada assembles vehicles for foreign owners. Countries that could fit into one of Canada's provinces have their own defence capability and independent defence industry. Canada's air force is, under the terms of NORAD (North American Air Defence Command), under the supreme command of a U.S. general; its defence industries manufacture parts for U.S. parents. Countries with a smaller population than Ontario have thriving cultural industries, including independent motion picture industries; Canada has surrendered its cultural expression to Hollywood.

This situation could quite easily be reversed with some political will and a coherent policy to do so. But Canada depends on the United States, or so goes the refrain, when in fact it is Canadian oil, gas, timber, minerals and electricity that drive the U.S. economy. Canada is making a terrible mistake giving these prized commodities away for virtually nothing.

Oh, but this is nationalism, the proponents of free trade and globalization reply, and nationalism is a reactionary, narrow-minded force, responsible for atrocities around the world. In fact, Canada's patriotism for the most part has been a defensive reaction to the threat of absorption by the United States, not an attempt to raise the Canadian flag over other nations. And if we do not have more lively, active, fighting patriotism, in the healthy sense of the word, we will not succeed in holding the border. Donald Creighton, one of Canada's leading historians, has made the observation that it is imperialism, not nationalism, which poses the greatest threat to the peace of the world. And from India it was Gandhi who said: "It is impossible for one to be an internationalist without being a nationalist. Internationalism is possible only when nationalism becomes a fact."

For Canada, "globalization" is really another word for Americanization. And it is no more inevitable today than in 1812 or any other time in our history.

Canadians have overcome great obstacles in the past. As we have seen, Canada turned back the United States in that country's major invasions of our territory as well as in its previous and repeated attempts for economic control in the name of free trade. This latest attempt can be defeated as well. Whenever Canadians have actively resisted Americanization, they have achieved dramatic results, whether in the war of 1690, of 1775, or of 1812; or through the National Policy of John A. Macdonald, the entry of the West negotiated by George-Étienne Cartier, the introduction of medicare by T.C. Douglas and Woodrow Lloyd in Saskatchewan, or the National Energy Program of Pierre Trudeau. However, if the FTA and NAFTA are allowed to take full effect — with a common currency and the assimilation of Canada into the United States to follow — then the work of all those who fought for Canada's survival over the past 400 years will be lost.

Canada is a sleeping giant. Whether she has the chance to awaken and take her place on the world stage depends on the work of her citizens in the months and years ahead.

When Isaac Brock fell at Queenston Heights, Tecumseh at Moraviantown, Riel in Regina, and when thousands of other men and women who in less spectacular, or less well-known ways, gave their lives for Canada, the responsibility passed to us.

Canada has gone from being a colony of France, to being a colony of Britain, to being a colony of the United States. It is time now to become a nation. We have the opportunity and all the tools needed to do precisely that.

Notes

Chapter 1 / A New Breed of People

1. Cartier's diary, quoted in Stephen Leacock, *The Mariner of St. Malo: A Chronicle of the Voyages of Jacques Cartier* (Toronto: Glasgow, Brook, 1922), pp. 72-77; and David R. Wrone and Russell S. Nelson Jr. (eds.), *Who's the Savage? A Documentary History of the Mistreatment of the Native North Americans* (Greenwich, Conn.: Fawcett, 1973), pp. 39-40.

2. Cotton Mather's "Decennium Lucituosum," quoted in I.K. Steele, *Guerillas and Grenadiers: The Struggle for Canada, 1689-1760* (Toronto: Ryerson Press, 1969), p. 27.

3. W.L. Morton, *The Kingdom of Canada: A General History from Earliest Times* (Toronto: McClelland and Stewart, 1963), p. 82.

4. Steele, *Guerillas,* p. 30.

5. Charles W. Colby, *The Fighting Governor: A Chronicle of Frontenac* (Toronto: Glasgow, Brook, 1922), p. 129.

6. Steele, *Guerillas,* p. 30.

7. *Ibid.,* p. 40.

8. June Callwood, *Portrait of Canada* (Markham, Ont.: Paperjacks, 1983), xxviii.

9. Washington, quoted in F.X. Garneau, *History of Canada from the Time of Discovery Till the Union Year 1840-41,* vol. 1 (Montreal: John Lovett, 1862), p. 490.

10. Stanley B. Ryerson, *The Founding of Canada: Beginnings to 1815* (Toronto: Progress Books, 1963), p. 186.

11. Belcher and Winslow, quoted in R. Howard, et al., *A New History of Canada,* vol. 3, *A Losing Game, 1701-1760* (Montreal: Éditions Format), pp. 255-57.

12. Lawrence, quoted in Arthur G. Doughty, *The Acadian Exiles: A Chronicle of the Land of Evangeline* (Toronto: Glasgow, Brook, 1922), p. 138.

13. *Ibid.,* p. 137.

14. Dobbs, quoted in Guy Frégault, *Canada: The War of the Conquest* (Toronto: Oxford University Press, 1969), p. 73.

15. Vaudreuil, quoted in *ibid.,* p. 110

16. Wrone and Nelson, *Who's the Savage?,* p. 135.

17. Frégault, *Canada,* p. 235.

18. *Ibid.,* p. 208.

19. *Ibid.* (both quotes), pp. 226-27.

20. Callwood, *Portrait,* p. 47.

21. Garneau, *History of Canada,* vol. 2, p. 51; and Ryerson, *Founding of Canada,* p. 192.

22. Frégault, *Canada,* p. 251.

23. Wolfe, quoted in W.J. Eccles, *France in America* (New York: Harper & Row, 1972), p. 200; and Frégault, *Canada,* pp. 244-45.

24. Lévis quoted in Frégault, *Canada,* p. 279; Cooper, quoted in Frégault, p. 262; Philadelphia *Gazette,* September 25, 1760, and Boston *News Letter,* both quoted in Frégault, p. 291; Foxcroft and Franklin, both quoted in Frégault, p. 293.

25. Murray, quoted in Mason Wade, *The French Canadians 1760-1967, vol. 1* (Toronto: Macmillan, 1968), p. 48.

26. Garneau, *History of Canada,* vol. 2, p. 90; and Murray, quoted in Wade, *French Canadians,* vol. 1, p. 56.

27. Murray, quoted in Wade, *French Canadians,* vol. 1, p. 56.

28. Callwood, *Portrait,* p. 62.

Chapter 2 / The Fourteenth Colony

1 . Robert M. Hatch, *Thrust for Canada: The American Attempt on Quebec in 1775-1776* (Boston: Houghton Mifflin, 1979), p. 97.

2. Montgomery, quoted in Justin H. Smith, *Our Struggle for the Fourteenth Colony: Canada and the American Revolution,* vol. 2 (New York: Putnams, 1907), p. 39.

3. Mason Wade, *The French Canadians 1760-1967,* vol. 1 (Toronto: Macmillan, 1968), p. 66.

4. Smith, *Our Struggle,* vol. 2, p. 106.

5. *Ibid.,* p. 22.

6. Arnold, quoted in Hatch, *Thrust for Canada,* p. 117.

7. William Wood, *The Father of British Canada* (Toronto: Glasgow, Brook, 1922), p. 91.

8. Wood, *The Father of British Canada,* p. 92; and Smith, *Our Struggle,* vol. 2, p. 95.

9. George F.G. Stanley, *Canada Invaded, 1775-1776* (Toronto: Hakkert, 1973), p. 87. Also Smith, *Our Struggle,* vol. 2, p. 96.

10. Copp and Montgomery, quoted in Smith, *Our Struggle,* vol. 2, p. 113; Smith, *Our Struggle,* vol. 2, p. 111 and 42; Stanley, *Canada Invaded,* p. 90.

11. Smith, *Our Struggle,* vol. 2, pp. 128-29.

12. Alfred L. Burt, *The Old Province of Quebec* (Toronto: Ryerson, 1933), p. 226.

13. Schuyler, quoted in Smith, *Our Struggle,* vol. 2, p. 164.

14.   Adams, quoted in Bruce Hutchison, *The Struggle for the Border* (Don Mills, Ont.: Longman, 1955), p. 147.

15.   Washington, quoted in Stanley, *Canada Invaded,* p. 107; and in Smith, *Our Struggle,* vol. 2, p. 189.

16.   Stanley, *Canada Invaded,* pp. 114-18.

17.   Smith, *Our Struggle,* vol. 2, pp. 343, 357.

18.   Physician and Adams both quoted in Stanley, *Canada Invaded,* p. 133.

19.   W.L. Morton, *The Kingdom of Canada: A General History from Earliest Times* (Toronto: McClelland and Stewart, 1963), p. 172.

20.   Donald Creighton, *The Empire of the St. Lawrence* (Toronto: Macmillan, 1956), p. 79.

21.   *Ibid.,* p. 80.

22.   Morton, *Kingdom of Canada,* p. 173.

23.   *The Canadian Encyclopedia,* vol. 2 (Edmonton: Hurtig, 1988), p. 1270.

Chapter 3 / To Rival the Exploits of Rome

1 .   Jefferson, quoted in Henry Adams, *History of the United States During the Administration of James Madison,* book 6 (New York: Boni, 1930), p. 337.

2.   Eustis, quoted in Bruce Hutchison, *The Struggle for the Border* (Don Mills, Ont.: Longman, 1955), p. 230.

3.   Morris, quoted in Stanley B. Ryerson, *The Founding of Canada: Beginnings to 1815* (Toronto: Progress Books, 1963), p. 272.

4.   Clay, quoted in Ryerson, *Founding of Canada,* p. 294; and in Hutchison, *Struggle for Border,* p. 230.

5.   Hunter and Harper, quoted in Ryerson, *Founding of Canada,* pp. 271-72.

6.   Jackson, quoted in Richard Hofstadter, William Miller and Daniel Aaron, *The United States: The History of the Republic* (Englewood Cliffs, NJ: Prentice Hall, 1957), p. 173. Also, Hugh Keenleyside, *Canada and the United States: Some Aspects of the History of the Republic and the Dominion* (New York: Knopf, 1929), p. 77.

7.   Randolph, quoted in Adams, *History of U.S. During Madison,* book 6, p. 146.

8.   D.B. Read, *Life and Times of Sir Isaac Brock* (Toronto: William Briggs, 1894), p. 125. See also Pierre Berton, *The Invasion of Canada 1812-1813* (Toronto: McClelland and Stewart, 1980), pp. 129-30.

9.   Brock, quoted in Berton, *Invasion of Canada,* p. 166.

10.   Brock, quoted in Ryerson, *Founding of Canada,* p. 294.

11.   Keenleyside, *Canada and United States,* p. 81 (footnote).

12.   McGill, quoted in Ryerson, *Founding of Canada,* p. 275.

13.   Brock, quoted in Luella B. Creighton, *Tecumseh: The Story of the Shawnee Chief* (Toronto: Macmillan, 1965), p. 114; also in Berton, *Invasion of Canada,* p. 166.

14. Read, *Life and Times of Brock,* pp. 158, 196, 228.

15. George Rideout, quoted in Berton, *Invasion of Canada,* p. 252.

16. James, quoted in David R. Wrone and Russell S. Nelson Jr. (eds.), *Who's the Savage? A Documentary History of the Mistreatment of the Native North Americans* (Greenwich, Conn.: Fawcett, 1973), p. 234.

17. Crockett, quoted *ibid.,* pp. 230-31.

18. FitzGibbon, quoted in J.M. Hitsman, *The Incredible War of 1812: A Military History* (Toronto: University of Toronto Press, 1965), p. 138; also, Ruth McKenzie, *Laura Secord: The Legend and the Lady* (Toronto: McClelland and Stewart, 1971), p. 129.

19. Cockburn, quoted in C.P. Lucas, *The Canadian War of 1812* (Oxford: Clarendon Press, 1906), pp. 225-26.

20. Hutchison, *Struggle for the Border,* p. 254.

21. Montreal *Herald,* April 15, 1815, quoted in Keenleyside, *Canada and United States,* pp. 100-101.

22. Clay, quoted in Albert K. Weinberg, *Manifest Destiny: A Study of Nationalist Expansionism in American History* (Baltimore: Johns Hopkins Press, 1935), p.49.

23. Keenleyside, *Canada and United States,* p. 180.

24. Baring, quoted in Callwood, *Portrait of Canada* (Markham, Ont.: Paperjacks, 1983), p. 113.

25. Maury in the *National Intelligencer,* May 20, 1845, quoted in Stanley B. Ryerson, *Unequal Union: Confederation and the Roots of Conflict in the Canadas, 1815-1873* (Toronto: Progress Books, 1975), p. 225.

Chapter 4 / 54°40' or Fight

1 . Richard Hofstadter, William Miller, and Daniel Aaron, *The United States: The History of the Republic* (Englewood Cliffs, NJ: Prentice Hall), 1957, p. 271.

2. *Ibid., p.* 279.

3. O'Sullivan in the New York *Morning News,* December 27, 1845, quoted in Albert K. Weinberg, *Manifest Destiny: A Study of Nationalist Expansionism in American History* (Baltimore: Johns Hopkins Press, 1935), p. 145. And July 7, 1845, quoted in Stanley B. Ryerson, *Unequal Union: Confederation and the Roots of Conflict in the Canadas, 1815-1873* (Toronto: Progress Books, 1975), p. 227.

4. Baker and Sawyer, quoted in Norman A. Graebner (ed.), *Manifest Destiny* (New York: Bobbs-Merrill, 1968), xxxix.

5. Adams, quoted *ibid.,* pp. 103-105; Kennedy, *ibid.,* xlii.

6. Polk, quoted *ibid.,* xlv.

7. New York *Herald,* July 27,1846, quoted in Weinberg, *Manifest Destiny,* p.168; Houston, quoted in Weinberg, p. 178; Dickinson, quoted in Weinberg, pp. 174, 180.

8. Buchanan, quoted in Graebner, *Manifest Destiny,* lii.

9.   *Democratic Review,* xx (1847), p. 100; quoted in Weinberg, *Manifest Destiny,* pp. 168-69.

10. New York *Evening Post,* December, 1847; quoted in Graebner, *Manifest Destiny,* lvii; *American Review* March, 1847, in Graebner, lii.

11. Cass, quoted in Graebner, *Manifest Destiny,* li-lii.

Chapter 5 / The American Warning

1.   Lord Elgin, quoted in Oscar D. Skelton, *The Canadian Dominion: A Chronicle of Our Northern Neighbor* (New Haven, Conn.: Yale University Press, 1919), p. 109.

2.   Cephas D. Allin and George M. Jones, *Annexation, Preferential Trade, and Reciprocity: An Outline of the Annexation Movement of 1849-50* (Toronto: Musson, 1911), pp. 106-14.

3.   *Ibid.,* p. 131.

4.   *Ibid.,* p. 145.

5.   Donald E Warner, *The Idea of Continental Union: Agitation for the Annexation of Canada. to the United States 1849-1893* (Lexington, Ky: University of Kentucky Press, 1960), p. 22.

6.   *The Examiner,* November 14,1849, quoted in Allin, *Annexation,* p. 155.

7.   Abbott, quoted *ibid.,* p. 115, footnote.

8.   Andrews, quoted in Lester Burrell Shippee, *Canadian-American Relations 1849-1874* (New Haven, Conn.: Yale University Press, 1939), p. 75.

9.   *Ibid.,* p. 75.

10. Stanley B. Ryerson, *Unequal Union: Confederation and the Roots of Conflict in the Canadas, 1815-1873* (Toronto: Progress Books), 1975, p. 242.

11. Little, quoted in A.R.M. Lower, *The North American Assault on the Canadian Forest: A History of the Lumber Trade between Canada and the United States* (Toronto: Ryerson Press, 1938), p. 146.

12. *Ibid., pp.* 139,121.

13. Ryerson, *Unequal Union,* pp. 241-242.

14. Edward Watkin, quoted in *ibid,* p. 242.

15. New York *Herald,* September 26,1861, quoted in Shippee, *Canada-American Relations,* p. 185.

16. Hugh Keenleyside, *Canada and the United States: Some Aspects of the History of the Republic and the Dominion* (New York: Knopf, 1929), p. 139.

17. Chicago *Tribune,* quoted in Ryerson, *Unequal Union,* p. 339.

18. Ryerson, *Unequal Union,* p. 340.

19. W.L. Morton, *The Kingdom of Canada: A General History from Earliest Times* (Toronto: McClelland and Stewart, 1963), p. 315.

20. P.B. Waite, *The Life and Times of Confederation 1864-67* (Toronto: University of Toronto Press, 1962), p. 44.

21.   Brown, quoted in J.H. Stewart Reid, Kenneth McNaught, and Harry S. Crowe (eds.), *A Sourcebook of Canadian History* (Don Mills, Ont.: Longman, 1959), pp. 200-201.

22.   Taché and Langevin, quoted in Ryerson, *Unequal Union*, pp. 366-67.

23.   McGee, quoted in Bruce Hutchison, *The Struggle for the Border* (Don Mills, Ont.: Longman, 1955), p. 8; and in Ryerson, *Unequal Union*, p. 366.

24.   McGee in *Parliamentary Debates on the Subject of the Confederation of the British North American Provinces* (Quebec: February 9, 1865), p. 135.

25.   Cartier, to the Legislative Assembly, February 7, 1865. Quoted in Janet Morchain, *Sharing a Continent: An Introduction to Canadian-American Relations* (Toronto: McGraw-Hill Ryerson Ltd. 1973), p. 121.

26.   Seward, quoted in Shippee, *Canadian-American Relations*, p. 200.

27.   Keenleyside, *Canada and the United States*, pp. 146-47.

28.   Heffernan, quoted in Hutchison, *Struggle for the Border*, p. 356.

29.   Waite, *Life and Times of Confederation*, pp. 304-305.

30.   Donnelly, quoted in Alvin C. Gluek Jr., *Minnesota and the Manifest Destiny of the Canadian Northwest* (Toronto: University of Toronto Press, 1965), p.215.

31.   Reginald George Trotter, *Canadian Federation: Its Origins and Achievement, a Study in Nation Building* (London: J.M. Dent, 1924), p. 138.

32.   Sumner, quoted in John Bartlett Brebner, *North Atlantic Triangle: The Interplay of Canada, the United States and Great Britain* (New York: Columbia University Press, 1945), pp. 170, 171; Chandler quoted in Shippee, *Canadian-American Relations*, p. 204.

33.   Morton, *Kingdom of Canada;* p. 333.

Chapter 6 / Prophet of the New World

1.   Ramsey's bill, quoted in Alvin C. Gluek Jr., *Minnesota and the Manifest Destiny of the Canadian Northwest* (Toronto: University of Toronto Press, 1965), p. 211.

2.   Resolution, quoted in Donald F. Warner, *The Idea of Continental Union: Agitation for the Annexation of Canada to the United States 1849-1893* (Lexington, Ky: University of Kentucky Press, 1960), p. 111.

3.   Spaulding, in *Congressional Globe,* 40th Congress, Session 2, July 7, 1868, p. 3810.

4.   Fish's diary, quoted in Gluek, *Minnesota and Manifest Destiny, p.* 279.

5.   Taylor, quoted in Stanley B. Ryerson, *Unequal Union: Confederation and the Roots of Conflict in the Canadas, 1815-1873* (Toronto: Progress Books, 1975), p. 340; also, Taylor's report, "Commercial Relations with British North America," quoted in Gluek, *Minnesota and Manifest Destiny,* p. 207.

6.   St. Paul *Press,* quoted in Gluek, *Minnesota and Manifest Destiny,* p. 262; Donnelly, quoted in Joseph K Howard, *Strange Empire: The Story of Louis Riel* (New York: William Morrow, Swan Edition, 1965), p. 123.

7.   Malmros, quoted in Gluek, *Minnesota and Manifest Destiny*, pp. 267-68; and Warner, *Idea of Union*, p. 117.

8.   *The New Nation*, vol. 1, no. 1 (January 7, 1870).

9.   *Ibid.*, vol. 1, no. 3 (January 21, 1870).

10. Macdonald, quoted in Sir Joseph Pope, *Correspondence of Sir John Macdonald* (Toronto: Oxford University Press, 1921), p. 124.

11. Chandler, in *Congressional Globe*, 41st Congress, 2nd Session, April 22, 1870, pp. 2888-89.

12. Begg, quoted in Gluek, *Minnesota and Manifest Destiny*, p. 269.

13. Malmros, quoted in Warner, *Idea of Union*, p. 120.

14. Langford, quoted in Peter Charlebois, *The Life of Louis Riel* (Toronto: New Canada Press, 1975), p. 62.

15. Howard, *Strange Empire*, p. 188.

16. Langford to Taylor, June 12,1870 (Taylor papers), quoted in Warner, *Idea of Union*, p. 119, footnote.

17. Irvine, quoted in Howard, *Strange Empire*, p. 196.

18. Archibald, quoted *ibid.*, p. 195.

19. Archibald, quoted *ibid.*, p. 197.

20. W.L. Morton, *Begg's Journal and Other Papers Relative to the Red River Resistance of 1869-1870* (Toronto: The Champlain Society, 1960), p. 148.

21. Butler, quoted in Howard, *Strange Empire*, p. 134.

22. George F.G. Stanley, *The Birth of Western Canada: A History of the Riel Rebellion* (Toronto: University of Toronto Press, 1961), p. 165; and Howard Adams, *Prison of Grass: Canada from a Native Point of View* (Saskatoon: Fifth House Publishers, 1989), p. 59, 185.

23. Archibald, quoted in Howard, *Strange Empire*, p. 185.

24. A.H. de Trémaudan, *Hold High Your Heads (History of the Métis Nation in Western Canada)* (Winnipeg: Pemmican Publications, 1982), p. 104.

25. David R. Wrone and Russell S. Nelson Jr. (eds.) *Who's the Savage? A Documentary History of the Mistreatment of the Native North Americans* (Greenwich, Conn.: Fawcett, 1973), p. 411.

26. Adams, *Prison of Grass*, p. 68.

27. Howard, *Strange Empire*, p. 380.

28. *Ibid.*, pp. 382-83.

29. Riel quoted in Howard, *Strange Empire*, p. 452. Lawyer Francois-Xavier Lemieux, leader for the defence, quoted in D. Morton, ed., *The Queen v Louis Riel* (Toronto: University of Toronto Press, 1974), p. 311.

30. Riel's speech from Morton, *Queen v Riel*, pp. 311-63. Excerpts selected and abridged by the author.

31. Macdonald, quoted in Howard, *Strange Empire*, p. 456.

32. Charlebois, *Life of Riel*, p. 235.

33.   Laurier and Mercier, quoted in Mason Wade, *The French Canadians:* 1760-1967, vol. 1 (Toronto: Macmillan, 1968), p. 417.

34.   Gluek, *Minnesota and Manifest Destiny, p.* 291.

Chapter 7 / The Uncrowned King of the Masses

1 .   Polk, quoted in Norman A. Graebner (ed.), *Manifest Destiny* (New York: Bobbs-Merrill), 1968, xlv.

2.   P.B. Waite, *The Life and Times of Confederation 1864-67* (Toronto: University of Toronto Press, 1962), p. 26.

3.   Stanley B. Ryerson, *Unequal Union: Confederation and the Roots of Conflict in the Canadas, 1815-1873* (Toronto: Progress Books, 1975), p. 408.

4.   Roland Wild, *Amor De Cosmos* (Toronto: Ryerson Press, 1958), p. 37.

5.   Macdonald, quoted in Bruce Hutchison, *The Struggle for the Border* (Don Mills, Ont.: Longman, 1955), p. 386.

6.   George Woodcock, *Amor De Cosmos: Journalist and Reformer* (Toronto: Oxford University Press, 1975), p. 1.

7.   Wild, *De Cosmos,* pp. 19, 30, 36, 49.

8.   Woodcock, *Amor De Cosmos: Journalist,* p. 61.

9.   De Cosmos, quoted in Ryerson, *Unequal Union,* p. 410.

10.   De Cosmos, quoted in Wild, *Amor De Cosmos,* p. 117.

11.   Above quotations in Woodcock, *Amor De Cosmos: journalist,* pp. 124,122.

12.   Dr. Helmcken, quoted in *ibid.,* pp. 168,162.

13.   The *Times-Colonist,* quoted in Wild, *Amor De Cosmos,* pp. 140-41.

Chapter 8 / The Lightning Striker

1 .   Of these exiles, the young Antoine Gérin-Lajoie wrote his famous and haunting song, "Un Canadien errant."

2.   John Ralston Saul, *Reflections of a Siamese Twin: Canada at the End of the Twentieth Century* (Toronto: Viking Press, 1997), p 111.

3.   *Ibid.,* p. 112.

4.   John Boyd, *George-Étienne Cartier* (Toronto: The MacMillan Company of Canada, 1914) p. 96.

5.   *Ibid.,* p. 176.

6.   *Ibid.,* p. 359.

7.   *Ibid.,* p. 359.

8.   *Ibid.,* p. 202.

9.   *Ibid.,* p. 218.

10.   *Ibid.,* p. 273.

11.   *Ibid.,* p. 292.

12.   *Ibid.,* p. 291.

13. Alastair Sweeny, *George-Étienne Cartier* (Toronto : McClelland & Stewart, *1976), p. 182.*

14. *Ibid.,* p. 230.

15. *Ibid.,* p. 301.

16. W.E. Ireland, *Helmcken's Diary of the Confederation Negotiations, 1870* (BCHQ IV, 2: 1940), pp. 111-123.

17. John Boyd, *George-Étienne Cartier,* p. 307.

18. Alastair Sweeny, *George-Étienne Cartier,* p. 226.

19. Pierre Berton, *The National Dream* (Toronto: McClelland & Stewart, *1974)* p. 6.

20. Margaret A. Ormsby, *British Columbia, A History* (Toronto: Macmillan of Canada, *1958),* p. 249.

21. W.E. Ireland, *Helmcken's Diary of the Confederation Negotiations, 1870,* p. 128.

22. Alastair Sweeny, *George-Étienne Cartier,* p. 276.

23. *Ibid.,* p. 277.

24. *Ibid.,* p. 280.

25. *Ibid.,* p. 298.

26. *Ibid.,* p. 314.

27. John Boyd, *George-Étienne Cartier,* p. 364.

28. *Ibid.,* p. 363.

29. *Ibid.,* p. 391.

30. *Ibid.,* pp. 393-94.

31. *Ibid.,* p. 320.

32. *Ibid.,* p. 404.

Chapter 9 / Veiled Treason

1. Donald Creighton, *John A. Macdonald: The Old Chieftain* (Toronto: Macmillan, 1965), p. 215.

2. *Ibid.,* p. 306.

3. Macdonald, quoted in *ibid.,* p. 308.

4. Alexander Morris, quoted in *ibid.,* p. 309.

5. Macdonald, quoted in *ibid.,* p. 459.

6. Thomas A. Bailey, *A Diplomatic History of the American People* (New York: Meredith, *1969),* pp. 374-75.

7. Macdonald, in *House of Commons Debates,* quoted in Creighton, *John A. Macdonald,* p. 474.

8. Creighton, *John A. Macdonald,* p. 487.

9. All quotes from Goldwin Smith, *Canada and the Canadian Question* (reprint; Michael Bliss, ed.) (Toronto: University of Toronto Press, 1971), pp. 203-234.

10. Smith, quoted in Mason Wade, *The French Canadians 1760-1967*, vol. 1 (Toronto: Macmillan, 1968), p. 449.

11. Wiman, quoted in Charles Tansill, *Canadian-American Relations 1875-1911* (New Haven: Yale University Press/Toronto: Ryerson Press), 1943, p. 392 and footnote.

12. Sherman, in *Congressional Record – Senate, 50th Congress, Session 1* (August 7, 1888, p. 7286 and September 18, 1888, pp. 8670-71).

13. Chicago *Tribune*, September 26, 1888, quoted in Colonel George T. Denison, *The Struggle for Imperial Unity: Recollections and Experiences* (London: Macmillan, 1909), p. 103.

14. New York *World*, December 1, 1888, quoted in Denison, *Struggle*, pp. 104-105, 108.

15. Butler, quoted in Denison, *Struggle*, p. 105.

16. Donald F. Warner, *The Idea of Continental Union: Agitation for the Annexation of Canada to the United States 1849-1893* (Lexington, Ky: University of Kentucky Press, 1960), p. 194.

17. J. Castell Hopkins, *The Story of the Dominion. Four Hundred Years in the Annals of Half a Continent. A History of Canada from Its Early Discovery and Settlement to the Present Time; Embracing Its Growth, Progress and Achievements in the Pursuits of Peace and War* (Philadelphia; John Winston, 1901), p. 500.

18. Macdonald, quoted in Tansill, *Canadian-American Relations*, p. 401.

19. P.B. Waite, *Arduous Destiny 1874-1896* (Toronto: McClelland and Stewart, 1971), p. 224.

20. The Toronto *Empire*, February 18, 1891, quoted in Edwin C. Guillet, *You'll Never Die, John A!* (Toronto: Macmillan, 1967), p. 126.

21. Creighton, *John A. Macdonald* p. 526; and Macdonald, quoted in R. Howard, J. Lacoursière, and C. Bouchard, *A New History of Canada*, vol. 8, *Movements West, 1887-1908* (Montreal: Éditions Format, 1973), p. 691.

22. Howard et al., *New History*, vol. 8, p. 691.

23. Macdonald, quoted in Creighton, *John A. Macdonald*, p. 555.

24. Hopkins, *Story of the Dominion*, p. 502.

25. Blaine, quoted in Warner, *Idea of Union*, p. 218. See also Alice Feld Tyler, *The Foreign Policy of James G. Blaine* (Minneapolis: University of Minnesota Press, 1927), p. 351.

26. Waite, *Arduous Destiny*, p. 226.

27. Bruce Hutchison, *The Struggle for the Border* (Don Mills, Ont: Longman, 1955), p. 424.

28. Macdonald, quoted in Donald Creighton: *Dominion of the North: A History of Canada* (Toronto: Macmillan, 1957), p. 375.

29. Macdonald, quoted *ibid.*, p. 375.

30. Blake, quoted in Robert C. Brown, *Canada's National Policy 1883-1900: A Study in Canadian-American Relations* (Princeton, NJ: Princeton University Press, 1964), p. 406.

31. Guillet, *You'll Never Die,* p. 90.

32. Warner, *Idea of Union,* p. 235.

33. Denison, *Struggle for Unity,* p. 192.

34. *Ibid.* pp. 191-92.

Chapter 10 / The Yankee to the South of Us

1. Hay, in a letter to Ambassador Choate, August 18, 1899, quoted in Charles Tansill, *Canadian-American Relations 1875-1911* (New Haven: Yale University Press/Toronto: Ryerson Press), 1943, p. 202. And to Senator Davids, August 4, 1899, quoted in *ibid.,* p. 200.

2. Hay, in a letter to Roosevelt, quoted in Tansill, *Canadian-American Relations,* p. 225.

3. H.P. Angus (ed.), *British Columbia and the United States: The North Pacific Slope from Fur Trade to Aviation* (Toronto: Ryerson Press, 1942), pp. 370-72.

4. Roosevelt, quoted in Tansill, *Canadian-American Relations,* p. 243.

5. Roosevelt to A.S. Raikes of the British embassy, May 1902, quoted in Norman Penlington, *The Alaska Boundary Dispute: A Critical Reappraisal* (Toronto: McGraw Hill-Ryerson, 1972), p. 127, footnote 27.

6. Roosevelt, quoted in John Bartlett Brebner, *North Atlantic Triangle: The Interplay of Canada, the United States and Great Britain* (New York: Columbia University Press, 1945), p. 261.

7. Hay, quoted in Richard Hofstadter, William Miller, and Daniel Aaron, *The United States: The History of the Republic* (Englewood Cliffs, NJ: Prentice Hall, 1957), p. 561.

8. Hay, quoted in Lawrence Martin. *The Presidents & the Prime Ministers – Washington and Ottawa Face to Face: The Myth of Bilateral Bliss 1867-1982* (Toronto: Paperjacks, 1983), p. 64.

9. Tansill, *Canadian-American Relations,* p. 451, footnote.

10. *Ibid.,* p. 459.

11. Root to J.H. Wilson, quoted in Tansill, *Canadian-American Relations,* p. 460; and Robert E. Hannigan, "Reciprocity 1911: Continentalism and American Weltpolitik," *Diplomatic History* (winter 1980), p. 10.

12. Hannigan, "Reciprocity," p. 13. And Charles M. Pepper, "The Open Door to Canada," quoted in Hannigan, p. 12.

13. Hannigan, "Reciprocity," p. 3.

14. Ambassador Bryce to Lord Grey, May 12, 1910, quoted in Tansill, *Canadian-American Relations,* p. 461.

15. Taft to Bradley, February 27, 1911, quoted in Ethan Ellis, *Reciprocity 1911: A Study in Canadian-American Relations* (New Haven: Yale University Press, 1939), p. 92; also, Taft quoted in Tansill, *Canadian-American Relations,* p. 462; and Taft to Roosevelt, January 10, 1911, quoted in Hannigan, "Reciprocity 1911," pp. 16-17.

16. Montreal *Herald,* January 27, 1911, quoted in Paul Stevens, *The 1911 General Election: A Study in Canadian Politics* (Toronto: Copp Clark, 1970), p.6.

17. Borden, quoted *in* Paul Stevens, *1911 General Election,* p. 86.

18. *House of Commons Debates,* February 9, 1911, and February 14, 1911, in H of C Debates 1910-1911, pp. 3327-3563.

19. Lord Grey, quoted in Stevens, *1911 General Election,* p. 2.

20. *House of Commons Debates,* February 28, 1911, in H of C Debates 1910-1911, quoted in Stevens, *1911 General Election,* pp. 38-46.

21. Van Horne, quoted in Ellis, *Reciprocity 1911,* p. 153.

22. Davis, quoted in Albert K. Weinberg, *Manifest Destiny: A Study of Nationalist Expansionism in American History* (Baltimore: Johns Hopkins Press, 1935), p. 375.

23. Clark in the *Congressional Record, 61st Congress, 3rd Session,* February 14, 1911, quoted in Thomas A. Bailey, *A Diplomatic History of the American People* (New York: Meredith, 1969), p. 538.

24. Prince and McCumber, quoted in Hugh L. Keenleyside, *Canada and the United States: Some Aspects of the History of the Republic and the Dominion* (New York: Knopf, 1929), pp. 316-317.

25. Ellis, *Reciprocity 1911,* p. 149.

26. Winnipeg *Free Press,* June 20, 1911, and *Grain Grower's Guide,* June 28, 1911; quoted in *ibid.,* p. 161.

27. Montreal *Daily Star,* August 7, 1911, quoted in Stevens, *1911 General Election,* p. 135.

28. Victoria *Times-Colonist,* September 20, 1911, quoted in Keenleyside, *Canada and the United States,* p. 319.

29. Leacock, quoted in Stevens, *1911 General Election,* p. 148.

30. Pauline Johnson, *Flint and Feather* (Toronto: Musson, 1913), p. 82.

31. Montreal *Daily Star,* September 16, 1911, quoted in Stevens, *1911 General Election,* p. 118.

32. *Daily Mail and Empire,* September 19, 1911, quoted in Stevens, *1911 General Election,* p. 119.

33. Creighton, *Dominion of the North,* p. 436.

34. Toronto *Globe,* September 22, 1911, quoted in Keenleyside, *Canada and the United States,* p. 321.

35. Sifton, quoted in Stevens, *1911 General Election,* pp. 192-93.

36. King, quoted in *ibid.,* p. 171.

Chapter 11 / Working for Mr. Rockefeller

1. Knowlton Nash, *Kennedy and Diefenbaker: Fear and Loathing Across the Undefended Border* (Toronto: McClelland and Stewart, 1990), p. 31.

2. Phillips to Franklin D. Roosevelt, November 7, 1935. Franklin D. Roosevelt Library, President's Secretary's File (PSF) 25, Diplomatic Correspondence, "Canada."

3. King to Armour, October 24 and 25, 1935, quoted in Marc T. Boucher, "The Politics of Economic Depression: Canadian-American Relations in the Mid-1930s," *International Journal* (winter 1985-86), p. 29.

4. Armour to Phillips, memo dated October 22,1935, Franklin D. Roosevelt Library, PSF 25.

5. State Department memo by LaVerne Baldwin, November 9, 1935, quoted in Boucher, "Politics of Depression," p. 35.

6. King, quoted in Boucher, "Politics of Depression," p. 35.

7. King, quoted in J.L. Granatstein and Norman Hillmer, *For Better or for Worse: Canada and the United States to the 1990s* (Toronto: Copp Clark Pitman, 1991), p. 173.

8. Willoughby, quoted *ibid.*, p. 172.

9. Deutsch, quoted *ibid.*, p. 171.

10. *Time,* February 1948, quoted in Richard Gwyn, *The 49th Paradox: Canada in North America* (Toronto: Totem, 1986), p. 53, footnote.

11. *Life,* March 15,1948; *Financial Post, Globe and Mail,* and King quoted in Donald Creighton, *The Forked Road: Canada 1939-1957* (Toronto: McClelland and Stewart, 1976), p. 155.

Chapter 12 / Comic Union

1. Richard Gwyn, *Smallwood: The Unlikely Revolutionary* (Toronto: McClelland and Stewart, 1972), p. 5.

2. *Ibid.,* p. 97.

3. Harold Horwood, *Joey: The Life and Political Times of Joey Smallwood* (Toronto: Stoddart, 1989), p. 116.

4. Richard Gwyn, *Smallwood,* p. 78.

5. J. Smallwood, *I Chose Canada: The Memoirs of the Honourable Joseph R. "Joey" Smallwood* (Toronto: Macmillan, 1973), p. 314.

6. Ewart Young, quoted in Gwyn, *Smallwood,* p. 112.

Chapter 13 / In a Class of Its Own

1. Howe, quoted in Greig Stewart, *Shutting Down the National Dream: A.V. Roe and the Tragedy of the Avro Arrow* (Toronto: McGraw Hill-Ryerson, 1988), p. 13.

2. Dobson, quoted *ibid., p.* 29; and in E.K. Shaw, *There Never Was an Arrow* (Ottawa: Steel Rail Educational Publishing, 1981), p. 32.

3. Dobson, quoted in Stewart, *Shutting Down,* p. 44.

4. *Aviation Week,* October 21, 1957, and *Flight,* October 25, 1957, quoted in Palmiro Campagna, *Storms of Controversy: The Secret Arrow Files Revealed* (Toronto: Stoddart, 1992), p. 54.

5. Shaw, *There Never Was,* pp. 57-58.

6. Stewart, *Shutting Down,* p. 2; and Morley quoted in Stewart, p. 267.

7. Campagna, *Storms,* p. 69.

8. Rummel, quoted in *ibid.*, p. 8.

9. Smye, quoted in Stewart, *Shutting Down,* p. 270.

10. Shaw, *There Never Was,* p. 40.

11. Diefenbaker, quoted in Campagna, *Storms,* p. 1.

12. Stewart, *Shutting Down,* pp. 261, 273, 274.

13. Shaw, *Never Was,* p. 100.

14. *Ibid.,* p. 89.

15. *Ibid.,* p. 110.

16. *Ibid.,* pp. 173,167.

17. Campagna, *Storms,* p. 100.

18. Judith Robinson, "Rabbits for the Eagle," Toronto *Telegram,* February 10, 1959, quoted in Shaw, *Never Was,* p. 127. (Shaw relates that after this article, the *Telegram* dropped Robinson's column and did not reinstate it until she dropped all references to the Arrow or to defence.)

19. New York *Times,* quoted in Shaw, *Never Was,* pp. 174-75.

20. Stanley B. Ryerson, *The Founding of Canada: Beginnings to 1815* (Toronto: Progress Books, 1963), p. 161.

21. Campagna, *Storms,* p. 198.

22. Zurakowski, quoted in Shaw, *Never Was,* and Stewart, *Shutting Down,* xii.

23. Campagna, *Storms,* p. 170.

Chapter 14 / We Were Fighting for Canada

1. John Stanton, *Life and Death of the Canadian Seamen's Union* (Toronto: Steel Rail, 1978), p. 28.

2. Bengough, quoted in Charles Lipton, *The Trade Union Movement of Canada, 1827-1959* (Toronto: New Canada Publications, 1964), p. 276.

3. Stanton, *Life and Death,* p. 122.

4. *Ibid.,* p. 37.

5. Grabek, quoted in Peter Edwards, *Waterfront Warlord: The Life and Violent Times of Hal C. Banks* (Toronto: Key Porter, 1987), p. 22.

6. Murray, quoted in Stanton, *Life and Death,* p. 25.

7. *Ibid.,* p. 15.

8. Banks, quoted in William Kaplan, *Everything that Floats: Pat Sullivan, Hal Banks, and the Seamen's Union of Canada* (Toronto: University of Toronto Press, 1987), preface.

9. Banks, quoted in Edwards, *Waterfront Warlord,* p. 23.

10. *Ibid.,* p. 29.

11. Banks, quoted in Jim Green, *Against the Tide: The Story of the Canadian Seamen's Union* (Toronto: Progress Books, 1986), p. 270.

12. Banks, quoted in Edwards, *Waterfront Warlord,* p. 73.

13.   *Ibid.,* p. 61.

14.   *Ibid.,* p. 31,130.

15.   Schlesinger, quoted in *ibid.,* p. 104.

16.   *Ibid.,* p. 63.

17.   Kaplan, *Everything that Floats,* p. 142.

18.   Edwards, *Waterfront Warlord,* p. 132. And T.G. Norris, "Report of Industrial Inquiry Commission Concerning Matters Relating to Disruption of Shipping on the Great Lakes, the St. Lawrence River System and Connecting Waters," quoted in Green, *Against the Tide,* p. 292.

19.   Marrinan, quoted in Edwards, *Waterfront Warlord,* p. 70.

20.   Norris, quoted in *ibid.,* p. 200.

21.   Rusk, quoted in *ibid.,* p. 172.

22.   Edwards, *Waterfront Warlord,* p. 57.

Chapter 15 / "You Pissed on My Rug"

1.   Peter Wyden, *Bay of Pigs: The Untold Story* (New York: Simon & Schuster, 1979), p. 27.

2.   Richard Gwyn, *The 49th Paradox: Canada in North America* (Toronto: Totem Books, 1986), p. 112.

3.   Diefenbaker and Douglas, quoted in Lawrence Martin, *The Presidents and the Prime Ministers: Washington and Ottawa Face to Face — the Myth of Bilateral Bliss, 1867-1982* (Toronto: Paperjacks, 1983), pp. 199-200.

4.   Knowlton Nash, *Kennedy and Diefenbaker: Fear and Loathing across the Undefended Border* (Toronto: McClelland and Stewart, 1990), p. 15.

5.   Diefenbaker, January 31, 1963, quoted in R. Howard, J. Lacoursière, C. Bouchard (eds.), *A New History of Canada: Quiet Revolution 1960-67* (Montreal: Éditions Format, 1973), p. 1215.

6.   Trudeau, quoted in Gwyn, *49th Paradox,* p. 111.

7.   Thompson, quoted in Martin, *Presidents and Prime Ministers,* p. 204.

8.   "Canada's Diefenbaker, Decline and Fall," *Newsweek,* February 18, 1963.

9.   Grant, quoted in Nash, *Kennedy and Diefenbaker,* p. 274.

10.   Diefenbaker, quoted in Martin, *Presidents and Prime Ministers,* p. 207. And in J.L. Granatstein and N. Hilmer, *For Better or For Worse: Canada and the United States to the 1990s* (Toronto: Copp Clark, 1991), p. 210.

11.   Granatstein and Hilmer, *For Better or Worse,* p. 212.

12.   Gwyn, *49th Paradox,* p. 111.

13.   *Ibid.,* p. 113.

14.   Johnson, quoted in Martin, *Presidents and Prime Ministers,* p. 212.

15.   Barry Weisberg, *Ecocide in Indochina: The Ecology of War* (San Francisco: Canfield/Harper and Row, 1970), p. 34.

16.   Westmoreland, quoted in *ibid.,* p. 39.

17. Johnson, quoted in Joseph A. Amter, *Vietnam Verdict: A Citizen's History* (New York: Continuum Publishing, 1982), p. 101.

18. Eisenhower, August 4, 1953. Quoted in Felix Greene, *Vietnam! Vietnam!* (Harmondsworth, U.K.: Penguin, 1966), p. 126.

19. Johnson, quoted in Amter, *Vietnam Verdict,* p. xiv.

20. Lemay, quoted in Greene, *Vietnam!,* p. 154; and in the documentary film, *In the Year of the Pig,* Emile De Antonio, 1968.

21. Jean-Paul Sartre, "On Genocide,"in Weisberg, *Ecocide in Indochina, p.* 45.

22. Arthur Westing, "From Poisoning Plants for Peace," in Weisberg, *Ecocide in Indochina,* p. 72.

23. *Aviation Week,* March 21,1966, quoted in Weisberg, *Ecocide in Indochina,* p. 186.

24. Martha Gellhorn, *The Face of War* (New York: Atlantic Monthly Press, 17th, ed., 1988), p. 271.

25. Noam Chomsky and Edward S. Herman, *The Washington Connection and Third World Fascism* (Montreal: Black Rose Books, 1979), p. 314.

26. Jonathan Schell, *The Military Half: An Account of Destruction in Quang Ngai and Quang Tin* (New York: Random House, 1968), p. 141.

27. Chomsky and Herman, *Washington Connection,* pp. 325-26.

28. *Le Monde,* July 1968, quoted in Weisberg, *Ecocide in Indochina,* p. 97.

29. Martin, *Presidents and Prime Ministers,* pp. 2, 226, 227.

30. Claire Culhane, *Why Is Canada in Vietnam? The Truth about Our Foreign Aid* (Toronto: New Canada Press, 1972), p. 8.

31. Lenny Glynn, "The Sovereign State of Kissinger Inc.," *Report on Business* (July/August 1985), p. 60.

32. Bundy in a PBS TV interview, April 30, 1985.

Chapter 16 / The Rabid Nationalist

1 . Stephen Clarkson, *Canada and the Reagan Challenge: Crisis and Adjustment, 1981-85* (Toronto: Lorimer, 1985), p. 60.

2. *Ibid.,* p. 21.

3. *Ibid.,* p. 27.

4. *Ibid.,* p. 35.

5. *Ibid.,* pp. 39-40, 41.

6. *Ibid.,* p. 44.

7. *Ibid.,* p. 37.

8. Richard Gwyn, *The 49th Paradox: Canada in North America* (Toronto: Totem Books, 1986), p. 96.

9. Clarkson, *Canada and Reagan,* p. 82.

10. Paul Robinson in a speech to "Current Insight Newsmagazine," broadcast by Rogers Cable TV, Vancouver, B.C., December 1989; and in Mel Hurtig, *The Betrayal of Canada* (Toronto: Stoddart, 1992), p. 200.

11. Camp, quoted in Vancouver *Sun,* February 1, 1983.

12. Mulroney, quoted in the Toronto *Star,* June 3, 1983; and in Claire Hoy, *Friends in High Places: Politics and Patronage in the Mulroney Government* (Toronto: Key Porter, 1987), p. 162.

13. Crombie, Wilson and Clark quoted in "What They Stand For," *Maclean's,* June 13, 1983.

14. D. Bercuson, J.L. Granatstein, W.R. Young, *Sacred Trust? Brian Mulroney and the Conservative Party in Power* (Toronto: Doubleday, 1986), p. 275.

15. Merkin, quoted in *ibid.,* p. 275.

16. Donald Macdonald to Prime Minister Mulroney, September 7, 1984; and Mulroney to Macdonald, November 2, 1984. Reprinted in *Report of the Royal Commission on the Economic Union and Development Prospects for Canada* (Ottawa: Queen's Printer, 1985), appendix A, pp. 571, 573.

17. Saskatoon *Star-Phoenix,* May 16, 1985.

18. Prime Minister's Office, "Communications Strategy for Canada-U.S. Bilateral Trade Initiative." Reprinted in Duncan Cameron (ed.), *The Free Trade Papers* (Toronto: Lorimer, 1986), pp. 4-8.

19. *Ibid.,* pp. 4-8.

20. *Ibid.,* pp. 4-8.

21. *Maclean's,* November 11, 1985, pp. 18-19.

22. *Ibid.,* p. 15.

23. *Ibid.,* p. 19.

24. *Ibid.,* p. 19.

Chapter 17 / The Most Critical Date on this Continent

1. Senator Richard Lugar (Indiana, former Republican Chairman of the Senate Foreign Relations Committee) on CBC-TV *News,* September 10, 1987.

Chapter 18 / Crusaders for the Deal

1. Mulroney, House of Commons *Hansard,* October 5, 1987, pp. 9631-33.

2. Turner, *ibid.,* pp. 9634-36.

3. Broadbent, *ibid.,* p. 9637.

4. Reisman, quoted in the *Financial Post,* July 25, 1988. Quoted in Paul Shuttle, "How the Canada-U.S. Free Trade Deal Affects You" (Saskatoon: mimeographed document, 1988).

5. L.G. Bonar, "U.S. Uranium Mines Won't Be Allowed to Shut the Door on Canada," in Earle Gray (ed.), *Free Trade, Free Canada: How Free Trade Will Make Canada Stronger* (Woodville, Ont.: Canadian Speeches, 1988), p. 140.

6. Edward A. Carmichael, "Energy," in John Crispo (ed.), *Free Trade: The Real Story* (Toronto: Gage, 1988), p. 73.

7. Carney, quoted in *Globe and Mail,* July 7, 1988.

8.   Morris, quoted in Linda McQuaig, *The Quick and the Dead: Brian Mulroney, Big Business and the Seduction of Canada* (Toronto: Viking Press, 1991), p. 173.

9.   Yager, quoted in Hurtig, *The Betrayal of Canada* (Toronto: Stoddart, 1992), p. 213.

10.   Cedric Ritchie, quoted in McQuaig, *The Quick and the Dead,* p. 179.

11.   Peter Martin, "The Canada-U.S. Free Trade Agreement: Point Form Summary and Preliminary Evaluation" (McLeod Young Weir, October 19, 1987), appendix 1, p. 8.

12.   Dan Morgan, *Merchants of Grain* (New York: Viking Press, 1979), p. 250.

13.   Mel Clark, speech before the Ontario Standing Committee on Finance and Economic Affairs, June 15, 1988.

14.   Crosbie, quoted in Wendy Holm (ed.), *Water and Free Trade* (Toronto: Lorimer, 1988), p. 8.

15.   Simon Reisman, "Trade Policy Option in Perspective," Speech before the Ontario Economic Council, April 1985.

16.   Grandy, quoted in Holm, *Water and Free Trade,* p. 18.

17.   "Canada Warms up to U.S. Business," *Fortune,* March 4, 1985, quoted in Holm, *Water and Free Trade,* p. 13.

18.   "Notes for the Assembly of First Nations Presentation to the Legislative Committee on Bill C-130: Canada-USA Free Trade Agreement," Presented by Konrad Sioui, then Vice-Chief, Quebec Region, July 18,1988.

19.   Anthony Smith, "The Geopolitics of Information: How Western Culture Dominates the World," quoted in Manjunath Pendakur, *Canadian Dreams and American Control: The Political Economy of the Canadian Film Industry* (Toronto: Garamond Press, 1990), p. 276.

Chapter 19 / Everything We Wanted

1.   Cohen, quoted in the Toronto *Star,* December 28, 1987.

2.   Yeutter, quoted in the Toronto *Star,* October 6, 1987.

3.   "U.S.-Canada Free Trade Agreement Briefing Paper for Secretary Baker and Ambassador Yeutter" (Confidential Appraisal of U.S.-Canada Pact presented to Treasury Secretary James Baker and Trade Ambassador Clayton Yeutter) (Washington, September 1987). Photocopy of document obtained by *Inside U.S. Trade,* pp. 12, 4,18.

4.   William Randolph Hearst Jr., Editorial, reprinted in the Toronto *Star,* October 11, 1987.

5.   Duncan Cameron, ed., *The Free Trade Papers* (Toronto: Lorimer, 1986), p. 4.

6.   Mayer, quoted in *Globe and Mail,* November 4, 1988.

7.   Mulroney, quoted in Mel Hurtig, *The Betrayal of Canada* (Toronto: Stoddart, 1992), p. 156.

8.   Mulroney, quoted by Alexander Cockburn in *The Nation,* April 18, 1987.

9.   Photocopy of RCMP document, in author's possession.

Chapter 20 / The Sale of Canada Act

1.   Turner, House of Commons *Hansard,* June 29, 1988, pp. 16942-51.

Chapter 21 / It Is Manifest Destiny

1.   Bate and Foraker, quoted in Manuel Maldonado-Denis, *Puerto Rico: A Socio-Historic Interpretation* (New York: Random House, 1972), pp. 88, 89-90.

2.   Cooper, quoted in *ibid.,* pp. 105-106.

3.   de Diego, quoted in *ibid.,* pp. 109, 111.

4.   Marin, quoted in Adalberto López, *The Puerto Ricans: Their History, Culture and Society* (Cambridge, Mass.: Schenkman, 1980), p. 177.

5.   Stevens, quoted in Thomas A. Bailey, *A Diplomatic History of the American People* (New York: Meredith, 1969), p. 430.

6.   *Ibid.,* p. 431.

7.   *Ibid.,* p. 432.

8.   McKinley, quoted in Weinberg, *Manifest Destiny. A Study of Nationalist Expansionism in American History* (Baltimore: Johns Hopkins Press, 1935), p. 263; and in Bailey, *A Diplomatic History, p.* 435.

9.   Pinhas Dror, quoted in Regina *Leader-Post,* October 21, 1987.

Chapter 22 / Closure on Christmas Eve

1.   Chief Electoral Officer of Canada, *Thirty-fourth General Election. Report of the Chief Electoral Officer, Pursuant to Section 193 of the Canada Elections Act,* 1988.

2.   Crosbie, House of Commons *Hansard,* December 15, 1988, p. 117.

3.   Broadbent, *ibid.,* p. 129.

4.   Turner, *ibid.,* pp. 124-25.

5.   Broadbent, quoted in the *Globe and Mail,* July 23, 1988.

6.   Fingerhut, quoted in Linda Diebel, "NDP Got Proper Advice Their U.S. Pollster Insists," Toronto *Star,* December 9, 1988.

7.   Broadbent, quoted in the *Globe and Mail* and *La Presse,* November 23, 1988.

8.   Turner, quoted in the Ottawa *Citizen* and the Toronto *Sun,* November 23, 1988.

Chapter 23 / The First Four Years

1.   Claire Hoy, *Friends in High Places: Politics and Patronage in the Mulroney Government* (Toronto: Key Porter, 1987), p. 174.

2.   *Business Week,* July 17, 1991, pp. 76-77.

3.   Pattison, quoted in *Maclean's,* March 18, 1991, p. 40.

4.   Gordon Ritchie, quoted in "High dollar costs jobs, Ritchie says," The Toronto *Star,* March 24, 1990.

5.   Mulroney, Wilson and Reisman, quoted in Mel Clark, "Notes: The FTA, Medicare and a Social Charter," December 17, 1991, pp. 4-5. Mimeographed document

6.   Crosbie, quoted in Montreal *Gazette,* October 14, 1988.

7.   Clark, *Notes: FTA,* pp. 4-6.

8.   Decker, quoted in Rod Mickleburgh, "Ministers pessimistic about Medicare," *Globe and Mail,* June 17, 1992.

9.   Bégin, quoted in Clark, *Notes: FTA,* p. 3.

10. Mazankowski, quoted in the Toronto *Star,* February 10, 1990.

11. *The Ganada-U.S. Free Trade Agreement and Canadian Consumers: An Assessment* (Ottawa: Consumer and Corporate Affairs, 1988), pp. 16, 25.

12. Crosbie in "The Simon Fraser Debate" (Vancouver: Simon Fraser University, December 3, 1987). Videotape distributed by Citizens Concerned About Free Trade, 1988.

13. John L. Orr, "Canada's Free Trade Dilemma: Renegotiate or Abrogate?" *The New Federation* (July/August 1992).

14. Jeffrey Hawkins, "The Canada-U.S. Free Trade Agreement: An Interim Assessment," *Business America* (a publication of the U.S. Department of Commerce: April 20, 1992).

15. McNaughton, quoted in Richard Bocking, *Canada's Water: For Sale?* (Toronto: Lorimer, 1972), p. 118.

16. A.G.L. McNaughton, "A Monstrous Concept – A Diabolical Thesis," quoted in *ibid.,* p. 72.

17. Dale, quoted in Vancouver *Sun,* May 8,1992, and in *B.C. Report,* May 25, 1992.

18. Rush, in telephone interview with the author, February 19, 1993.

19. Gordon Ritchie quoted in "High dollar costs jobs, Ritchie says," The Toronto *Star,* March 24, 1990.

20. De Cuellar, quoted in David Cox, "Canada's UN Policy after the Gulf War," cited in Lloyd Axworthy, *Canada and the Newly Developing Democracies;* Speech, International Relations Society (Toronto: Trinity College, University of Toronto, November 20, 1991), mimeographed document, p. 4.

Chapter 24 / Prying Open Mexico

1.   Robert Ryal Miller, *Mexico: A History* (University of Oklahoma Press, 1985), p. 267.

2.   Rojas, quoted in Ramón Eduardo Ruiz, *The Great Rebellion: Mexico 1905-1924* (New York: Norton, 1980), p. 391.

3.   John Womack Jr., *Zapata and the Mexican Revolution* (New York: Knopf, 1969), p. 186.

4.   LaGuardia, and the New York *Times,* February 1, 1921, quoted in Ruiz, *Great Rebellion,* p. 405.

5. Andrew Reding, "Favorite Son," *Mother Jones* (November 1988), pp. 35-37, 44-45.

6. "U.S.-Canada Free Trade Agreement Briefing Paper for Secretary Baker and Ambassador Yeutter" (Confidential Appraisal of U.S.-Canada Pact presented to Treasury Secretary James Baker and Trade Ambassador Clayton Yeutter) (Washington: September, 1987). Photocopy of document obtained by *Inside U.S. Trade*, p. 6.

7. Canadian Centre for Policy Alternatives, *Which Way for the Americas: Analysis of NAFTA Proposals and the Impact on Canada* (Ottawa: 1992), p. 23.

8. *Ibid.*, p. 77.

9. Clinton, October 4, 1992, quoted in *ibid.*, p. 98.

10. "Confidential Appraisal," p. 11.

11. Negroponte in a memo to U.S. State Department, quoted in Canadian Centre for Policy Alternatives, p. 99.

12. Rosselló, quoted in New York *Times*, January 3,1993.

13. Bram Garber, letter to the Editor, *Globe and Mail*, Sept. 20, 1990.

14. Bush, quoted in *Globe and Mail*, December 18,1992.

15. "Rich Get Richer," *Globe and Mail*, April 22,1992.

Chapter 25 / We Don't Scare Easily

1. Pawley, quoted in Pierre Trudeau, "We, the People of Canada," in Donald Johnston (ed.), *Pierre Trudeau Speaks out on Meech Lake* (Toronto: Stoddart/General Paperback, 1990), p. 93.

2. Pierre Trudeau, "Say Goodbye to the Dream of One Canada," *ibid.*, pp. 11-22.

3. Devine, quoted in Dale Eisler column, Regina *Leader-Post*, July, 1990.

4. Native Women's Association of Canada, Press Release: "Native Women's Association Forms 'No' Committee," September 17, 1992.

5. Union of B.C. Indian Chiefs, "Termination – Not Self-Determination!" (Leaflet. Vancouver, September 1992).

6. Pierre Trudeau, A *Mess that Deserves a Big NO* (Toronto: Robert Davies Publishing, 1992), pp. 12, 33, 60-63, 69.

7. Montreal *Gazette*, July 14, 1992.

8. Henri Bourassa, "Language and Nationality," 1913; and "French and English," 1914; reprinted in Joseph Levitt, *Henri Bourassa on Imperialism and Bi-culturalism, 1900-1918* (Toronto: Copp Clark, 1970), pp. 135, 137, 149-50.

9. Pierre Trudeau, "New Treason of the Intellectuals," *Federalism and the French Canadians* (Toronto: Macmillan, 1968), p. 167.

10. Big Bear, quoted in a reconstruction of dialogue, based on historical documents, Rudy Wiebe: *The Temptations of Big Bear* (Toronto: McClelland and Stewart, 1973).

11. Mercredi in a public meeting in Vancouver, B.C., October 15, 1992.

12. Wilson on CBC-TV phone-in program, "On the Line," May 1992.

13. Mitchell on CBC Radio, Saskatchewan, August 24,1992.

14. Allard on CBC radio phone-in show, "Cross Country Check-Up," July 12, 1992.

15. Michael Doxtater; "Wampum Wisdom: Why Many Natives Viewed the Charlottetown Accord as a Con," *This Magazine* (January/February 1993), p. 24.

16. Eileen and Graham Linklater, Saskatoon, January 15, 1993. Audio tape interview (in author's possession).

Chapter 26 / "You Know We'll Abrogate"

1. Jean Chrétien, *Straight from the Heart* (Toronto: Key Porter Books, 1985), p. 90.

2. House of Commons *Hansard,* May 11, 1992.

3. James J. Blanchard, *Behind the Embassy Door: Canada, Clinton and Quebec* (Toronto: McClelland & Stewart, 1998), p. 81-83.

4. *Ibid.,* p. 98.

5. Marci McDonald, *Yankee Doodle Dandy: Brian Mulroney and the American Agenda* (Toronto: Stoddart, 1995), p. 292.

Chapter 27 / The Great Canadian Train Robbery

1. Harry Bruce, *The Pig That Flew: The Battle to Privatize Canadian National* (Vancouver: Douglas & McIntyre, 1997), p. 3.

2. Kenneth McNaught, *The Penguin History of Canada* (London: Penguin Books, 1988), p. 221.

3. MacKay & Perry, *Train Country* (Vancouver: Douglas & McIntyre, 1994), p. 71.

4. Harry Bruce, *The Pig That Flew,* p. 4.

5. *Ibid.,* p. 6.

6. *Ibid.,* p. 105.

7. *Ibid.,* p. 149.

8. *Ibid.,* p. 26.

9. *Le Monde,* November 5 & 6, 1995, quoted in Montreal *Gazette,* November 25, 1995.

10. Montreal *Gazette,* November 25, 1995.

Chapter 28 / 10 Years After

1. Jean Chrétien, letter to Don Mazankowski, House of Commons, April 17, 1991. See also Jean Chrétien's press release of same date.

2. Sergio Marchi, minister of environment, House of Commons, September 25, 1996.

3.   *Globe and Mail,* July 25, 1998.

4.   Toronto *Star,* March 18, 1998.

5.   Settling Trade Disputes: When the WTO Forum is Better than the NAFTA, C.D. Howe Institute, Commentary III, by Robert Howse, C.D. Howe Institute, Toronto, June 1998, p. 5.

Chapter 29 / The Sleeping Giant

1 .   Marci McDonald, *Yankee Doodle Dandy: Brian Mulroney and the American Agenda* (Toronto: Stoddart, 1995), p. 227.

2.   Marvin Cetron and Owen Davies, *American Renaissance: Our Life at the Turn of the 21st Century* (New York: St. Martin's Press, 1989), p. 7.

3.   *Ibid.,* pp. 221-23.

4.   Mel Clark, "Memorandum: Canada and the Free-Trade Agreement," December 6, 1991, mimeographed document, p. 7.

Index